The
Underside
of History

Revised Edition   Volume 2

To all the women,
of every time and space,
who are this book

The Underside of History

Revised Edition   Volume 2

A View of Women Through Time

Elise Boulding

Original line drawings by *Helen Redman*

SAGE Publications
International Educational and Professional Publisher
Newbury Park   London   New Delhi

For information address:

 SAGE Publications, Inc.
2455 Teller Road
Newbury Park, California 91320

SAGE Publications Ltd.
6 Bonhill Street
London EC2A 4PU
United Kingdom

SAGE Publications India Pvt. Ltd.
M-32 Market
Greater Kailash I
New Delhi 110 048 India

Printed in the United States of America

Library of Congress Cataloging-in-Publication Data

Boulding, Elise.
   The underside of history: a view of women through time / Elise Boulding.—Rev. ed.
   v. cm.
   Vols. 1-2 include bibliographical references and indexes.
   ISBN 0-8039-4768-2 (v. 1).—ISBN 0-8039-4816-6 (v. 2).—ISBN 0-8039-4769-0 (v. 1: pbk.).—ISBN 0-8039-4817-4 (v. 2: pbk.)
   1. Women-History. I. Title.
HQ1121.B64 1992
305.4'09—dc20   92-28926

92 93 94 95 10 9 8 7 6 5 4 3 2 1

Sage Production Editor: Diane S. Foster

Contents

List of Tables

List of Figures

Foreword

With humankind, female and male, standing on the threshold of
the third millennium, it seems particularly appropriate in this
decade of the 1990s to begin the second volume of *The Underside of
History* with the onset of the second millennium. The themes have not
changed all that much in the past 1,000 years. In the late 900s, as today,
people hoped for a New World Order and, at the same time, feared that
judgment day (for our times, read: accidental nuclear holocaust, global
climate warming, environmental destruction) was coming.

By the 1100s, it seemed probable that reprieve had been granted. The
human race still had time. Throughout Eurasia, the male half of the
species put great energies into the development of new administrative
structures of church and state and new technologies, which were to lead
some centuries later to the industrial revolution in the European part
of the sprawling continent. These were not good times for women,

AUTHOR'S NOTE: *The Underside of History*, Volume 1, contains the author's Preface to
the original edition of this book, in which I describe my reasons for undertaking the
challenging and difficult task of presenting a view of women through time as a counter-
balance to more conventional, male-centered, treatments. For those readers who want to
understand my motivation, I recommend that you read this material. I would also like to
note the Acknowledgments for *The Underside of History* (also printed in Volume 1). My
gratitude for those who helped me in this enormous endeavor is documented therein,
together with my recognition of the numerous intellectual debts incurred in an undertaking
of this magnitude.

however. In the West, upper-class women gradually found themselves squeezed out by the new bureaucracies of church and state, losing the autonomy they had under feudalism. Women of the artisan classes found their working day growing longer and longer over the centuries, and their living conditions poorer, as cities came to absorb an ever larger part of the population. These were not good times for women elsewhere either. As Western colonial penetration of other continents began in the 1400s, what in later centuries came to be designated as the "Third World" similarly suffered a decline in living conditions, a decline women as always were the first to feel.

Part I of this volume begins with my favorite period of history, 1000 to 1800 C.E. The intellectual, social, and political excitement generated in anticipation of the year 1000 in Christian Europe, and similar transformations of awareness noted on every continent in these centuries, affected women every bit as much as men. This excitement released waves of creativity within already rich women's cultures that are only now being rediscovered; that creativity continued in the post-Renaissance period—not only in convents and salons and at family hearths but among women adventurers who sought new experiences in far-off lands.

The new Part II of this volume includes the 1800s as well as the 1900s, as transition centuries. This makes good sense conceptually as we prepare to move into the twenty-first century. The tremendous surge in women's activism in the twentieth century cannot be understood properly without knowledge of the women revolutionaries, workers, and reformers, women intellectuals, scientists, and artists, and the intrepid, down-to-earth visionaries who laid the foundation for the contemporary peace and women's rights movements of our own times.

Once again, I apologize to my sisters in the "Two-Thirds World" for the unseemly dash through the story of women's lives in Africa, Asia, and Latin America necessitated by the Western bias of the previous chapters. At least Chapter 5, largely a new chapter, treats contemporary women's movements in a more appropriately international context.

It has always seemed to me that the energy of the male overside in the West had its counterpart in the creativity of women on the underside. The chorus of dissent against ancient customs of subjugation finally found public voice and some public response by the closing centuries of this second millennium.

Strong female energies are unleashed on every continent by the 1990s, although the structures of male dominance are still in place. The new material in Chapter 5 uses a different approach than that used in the other chapters, in not depending on a name roster but shifting instead to women's networks. I believe this reflects the new ways in which women are able to function in modern times.

The epilogue turns to the future. In it, we explore possibilities for very different human relations in the next millennium, through the bursting forth of a women's culture that helps dismantle militarism, that enables the maturing of partnerships across gender, age, ethnic, and cultural lines as well as a maturing of our partnership with the earth itself, on all continents. The continuing development of our understanding of how women are participating—and can increasingly participate—in reshaping the sorry existing social order is what keeps me an optimist about the future.

This is an exciting time in women's studies, one filled with challenge, diversity, and conflict and one that will test our analytic and sisterhood skills to the utmost. I am pleased that these volumes are once again available to my sisters—especially the younger generations. It is important that you know you are standing "on the shoulders of giants"[1]—but *giants* in a different sense than male scholars have conceived them. These giants are the heroic women of the underside, peasants and poets, jugglers and queens, *hetaira* and nuns, adventurers and scientists, and always mothers and daughters from the time of knowledge-seeking Eve to the current time. These giants have not only provided history with its hidden undergirding structures but have unfailingly passed on to each succeeding generation the love, courage, and imagination that has helped to keep humanity, with all its failings, open to new beginnings. Sisters, climb up where you belong so you can see where to go!

Note

1. This is a reference to Newton's epigram, "If I have seen farther, it is by standing on the shoulders of giants," delightfully pursued by Robert Merton in a book by that title (1965).

From the Millennium to a Century of Revolutions: 1000-1800 C.E.

Introduction

Part I begins with a night of terror: December 31, 999. When the church bells rang at midnight, the lords and peasants of Europe were on their knees, for this was to be the end of the world. For months, women and men had been bringing wagonloads of possessions, parcels of land deeds, valuable jewels, and manuscripts to the monasteries and churches of Christendom. People wanted to be ready and in good standing on Judgment Day. Part I ends with a Reign of Terror, as first Queen Marie Antoinette, and later even some of the leading citizenesses of the French Revolution, ended their lives at the guillotine. This extraordinary sweep of years takes us through the Middle Ages, the Renaissance, the beginnings of the Enlightenment, and the revolutions that ushered in the modern world. It takes us through a great civilizational flowering and mystical fervors on all continents during the "greatest of centuries"—the thirteenth. It also takes

us through the crusades, the Hundred Years' War, plague and famine, and the slowly
swelling parade of ships from Europe to other continents to "discover" worlds far
older than their own. Women were everywhere in the action through these centuries,
but, with the exception of the "great queens," worked invisibly as usual, from the
underside. First, we will have some historical background.

1000 to 1450 C.E.

On the surface, the first century of the second millennium seemed peaceful
enough. In the flood of emotional relief that followed the postponement of Judgment
Day, there was an orgy of church building all over Europe, especially in France and
Germany. The most visible signs of the fervor lay in the beginnings of the great
cathedrals. "The world was shaking herself, throwing off her old garments, and
robing herself in a white mantle of churches" (Baldwin 1971: 15). Underneath the
mantle, battles raged between popes, kings, and emperors competing for legitimacy
and power, but the respite was, in a sense, real. The Viking depredations were over.
Feudal society, for so long locked in its walled castles, began trickling out into the
countryside. The church was strong enough to declare and enforce the Truce of God,
spelling out when and where fighting could take place. No fighting was permitted

> from Wednesday evening to Monday morning every week, leaving only
> three days and two nights per week for . . . private wars. Even these three
> days were ruled out during Lent, Advent, and the great feasts of Our Lady,
> the feasts of the Apostles and certain other saints. (Nickerson 1942: 31)

It was forbidden to charge interest on military loans (a policy worth some
consideration in the twentieth century), and soldiers could not fight on land
belonging to the church; nor could they attack pilgrims, merchants, women,
peasants, cattle, agricultural implements, clerics, or students.

The war-control measures contributed substantially to the conditions in which
agricultural and craft productivity and trade could develop. New agricultural land was
cleared; new towns sprang up on old and new trade routes. Merchant guilds formed,
and their spinoffs, craft guilds, multiplied. New monasteries opened to absorb surplus
populations. What had been miserable towns in 1000 were flourishing cities by 1350.

Before 1000, what bureaucracies existed had belonged to the church. But, by the
thirteenth century, something new had happened: an amazing multiplication of the
number of lay officials throughout Europe. Strayer (1964) calls it one of the most
striking phenomena of the thirteenth century:

> In every country the conservatives protested again and again that there
> were too many officials and in every country the number of officials went
> right on increasing in spite of protest. . . . The fact that such men [the

officials] could brutally disregard the church's rights and still keep their positions must have convinced many people that lay governments were going to be supreme. Finally, with the steady increase in the number of government jobs a new career was opened up for able men of all classes. The church could no longer count on securing the services of the great majority of educated and intelligent men. (107-8)

This development represented a significant new power base for the lay citizenry. As the quotation from Strayer suggests, the new bureaucracies were for men. Women remained on the underside of the church bureaucracy in such posts as were available to them through the religious orders. The new network of secular officials had no place at all for women. The absence of women from these new roles was to have important consequences for women's economic position when the craft guilds began to decline.

In the early Middle Ages, this did not appear to be a problem. We have already seen in the last chapter that women administered up to one-fifth of the landed estates of Europe. They were also involved in the growth of the urban centers, as craft workers in and outside the guilds and as teachers. Towns with populations of 10,000 and less were soon supporting schools—some under the care of local monasteries and convents and some under the care of newly prosperous craft guilds. Cathedral towns had larger and better equipped schools, and these, along with guild schools, became the nurseries of the universities born in the 1200s.

The knowledge explosion, however, excluded women, given that only clerics—men vowed to the church and to the priesthood—could enter these schools. Only in Italy and Spain, where universities had a more ancient organizational base, did this not apply. The chief role left to women in relation to the new learning through most of Europe

Figure I.1. Nuns Working on Manuscripts, 1341 C.E., Gothic. Redrawn by HBR.

was as copyists, because there was a great demand both in the cathedral schools and among the aristocracy for libraries. The fingers of copyists, both women and men, flew to provide manuscripts to meet this demand of newly literate folk.

People were on the move and ideas were on the move. Even while new land was being tilled, cities and feudal armies were filling up with former peasants and serfs who sought to free themselves from bondage to the land. The discontented peasant became the discontented city dweller, for the new towns could not absorb and employ all who came there. *Vagantes*, unemployed clerics, wandered everywhere. So did female vagabonds. Restless Norman war bands also wandered about Europe, spoiling for conquests. They were a problem to Europe and to the pope.

When a shower of meteorites fell over Europe in the spring of 1095, it was thought to be a clear signal from God that the Norman armies should be used in a Crusade. The wide outburst of Christian fervor that followed the declaration of the Crusade was matched only by the parallel outburst of exuberant greed. The Crusades offered something for everyone. Women, men, and children all set out, on foot or on horseback, in rags or in glittering armor.[1] Wave after wave of Crusaders poured out of Europe, in a series of 39 different crusades covering a 400-year period (Hazard 1931: 36). It all began with the premature setting out of Peter the Hermit in 1096 with thousands of ragtag and bobtail followers before the regular Crusader knights had assembled. The carnage of that "people's crusade," with gone-wild followers massacring Jews everywhere on the way, was matched only by the tragic Children's Crusade in 1212, which ended in slaughter or enslavement for the entire children's army (Hazard 1931). The final crusade, 1462 to 1492, drove the Moslems out of their last European stronghold, Granada. What came from the Crusades? Power and wealth for the few, suffering, enslavement, and death for the many, on both sides of the movable fighting lines. The land reform and social redistribution movements we noted in the empires of antiquity were replaced by land-grab movements. War is a poor teacher. During the last century of Crusades, Europe turned on itself in the Hundred Years' War and smothered the last bits of millennialist fervor in its population.

It is not possible to make sense of the years from 1000 to 1450, which include both the High Middle Ages and the later Middle Ages, and the role that women played in those years, without taking account of millennialism, the agony of the Crusades abroad, and the Hundred Years' War at home. Wars were not the only problem. Poor agricultural practices and expanding population led to soil exhaustion; there were long cold spells and years of such excessive rainfall that crops could not ripen. The first famine was in 1140, and, from 1272 to 1348, there were repeated periods of extreme cold and heavy rainfall, with accompanying famines. When the plague bacillus hit Europe in 1348 from the East, it struck a population already weak from famine and cold. Within the next half-century, the population of Europe dropped by perhaps one-third (various estimates from Zeigler 1969: 232-39; Hollingsworth 1969).

The horror of the plague was not just in the dying but in the physical agony of the dying and the effect on survivors of seeing dead and dying bodies everywhere.

Instead of the millennium, there was death. Death from war; death from famine; and, most horribly, death from plague.

It would be easy to go on and on painting the terror of the Middle Ages, but of course we all know that is not the whole story. This is also the age of courtly love and the era of the cult of the Virgin. The phenomena included under these labels range all the way from absurd swashbuckling chivalry, passionate amours, and convenient if somewhat salacious miracles performed by the Virgin Mary, to the sad and tender love described by Christine de Pisan in *The Book of the Duke of True Lovers* (1966). Boccaccio's *Concerning Famous Women* (1963) falls somewhere in between the extremes. The touching story of the knight who was so lost in prayer in a wayside chapel that he never got to the tournament he was headed for and found afterward that the Virgin had taken his place in the lists and won him great honors (Adams [1905] 1933: 263-64) brings together in one vignette the extremes of medieval sentiments. To confuse things still further, there is the semierotic mysticism found in the popular Tristan and Lancelot legends.

The final blow to the comprehensibility of the Middle Ages comes when one reads the lives of the saints and the mystics side by side with those of the religio-political activists, the chiliasts, and the revolutionaries. The heretics sometimes turn into saints, sometimes into lusty free livers, and sometimes into petty tyrants who create their own private reigns of terror. The three best known religious movements of the Middle Ages outside the institutional church—the Cathari, the Beguines/ Beghards,[2] and the Brethren of the Free Spirit—all encompassed the full range from sainthood to bestiality. Four popular, yet scholarly, books aimed at trying to interpret this confusing period, by Denis de Rougemont (1956), Johan Huizinga (1924), Henry Adams ([1905] 1933), and Norman Cohn (1970), all manage resolutions of the conflicting patterns along lines suiting their particular training and perspective. Needless to say, they are all quite different than each other. Although each of these writers must perforce deal with women in their books, none of them is able to move very far from conventional representations of women. It is our business to rectify that here.

How was it possible for wars, famines, and plagues to exist side by side with the whole set of phenomena revolving around erotic indulgence on the one hand, religious asceticism and new ideals of service and love on the other, and still make room for utopianism, revolution, and a knowledge explosion? This was an axial period in human history, a time when physical, intellectual, and spiritual resources came together in such a way as to put humankind again on the threshold of new developments. It was an age akin to the time of the first emergence of world religions in the closing centuries B.C.E.

It also led to the rise of the new European universities. In the long interregnum from the fall of Rome to the end of the first millennium of the Common Era, only Italy and Spain kept their ancient schools and Mediterranean-wide knowledge networks intact. From the tenth century on, it was the Moslem universities that represented the great knowledge centers along with the universities of China and

India. With the rebirth of the university in Europe, there was a great busyness with the collection and circulation of manuscripts, the establishment of new libraries, and the gathering together of scholars. By 1445, when guild resistance was overcome and printing presses established, the growing demand for primary schools provided new occupations in teaching for the unemployed army of copyists, both male and female. The thirteenth century in particular was the age of the great schoolmen, the synthesizers of knowledge: Thomas Aquinas, who wrote the summa of theology; Hostiensis, who created the summa of canon law; Vincent of Beauvais, encyclopedist; Roger Bacon, natural philosopher; Albertus Magnus and Duns Scotus, philosophers; Bonaventura, mystic—the names go on, all clerics, and so of course no woman is found in these lists. But we shall make our own list of learned women, for they too participated in the knowledge synthesis.

Alongside the universities, the old guild movement took on new life and new institutional forms in response to the requirements of a new scale of social organization with increased population and a new urbanism. "Brethren and sistren" mingled freely in these guilds until changing economic circumstances forced the "sistren" out.

Finally, as Mujeeb (1960) notes, mysticism flourished everywhere in the world. Why that kind of response, at this particular time? Again, it was a response to the challenge of a changing scale of social organization. When the world religions were first founded, they consisted of small communities of the faithful living relatively close to the traditions of the founder. But

> the idea of the religious world-state among Muslim and Christians expanded the religious community to such dimensions that it became spiritually necessary to organize small units of like-minded people who could live the ideal life for themselves. The monastery, and its Muslim form, the *Khanqah*, appear inevitably as the social, and in many cases, the economic expression of the mystic tendency. (Mujeeb 1960: 153)

In addition to the *khanqah*, in which the Sufi devotion to the *Tariqah*, or "Path," was central, there were also the reform movements dedicated to *futuwah*, sometimes translated as "chivalry." In the Middle Ages, these were a combination of guild and religious order, and there were as many different movements as there were occupations.[3]

One accompaniment of the mysticism of the Middle Ages was its futurism. The millennium had not come in 1000, but, writing in the next century, Joachim de Fiore (1135-1202) expected it in 1200. After his death, his writings were used repeatedly to predict the millennium. Identifying, alternately, the Anti-Christ and the Savior King, both potential heralds of the millennium, was a favored occupation throughout the Middle Ages. Along with predictions of the millennium came the visions of what the new era would be like. De Fiore painted it as the postbureaucratic age, with all institutional structures of church and state crumbled away. Every revolutionary futurist in the next four centuries was to cite Joachimite writings; the radical

Franciscans, especially, espoused Joachimite doctrines. Saint Clare, Saint Francis, and Joachim, the gentlest collection of apocalyptic figures imaginable, guarded the gateway to the new Age of the Holy Spirit.

Yet the flames of the Inquisition eventually roared on the other side of the gateway. By the late 1400s, Dominican and Franciscan inquisitor-monks were pushing the futurists—peasants, peddlers, and duchesses—through that gateway as heretics that required burning. The apocalyptics were seen as part of a gigantic world conspiracy of "wild fanatics who fostered the most subversive and abominable ideas . . . to establish communities and remodel whole territories according to *the programme*" (Summers 1948: xvii). What was the program? It was "the abolition of monarchy, the abolition of private property and of inheritance, the abolition of marriage, the abolition of order, the total abolition of all religion" (Summers 1948: xviii). The hard-pressed church, guardian of law and order, concluded that there was a "society of witches . . . nothing less than a vast international of anti-social revolutionaries" (Summers 1948: xxv). At first, it was only kings and clerics who believed this. Gradually, the frightened bourgeoisie were drawn into the conspiracy view, and finally even peasants turned on each other. What started in 1232 as a program against political sedition ended as mass hysteria in the late 1400s and the 1500s. It was the followers of the gentle Francis and the learned Dominic who unleashed and presided over the fury.

During this entire period, there was an underlying shift from land to money as a power base. Society was pressing against its traditional means of subsistence and had to find new resources (Wilkinson 1973). In the short run, this shift away from feudal toward commercial power structures apparently favored the development of both social equality and spiritual discernment, because reformers, revolutionaries, and mystics alike seemed to flower in this climate. Certainly women flowered, as we shall see. So, very shortly, did the Inquisition. The decline of religious orders and the decline of the workers' orders—that is, guilds—were only to become evident toward the end of this period. The struggle between the craft and trade guilds over the development of new high-production technologies that pushed wages down for some groups of artisans foreshadowed, toward the end of the Middle Ages, the even more bitter struggle to come, at the dawn of the industrial revolution.

The year 1450 already heralded the modern era. Waterpower and windmills had been developed in the twelfth and thirteenth centuries. All kinds of clockwork mechanisms and precision instruments were available in the fourteenth century. Even the Crusades, the plague, and the economic recession of the fourteenth and first half of the fifteenth centuries could not stem the forward thrust. By 1500, Europe was at takeoff and had become the "workshop of the world" (Clough 1951: 168). The flowering of the Middle Ages was real. It was possible for this to take place side by side with wars, famines, and plagues in part because medieval society was still primarily a *local* society. While some localities were wiped out by calamity, others were untouched. Wars, even the destructive Hundred Years War, were far more limited in scope than are modern wars. Under feudal law, vassals only had to fight

40 days a year for their lords and, when 40 days were up, a vassal often simply went home, no matter what battle was raging. The lives of most of the women and men of the Christian and Moslem world, and the Far East, were untouched by war. Crop failures were not as widespread or calamitous as is sometimes pictured (Ladurie 1971), and, even during the worst of the plague, in large areas of the countryside, no one even knew it was occurring. The women we will be writing about, however, were not village ignoramuses; they understood the character of their times pretty well; they were in touch with the crosscurrents and responded creatively to them.

1450 to 1800 C.E.

The period 1450 to 1800 in Europe saw the reigns of three outstanding women rulers who not only brought their own countries out of feudalism but also built the foundations of a new *oecumene*, a Western-based imperial order that was to span all the continents.

The year 1450 also was the occasion of the birth of the Iroquois League, an important political invention in pre-Columbian North America. Because the league was developed by matrilineal tribes, it was partly shaped by the women who served as advisers to the male tribal councils. Unlike the queens, these women worked from the underside and remain nameless in the history books.[4]

Of the women monarchs, the first was Isabel of Castile, who, in the year 1469, moved toward creating a united and imperial Spain by marrying a conservative, provincial-minded neighboring king, Ferdinand of Aragon. A little short of a century later, the second monarch, Elizabeth Tudor, stepped from prison to the throne to build a powerful and united England. Still another century later, the third monarch, Catherine II, moved to the throne of the czars to preside over the imperial expansion of a new world power, Russia.

It would be perfectly possible for a historian to write the history of the three and a half centuries in terms of the lives of these three women and the consequences of their reigns, with footnotes now and then on France and the Austrian empire. Such a history would do at least as much justice to the facts as most standard histories do. It would cover the transition of Europe from a land-centered oecumene ("imperial order") to a sea-based one. It would cover the incorporation of North America and Russia (culturally speaking) into Europe. It would further cover the beginning of the annexation of Latin America and parts of Africa and Asia as appendages to Europe. It would cover much of the drama of the Reformation and Counter-Reformation and the rise of the new humanism. Such a three-monarch focus would leave out the Thirty Years War, the American and French revolutions, and the development of modern mass armies. It would leave out the fall of Constantinople and the stream of Greek artist and scholar refugees that fled to Europe rather than live under the Turks. It would leave out the still-expanding Moslem world those refugees left behind. It would also leave out some aspects of the rise of the new international banking system and of the scientific and industrial revolutions. It would include, however, the gradual development of new solutions to the welfare problems that came with increasing urbanization and industrialization. The poor laws of England came to birth under Elizabeth. The legislative commission, intended to abolish serfdom and deal with the problems of the poor in Russia, was set up under Catherine.

Can one justify lumping all these centuries together? We are leaving behind the medieval world in which each continent supported its own kingdoms and empires. The more ambitious rulers tended to push against one another, particularly between the Moslem and the Christian world, but no one seriously developed imperial policy to deal with the whole known world. The futurists were Joachimites and dreamt of a universal age of the Holy Spirit, but they had no blueprints—they only waited. These middle centuries of the second millennium that we are now inspecting, however, not only expanded the extent of the known world, they saw the birth of a set of double and contradictory visions: one was of an expansionist imperial world undreamed of even in the heyday of the Roman Empire and the other was of the nonimperial utopian world community.

Individualism and autonomy were the key concepts of the Renaissance. The very struggle for autonomy inevitably led to a questioning of the limits of autonomy. The struggle was at first a purely European affair. The wars for religious freedom were superseded by wars for national freedom. National freedom then expanded to include the right to annex portions of other continents.

If it was the queens who helped build the imperial structures that at first overburdened the world oecumene, it was women of all classes who set themselves to breaking down the imperial walls. Women of the upper classes worked within the system. Women of the middle classes worked partly within the system and partly in alliance with their working-class sisters outside the system. The latter were a revolutionary sisterhood whose primary commitments were other than to the nation-state system.

The intellectual and emotional harassment of women characteristic of most of this period began in the Renaissance, with the new "male" humanism. Is it justified to speak of the Renaissance as "harassing" women? We do after all witness a flowering of women's culture in the Renaissance, particularly in Italy but also spreading from there to the rest of Europe. Therefore referring to this period as a Dark Age, as I was tempted to do in the first draft of Part I, may somewhat overemphasize the male backlash against the education of women and against their ventures into the cultural arena. The mental suffering of many educated women as the backlash developed was, however, great. The sudden and rapid spread of syphilis in Europe beginning in the 1500s compounded the backlash.[5] The syphilis scourge led to viciously punitive regulations aimed entirely at women. These regulations affected many single women, prostitutes or not, and created the atmosphere of horror that still surrounds the label "prostitute."

Reich has written about the "nebulous personality" of the Renaissance woman, complaining that it is "more difficult to visualize a famous woman of the Renaissance, more difficult to grasp her individuality, than in most other periods of which we have knowledge" (1908: 227). The reason is not hard to find. The new interest in the individuality of the human being that lay at the heart of the Renaissance was an interest in the male human being. The entire Renaissance was one long song of rejoicing over this remarkable new male individuality. Because women of the culture could and did read the same things the men were reading, and would themselves be affected by the tremendous intellectual excitement engendered by the new humanist writings, they naturally began wondering where they fit. When they raised these questions, the answers were scarcely comforting. Not that answers were lacking. Kelso's *Doctrine for the Lady of the Renaissance* (1956) contains a bibliography of 890 items all written between 1400 and 1600 on the subject of the education of women. With varying degrees of cruelty or refinement, these items indicate that the purpose of education for women is to make women perfect wives, however unworthy their husbands. Latin and Greek, those foundation stones of all learning in the 1500s, were described as dangerous because they might distract a woman's mind and render her unfit for wifehood. The Dutchman Erasmus, the Englishman Thomas More, and the Spaniard Luis Vives (the latter a tutor to the royal women of England) all held to this view. There was a spectrum of opinion on how much learning a woman's mind could be exposed to without danger, and it is small comfort to know that Erasmus and More were among the most liberal of their time in this regard. More's famous school for his own daughters exemplified the adage that, in the country of the blind, the one-eyed man is king.

In Italy, there was a special set of niches for women, spaces that had been carefully protected for centuries. They were good niches, and women scholars, scientists, and artists who found life too harsh elsewhere fled to Italy to recover their sense of identity. This process went on right into the 1800s. These niches did not, however, answer the basic needs of the times.

The only widely read male exponent in the 1500s of the idea that the new humanism applied equally to women and men was Agrippa von Nettesheim (sometimes called Cornelius Agrippa), who said boldly: "Women and men were equally endowed with the gifts of spirit, reason and the use of words; they were created for the same end, and the sexual differences between them will not confer a different destiny" (O'Faolain and Martines 1973: 184).

The Reformation was no help at all. In fact, it provided another set of reinforcements for the concept of second-class mental and spiritual equipment for women. Luther and Calvin set back at least 100 years the progress that had been made in the Middle Ages in education for women, largely in convents, by their ideology of destruction of convents and abolition of the roles of monks and nuns. What they substituted for convent education, which had always included some classical learning, was a narrow vocational education that would fit women for their household duties. In fact, the chief argument for teaching women to read at all was to equip them as Sunday school teachers to impart scriptural knowledge to children. Women could have no other use for literacy.

It is painful to move through the literature of the 1500s and 1600s and see how widely the insights of humanism were denied applicability to women. Christine de Pisan's strong voice from the early 1400s was forgotten. I suggest that this period was much worse for women than the medieval period when the church regularly fed them the "woman as the source of all evil" doctrine, because that doctrine was simply part of the cultural furniture of the church. There were many other sources for a different image of women—within the church and outside it—in the Virgin Mary, in the saints, in nuns (especially the prophetess nuns that are described in Chapter 1 of this volume), and in the many devout women in the Beguine and other movements who lived secure and self-sufficient lives untouched by "Eve" doctrines. The Renaissance, however, created a new situation. There was a rediscovery of the nature of humanness, and there was a group of educated, cultured women in every country who would have every reason to expect to participate in that rediscovery. But their platforms were gone, their niches were gone, and their role models were gone. All they had were the bleak pronouncements that the new discoveries did not apply to them. The abject humility with which many women authors in the next two centuries wrote prefaces to their books, apologizing for presuming to write on any subject, is a direct outcome of the shock of this exclusion from the Renaissance. We have to realize how universal the male message was in this regard[6] to understand why it took women so long to develop the courage to claim their own nature.

The women who survived the 1500s best were the nonintellectuals. In England, they carried on for some time a robust involvement with estate management. Many middle-class women were still involved in merchandising and workshop partnerships, though the number was dwindling. Women of the Elizabethan era knew they had a strong queen, and the general status of women in society was not unaffected. By the time women managers and artisans were shifted out of former occupational statuses, intellectual women had found their tongues and begun the long campaign for their rights. By the 1600s, the upper-class women of France had invented their own version of an earlier Moslem, and then Italian, institution: the salon.

The salons were in a way the delayed entry of women into the Renaissance, although it was the Age of Enlightenment they were in fact entering. Renaissance humanism had always been rather self-centered and never concerned itself, either in Italy or in its transalpine forms, with social problems or the situation of the working classes (Hyma 1930). The salon movement similarly was a narcissistic exercise in the use of human wit. To a degree, it was also an exercise in the use of political power from the underside. Little social conscience developed there. To be fair, however, the salons developed more than wit and political maneuvering. Women artists, writers, and musicians flourished in the new environment, and there was a kind of cultural rebirth for many gifted women as a result.

The religious and social ferment involved in the Reformation, the Counter-Reformation, and the dissenting movements outside the Church of England cut across the issues of the new humanism and created another set of hardships for women. These hardships were much more immediate than the deprivation of education resulting from the closing of convents. They stemmed from the political alignments and military obligations on the Continent that went with being a Huguenot or a Catholic. Often, families were divided in their allegiances, and women had to find ways to be loyal to their family obligations without doing violence to their personal beliefs; also, they had to mediate between other family members. On the Continent, there was little that was positive that came out of the feuds, massacres, and continuing wars that lasted from the 1520s until the deportation of the Huguenots from France in 1687. In England, the dissenting sects were not so violently dealt with, and women came to play significant roles in their development. The Quakers, for example, institutionally organized by 1660, were notable for continuing the earlier artisan tradition of the participation of women in the common life. The Quaker group thus became a source of female leadership in England for several centuries to come. The jail terms regularly meted out to them only seemed to whet their appetites for action.

In the eighteenth century, women of all classes began to find their bearings in a more urban world. By 1700, 25% of the population of England was living in London and the larger towns. It took another century before the same was true in Western Europe (Laslett 1965).[7] It was a world full of new problems. Increasing population densities since the end of the black death, plus the new trade on the seaways of the world, meant another shift in the scale of social organization. Fuel shortages were already serious in the 1500s as local forests were everywhere depleted, and the 1600s saw the introduction on a large scale of the use of coal and coke (available but little used since the 1100s). Urban housing shortages and lack of sanitation systems to deal with new urban densities were the nightmare problems of the next three centuries.

The 1600s saw the first of the enclosure movements in England—the enclosure of common land for grazing the sheep of the gentry and large landowners. This first enclosure movement worked great hardship on the women and men of the cottager class, leaving them with shrunken subsistence opportunities. The second enclosure movement, extending approximately from 1750 to 1850, had different and more complex effects. By this time, there was a population explosion in process, and the countryside was swarming with labor. The second enclosure was associated with a new practice of extensive cultivation of wheat, which at harvest time required massive amounts of labor. A new class of migrant laboring families was created and led to the phenomenon of the family work gang. By the early 1800s, 50% of all rural labor was at least semi-migrant, and women and children suffered all the hardships of life in the open even while they "benefited" from ample opportunities for rural employment.

The story of the lot of rural women from the later Middle Ages to the industrial revolution is one of increasing work loads and increasing severity of working conditions. Life was hard for urban women too, but their situation had more social visibility. Middle-class urban women with entrepreneurial abilities, less involved than formerly in economic activity, turned their energies to the development of new approaches to work and housing relief, the education of children, and general aid to the poor. By the 1800s, as we will see in Part II of this volume, these activities were well organized and were accompanied by the appearance of a large number of women's magazines and women's organizations dealing with these new interests. Within the Catholic church, a new set of religious orders had developed enabling women to engage in the active teaching and welfare work denied them during the monastic enclosure movement of the 1500s. The Beguines paved the way for this. Having become "respectable," they were no longer persecuted for "errors in doctrine and moral aberration" and were now chiefly attacked by local guilds as sources of privileged competition. In fact, many beguinages by the beginning of the 1500s operated as urban poorhouses, meeting urgent welfare needs (McDonnell 1969: 573-74).

The unemployment of women was a new problem. It is hard to know who among working-class women were the worst off: the laboring rural poor or urban women working in factories for starvation wages. A new unemployed sector was the single gentlewoman, starving in quiet desperation between underpaid governess jobs. Surprising numbers of these "helpless" ladies joined the great stream of migrations to the Americas and later to Australia. The story of these pioneer women on the frontiers of expansionist Europe is the story all over again of the building of new systems of education and welfare under conditions of hardship and savagery,[8] a repetition of the dramas in the days of the old Germanic kingdoms after the fall of Rome.

The voluntary unemployment of women among the middle classes turned many of them toward the "conspicuous consumption" life-style characteristic, as we have seen, of a small group of women in every society with any kind of urban center. What was new in the eighteenth century, and even more in the nineteenth, was that much larger numbers of women entered this group.

As women left former employments, increasingly restrictive legal interpretations of the rights of married women to engage in business prevailed, particularly in England. Middle- and upper-class women had less and less to do as estate management also shifted into the hands of men. Married women lost control over their property, their persons, their children, and their beliefs.

Because we have no time budgets for women of these centuries, we do not know how much "free time" any of them really had. What we can observe from the record is that one fairly visible sector found alternative activities. Among upper-class women, the traditional manor house role was never wholly given up but was gradually transformed into community service roles. Urban middle-class women with energy and initiative followed the manor house pattern. The more problems women took on in dealing with urban and rural misery, the more they realized that the decision-making powers needed to carry out their work were not available to them. With or without Queens, women as civic beings were invisible in the public spaces of society. The deliberate campaign by women to obtain civic rights did not begin systematically until the 1800s and is the story in Part II. It actually began as a by-product of their other efforts. It was only when they were handicapped in their work for schools, for the poor, and for control of conditions of emigration for women as well as in their campaigns against slavery and alcoholism—handicapped because of their legal status as females—that they finally were pushed into fighting long-endured limitations. The trauma of the Renaissance was over.

This section again centers mainly on Europe, where industrialization, nationalism, and imperialism developed. The settlement of North America is also included, but the whole South American story is left out as well as that of the other continents. There is little excuse for excluding South America except the inability to master the necessary scholarship. The settlement of Peru and New Granada by Spain, and of Brazil by Portugal, in the 1500s deserves special study because women's roles developed differently there, both the Spanish and the Native American roles. The tale of colonialism in South America, Africa, and Asia from the 1500s on, and what it meant for the women who were colonized and the women who were colonizers, will have to wait for another book. Spotty as the presentation of these centuries will be, they do bring us after a fashion to the last two centuries of the second millennium, the transition centuries, with all the discomforts of their imperfectly conceived globalism.

Notes

1. Western accounts of the Crusades do not normally emphasize women's roles. Francesco Gabrieli's *Arab Historians of the Crusades*, however, brings out the fact that there were a number of women soldiers in the Frankish armies, as well as queens with their own all-women's battalions, and that the same phenomenon held for the Moslem side (Gabrieli 1969: 204).

2. The Beghards are the male counterpart of the Beguine movement, but they never attained anything like the size and significance of the Beguines. Apart from noting their existence, they will not be further discussed in this chapter.

3. Comparable developments in Asia include the *Ramanujachary*, which gave a new direction to the *bhakti* movement in India in the 1100s. The latter was a devotional movement that developed in the early Middle Ages as a "defense" against Buddhism and Jainism. In China, there was the appearance of Amida Buddhism and, in Tibet, the reform of a lax religiosity by the establishment of a new priest-state under the dual rule of a Dalai Lama and a Tashi Lama.

4. They were nameless, that is, unless the legendary peacemaker queen Genetaska of the Seneca nation was actually a historical character (see "The Peacemaker," in Canfield 1902: 149-54).

5. At one time, it was thought that the explorers brought syphilis to Europe from the Americas. It is now, however, generally considered that the disease was present in Europe all along and that there was a sudden and unexplained increase in infection rates.

6. Sheila Johansson (personal communication, 1975) feels I am making too much of a "stream of essays by male authors saying that women shouldn't be highly educated, even

[while] they were in fact getting a lot of education in the privileged classes. A few essays never stopped anybody." There may indeed have been, and probably were, many more men supportive of the education of women than the polemic literature implies. There is, nevertheless, such a thing as a climate of opinion. However unrepresentative of a society the creators of that climate are, they leave traces in social thought that to a degree constrain behavior.

7. By 1800, 20% of the population of Western Europe was in towns with more than 2,500 population. The United States, by contrast, was still predominantly rural, with only 5% of its population in urban areas.

8. The savagery refers to the white man, not the natives. McNeill (1963) in *The Rise of the West* makes it startlingly clear that the success of the expansionism of Europe was due to the superior savagery of the Europeans, who treated natives with a ruthlessness that Indians and blacks were culturally incapable of reciprocating (at least not until it was too late).

References

Adams, Henry. [1905] 1933. *Mont Saint-Michel and Chartres*. Boston: Houghton Mifflin.

Baldwin, John. 1971. *The Scholastic Culture of the Middle Ages*. Lexington, MA: D. C. Heath.

Boccaccio, Giovanni. 1963. *Concerning Famous Women*, translated by Guido A. Guarino. New Brunswick, NJ: Rutgers University Press.

Canfield, William W. 1902. *The Legends of the Iroquois*. Port Washington, NY: Ira J. Freidman.

Clough, Shepard B. 1951. *The Rise and Fall of Civilization: How Economic Development Affects the Culture of Nations*. New York: McGraw-Hill.

Cohn, Norman. 1970. *The Pursuit of Millennium*. New York: Oxford University Press.

de Pisan, Christine. 1966. *The Book of the Duke of True Lovers*, edited by Laurence Binyon and Eric R. D. Maclagan; translated by Alice Kemp-Welch. New York: Cooper Square.

de Rougemont, Denis. 1956. *Love in the Western World.* New York: Pantheon.

Gabrieli, Francesco, ed. 1969. *Arab Historians of the Crusades*, translated by E. J. Costello. Berkeley: University of California Press.

Hazard, Harry W. 1931. *Atlas of Islamic History.* Princeton, NJ: Princeton University Press.

Hollingsworth, Thomas Henry. 1969. *Historical Demography.* Ithaca, NY: Cornell University Press.

Huizinga, Johan. 1924. *The Waning of the Middle Ages.* New York: St. Martin's.

Hyma, Albert. 1930. *Erasmus and the Humanists.* New York: F. S. Crofts.

Kelso, Ruth. 1956. *Doctrine for the Lady of the Renaissance.* Urbana: University of Illinois Press.

Ladurie, Emmound LeRoy. 1971. *Times of Feast: Times of Famine.* Garden City, NY: Doubleday.

Laslett, Peter. 1965. *The World We Have Lost.* London: Methuen.

McDonnell, Ernst W. 1969. *The Beguines and the Beghards in Medieval Culture.* New York: Octagon.

McNeill, William H. 1963. *The Rise of the West: A History of the Human Community.* Chicago: University of Chicago Press.

Mujeeb, M. 1960. *World History: Our Heritage.* Bombay: Asia.

Nickerson, Hoffman. 1942. *The Armed Horde: 1793-1939.* 2nd ed. New York: Putnam.

O'Faolain, Julia and Lauro Martines, eds. 1973. *Not in God's Image: A History of Women in Europe from the Greeks to the Nineteenth Century.* New York: Harper & Row.

Reich, Emil. 1908. *Woman Through the Ages.* 2 vols. London: Methuen.

Strayer, J. R. 1964. "The Laicization of French and English Society in the Thirteenth Century." Pp. 103-15 in *Change in Medieval Society: Europe North of the Alps, 1050-1500,* edited by Sylvia L. Thrupp. New York: Appleton-Century-Crofts.

Summers, Rev. Montague, translator. 1948. *The Malleus Maleficarum of Heinrich Kramer and James Sprenger.* New York: Dover. (First published 1486.)

Wilkinson, Richard G. 1973. *Poverty and Progress: An Ecological Model of Economic Development.* London: Methuen.

Zeigler, Philip. 1969. *The Black Death.* London: Collins.

1

Millennialism and New-Old Roles for Women in the Middle Ages: A European Story, 1000 to 1450 C.E.

An Overview of Roles of Women in the Middle Ages: Queens, Prophets, Reformers, and Revolutionaries

The Middle Ages are confusing in regard to the status of women. Women had to remain in their own niches inside declining religious bureaucracies while men filled the new secular bureaucracies of the state. The linking of higher education with training for the priesthood effectively barred them from preparing for entry into the new state machinery. Yet, in the short run, "women religious," particularly the prophetesses, rose to a kind of zenith in social status and public recognition. But, when the vogue for prophecy had passed, they went to the stake. There was a gradual economic decline in the women's orders during this period because they were not organized to participate in the general shift toward a monetized economy. The church itself, moreover, used this economic transition to further limit the autonomy of the women's orders. A parallel development of long-run importance to women was the emergence of secular alternatives for the unmarried. Linked to the craft guild movement, yet separate from it, the Beguine

movement outlasted the guilds and gave working women an autonomous niche in urban society that the mixed guilds never provided.

The Crusades, urbanism, and statism are perhaps the major forces
affecting women in these centuries. The reemergence of the old prophecy tradition was in one sense, perhaps, an immediate outcome of the
year 1000's millennialist fervor; in a larger sense, it was a response to
continuous social upheaval. The charismatic face of the church could
smile on the woman visionary even while the bureaucratic face was
trying to clamp down on women's initiatives. The result was almost a
reincarnation of the old sibylline sisterhood.

The royal abbeys in particular produced distinguished abbesses and
clairvoyant nuns who advised heads of state. At the same time, the
woods of Europe, and more particularly England, were full of anchoresses who lived ascetic and solitary lives in little hermitages. These
anchoresses often also rendered local services, including healing, and
were both revered and feared by local communities as sources of knowledge closed to others. Many a local functionary had his own private
anchoress-consultant on local affairs. It was a routine matter for anyone
who had a decision to make about affairs of state, from the local squire
to the pope and the emperor, to consult with a known woman religious
before taking any action. This was notably true from the time of the
second Crusade forward. (The second Crusade might never have been
launched if Mechthild of Magdeburg had not taken it as her own
particular "cause.") The nun-prophetess, the cult of the Virgin, and the
phenomenon of the rediscovery of the pagan sibylline books can from
one point of view be seen as the revenge that a society, deprived since
pagan days of significant female leadership, took on the patriarchal
Christian church. This is the way Henry Adams ([1905] 1933) puts it,
and in a sense he is right, although his conception of female leadership
leaves something to be desired. His "Mary-image" of the female involves an ingenious compound of woman the inspirer and woman the
capricious mistress, leaving out any task-oriented capacities.

One example of this need to turn to women is found in the recurring
Pope Joan legends. The legend of a woman pope, supposed to have
reigned in the 850s C.E., became very popular in the Middle Ages. It
looks as if the original legend was a positive, "pro-woman" one. By the
time medieval chroniclers got through with it, however, Joan was the
dreaded Anti-Christ, to be welcomed as much as feared because she
would usher in the reign of Christ. The medieval mind never got its
feelings straight about the savior-queen/king versus the Anti-Christ,
as to which one or both were expected; frequently, the same person is

presented both ways. Here is one of the earlier forms of the Pope Joan legend, given by Martin Polonus in 1282:

> After Leo IV, John Angelus, a native of Metz, reigned two years, five months and four days. . . . He died in Rome. He is related to have been a female, and, when a girl, to have accompanied her sweetheart in male costume to Athens; there she advanced in various sciences, and none could be found to equal her. So, after having studied for three years in Rome, she had great masters for her pupils and hearers. And when there arose a high opinion in the city of her virtue and knowledge, she was unanimously elected Pope. But during her papacy she became in the family way by a familiar. Not knowing the time of birth, as she was on her way from S. Peters to the Lateran she had a painful delivery, between the Coliseum and S. Clements Church, in the street. Having died after, it is said that she was buried on the spot. . . . She [is not] placed in the catalogue of the Holy Pontiffs, not only on account of her sex, but also because of the horribleness of the circumstances. (Baring-Gould 1896: 172-73)

Although scholarship indicates no missing dates in the papal history during which this person could have sat on the throne, the record could have been rewritten. We have already noted some instances of holy men in the history of the church who were accidentally discovered to be holy women. If one or more of the popes of recorded history was actually a woman, we shall never know it![1]

Whatever the merits of Pope Joan, the sibylline sisterhood was certainly being courted. I have already mentioned that the pagan sibylline books were rewritten to help the conversion of the pagans and the Jews to Christianity. The oldest such manuscript known to medieval Europe was the Oracle of Sibilla Tiburtina. Written in the mid-300s C.E., it proclaimed Constantine as the Last World Emperor who would fight the Anti-Christ and usher in the Second Coming. The Last World Emperor theme was too useful to discard, and countless versions of it, under the labels of the sibyls Tiburtina, Samia, and Cumae, were circulated by medieval prophets and prophetesses with various interpretations as to who was meant (Reeves 1969). Given that the prophecies were supposed to have been originally written by women, women had a special role in their interpretation, although most of the interpretive manuscripts that have survived were written by men.

It is hard to sort the wheat from the chaff in looking at these materials. The political pronouncements of well-educated monastic women experienced in political affairs, such as Hildegarde of Bingen, or the imperious but knowledgeable Brigitta of Sweden, cannot be set side by side with those of unstable but charismatic figures such as Prous Boneta, who thought she was the incarnation of the new age, or Manfreda, "candidate" for the papal chair. Unfortunately, however, not even the pronouncements of the scholarly women can be considered reliable. We are well enough aware today that scholarly training does not in itself produce good political judgment; neither did it in those days. What is important to note is that women were being consulted in matters of public policy, and their judgments were based on the same worldview that their male colleagues held. This was "overlife activity," and there was no distinctive "woman's point of view," for good or ill, in the world situation.[2]

The queens and princesses of the Middle Ages often joined forces with the abbesses both on issues of public affairs and in support of the continuously developing educational and service institutions that convents offered. At least one queen achieved greatness, as we shall see.

A different and quieter leadership role for women is seen in the writings of Mechthild of Magdeburg and other Beguine mystics and in anchoresses like Julian of Norwich. These women were concerned at a very deep level with the interior work of transformation of mind and spirit yet dealt with the human soul in an allegorical fashion with more or less direct political implications. Some of these women, like Mechthild, addressed directly the corruption of the priesthood and of society. That corruption and the prevalent practice of priests keeping one or more "concubines" or "priestesses" have to be remembered when we read the visions of these women. Ironically, much of their work surfaces in Dante, while they themselves remain unknown. Many passages in the *Divine Comedy* are reminiscent of descriptions of hell and heaven in the writings of these mystics (Kemp-Welch 1913: 70-82).

It is no accident that Dante lived in Italy, a country that gave an honored place to nonreligious women intellectuals in its universities and its public life throughout the entire Middle Ages. Perhaps his study of the formation of the interior life, *Vita Nuova*, would not seem unique if we were more familiar with his women contemporaries.[3] He must have interacted a fair amount with them, and he must also have been familiar with the writings of the Beguine mystics. In fact, either Mechthild of Magdeburg or Mechthild of Hackeborn is supposed to have been the original of his Matilda (Kemp-Welch 1913). And Dante's Beatrice, both as historical person and as symbol of the inward guide, may also represent something else: the internalized teachings of Dante's women colleagues.

One of the tragic accompaniments of turning to seers, male or female, was the resurgence of the old fear of demonism and sorcery, an undercurrent in every society from hunting-gathering bands to sophisticated civilizations. The witchcraft mania did not at all begin by pointing at women. In England, two major witchcraft trials, one in 1232 and one in 1324, involved, respectively, a chief justice and the leading burghers of the town of Coventry. In France in 1308, a bishop was accused of witchcraft, and, in 1315, the chamberlain, privy councellor, and chief chamberlain of the king fell under the same accusation. Needless to say, these were political trials aimed at uncovering treason. Most of them were cases of suspected poisoning of a king (Summers 1948).

From the time of the kings of Israel and before, people in high places were accustomed to calling in soothsayers to forecast futures, and it has always been but a step from asking for forecasts to asking for the means to implement or prevent the predicted outcomes. The forecasters were often also herbalists who knew both healing and poisonous plants. Forecasting, poisoning, and healing thus became inextricably mixed.[4] High-class witches, or warlocks, tended to be men. But, when suspicion started to descend the social ladder, the large group of middle- and lower-class women herbalists and healers began to be caught in the nets. Because these were the traditional medical practitioners for the masses of society, and were generally excluded as women from the possibility of getting formal medical degrees, there was no protection for them if a disgruntled patient or neighbor chose to accuse one of them of witchcraft.

While it is an oversimplification to say that the witchcraft mania was a plot on the part of male doctors to get rid of their more popular female competition (Ehrenreich and English 1973), many doctors no doubt enthusiastically took part in the accusation process. By 1460, the date at which the University of Paris made provision for (male) students to matriculate in medicine, witchcraft accusations against women healers were reaching their height.

The social and intellectual environment that fostered this combination of demonism and learning was not friendly to learning for the female. Women scholars did flourish, however, in some protected niches, particularly in the German convents, which already had long traditions of female scholarship. We also find them, with surprise, at royal courts, and we find them at the Italian universities. This is partly due to the early development of the Renaissance in Italy, partly due to continuing contact with an older tradition of women scholars in Moslem Spain.

It is one of the ironies of history that the rise of the universities as well as the great mendicant religious orders and the establishment of the Inquisition all happened within a short space of time in the 1200s. Each set of institutions was individually chartered by the pope himself. While none of them set out to victimize women, in fact all three contributed to that process over the next couple of hundred years.

None of the limitations placed on women in this period stifled their creativity as related to one of the major contributions of women not only to the Middle Ages but to the whole sociocultural development of urban life in the West: the Beguine movement. A religiously oriented laywomen's movement led by upper- and middle-class women who were moving from rural areas to the towns and cities of Europe, it provided autonomy for single women of all classes moving in from the countryside. It created for women a third alternative to the existing ones of marriage or religious seclusion. It also provided a new kind of urban social service network. Responding to the political and economic conditions of the times, it became entangled with numerous heretical movements. Nevertheless, the core of the Beguine movement steered clear of too close an identification with the church, the libertines, or the revolutionaries. The movement continues in Europe today. (See the section "The Women's Movement in the Middle Ages: The Beguines," below, in this chapter, for a further description of the Beguines.)

One learns only indirectly of the role of women in the many revolutionary and heretical movements. Rodney Hilton, in discussing rural communal movements in Europe in the Middle Ages, comments that "the majority of [the movements'] supporters were artisans, workers and peasants from the mountain and the plain (and amongst these, as in other heretical sects, a high proportion of women)" (1973: 107). This parenthetical statement is almost his only mention of women in his entire fascinating study of medieval peasant uprisings. We learn more about them in the urban revolutionary movements, partly because the women leaders in these movements were often from the upper classes. The revolutionary unrest that developed as the craft guilds weakened and the wealthy mercantile guilds became the new oppressors often led to an alliance of idealistic merchants and landholders with oppressed workers. As in the beginning of the Christian era, the houses of women of wealth sheltered many utopian enterprises and charismatic religious sects. Even the flagellants, who scandalized and hypnotized Europe with their bloody public scourgings, were initially solid middle-class women and men concerned with bringing to an end the destructive plagues, wars, and Crusades and with helping the urban poor (Le Goff 1968).[5]

The religious utopian movements and the more directly political movements were all treated by the authorities as part of a conspiracy involving heresy and witchcraft. Far from being one huge interrelated conspiracy, however, these movements were highly local in orientation. This is one reason it was easy for women to be active in them. If one wonders how middle- and lower-class women could be attracted to the crudely authoritarian millennialism represented in many of the movements—"Obey me and I will bring you paradise on earth"—it should be remembered that women were already "trained" to obedience by the church, the state, and their husbands and fathers. Some of the movements were indeed frighteningly totalitarian, others astoundingly libertine. Most women who were prepared to step out of conventional roles, however, entered the Beguines, who represented the great, solid center of the urban social-change movement. We will look at the women in the extremist groups but also give serious attention to the Beguines.

Outside of the Beguines, the only major social institution available to working-class women was the guild, and we will explore the extent to which women were active in guilds and independent economic enterprises. The Middle Ages represent the peak period of women's guild involvement, and the Renaissance will usher in the long decline in the status of the working woman in Europe.

The context in which the prophesying abbess, the reforming Beguine, and the rebellious peasant women were living out their lives was one in which queens and princesses moved to more overtly political roles than women of the royalty had had before. These noblewomen no longer had the exciting task of taming crude societies for the church—the crudeness was now inherent in the church itself. They headed instead into a protracted balance-of-power game in a new statist-conscious Europe; marriage alliances played the crucial role in keeping the balance. What excitement there was for the female nobility of the Middle Ages lay in games of chivalry and the Crusades. At the same time, the earlier work of supporting convents and the educational and medical activities associated with them continued. In fact, queens and princesses joined forces with abbesses in fighting to keep independent power for the convents in the face of a concerted attack by lower levels of the church bureaucracy and state officials. We will now turn to an examination of individual women in each of the categories we have discussed above, beginning with royal women.[6]

Women of the Aristocracy

The Princesses of England

The skills of elite women in marriage diplomacy were first mentioned in describing women's roles in the ancient empires of the Middle East. The Middle Ages is the first period for which we have the materials to examine the phenomenon in some detail. M. A. E. Green's six-volume study (1850) of the princesses of England from 1035 to 1482 makes it possible to look at diplomatic alliances in a particularly interesting subset of the aristocracy—princesses of the royal blood who did not themselves become queens in their own land. In a way, this is the "underlife" of royalty, although it is the overlife of England in respect to its international alliance system in the Middle Ages.

Table 1.1, which provides data on 48 English princesses, shows clearly that the lives of these princesses were totally geared to alliance structures. This was a period of protracted power struggles between European kingdoms, particularly between England and France, and every daughter was worth an army if "deployed" in the right way. Out of 48 princesses, 3 were vowed to convents in infancy or early childhood, and 14 died before they could be married (of these, 3 had been betrothed, and the others died in early infancy), leaving 30 to conduct actual diplomacy on behalf of their fathers' kingdoms after marriage.

The amount of time and care given to the betrothal negotiations themselves are indicated by the fact that, out of a total of 26 betrothals (a subset of the betrothals from Table 1.1), only 12 involved negotiations with only one country; 3 betrothals called for negotiations with two countries; and 11 involved more than two countries (some almost up to a dozen). The betrothal process began for most princesses between the ages of 1 and 9. The total number of principalities dealt with was 15. The importance of adequate preparation for carrying on diplomacy after marriage can be seen by the fact that five of the princesses were educated in the courts of their husbands-to-be before marriage, and two of the husbands were educated in the English court before marriage (not shown in Table 1.1). Many betrothal negotiations involved court appearances for the girls before the age of 9. Age at marriage was as follows:

Age	Number of Princesses
9 or under	2
10-12	4
13-15	9
16-17	5
18-19	4
20 or older	6
Total	30

There can be no doubt about what these princesses were expected to be able to do in addition to providing babies; 17 of them took active ruling

text continued on page 28

TABLE 1.1 The Princesses of England from William the Conqueror to Charles I (1035-1482)

	Age at Betrothal	Country of First Marriage Alliance	Age at First Marriage	Age at Birth of First Child	Age at Death	Political Cultural Activities
William the Conqueror:						
Caecilia[a]	Negotiations at birth	—	—	—	—	Convent life
Adeliza	Childhood	—	—	—	Childhood	—
Matilda	Childhood and teens	—	—	—	Teens	—
Constance	Late 20s	Castile	29	?	33	Founded many institutions
Adela	13	Blois	18	?	Old age	Active coruler, also regent, founded many institutions
Henry I:						
Mathilda	7	Germany	12	?	?	Very active and very ambitious
Stephan:						
Matilda and Mary	No information					
Henry II:						
Matilda	Many early, final at 9	Saxony	18	19	33	Politically unskilled but met demands
Eleanore	Childhood	Castile	19	19	59	Loved political activity, regent, mediator
Joanna	Many	Sicily	11	17	36	Loved political activity, participated in Crusades
King John:						
Isabella	Very many	Germany	21	27[b]	27[b]	Lived secluded harem existence
Eleanore	5	England	15	?	59	Active by choice, poor administrator
Henry III:						
Margaret	Infancy	Scotland	10	18	34	Imprisoned age 10-15, wise, coped well, became loved queen
Beatrice	Three negotiations, 11-16	Brittany	17	20	32	Not independently active, did go on Crusades
Katherine	Died at age 3½					
Edward I:						
Eleanora	Many negotiations, childhood, teens	France	27	—	?	Hard life, wars, imprisoned by husband

continued

TABLE 1.1 Continued

	Age at Betrothal	Country of First Marriage Alliance	Age at First Marriage	Age at Birth of First Child	Age at Death	Political Cultural Activities
Joanna	Ages 5, 13	Italy	19	?	35	Retiring life
Margaret	3	Brabant	15	?	?	Marriage was trade alliance, skillful negotiator
Beringaria	Died in infancy					
Mary[a]	7	—	—	—	?	Convent life, active as royal nun, many good works
Elizabeth	Ages 2, 5	Holland	15	34[b]	34[b]	Turned out as good politician, unexpected
Eleanora	Died at age 5					
Edward II:						
Eleanora	Three negotiations in teens	France	15	16	?	Unskilled, did her best as regent, crowned queen at 10
Joanna	8	Scotland	8	—	41	Ruled well in difficulties
Edward III:						
Isabella	Many negotiations, age 2-15	France	33	—	?	Tragic life, left loved husband when countries at war
Joanna	Ages 2, 6, and 13	Spain	17	—	17	Tried hard, life of failures
Blanche	Died at birth 1					
Mary	Several early negotiations	Brittany	17	—	17	Died three months after marriage
Margaret		England	14	—	15	Died shortly after marriage
Henry IV:						
Blanche	Many negotiations in teens	Bavaria	13	15	19	Died in third childbirth
Philippa	9	Sweden	13	—	37	Active ruler of Norway, Sweden, Denmark; king deferred to her
Edward IV:						
Mary	Many negotiations	Died before marriage			16	—

Name		Country				Description
Cecelia	4	England	20	21	38	Death of Edward IV removed her from alliance system
Margaret	Died in infancy					
Anne	Negotiations, age 4 to 5	England	22	?	36-37	Obscure, poor health
Catherine	Negotiations began at 4	England	16	18	49	Managed estate
Bridget[a]		—	—	—	23	Religious seclusion
Henry VII:						
Margaret	6	Scotland	—	18	53	Intense political activity and turmoil, regent of Scotland for a time
Elizabeth	Died at age 3					
Mary	11	France	18	21	37	Personal political activity, for love, marriage, friends, and relatives
Catherine	Died in infancy					
James I:						
Elizabeth	16	Germany	17	17	66	Intense political activity, defender of Protestant cause
Sophia	Died in infancy					
Charles I:						
Mary	10	Holland	10	19	30	Active in political sphere Brilliant and intellectual, lived in seclusion after death of father, poor health
Elizabeth		—	—	—	15	
Anne	Died in infancy					
Catherine	Died in infancy					
Henrietta Anne	16	France	17	18	26	Diplomacy between brother Charles II and brother-in-law Louis; also liked courtly gaiety, ballets, and so on

NOTE: Princesses who later became queens of England are excluded.
a. Vowed to convent.
b. Died in first childbirth.

responsibilities. Some, like Joanna, who married David the Bruce, began as early as the age of 10 as crowned queen. Philippa, at the age of 13, had three countries to rule: Norway, Sweden, and Denmark; her husband didn't like ruling, so he turned the job over to her.

Edward I's daughter Margaret married the Duke of Brabant at age 15 in what was essentially a trade alliance, and she successfully monitored and increased trade relations between England and Brabant. Some of the princesses participated actively in wars and went along on the Crusades, although most did not enjoy that aspect of ruling. The saddest fate came to Isabella, daughter of Edward II, who left her much-loved husband, de Coucy of France, when war broke out between their two countries, perceiving that her primary loyalties lay with England. This gives an inkling of the tensions under which these princesses lived, having diplomatic responsibilities for relations with their native country, immediate responsibility for the government of the countries they married into, and, in addition, the responsibilities of motherhood. Babies began to come to most of these women in their teens.

On the whole, they did not live very long. Of the ones who married, a majority died before the age of 40. With 14 the modal age of marriage and 35 the modal age of death, most of these women packed a lot of activity into an average 21 years of diplomatic married life. Most were active on their own initiative, and most of those who were active enjoyed it. Those who enjoyed their political activity were generally those who had a talent for it. Those who did their best, but with difficulty, are considered to have acted out of "noblesse oblige." Given the few options open to these princesses, it is amazing that only three felt actively hostile to their role. The inactive ones were partly those who died too young to have an activity record and partly those who had no talent for politics and found a way to live in domestic retirement at court. Two nuns are also included in this group: One lived a secluded life, but the other took full responsibility as a royal nun, getting support for enterprises important to her order.

The family and court life of these princesses in early childhood was probably typical of other royal families of Europe of the time. Some fathers, like Edward III, swore they would not sacrifice their daughters' happiness to diplomatic necessity, yet Edward himself was one of the most active marriage negotiators in this set of fathers. He could not avoid dealing with a knotty balance-of-power problem with the only tools he felt he had. Sons were equally caught up in the alliance problem and had no more choice than their wives-to-be, so one could hardly say that the system discriminated against women.

What I find of particular interest in pondering the lives of these women is the amount of individuality and autonomy they displayed in a life situation hedged with many restrictions. I have given no details of their political and cultural activities, but they were certainly on the order of the activities a secretary of state of a small nation might undertake today, with the duties of minister of cultural affairs added. One striking feature of their lives is how early they began their public responsibilities. It is almost impossible to imagine 10- to 15-year-old girls in Western societies having the necessary training and self-discipline to undertake roles the princesses took for granted. The success of the medieval princesses in their diplomatic roles is all the more remarkable when one considers that nearly every one of them had to make her home in a foreign country and function in a language not her native tongue, with a set of customs alien to her own upbringing. There was no running home to mother. Not a single one of these princesses was considered outstanding in her own time or later. Nonetheless, these women often performed key functions that history ascribes to their less capable husbands, due to the convention of recording history in terms of reigning kings.

Other Princesses and Queens

The story of women in the Middle Ages is often overshadowed by the story of Eleanor of Guienne, or Aquitaine (1122-1204), the richest woman in Europe and the most dominant personality among medieval queens. If the princesses described above represent the underside of the diplomatic marriage system, Eleanor of Aquitaine represents the over-side. A woman of towering capabilities and ruler of her own kingdom of Aquitaine in France, she was twice unequally yoked with kings of lesser ability and struggled until the end of her long life to harness her ideas and her political skills to the intractable realities of her situation as queen of a small principality.[7]

Allied to France as the queen of Louis VII at the age of 15, she accompanied him to the Holy Land on the Crusade of 1147 and discovered there the exciting intellectual and cultural world of the Mediterranean, unknown to the Europe of her time. She also discovered that she had married a pious, retiring man with no political or cultural interests and, after 15 years of marriage, divorced the king to return to her own kingdom.

Her second marriage at the age of 30 to Henry II of England linked her with a ruler as politically ambitious as she but without her breadth of intellect and wisdom. Bearing and rearing 10 children in her 50 tumultuous years as queen of England, she was often allied with her sons, including the later kings Richard and John, against her husband. In protest against his politics and his very public amours, she determined to return to her own kingdom of Aquitaine. Seized and imprisoned by Henry while in flight, she endured 14 years of house imprisonment without ever losing her hold on political affairs and successfully defeated Henry's attempts to divorce her and force her into a convent so he could seize her kingdom. She was finally released by her son Richard when Henry died. In her last years, she lived quietly and ruled well, serving as regent of England while Richard was away at the Crusades. She died at 83. Her last signature on a public document read "Eleanor, by the wrath of God, Queen of England."

She shaped much of the culture of her times, as both Kelly (1950) and Henry Adams ([1905] 1933) show. She undertook many institution building enterprises, educational and religious, including the endowment of Fontrevault, which became one of the major religious houses of Europe. Eleanor was also a notable contributor to the great medieval institution of the Court of Love, which her daughter Mary of Champagne developed further at Troyes. Eleanor might, among other things, be called the Mother of the Century, given that she reared and educated a most extraordinary group of sons and daughters who in their turn shaped the institutions of Europe in the next generation. Most notable were Richard, John, Mary, and Leonore. Mary created the rules for the Court of Love and brought together poets and troubadours to set a high cultural standard for this new artistic medium. She supported Chrétien de Troyes as her court poet. Leonore married the king of Spain. The daughter of that union, Blanche of Castile, became one of the great queens of France after marrying Louis VIII at the age of 12. Queen Blanche served as regent of France twice in her lifetime, saw to the sound management of the country, and produced the son who was to become St. Louis of France.

Another group of royal women, as inconspicuous for the most part as the princesses of England, and in style totally different than the Court of Love queens, are the princesses of Germany, Czechoslovakia, Poland, and Hungary: Matilda, Hedwig, Anna, Agnes, Elizabeth, and, somewhat later, Jadwiga. These were all wives and daughters of kings and all devout Christians who carried on the work of caring for the sick and the poor begun by their royal sisters of the earlier Middle Ages. Two of these royal women are famous: Jadwiga of Poland (1371-99) and St. Elizabeth of Thüringen (1207-31).

Jadwiga belongs in the tradition of the heroic Christianizing queens of the earlier Middle Ages. She was betrothed at age 7 to the son of the archduke of Austria. When she was crowned queen of Poland at 16, she was forced by her subjects to give up a by-then unwelcome alliance and marry the boisterous pagan Jagiello of Lithuania. The marriage involved an agreement for the mass conversion of Lithuania. A deeply religious person herself, Jadwiga worked at "taming" Jagiello. She was also a strong political leader and led her army into the field when border disputes erupted. Her most noteworthy accomplishments were a serious effort to contain the dangerous Order of Teutonic Knights by peaceful negotiation and the founding of the University of Cracow. The university was to a considerable extent the product of her own personal planning and activity. Working with a committee of duchesses and governors' wives, she studied existing university models at Padua, Bologna, and Paris carefully before deciding on Cracow's format. She died in childbirth at 28 and is still revered as one of the great rulers and great saints in Polish history (Kellog 1932).

St. Elizabeth of Thüringen, who lived much more quietly and died at an even younger age than Jadwiga, is nevertheless one of the most written about royal saints of Europe. The daughter of a Hungarian king, Elizabeth was raised in her husband-to-be's court from the age of 4 and married at 13. She had three children, and the fourth died at birth at the very time that her husband was killed in the Crusades. As a child in her husband-to-be's court, Elizabeth used to walk about the narrow streets of the town outside the castle walls, carrying food to distribute to the poor. Her mother-in-law was unfriendly to her activities, but Elizabeth persisted in works of charity. All through her teens, she continued this process of visiting in the families of the poor and nursing the sick. She evidently had a radiant presence. Only 20 when her husband died, she was more or less chased out of the castle by hostile brothers-in-law. She found refuge in the town and continued to work among the poor until she died three years later, at the age of 24 (Ancelet-Hustache 1963; Bordeaux 1937).

Eleanor, Jadwiga, and St. Elizabeth were very different kinds of persons, but all were in one way typical of royal women: betrothed in childhood, married in the teens, removed from normal personal family supports, finding a way to live an active public life according to their *own pattern*, determined by their own values and interests.

In Byzantium during the early 1100s, the scholar princess Anna Comnena, known as a "pious, learned and passionate" mistress of classical learning, wrote the *Alexsiad*, a vivid documentary of the reign of her father, Emperor Alexius I. She was a good historian and is also supposed to have founded and taught in a medical school in Constantinople. In fact, she was a sad, complaining figure. She had been reared by her father to succeed him as reigning empress, "born to the purple," as she put it, but circumstances (and a younger brother) intervened, and she had to content herself with second-rate status and a second-rate husband. She never accepted this, and her writings are interspersed with personal laments. It is not hard to sympathize with her situation, given that her sex-imposed alternative life was a dull one. She did exercise her considerable talents to good purpose in her scholarly work, however. As an eyewitness of the Crusades and the barbarian invasions into Byzantium, she brought more than detached scholarly interest to her writing (Diehl 1963; Buckler 1929).

The 1100s in Byzantium witnessed a period of great effort to create alliances by marriage between the Eastern empire and Western Europe. Emperor Manuel married the German princess Bertha of Sulzbach. The unlucky Alexius, who had been betrothed to Agnes of France as a child, was murdered, and Andronicus, who took the throne instead, married Agnes when she was 12. Constance of Hohenstaufen, daughter of Frederick II, married Emperor John in 1244. Then there was Yolanda of Monterray, who married Andronicus II, and Anna of Savoy, who married Andronicus III. In each of these cases, the lives of the women were lives of stark tragedy, because of the tension and actual warring between Byzantium and Europe during the Crusades. Each woman in turn was totally abandoned to her fate by her European family (Diehl 1963).

In spite of all the personal and public tragedies that the princesses and queens of the Middle Ages suffered, on the whole they performed remarkably as competent state functionaries. Many of them were women of great individuality and assertiveness, yet they are but infrequently present on the pages of history.

Other Aristocrats

The life of women of the aristocracy outside the royal ruling family was to varying degrees like that of the princesses. Aristocratic women had two major duties: the management of the family estates and attendance at court. Depending on their temperament and abilities, they could devote themselves to the productivity of the estate, to public works on behalf of the court, or to a life of social activity centering on the Courts of Love and tournament watching. Occasionally, groups of more robust ladies, bored with the spectator roles of social life at court, scandalized the local countryside by arriving at tournaments dressed to enter the lists themselves. This kind of activity reached a fever pitch around the time of the black death—perhaps a replay of the restless last days of Rome when women went into the circus as gladiators (Ziegler

1969: 36). During prolonged absences of the men of a region at Crusades, women sometimes carried on tournaments themselves, dressed as their husbands and jousting under their husbands' names (Reich 1908: 184).

Women of the aristocracy could also take military training if they chose, and they often did. Among the outstanding aristocratic women warriors of the Middle Ages, we find Matilda of Tuscany, who at 15 rode beside her mother Beatrix and father Godfrey of Lorraine at the head of the Tuscan forces, to repel Norman invaders (Reich 1908: 174). Spain had several famous women warriors, including, a little later than this period, the "nun-ensign" Dona Catalina de Eraus, who is said to have turned the tide of many a battle by appearing as the soldiers were getting ready to fight (de Beaumont 1929: 59). Eleanora di Arborea of Sardinia took the field after her brother's murder and successfully suppressed a domestic rebellion, then went on to defeat the king of Aragon in battle (Castellani 1939: 22). The heroines of the defense of Vienna in 1554 were a 3,000-woman army, which fought in three regiments under Forteguerra, Piccolonimini, and Fausti (Castellani 1939: 27).

The cavalieressi of Italy were not all of the nobility, but they belong to the tradition of medieval women warriors, to the romantic tradition of chivalry. Among them were "the very noble Luzia Stanga"; Margheritona, the courtesan who served as a paid trooper in Count de Gaiazzo's light horse squadron; and the courtesan Malatesta (de Beaumont 1929: 57). French women warriors in this period were either duelists who made themselves locally famous in France or hard-fighting Crusader soldiers who usually died unidentified—and therefore unhonored.

The most famous woman warrior of the Middle Ages was not of the aristocracy at all but a peasant girl of France. She does not belong in this section, but she does not belong in any other section of this chapter either. There have been many different historical portrayals of Joan of Lorraine.[8] Common to them all is the picture of a robust peasant girl with mystical leanings who became convinced that she was to "save France." She was not well educated and had neither geographic sense (about where battlegrounds were) nor political understanding, but she had native intelligence and tenacity and managed to persuade a relative into introducing her to the local lord who could send her on to the king.

At each step of the way, Joan's story seems fantastically unlikely. She learned to ride and gained a smattering of military tactics in her early teens during a period when her own community was overrun by a hostile neighboring army. This is how it was possible for her to handle herself creditably on horseback when she later actually rode with an army. The local nobleman of her hometown tried to put Joan off but finally shipped her away to the king as a political maneuver. The king in turn sent her away with a small retinue of soldiers to placate her, never intending that she should lead an army. Encamped with the main French army, she was completely ignored by the officers. Infuriated, she literally seized an opportunity and rode off with the army sans officers on the famous occasion of her first battle. The peasants and the common soldiers already revered her, having heard and believed the story of her mission, so she had no difficulty getting followers en route to battle. When the officers discovered that she had ridden off with their men, they did the only thing possible—dashed after the army, took over a battle they hadn't intended to fight, and, to everyone's surprise, won it (Guillemin 1972; see also Reich 1908). Joan moved through all this as a charismatic figure who never really understood what she was doing but did it with a simplicity and faith that make her come through as "believable" no matter how unfriendly her chronicler. As a historical figure who happens to be a woman, her significance lies in the fact that she acted out a major role in a crucial portion of French national history out of an initial unawareness of the limitations and weaknesses that went with her situation as a woman—and she was therefore not constrained in her behavior by those limitations. The awareness of the limitations came to her later and tragically, after her part had been played, as she suffered imprisonment and the Inquisition. But the courage of one who acts as if there are no limitations continues to capture us, centuries later. She evidently did not seem as unusual to her own countrymen as she does to the twentieth century, which suggests that more of a woman warrior tradition than we know of was extant in her time.

Joan did not start a social movement. She was rather a demonstration that a charismatic peasant can have as much as or more impact on society than can a queen. While the lonely Joan was playing her part, however, the Middle Ages were seething with social movements. One significant set of them, known as the "women's movement," developed an interesting alliance between former peasants and the urban middle classes. This is the phenomenon we shall look at next.

The Women's Movement in the Middle Ages: The Beguines

The term *Frauenbewegung* (women's movement) is often used in referring to the activities of upper- and middle-class laywomen who took leadership in promoting the transition to urbanism that began in

Europe in the 1100s. It is appropriate to call it a social movement in that it began spontaneously in a number of different locations at the same time, all over the Low Countries. It spread to the rest of Europe very quickly. Colledge calls the *Frauenbewegung* "that great and victorious revolt of pious women, everywhere in Europe, against the reactionary traditions which would have condemned them in the cloisters as well as in the world to a role of subordination and silence" (1961: 7).

It is difficult to give a balanced picture of the movement because some studies treat it primarily as a lay religious movement (McDonnell 1969) and others as a strictly pragmatic development associated with the women's guilds (Bücher 1910). Because there was a high background level of religiosity in the Middle Ages, especially for women, even the most pragmatic guild-associated beguinages (a type of women's commune) also had some group religious practices. The guild movement itself had a strong religious component in its ceremonial observances; according to some authorities, this developed out of earlier religious associations of workers in the same craft that were similar to, if not actually descendants of, the religious mutual aid associations of Greece and Rome. While the craft guilds became increasingly secular, the Beguines kept more of a religious emphasis. The women who became outstanding in the Beguine movement were in fact religious leaders. These women were also leaders of a movement for social and economic justice and against institutional corruption, however, and this must not be forgotten when we look at the more spiritual aspects of their work. Those who emphasize the religious aspect of the Beguine movement say that it is the women's lay counterpart of the Franciscan and Cistercian movements. Even the most deeply religious of the Beguines, those known as the ecstatics, however, sought cloistered life but rarely.

As a social movement, Beguinism is unique in that it used the old traditions of the all-women's workshops that we discovered in antiquity as a device for establishing autonomous working and living spaces for single women in a postslave society. If the beguinage had some similarity to the workshops run by the matrons of antiquity in the *gynaeceum*, or by the ladies of the manor houses in the Middle Ages (see the section "The Manor," below, in this chapter), it was also very different because it was not part of a male-headed estate. No men ever had authority roles of any kind in a beguinage. Even more important, the women were free women, neither slaves nor serfs.

The beguinages were started by well-to-do women with property in both countryside and city who built special houses on the edges of cities for unmarried women workers moving into the cities. These larger houses, called beguinages,[9] can be related to two other social models, one earlier, one contemporaneous. One is the gynaeceum workshop already mentioned. The other is the *frèrêche*, a kind of extended-family household that was occasionally formed in the fourteenth and fifteenth centuries in rural southern France in response to economic difficulties. The frèrêche was a *communeauté familiale* consisting "of brothers sharing their patrimony and their households. . . . sister's husbands and sisters themselves, other relatives, and even strangers, could become incorporated" (Laslett 1972: 14). Similar familial communities have been found in earlier and later times in Italy, Spain, and Poland, as well as in France, and were usually associated with economic recession. The surplus of women associated with the aftermath of the Crusades, and their concentration in cities where there was a dearth of residences and jobs, could very naturally trigger the formation of "*soeurêches.*" Whatever relationship the beguinage might have had conceptually or historically to the gynaeceum and the frèrêche, it was nevertheless a remarkable social innovation.

The women who entered into these all-women households took no special vows. They were simply entering into a congenial and practical living arrangement. Working women went on with their former trades; upper-class women stirred by the Frauenbewegung left their manor houses to join the working women in their workshops. They gave up fancy clothes, lived on the simplest food, and rose early for prayers before work. Scholars agree that the movement had no place of origin and no single initiator. One group began with a couple of sisters and soon had 300 women living all crowded together (McDonnell 1969: 109-10). Groups of 3 and 4 expanded to 25 and 50. The rapid expansion was due to the need of increasing numbers of unmarried women workers in the cities to have a place to live and work. Part of the movement thus became almost indistinguishable from women's trade guilds, although religious practices were always maintained. The combination of a surplus of women[10] and substantial urban poverty meant that some of the beguinages functioned in fact as poorhouses, where unpartnered women (and children) could be guaranteed shelter, food, and some work to do.

After the initial period of spontaneous formation of small groups, there was an inevitable second stage of "organizing the movement." Women developed rules about living together, appointed councils of women to administer their affairs, and finally installed a "grand mistress." By this time, the church was alarmed, because here were groups of pious women out of the control of the church. In the struggle that followed, the women by and large kept cool heads and won recognition as secular institutions with their own rules; in that heresy-conscious age, they needed recognition by the church if they were to go on living together safely. Many Beguines simply "took over" their own religious life, organized their own prayers and rituals, and even heard each other's confessions. They went to church dutifully enough but did not feel dependent on priests. This kind of autonomy made the priests and the teaching orders, which were ordered by the church to "look after" the women, very uneasy. The women might develop heresies.

The main body of the Beguines was not antichurch and accepted the idea of being organized into parishes. This meant recognizing the authority of a bishop, but nothing more. After all, everyone lived in parishes, and all parishes were connected to bishoprics. There were localities in which considerable pressure was applied to get Beguines to adopt an enclosed way of life. This they resisted successfully in the Middle Ages, although, at a later time, beguinages became a kind of secular cloister.[11] During the 1200s and 1300s, the requirements of the Flemish cloth industry were such that the beguinages "were interlaced . . . with guild organization" (McDonnell 1969: 85).

It is undeniable that many of the Beguines had a strong religious character. They produced a group of mystics whose spiritual classics, predating the famous Rhineland mystics (all men), are of the same literary and spiritual quality as those of their better known male successors. Here again, we tap the worldwide vein of mysticism. Because the Beguine movement was also oriented to the reconstruction of society, it ran schools, hospitals, and workshops for the poor. The Beguine schools were so highly respected that many little girls were sent to them by ambitious parents with no religious interests. Because the little girls usually wanted to become Beguines—a role that must have seemed both glamorous and exciting to girls from conventional homes—an expanding supply of Beguines was assured for several centuries. The outstanding mystics, such as Mechthild, Beatrice, and Hadewijch, all came from worldly backgrounds and were sent to Beguine schools. Each chose to become a Beguine, over varying degrees of parental resistance, between the ages of 9 and 12.

All sorts of interesting problems arose in the relationship of these women's groups to the church. The church wanted to control them, but the Dominicans were already overloaded with pastoral work because of the large influx of women into Cistercian convents;[12] many Dominican writings of the time complain of the overload in counseling women. A further overload was created by the fact that the pope continually put whole towns, sometimes whole countries, under papal interdict in the course of power struggles between church and state. An interdict meant that no mass could be said in the affected area. The Beguines, with their independence, could cope with this much better than either nuns or family women, who often felt real terror when the Mass was denied them. The Beguines clearly felt that they could get along without the church when necessary.

It is evident that the Beguine movement was almost perfectly adapted to cope with the economic, social, and religious problems of the times. Within the church, however, the ideology of male dominance won out over the pragmatic usefulness of Beguine independence. The Dominicans forbade women to write their own Psalters (they had been doing just this) and clamped down on the tendency of some beguinages to install their own women preachers and confessors. Finally, in 1274, the pope forbade new religious associations of any kind (although this did not outlaw existing beguinages).

The natural tendency for able women organized in their own living communities to take responsibility for their own lives, both in economic and in religious terms, sometimes led these women in unusual directions. It also served to blur the distinctions between Beguines, who generally accepted the ultimate authority of the church, and the heretic movements, which to varying degrees denied that authority. Given that being convicted of heresy meant being burned at the stake, this was not an academic issue. What the Beguines had in common with the heretics was a certain independent-mindedness, a general feeling that one's spiritual state did not depend very closely on ministrations by priests, and a high view of the perfectibility of human beings and of the possibility of being "oned" with God. Mystics of all ages have tended to hold these views, yet most of them stay in the bosom of the church.

What determined whether one stayed in the central Beguine fold, or went off with the Albigensians, the Waldensians, the Cathari, the Brethren of the Free Spirit, the Perfecti, or the more violently revolutionary Turlupins and other extremists? In fact, most people of the movements just listed were also loyal to the church but were committed to a more demanding demonstration of Christianity. There were two main forces that separated the heretics from the mainstream. One was a sense of alienation from corrupt society so profound that the individual must participate in destroying that society at any cost. The other was a low threshold of emotional suggestibility that led people to think they had already united with God, that they were already living in the millennium and could do no wrong.[13] The Beguines and the other mainstream groups were institution builders more than protesters. The Beguine movement was particularly important to the European scene because it linked practical problem solving with the development of healthy community life and high religious ideals.

What is definitely not true is that there were a large number of silly, emotional women running around causing problems for the church and for society. Let us look at the women who gave leadership to the Beguine movement.

The first to be associated historically with the movement is Mary d'Oignies. Of interest, the significance of her role was that she provided leadership to a group of men who then went out and helped create the support within ecclesiastical structures that made it possible for the women's movement to organize outside the religious orders. Mary is particularly interesting because she felt a strong call to preach yet did not do so. Other women who felt that call and followed it were burned at the stake, as we shall see. The church would not allow such activity. Mary rechanneled her own preaching drive into the teaching of a group of men who became her disciples. She had already raised a family when she felt the call to that life of austerity, devotion, and service—the Beguine "germ" that was to be so contagious. She got permission from her husband to leave home[14] and settle near a small independent "cenobium" (religious commune)—not a regular monastic house but a group of priests who had felt a call similar to her own—at Oignies. The male counterpart of the Beguine movement was the sprinkling of small groups of clerics in little cenobia around Europe who shared a similar longing for a greater purity of life and more service to the world than the church seemed to require. This was the untapped resource that made it possible for both the Franciscan and the Beguine movements to grow so rapidly.

Mary's "circle," as it is referred to, are the men from the Oignies cenobium who responded to her teachings. She trained them to analyze the world the way she did and to preach eloquently. Some of her students became leading bishops of the day, and they all became promoters of responsibility for women in the church and the community. Given that their letters and writings are filled with references to Mary, there is no doubt about the role she played in their work.[15]

Another woman known particularly for her teaching role in relation to clerics was Christine Stemmeln. At the age of 10, she had an inner experience that separated her from other children and, at 13, she ran away from her well-to-do family to the Beguines. She continually embarrassed the Beguines by her religious exaltations, because they were on the whole a practical-minded group of women. She finally found her niche living close to a Dominican center in Cologne, which more or less accepted her as a lay sister and de facto spiritual adviser. Like Mary, she "trained" men who became prominent supporters of women's activities, and we know about her through her correspondence with Friar Peter of Gothland and through several Dominican biographers, including her chaplain Master John. (Christine, incidentally, could not write—all her letters were dictated to willing Dominican brothers—so the Beguine educational system was evidently not effective with her.) The Franciscans detested her and called her the "seductress of Stemmeln." The Dominicans loved her as a holy woman. In other circumstances, she easily could have gone to the stake.

Mary and Christine both came from middle-class families. There were many ordinary village girls—daughters of farmers, millers, and artisans—who were also caught up in religious visioning in the thirteenth century. Ordinarily, they remained in their own homes, under the protection of their own families and a friendly local Dominican monastery. Because they were often illiterate, the monks would write down their visions and these would be passed from hand to hand among "movement" monasteries. Margrete from Ipern and Ludgard von Tonzern are two such relatively unknown local visionaries. This type of working-class piety, protected and revered in local communities, formed a kind of backdrop to the more visible and articulate activities of the women's movement (Weinhold 1882).

The primary role of leaders like Mary and Christine was to gain support for women among clerics already predisposed to the Beguine approach to life. Most Beguines lived more within a self-contained woman's world, a world that had a place for men but not too close a relationship with them. Mechthild of Magdeburg and Beatrice of Nazareth represent a generation raised within that women's community and are outstanding products of that religious culture. They were both sent to school to the Beguines by well-to-do families, and both chose to spend their lives in such communities. Mechthild went into a convent toward the end of her life, and her work will be discussed in the next section, on women's religious orders. Beatrice's *Of the Seven Manners of Loving* (Colledge 1965) is written with the skill and spiritual discernment that comes only to women steeped in religious experience. The same is true for Hadewijch of Antwerp. We know nothing about her except that she appears to have grown up among the Beguines, and her series of letters of spiritual instruction for young Beguines (Colledge 1965) have become a religious classic. The same clarity of perception and use of language to point to experiences beyond words, so characteristic of Beguine mystics, plus a fresh, spontaneous style, are found in her letters. Knowing more about the lives of these women would not add to the beauty of their writings, but one feels cheated to know so little about them.

With Marguerite of Porété, we move into the realm of heresy or of accusations of heresy. Marguerite was burned at the stake for persisting not only in writing but in circulating her manuscripts all over France. Even worse, she persisted in preaching in public in Paris. High church dignitaries protected her as long as they could, for they recognized her spiritual gifts. Her independent ways offended too many in the church, however, and the last time she was arrested she had to go to the stake. Mystical writings can easily be misinterpreted by those not prepared for them, and many devotional classics are prefaced by remarks that "this book is not for everyone."[16] Marguerite's book also had such a warning, but, for what others could write and be revered for, she was burned.

Apparently someone saved a manuscript at the time when Marguerite's writings were publicly burnt, because Professor Guarnieri has recently identified a medieval manuscript known as *The Mirror of Simple Souls*, ascribed to an obscure medieval writer, as actually being Marguerite's book (Cohn 1970). Marguerite was not only an activist preacher, she was also a scholar. One of the things that got her in trouble with the Inquisition was a translation she had made of the Bible. Marguerite was a Beguine but left the residential community of Beguines to engage in a more public life. We do not know what her sisters thought about her activities.

Another Beguine who moved outside the community was Bloemardinne. It is harder to judge her work, because we know about her chiefly through her enemies, who accused her of establishing a cult of libertinism. The fact that her circle of supporters included women of high position and presumably of educated judgment who considered her a saint, and that she was so venerated by the clerics of her own milieu that no one dared bring charges of heresy against her until after her death, suggests that she was in fact a woman of great personal sanctity. It is easy to burn people posthumously.

Another Beguine-type saint who was burnt posthumously was Guglielma of Milan, a Joachimite who founded a sect to inaugurate the Age of the Holy Spirit. She "died in the odour of sanctity" in 1282 but was dug up to be burned when her disciple Manfreda was moved to announce that she, Manfreda, was to usher in the new age as pope. (All her cardinals were to be women.) Manfreda came of a very distinguished Italian family, but it did not save her from the stake (Reeves 1969: 248). Prous Boneta was associated originally with the Beguines but had become an independent by the time she was burned for announcing that she was sent to inaugurate the Age of the Holy Spirit (Reeves 1969: 248).

Most of the women who were burnt are nameless. In our day, some of them would be considered harmless Pentecostals, others sensible social reformers. Many of them must have been literate beyond the average, because they were so often accused of producing and circulating new vernacular translations of the Bible. Their other major fault in

the eyes of the church, apart from Pentecostalism, was that their meetings were held (out of obvious necessity, once persecution had begun)
in secret (McDonnell 1969: 506-7).

From the fragments of stories that remain, it is hard to tell how
politically oriented these women were. Few of them could have been
much of a threat either to the church or to the state. Jeanne Dabenton,
an ex-Beguine, was perhaps more politically minded than most. She
seems to have done organizing work among the poor with a sect known
as the Turlupins. She and some companions, women and men, were
burned at the stake, presumably for being too effective in arousing the
poor (McDonnell 1969: 500-502; Cohn 1970: 169).

There seem to have been no women leaders among the obviously
totalitarian extremist movements that instituted reigns of terror in some
of the German cities, such as the groups led by Matthys and Bockelson
(Cohn 1970: 261-80). This is an indication, I think, of the essentially
libertarian approach of the Beguines to individual and social reform.
Certainly there were women followers of extremist movements, as
there were men followers, but the Beguines should not have to take the
blame for extremism as they are often made to do.

The problem with doing a "big-name" roll call of the Beguines is that
it misses what the Beguines were about. Their genius lay in the quality
of the local communes. They did have a rich inner life, and a richer sense
of the human possibility, than most of the people around them. I wish
some record remained of how they educated the children in their
charge. Some of the communities clearly bred revolutionaries.

While the Beguines were the secular underlife of the church, they
laid the basis for an overlife participation of women in urban society
that survived the expulsion of women from guilds; it was the Beguine
groundwork that enabled women to retain a foothold in society in the
face of the antifeminist elements of the Renaissance and the Enlightenment. We will see the other half of that story when we look at the
activities of women in guilds. But first, we will look at what was
happening with women within the institutional church itself.

Women Religious in the Middle Ages

Women in the Mainstream Religious Orders[17]

In the last chapter of Volume 1, we watched the rise of great women's
abbeys as independent power bases from the late seventh century

forward. By 800, German Saxony was one of the strongest centers of religious women, and the traditions that began in the great convents of Herford, Gandersheim, and Quedlinburg (Essen) flowered in the work of Hrotswitha, described earlier. Hrotswitha was really a transitional figure, belonging both to the earlier days of less demanding monastic scholarship and to the new era of intellectually more sophisticated medieval scholarship. There was a great revival of her work in the 1400s, at the beginning of the Renaissance. Germany continued as the major intellectual center of women's monasticism throughout the Middle Ages. In the 1100s, 100 new Benedictine convents were established there. French convents spread more slowly, and in England the Danish invasion in the 800s had brought monastic life for women almost to a standstill. By 1100, when convents began to spread again in England, all women prioresses were subject to male abbots, and the new convents had greatly reduced power compared with those that flourished earlier under St. Hilda. Lively nuns made the best of the situation, essentially using the convents as handcraft centers, producing embroidery, tapestries, weaving, manuscripts, and painting.

The eleventh century was a good one for the Benedictine women monastics. Not only did they spread in Germany, but abbeys opened in Bohemia, Poland, Hungary, and the Scandinavian countries. Many of these were royal convents, with a princess abbess who had the right to participate in the coronation of the queen. They often restricted admission to girls of the aristocracy, and abbesses were like peeresses of the

Figure 1.1. "Claricia." Detail, Self-Portrait From a South German Psalter, c. 1200 C.E. Redrawn by HBR.

realm. Like secular princesses, they were usually betrothed from the age of 4 to 8, but, in this case, they were brides of Jesus, not a secular prince. Like the princesses, they often undertook ruling duties at a very young age. Princess Urraca of Aragon became abbess at 11; many were appointed before the age of 20. One of the most renowned abbesses of the Middle Ages, Gertrude of Hackeborn, was appointed at the age of 19. As in the case of the princesses, one must admire the extent of education, self-discipline, and administrative ability exhibited by the abbesses at very young ages.

In Spain, which had an ancient pre-Benedictine Christian tradition untouched by European developments during the long Moslem rule, Queen Leonore (a daughter of Eleanor of Aquitaine) founded Las Huelges de Burgos on the Cistercian rule. Las Huelges was a true royal abbey, endowed with lands encompassing 60 villages and decreed to be head of all religious houses in Spain. Queen Leonore, who was betrothed to the king of Spain at the age of 9 and sent to his court to be brought up, had, before leaving home, been well trained by her mother for an institution-building role. She gave a lot of attention to the development of Las Huelges. The abbess was the absolute monarch of her 60 villages and could punish clergy for heresy and the king's officials for secular offenses. She also heard confessions. Monks vowed to the hospitals under the abbey's care took their vows of obedience directly to

Figure 1.2. Nuns Making Cloth, Italian Manuscript, 1421 C.E.

SOURCE: Photograph by K. F. Rowland (in Singer et al., *A History of Technology,* 1956: Vol. 2, p. 209; Imperial Chemical Industries Limited; used by permission).

her. The most famous choir school of Europe developed there. The Spanish royal abbey, with the support both of king and pope, held on to its power longer than any other convent in Europe—right up to the 1800s.

These larger abbeys we have been discussing had up to 500 nuns, including a number who had specialized jobs in addition to their regular work of prayer, devotional reading, liturgical service, and maintenance duties. In addition to the dean, cellarer, and wardrobe mistress, there would be the chantress, who directed the choir, composed the music and accompanying poetry, did the work of librarian, and supervised manuscript copying. The infirmarian held another important convent position. She would have special medical training and act as physician, pharmacist, and teacher of the art of healing to other nuns. Every convent had its own medical herb garden, which the infirmarian supervised. Some convents ran hospitals and old people's homes, so the infirmarian would have a whole staff of nuns working under her to provide nursing services. Every convent also had to have a magistra, to teach the children who came to the convent. If we add the other administrative and maintenance tasks of treasurer, almoner, portress, and sacristan, there were at least 10 specialist jobs in each monastery in addition to that of abbess. As long as Europe remained a land-based economy with a strong barter component, the convents thrived. But, with the shift to a monetary economy and the need for cash, abbeys declined rapidly. They were not organized to make that transition effectively and soon shrank to houses of 25 women from an earlier 100 to 500. The aristocracy lasted the longest in the monasteries, because they could bring ample dowries with them. The dowryless working-class women were the first to have to leave; the middle class held on longer. The Beguine movement played an important part in picking up the slack during this transition.

Figure 1.3. Detail of Scene From Sick Ward at Hotel-Dieu at Beaune, 1443 C.E. Redrawn by HBR.

Abbesses not only had to contend with economic transitions; they had to contend with the determined efforts of bishops to reduce the autonomy of convents. The famous double monasteries of the eighth and ninth centuries, where monks and nuns both served under an abbess, declined in the tenth century under church pressure and were replaced by monasteries with dependent convents attached. Here the nuns "served the monks by copying books and performing other services" (Hilpisch 1958: 23). It is obvious that nuns did not care much for this situation, because this type of dependent convent also disappeared by 1300. Women simply stopped applying to enter them.

At the same time, new independent religious houses for women were developing. In one form, this was a rebirth of the old double monastery, as in the case of the Order of Fontrevault. This order, in

Figure 1.4. Nun and Monk Tilting, From a Gothic Manuscript. Redrawn by HBR.

which monks served nuns under an abbess, spread all over Europe in the twelfth century, much encouraged by Eleanor of Aquitaine.[18] Other independent religious houses included the Congregation of the Paraclete, Heloise's convent, which established daughter houses around France. St. Sulpice de la Forest did the same, as did the congregation of Santa Anne de'Funari in Italy. This movement represented a renewed declaration of independence of religious women. As usual, the pope supported this. He understood the value of groups of independent women religious answerable only to him.

The struggle between women and men in the church continued throughout the Middle Ages. For every move toward independence of women, there was a new movement toward control by men. The enclosure movement, which had absolutely no basis in the Rule of St. Benedict, but that conformed to prevailing ideas about what was proper for women, kept erupting again and again from the times of the earliest religious houses. Enclosed nuns were never to leave the convent for any reason or to be seen by others even inside the convent—hence the use of the grille between nun and visitor in the monastery parlor. Church law moved steadily in this direction from 1100 onward, but sensible bishops allowed for exceptions. Strong-minded women religious with a vocation that required contact with the world never accepted enclosure.[19]

The Cistercian movement was a reform movement of Benedictines, who felt a need for more withdrawal from the world, for greater simplicity, a deeper prayer life, and rigorous manual work. It should not be confused with the enclosure movement, which was imposed from without. Cistercianism attracted many nuns as well as monks, and the Cistercian women's houses grew faster than any other order in the 1200s. In fact, the men tried to stop the women from forming houses, because they were obliged to visit them and provide spiritual counsel— and the work load for spiritual counsel was getting too heavy! It is impossible to have a full understanding of the significance of religious orders in the lives of medieval women if we do not recognize the differences in types of convents chosen by women: Some were scholarly, or liturgical, and "world-oriented" convents; others were secluded, prayer-oriented ones. It is the latter that reflect the new spirituality of the worldwide mystical movements of the Middle Ages. McDonnell (1969: 105) gives a vivid picture of the ardent and prayerful asceticism of women Cistercians.

A third type, the service-oriented convent, did not develop in the Middle Ages[20] but only after the Reformation. This is why the secular beguinages became so important. Neither the Franciscan nor the Dominican service and teaching orders had the imagination to permit women to serve outside the convent as men served, so those important male religious inventions of the thirteenth century did not open the doors for women in the ways that we might have expected.

Each type of religious house for women produced some outstanding women—outstanding in that their work has been noted by others outside the order. The real work of convents is not a visible work and may never produce manifestations that others can judge. Therefore, in choosing some nuns to discuss in this section, I would like to remind the reader that these few women happened to have special gifts for communication with the world.

The German convents have the longest tradition of autonomy and of scholarship, as we have seen from the previous chapter, so it is not surprising that the most notable scholars and prophetesses should come from there. St. Hildegarde, Abbess of St. Rupert at Bingen (1098-1178), was both scholar and seer. She entered convent life at 7, took vows at 14. The most voluminous woman writer of the Middle Ages, although by no means with the literary gifts of Hrotswitha, she was called the "sibyl of the Rhine" and the "marvel of Germany." Her convent, says Mozans, "became a Mecca for all classes and conditions of men and women. . . . Among her correspondents . . . there were simple monks and noble abbots; dukes, kings and queens; archbishops and cardinals and no fewer than four popes" (1913: 46). From this correspondence, 300 letters remain.

Her own major work consists of six to eight large volumes on theology, scripture, and science. It is not likely that she wrote all this herself. Eckenstein (1896) suggests, for example, that the volume of *Materia Medica* attributed to her was probably prepared under her direction by a group of nuns. Reeves (1969: 281-98) indicates that much of her work was done by dictation and rewritten and polished by her (male) secretaries. This was certainly true of other writers of both sexes and does not detract from the importance of her work in the history of science. Singer, the science historian, writes of how she related the cosmic and the human:

> The terms macrocosm and microcosm are not employed by her, but in her last great work, the *Liber Divinorum Operum*, she succeeds in most eloquent and able fashion in synthesizing into one great whole, centered around this doctrine, her theological beliefs and her physiological knowledge, together with her conception of the working of the human mind and the structure of the universe. (quoted in Saport 1975: 9)

The natural sciences, astronomy, and medicine, as well as classical learning, theology, and a study of the church fathers, were part of the curriculum for most of these scholar-nuns. Still, in our eagerness to admire their skills, we should not overestimate their learning. The standards of the day were not very high, either for men or for women. Reeves (1969: 365-87) gives a careful appraisal of this issue.

Figure 1.5. The Synagogue, Illumination From Hildegard Von Bingen's *Scivias*, 1165 C.E. Redrawn by HBR.

Much of Hildegarde's fame came from her political prophesying. The tradition of religious prophecy on political matters was, of course, an old one, encompassing the Old Testament prophets, the Revelations in the New Testament, and the German seeresses and the Near Eastern sibyls of the days of the Roman Empire. While it happened that the writings of Joachim de Fiore became the main vehicle for political prophecy in the Middle Ages, many hundreds of scholars were poring over Old and New Testament writings to try to discern the shape of events to come. Hildegarde, a contemporary of de Fiore, was one of these. To say that her prophesying was in the Joachimite style is only to say that she was steeped in the thinking of her times. She brought something more than intellectual curiosity to her search of scriptures, however, and it was her capacity to rework the past and envision the future in a way to which others resonated that made her so important in her time. She was charismatic, with great skill in speaking and writing.

Her most famous public project was mobilizing support for the Second Crusade, which she did jointly with Bernard of Clairveaux. Bernard himself attributes the main drive to Hildegarde. Her last writing, the *Book of Divine Doings,* included the views of an elder stateswoman (she was 80 when she died) on the future of Europe. Like many seers, she was convinced that she was the chosen mouthpiece of the Lord. Most of her contemporaries apparently agreed with her. In retrospect, the political naiveté of her efforts on behalf of the Crusades leaves some room for doubt about her political judgments. Nevertheless, she must be recognized as one of the ideological leaders of her time. Elizabeth of Schonau was an only slightly less well known scholar-nun who also had the gift of political prophecy.

Herrad, Abbess of Hohenburg in Alsace, was another contemporary of Hildegarde and perhaps more noteworthy as a scholar. She prepared a compendium of the current knowledge of the times—the *Hortus Deliciarum,* or *Garden of Delights*—for the education of her nuns. It may be the first encyclopedia of medieval Europe. Only fragments of the original have survived wartime depredations, but they are far ranging in content and delightful in style. Herrad was an accomplished classical scholar.

In the middle of the next century, a whole group of scholar-nuns who were also contemplatives and mystics were based at Helfta, in Saxony. Their abbess was the Gertrude of Hackeborn noted above as having been appointed at the age of 19. She developed one of the best monastic libraries in Europe and maintained that the vitality of spiritual life depended on the well-trained mind. Three books considered religious classics in their time come out of Helfta under Gertrude:

Mechthild of Magdeburg's *Flowing Light of the Godhead*, Mechthild of Hackeborn's book on grace, and Gertrude the Great's (not the abbess) *Herald of Divine Love*. Helfta was a Cistercian house and shows Cistercian spirituality at its best.

Mechthild of Magdeburg (1212-80) was of the aristocracy, as most of these women were. She first joined the Beguines at the age of 23 and did not enter the Cistercian convent at Helfta until she was nearly 60. She is therefore not a typical Cistercian. She is, however, the most quoted and discussed member of the Helfta group (Kemp-Welch 1913). Not one of the more scholarly nuns, she wrote in Low German because Latin was difficult for her. She was well read, however, and knew Joachim de Fiore's writings. She had been familiar with court life before becoming a Beguine, and much of her spiritual writing draws on the metaphors of courtly love. The combination of her own keen intellect, her past experience with court life, the accompanying understanding of political realities and feeling of political responsibility, and her own inner mystical drives produced a life full of anguish and tensions. She tried to speak to the public figures of her time and at the same time to provide spiritual guidance for the inward journey of ordinary persons. Because she was not a person of status in the religious world, as Hildegarde was, it was much more dangerous for her to speak out on public issues, but she continued to do so all her life. Her writing has depth and power and also continuing relevance.

Women in Independent Orders

The independent houses were not as different than the mainstream orders as one might expect. In fact, most of them were royal abbeys and reflected the autonomy of queens rather than any new drive toward independence on the part of women. Nevertheless, there had to be initiators, and perhaps the chief significance of these houses lies in the extent of women's entrepreneurship within the church they represent. Starting a new house, and writing one's own rule, takes a great deal of negotiating with church authorities. We would expect, then, that women who found new houses will be women of unusual ability and enterprise. Three outstanding new houses of the Middle Ages did indeed have unusual women associated with them: the Paraclete was founded by Heloise of Argenteuil, the Birgittine Order by St. Birgitta of Sweden, and Fontrevault, actually founded by Robert d'Abrissel, was largely piloted by Eleanor of Aquitaine.

The house that Heloise (1100-1164) founded, the Paraclete, is famous as the place that Abelard gave to Heloise so that she might establish her own convent after the Benedictines reclaimed Argenteuil, her convent home after her abortive marriage to Abelard. The Abelard-Heloise story is one of the most often told, and hotly debated, tales of the Middle Ages. The traditional version of the story has contributed much to the crude stereotype of nuns as women languishing for lost lovers. It is said that, while serving as Heloise's tutor, Abelard fell in love with her and seduced her, then honorably decided to marry her. After their marriage and the birth of a baby, her guardian uncle, in a belated rage at the deceit of Abelard, had him attacked and castrated. Abelard became a monk. Heloise retired to a convent and grieved in silence for 20 years, then suddenly sat down to write a series of passionate love letters to Abelard that he then published (Moncrieff 1929).

One major reinterpretation of the story appears in *Heloise: Dans l'Histoire et dans la Légende* (Charrier 1933), based on a reanalysis of Abelard's publications and other documents. In this version, Heloise, convent reared, did indeed come to Paris to live with her guardian uncle, a canon of Notre Dame, and took Paris by storm. Referred to as a second Hypatia, this girl in her early teens knew a number of languages and was widely read in both the classics and theology. She was able to dispute with all the learned masters who taught at the cathedral schools of Chartres and Paris. Mozans (1913) says she was a gifted mathematician. Hurd-Mead (1933) says she studied and taught medicine and practiced it later in her own convent.

According to this interpretation, Abelard made love to her as a potential intellectual rival, in hopes of heading off a career that threatened his own. He not only saddled his Hypatia with a baby and marriage but also was playing around with other women to an extent widely known in Paris at the time. Years later, he pieced together parts of letters actually written years before by Heloise, the heartbroken wife suddenly forced into a convent. These pieces are woven into a fabricated whole, and the letters and his autobiography, *Calamities*, were published as a device to bring him some favorable publicity during one of the periods when he was trying to make a comeback in Paris. Passionate love letters from a famous and brilliant nun who had been pining for him for years in a convent? It was a best seller at the time and has been ever since.

Whatever conclusions one draws about Heloise, there are a variety of sources to examine. There are a number of references to her in contemporary literature, and there is the extraordinary letter Peter the Venerable, abbot of Cluny, wrote to Heloise after Abelard died. Abelard died in disgrace, but under Peter's protection, at a Cluny-administered monastery. The letter is not about Abelard at all but about Heloise:

> I should have known how large a place of love for you in the Lord I keep in my heart. For truly I do not now first begin to love a person whom I remember that I have loved for a long time. I had not yet completely passed out of adolescence, I had not yet attained young manhood, when the fame, not yet indeed of your religion, but of your distinguished and praiseworthy studies became known to me.
>
> I heard then that a woman, although she was not yet disentangled from the bonds of the world, devoted the highest zeal to literary studies, which is very unusual, and to the pursuit of wisdom, although it was that of the world. . . . you, by your praiseworthy zeal, completely excelled all women, and surpassed almost all men.
>
> Soon . . . you exchanged this devotion to studies for a far better one. Now completely and truly a woman of wisdom you chose the gospel instead of logic, the Apostle in place of physics, Christ instead of Plato, the cloister instead of the Academy. (Worthington 1962: 180)

After more supportive comments about the difficult responsibilities of being an abbess, he finally mentions Abelard. He delicately refers to their earthly marriage many years ago and their possible reunion in heaven (standard theological doctrine at the time).

Heloise's letters to Peter at this time are brief and to the point and show no signs of a woman who has been languishing in a convent all her life for a lover.

Just how learned and brilliant Heloise actually was we do not know. She may have simply "closed up" after the disastrous initial outcome of her relationship to Abelard. In any case, she did marry him, apparently against her will, at 18. She also apparently managed to return to Paris to resume her career, leaving her baby in the country. The nature of their relationship after Abelard entered a monastery and ordered Heloise to take the veil is in dispute. In a version friendly to Abelard, Mary Martin McLaughlin (medieval historian, personal communication, 1975) suggests that the famous love letters were composed jointly by Heloise and Abelard as a kind of moral tale for young nuns. McLaughlin would place much more emphasis on the rest of the Heloise-Abelard correspondence, which deals with the status of nuns in the church, and on Abelard's authorship of the Paraclete Rule, which is essentially a utopian design for a double-monastery type of community (McLaughlin 1975). She points out that analysis of these writings reveals Abelard to have been one of the strongest promoters of feminism in the medieval church, although he also shared the ambivalence most clerics felt about women. In this interpretation, he throws himself heart and soul into a joint venture with Heloise in trying to make the Paraclete the realization of all his ideals about monasticism—ideals rejected by his fellow monks.

(He was thrown out of his own monastery because his monks did not like his reforms.)

Certainly Abelard wrote strongly feminist things about women in the early church, some of which have already been quoted in Chapter 8 of Volume 1. Certainly also he was a self-centered person. Unfortunately, none of the treatments of Abelard throws a great deal of light on Heloise: She is thrown into the shadows every time. What was *she* like? Did she deliberately repress great gifts? We know only that she was a good abbess.

The Paraclete became a model of an independent house not tied into the Benedictine network as well as a model of rigorous piety. It was reformist but conservative and prospered as an order. What else it might have been had Heloise taken her first religious vows freely, and not under orders from a hysterical, castrated husband, we shall never know.

Most of the developments we have seen in this section took place in the twelfth and thirteenth centuries. By the fourteenth century, things were even livelier. The Crusades were still in full swing, the Turks were invading Byzantium, the black death came to Europe, the Hundred Years War was on, and there were insurrections of weaver and other trade guilds all over Europe. One of the last major independent houses was founded at this time, the Order of St. Birgitta of Sweden. Birgitta (1303-73)[21] was one of the most strong-minded women of a strong-minded century. She married at 13 and had eight children, all brought up sternly with the rod. (One turned out to be a saint, the holy Katherine, another a black sheep, and we don't know about the rest.)

Already a pious ascetic during her years of motherhood, she took her own private vows at 31, when her husband died. At that time, she had the first of her famous revelations. She soon moved to Rome, where her rapidly developing talents could have better scope. Birgitta was the aristocrats' saint. She founded and patronized orders of knighthood so the Crusaders could fight more devoutly. From her bishop's-palace residence in Rome, she issued her *Revelations*—eight thick volumes in all—setting a new tone of aristocratic piety honored more in the breach than in the observance. Every student in the medieval universities of the time had to study these books. They are well written, in the style of a vivid imaging of events in the life of Christ, but they lack other substance. They were enormously popular in those cataclysmic times. She was also a renowned healer—whether by training or psychic gifts is not clear—with major royal cures to her credit. In any case, she played an important part in providing nursing services in Rome during the plague and developed hospital and nursing institutions and orphanages in both Sweden and Rome.

The order for women she founded in Sweden soon spread over Europe. The Birgittine houses became major cultural centers for European women of the aristocracy, and there were often monks attached to these convents. Birgitta was also active politically, working for a united Europe. Her political prophecies became the policy guides of popes and kings, and she was also active in promoting royal marriage alliances she thought would be beneficial to the peace of Europe. Known as "Christ's secretary" and the "mystic of the North," she was as sure of herself as St. Hildegard and rather more powerful. She was a politician and an organizer, rather than an intellectual or a mystic, and played an important role in upgrading the quality of the participation of church and aristocracy in the public life of the times.

Catherine of Siena (1347-80), Birgitta's contemporary, was both her opposite and her counterpart. Catherine was a "daughter of the people," an illiterate who only learned to write three years before her death and who dictated her correspondence to young noblemen who served as her secretaries. Her father was a dyer and her language retained a working-class flavor, which much enhances the spontaneity of her letters. These letters went to prisoners, queens, popes, soldiers, and village folk in trouble. They can be read today in *Saint Catherine of Siena as Seen in Her Letters* (Scudder 1905). A nun of extreme asceticism who experienced the stigmata and frequent levitations, toward the end of her life she was continually exhausted by overpowering physiomystical experiences. At the same time, she was known as a joyous, gay person—a characteristic notably absent from many in religious orders. She had, as Evelyn Underhill ([1911] 1961: 173) says, a national destiny. Her destiny was to reform the papacy, and she did in fact complete the task that Birgitta had set for herself, bringing back the pope from his "captivity" in Avignon. She had remarkably sharp political intuitions. She also, with Birgitta, played a major role in the nursing work in Rome during the plague. Catherine belongs in the tradition of the prophetess-political reformer of the Middle Ages. She also belongs in a rarer company, that company of saints Underhill writes of who breathe another air and have life from another source.

Nuns were unsung heroines of the plague. While Ziegler (1969) mentions that about half the clerics of Europe died as contrasted with a third of the total population—which means many of them must have died through exposure during nursing—he makes no estimate of nuns who died. Yet, frequent but casual mentions of nuns' activities tell us that most of them left the protection of the convents and went into the community to give heroic service during the plague.

Plans to organize pious women as noncelibate missionaries to the Holy Land were mentioned in contemporary writings from time to time. A Pierre Dubois in the mid-1200s published a political utopia, *De Recuperatione Terra Sanctae*, recommending that women should be educated and a select group of them sent to marry Crusaders, princes, and statesmen in the Holy Land and to be models to enslaved Turkish womanhood. Some of these women were also to be trained as medical missionaries (Schomanns 1911). Some efforts were evidently made in this direction, probably most actively by Birgitta, but the project never came to fruition.

The Counterculture Orders

While both the mainstream Benedictine and the independent orders provided to some extent an independent power base from which women could participate in the life of their times, these orders were on the whole supportive of the established institutions of society. The gap between the institutional church, often self-serving and corrupt in the face of human need, and the reality of large social injustices led some dissident young people to form groups that would own no property; members would live a life of service and maintain themselves by begging. These became the mendicant orders. Francis of Assisi (1182-1226) is the best known of those who dreamed of a return to the simple apostolic communities of early Christianity. A rich merchant's son with experience in trade, a soldier in Italy's wars, and launcher of a mediation attempt in Egypt between Moslems and Crusaders, he was by no means as naive and unworldly as he has often been presented. He was not a scholar, however, and probably never read Joachim, although his view of the coming of the postbureaucratic age coincided very much with Joachim's concept of the Age of the Holy Spirit.

Clare (1193-1253) joined Francis very early in his religious adventures. The story of Clare and Francis[22] is very different than the Heloise-Abelard story. Clare came out of the same rich Assisi merchant background that Francis did, and they had known each other as children. As soon as Francis had "permission" to have brothers living together in this new mendicant style, Clare arrived to be included in the order. Her joining was both dramatic and conventional—she is supposed to have fled her home in the middle of the night with Francis's connivance, but she was also put up very quickly at a local convent to avoid scandal. For respectable women to be wandering mendicants at that time was socially impossible; they could only be perceived as vagabonds and therefore prostitutes. It was questionable enough for men to be doing so. So Francis and Clare compromised by setting up the sister house of Poor Clares, a residential convent vowed to poverty, from which the Clares helped the brothers in ways traditional for women (cooking, mending, making clothes, and so on). The way of life of the Poor Clares did, however, represent a radical departure from conventional upper-class monasticism and a real alternative for women who were questioning the social order. Clare built her institution carefully, wrote her own rule, and fought all her life against efforts both of the church and of some of her own nuns to abolish the commitment to poverty. "The Blessing of St. Clare," in the *Legend and Writings of St. Claire* (Franciscan Institute 1953), is a beautiful document.

An even more radical departure from the religious convent was the establishment of the Third Order. This provided a Franciscan identity and commitment for both women and men who continued to live in the world and carry out family responsibilities and normal work roles. While Third Order identification has been important in the lives of many distinguished men, it has been even more important for women because it has enabled them to stay in family roles and yet feel an independent commitment outside the family, particularly to social service. It was probably Clare's insistence that made the Third Order open to women as well as men.

Clare was the senior stateswoman of the entire Franciscan Order, male and female. The more one reads about Francis, the more one realizes that he never made a major decision without consulting Clare. They built the order together, suffered together as the bureaucrats took over, and, most movingly, loved God together. Spiritual friendships between women and men that lead to mutual flowering of personalities are perhaps not so rare in real life, but they do not often appear on the pages of history books. When they do, they are frequently falsified. The Clare-Francis story still rings true.

Clare's letters show that she was in correspondence with women in public life, including the circle of devout queens of Eastern Europe mentioned earlier. These women were all Third Order Franciscans and turned to her for support for their deviant (for royalty) way of life. Her advice deals entirely with the practical and personal religious life—no political pronouncements or prophecies from Clare's pen. Her order continued to grow, however, when others went into decline.

The Independents: Anchoresses[23] and Pilgrims

The highways and byways of England (and, to a lesser extent, Europe) in the Middle Ages were dotted with crudely built shacks in each of which lived a hermit or hermitess. There were highway and bridge hermits, ferry hermits, and town hermits. Often the town hermit's shack was in a churchyard or at a frequented intersection, where it would be easy for passers-by to leave a penny or two for the recluse. More rarely, the shacks were in isolated places in the forests, or the hermit lived in a lighthouse on the coast. No one knows how many women lived this way, but no village was without at least one anchoress. The village herbalist and healer was very often an anchoress. Other anchoresses supported themselves by odd jobs such as weeding the churchyard or sweeping a busy intersection (Judserand 1890; S. Sitwell 1965). In general, anchoresses seem to have been valued people and were often given a pension by the local village or a higher authority. One fortunate woman got "a penny a day and a robe a year" from the king (S. Sitwell 1965: 31).

All kinds of different women chose this way of life, from the well-educated bourgeois to the women of the poorest classes. Sometimes they chose it in their youth, sometimes later in life, after widowhood. Their motivations were as mixed as their backgrounds, although the common features of living in solitude, celibacy, and simplicity gave an at least superficially religious cast to the hermitesses' lives. They were something of a headache to the church, which felt a need to control holiness—hermitesses could not easily be controlled. The most devout of the anchoresses were no problem. They attended church regularly, had an "authorized" spiritual guide, and were sometimes formally recognized and blessed by the church as women who had chosen a special way of life. Rules were written for them by leading religious writers, although they had no obligation to adopt any rules laid down by others. *The Ancrene Rule* (The Rule for Anchoresses), a medieval classic in itself, suggests the typical problems that troubled the advisers of hermitesses: "Gossiping, chattering women at the window of the anchorhold, the sin of possessions and notably of anchoresses keeping cattle, scandalous 'hospitality,' the advisability of appointing an old, grave confessor" (Colledge 1961: 30).

The anchoress movement became a significant spiritual movement that swept England, evolving as an individualistic counterpart to the Beguine movement that swept Europe. Why the hermitage sufficed for English women when beguinages were needed on the Continent is not entirely clear. Perhaps the pressure of the rural-urban transition was not as great at this time for women in England as for those on the Continent. It may be that both the gynaeceum and the frèrêche model were absent in England, so that the beguinage idea never developed. Economic independence and a mystical spirituality certainly characterized both groups.

Mother Julian (1343-1416), an anchoress of the church of St. Julian in Norwich, was one of the finest flowers of mysticism not only of the Middle Ages but of any age. Her *Revelations of Divine Love* (in Walsh 1970) is a distillation of the best of the religious imagination, refined and disciplined by years of reflective thought. Both as a spiritual guide and as a theological statement, it belongs with books better known and more widely used (D. Sitwell 1960). Far ahead of her contemporaries, and of most present-day theologians, she developed a conception of God as containing the masculine and the feminine, and used both sets of pronouns in referring to the deity. We do not even know whether she was literate; she may have dictated the book to others. Nevertheless, because she was recognized and widely revered in her own day, there is no doubt of the authorship of the *Revelations*.

How close these independent women could come to the appearance of heresy is vividly revealed in the *Book of Margery Kempe*. Margery, a contemporary of Julian, was a successful merchant wife and mother who in later life chose to live as anchoress and pilgrim. She was a colorful character and extremely outspoken. There were some priests who loved and protected her and others who kept calling her up for heresy trials. In her own account of her confrontation with the Archbishop of York:

> Then the Archbishop said to her: "I have received very bad reports about you. They tell me you are a very wicked woman." And she replied: "Sir, they tell me that you are a wicked man; and if you are as wicked as people say, you will never get to Heaven unless you change whilst you are here." (Colledge 1961: 301)

When Margery was not at home struggling with the authorities, she was off on pilgrimages. The pilgrimages to Rome and the Holy Land were another aspect of the lay religious movements of the Middle Ages and were almost a way of life for some women and men.[24] The line between the pilgrim and the vagabond was often difficult to draw, as was the line between the anchoress and the spiritual fraud who made money out of piety. One of the most delightful discoveries about the Middle Ages is how many interstitial, unclassifiable roles were open to women and what fluidity of movement there was between formal roles in the hierarchies of church and state and these self-appointed village helper roles. There was an active underlife, which had many dangers and drawbacks for women but gave a variety and color to their existence.

How many women there were who remained quietly in the towns, inwardly Julians of Norwich while outwardly conducting conventional

TABLE 1.2 Occupations of Religious and Laywomen From Butler's *Lives of the Saints*

Religious (52.7%)		Laity (47.2%)	
Occupation	Percentage	Occupation	Percentage
Hermit	12	Hermit	10
Abbess	30	Householder	23
Contemplative	16	Third order	10
Founder of Order	17	Royalty	6
Mystic	2	Laborer-servant	8
Nursing	2	Prostitute	4
Teaching	5	Unknown	39
Administration	3		
Missionary	2	Total	100
Writer	2		
Monk	2		
Unknown	5		
Total	100		

SOURCE: Data from McDannell (1975: 7).

household affairs, we can only guess. The Mabel Rich story hints at the religious underlife for the devout medieval housewife. Mabel Rich is a case of an individual woman capturing a historian's fancy and thus being placed on the pages of history. Who first started quoting the passage about Mabel Rich from the writings of her son St. Edmund I do not know, but she is now famous as the widowed tradeswoman who, when she sent off her two boys to the university,

> packed a hairshirt for each of them, which they were to wear occasionally according to their promise to her, to remind them that they must not look for ease and comfort in life, above all must not yield to sensual pleasures, but must be ready to suffer many little troubles voluntarily, in order that they might be able to resist temptation when severer trials came. (Walsh 1970: 327)

Her educational work with her boys, one of whom became archbishop of Canterbury, is worthy of the "Mother of the Gracchi" tradition. For us, what is most interesting about her is that she apparently lived an anchoritic life in the midst of London.

From what we have seen of the Beguines, the women in religious orders, and the anchoresses, we realize that the Middle Ages supported an astonishing variety of life-styles for an astonishingly diverse group of religiously oriented women. Table 1.2, from McDannell's (1975) study of Butler's *Lives of the Saints*, shows how diverse were the occupations and backgrounds of holy women recognized by the church.

TABLE 1.3 Social Class of Religious and Laywomen From Butler's *Lives of the Saints*

Class	Percentage
Royalty	36.2
Nobility	36.2
Middle class	10.1
Working class	5.8
Peasant	4.3

SOURCE: Data from McDannell (1975: 7).

While the majority of these women belonged to the privileged classes, peasants and laboring women made their way to holiness too (Table 1.3). While celibacy was strongly associated with sainthood, it was by no means a prerequisite: 68% of the women were single, 17% widowed, and 15% married. We may note that the church authorities who compiled lists of holy people did not record as many women's lives as they might have, given that only 18% of the saints in Butler's *Lives* are women.

In addition to the many women in the Middle Ages who lived religiously oriented lives, there are several important groups of secular women that have not yet been considered. One is the women intellectuals and artists; another is the "ordinary" middle-class and working-class women. We will turn to the scholars and artists next, noting first that a valuable recent source of information on women of learning for this period will be found in Brink (1980).

Women Intellectuals and Artists

The only place in Christian Europe during the Middle Ages where a woman intellectual could choose a scholar's role and stay both single and secular was Italy. Italy stayed in touch with the active intellectual currents of the Moslem world and read the "lost classics" of the Greco-Roman tradition, while the rest of Europe was struggling along without that stimulation. Moslem and Christian women scholars worked side by side in Italian universities. There were women professors and doctors in many of the major schools in the Moslem world at this time, in Baghdad, Cairo, Kairouan, Cordova, and Toledo, as well as in Constantinople. We have mentioned that in 1083 Anna Comnena founded a new medical school in Constantinople and taught and practiced medicine in addition to writing history. Even in conservative Persia, where women were very secluded by the thirteenth century, Princess Gevher Nesibe built a famous medical school and hospital in 1206, and Muneccime was a famous lady astronomer at the Seljuk court (Afetinan 1962: 24).

Salerno, the site of healing springs famous since Augustan times, had the best medical school in Europe at the beginning of the second millennium. A tradition of medical knowledge supposed to date from the time of Sister Scholastica and St. Benedict fed directly into the university from Monte Cassino, the Benedictine center. One of the most quietly remarkable women of the Middle Ages lived and taught in the eleventh century at the University of Salerno. She wrote a gynecological-obstetrical treatise that served as the major medical reference work for practitioners in Europe for centuries to come. She also raised a family and cowrote medical books with her husband and son. Her name is Trotula, of the noble family of Ruggiero, and she is known in English nursery rhymes as Dame Trot.

In other cultures, she might have emerged eventually as the goddess of healing, but in English culture we find her as the sprightly old lady who adds color and humor to children's tales. Only recently has it been verified that her basic manuscript, which was copied and recopied in whole and in excerpt, repeatedly incorporated piecemeal in other medical works, and ascribed to a variety of authors including "a man named Trotulus," was in fact the work of Trotula (see Hurd-Mead 1933, for a discussion of this). Its original title was *De Morbis Mulierum et Eorum Cura—The Diseases of Women and Their Cure.* Another book of hers on *The Compounding of Medicaments* was as famous and widely used as *De Morbis.* The project undertaken jointly with her husband and son, John Platearius Senior and Junior, was an encyclopedia of medicine.

There was evidently a whole group of women doctors at Salerno at the time, but others remained unnamed. The issue of the practice of medicine by women became an increasingly difficult one as the church, male doctors, and universities united to disqualify and penalize women at every opportunity.[25] An interesting tabulation by Muriel Joy Hughes (1943: app. 1) of all the references to women medical practitioners in public records during this period indicates the extent to which women continued to practice even in the face of stiff penalties. Table 1.4 is a brief summary of her tabulations, which reflects only a fraction of actual women practitioners and does not include Italian women associated with schools of medicine. The large number of women listed for France partly reflects the concentration of professionals of all kinds in France in this period and partly is a function of the kinds of records Hughes was able to find.

TABLE 1.4 Women Practitioners Mentioned in Public Records in Europe,
1100-1500

	France	Italy	Germany
Barbers[a]	22	—	—
Doctors	18	11	15
Surgeons	5	1	—
Empirics[b]	22	—	—
Midwives	8	5	1
Nurses	12	—	—

SOURCE: Data from Hughes (1943, app. 1).
a. Barbers practiced surgery and other types of healing.
b. An empiric would be a kind of general practitioner.

By the fourteenth century, women in France were forbidden to perform surgery, either as "barbers" or as "surgeons." At this point, there would have been many experienced women surgeons in France who had traveled with the Crusaders and performed extensive surgery on the battlefields. Bologna was another center renowned for its women medical scholars, including the legendary Alessandra Gilani, who was associated with Mondino, the "father of modern anatomy." Alessandra died at 19. The French decree against women surgeons was probably aimed at those groups of highly trained women who practiced in both France and Italy.

Jewish women doctors were also much in demand in Italy and France, particularly with prominent clerics, but it was "doubly illegal" for Jewish women to practice medicine. Jacobina Felicie, a Jewess native of Florence, was evidently the most popular doctor in Paris. She was brought to court repeatedly and fined for "illegal practice." (There was no way in which she could be legal.) At each trial, she was defended by highly placed clientele. Other women in her situation included Clarisse of Rouen, Jeanne Converse, and Clarice Cambriere. The Jewess Sarah of St. Giles conducted a large private medical school in Montpellier in the 1320s, providing one answer to where the women got their training.

The very omnipresence of references to prohibitions against women practitioners serves to underline the important role they must have played in the health care of the cities of the Middle Ages. The frequency with which Jewess doctors are mentioned points to a tradition of educating women in the Italian Jewish subculture akin to that already noticed in the Cairo Geniza records in the last chapter of Volume 1. Germany was less hostile to women than was France and, in 1394, 15 women were licensed to practice medicine in the city of Frankfurt. In the Netherlands, Beguines were practicing medicine very quietly without being troubled by the authorities.

Medicine for women, except in Italy,[26] was an underlife field. This makes it very difficult to document the extent of the activity. Hurd-Mead (1933) notes that the group practice of medicine by whole families was very common in the Middle Ages, so many women practiced anonymously within "family clinics." The involvement of queens and princesses with nursing and hospitals has been mentioned from time to time. How much training these women had is hard to know, but Beatrice of Savoy ordered the preparation of a medical encyclopedia that she carried with her when she visited her daughter queens, and Queen Blanche of Castile never traveled without a well-equipped medical kit. She did not trust local doctors.

Standards of medicine began to decline in the 1500s, and accusations of witchcraft contributed to this general decline and demoralization of the profession. Legal codes in all societies have provided for the punishment of doctors for malpractice when this can be demonstrated. Usually there are some safeguards for the doctors, but in the Middle Ages all safeguards disappeared. "No medical faculty of the sixteenth century would defend any of its pupils against persecutions for heresy" (Hurd-Mead 1933: 336). Women were hit harder than men, but sex was no guarantee of safety. This tended to push medicine underground and thus increased the involvement of women in it at the very time that they were also being punished the most heavily for that involvement. The fact that there were so many able women available to carry on practice under all these constraints is due to the apprentice tradition among surgeons, doctors, herbalists, and midwives, which meant that skills were being passed on from generation to generation no matter what was happening in the schools and universities. Hurd-Mead (1933) suggests that the nonschool medical knowledge was often superior to that being taught in the schools, because schoolmen were increasingly divorcing themselves from reality. Women had the advantage of being closer to their patients than the schoolmen were and therefore closer to the medical realities with which they were dealing. Nevertheless, this kind of separation left the women in the end very vulnerable to being pushed out of medical practice entirely when the medical sector finally modernized.

While some mother-daughter combinations were found in medicine, in law there seem to have been instead father-daughter combinations. At the University of Bologna, where women shone in law, in the 1300s Novella d'Andrea frequently took her father's place and lectured on canon law. Her predecessor Bettina Gozzadini is described as one of the greats in the field.

In general, women's scholarly and scientific identity has been lost to the men with whom they worked, no matter how outstanding their

work. Thus Tycho Brahe's sister may have been one of the great astronomers of her time, but we will never know about it. She worked side by
side with her brother, yet it is only his work we hear of (Mozans 1913).
The same "group practice" in medicine that hid the roles of women
doctors from society obtains not only for scholarly and scientific work
but also for artistic work. The Van Eycks' sister Margaretha sacrificed
her own artistic fame by painting portions of her brothers' pictures
(Waters 1904). No one knows for sure how much that came out of the
Van Eyck studios was Margaretha's. The gender identity of troubadours
at the famous medieval courts of love has similarly been lost in the
public record. The pioneering scholarship of Meg Bogin (1976), however, has brought the poetry of women troubadours to light and has
revealed some delightfully unconventional verse (and behavior).

One remarkable exception to the equivocal underlife existence of
women scholars and artists is Christine de Pisan, Italian-born poet,
novelist, historian, and writer on contemporary national and international affairs.[27] She grew up at the French court, where her father was
a distinguished scholar. Through a series of misfortunes, she was left
widowed with three small children and a mother to support after the
death of the men of her family and of the king who had been their
patron. In an exceedingly hostile environment, with the men of the
court trying to seize what properties still remained to her, she managed
to outwit the conspirators and to write poetry successfully for money.
Almost overnight, she became the most popular literary figure in France.

It is almost hard to believe in Christine de Pisan. She stands head
and shoulders above many others of her time in breadth of concerns
and range of scholarship. Was she really the author of the works that
carried her name? As long as she wrote ballads and romances, she was
"believable" and universally admired. When she began turning out
historical studies and serious works on the major issues of the day,
rumors began circulating that her manuscripts were really written by
clerics. Scholars are satisfied today that all 28 works listed in Table 1.5
are hers. Some of her works were so popular that more copies exist of
them than of any other writings of the 1400s. They were very popular
in England too, so we can read most of her work in Middle English as
well as in medieval French.

A study of Table 1.5 shows that she continued turning out her
best-selling romances after beginning her serious work. Her major
concerns were (a) the economic plight of widows and the need for
education for all women, (b) the political problems of France, (c) the
larger questions of historical destiny, and (d) problems of military
strategy and international law. Probably attuned to these kinds of

TABLE 1.5 Chronological Table of Works of Christine de Pisan

Data	Work	Description
1389	*Triggering Event: Death of husband, requiring de Pisan to support her family*	
1390	First prize-winning ballad	
1390-99	Cent Ballades	Songs of widowhood, in praise of marriage, love songs
1390s	Dits Moraux	Letters of instruction for son
1396	*Events: Children leave home; daughter becomes nun at Poissy, son becomes ducal aide*	
1399	Epistre au Dieu d'amour	Attacks Ovid, Roman de la Rose; polemics, satire
1400	Le Dit du Poissy	Rural pastorale; debate on love
1401	Epitre d'Othea à Hector	Historical romance drawing on many sources
1401	Debat des Deux Amants	Courtly romance, contemporary and historical
1402	Epistre sur le Roman de la Rose	Polemics on woman question
1402	Dit de la Rose	"Court of Love," held for serious discussion of woman question
1403	Chemin de Long Étude	Dantesque historical allegory using Cumean Sibyl
1403	Oraison à Nostre Dame	Religious poetry
1403	Dit de la Pastoure	Pastorale—a love story
1404	Mutacion de Fortune	Philosophical history of humanity's ups and downs
1404	Fais et Bonnes Moeurs de Charles V	Court-commissioned life of King Charles V
1404	Livre des Trois Judgments	"Problem" love stories
1404	Livre du Duc des Vrais Amant	Courtly romance, contemporary
1405	Le Cité des Dames	History of women
1405	Le Livre des Trois Vertus	Advice to women on public and private affairs
1406	Lavision Christine	Historical allegory, also a history of France
1406	Epistre à Isabeau	Political epistle to the queen about problems of the times
1407	Le Corps de Policie	Essay on policy, international law
1409	Livre des Faits d'Armes	Military history, international law
1409	Sept Pseaulmes Allégories	Religious meditations
1410	Lamentacions sur les Maux de la Guerra Civile	Commentary on political, civil strife in France
1412-14	Livre de la Paix	Nature of state, the politics of peaceableness
1416	Epistre de Prison de Vie Humaine	Reflections on human conditions in a troubled society
1417-18	*Event: Christine leaves Paris, now in acute state of civil conflict, for convent at Poissy*	
1420s	Heures de Contemplation de la Passion	Religious meditations
1429	Victory Poem to Joan of Arc	Christine probably died shortly after writing this poem

questions by her environment at court and her father's tutoring as a child, she was able to use the libraries of the palace, the library of the University of Paris (its chancellor, Jean Gershon, was her good friend), and the books her father left her in her explorations of history and contemporary issues. She evidently moved in the kind of overlife spaces usually open only to royal women, and her life and work were a product of unusual opportunities combined with unusual ability.

She is considered by specialists in French literature the best of the "minor writers" of the period. To me she seems something more than that. What is called for is a study of her historical, allegorical, and political works in the context of the agonizing crosscurrents of the Hundred Years War, the French Civil War, the proliferating workers' riots, and the declining position of women as reflected in the activities of the church and the trade guilds. Having grown up in a milieu that separated her completely from the Beguine movement and from the major convent-based intellectual centers, she was nevertheless a kind of distillation in her own person of the women's movement of the Middle Ages. Willard (1975) is, I think, right in saying that she was not a feminist, but she had a strong sense of the nature of the social and economic problems that faced women. She not only argued that they should be better educated, she spoke (in the *Livres des Trois Vertus*) to the differing educational needs of princesses, managers of large estates, wives of merchants and artisans in the city, and farmers' wives in the country. Her *City of Ladies* was the forerunner of many histories of women, the first to be written by a woman. She addressed questions of international relations long before Erasmus. In studying military strategy to see where the destructive potentials of war could be minimized, she anticipated much later approaches.

Figure 1.6. Christine de Pisan, La Cité des Dames. Redrawn by HBR.

Christine accepted the court conventions of her environment and was willing to spend a lot of her time both living and writing about a courtly existence that was already considered very old fashioned. When she did get roused about social issues, she dressed her arguments in heavy historical allegories that she knew her audience would love. I suspect that she liked court life, or she could not have written so charmingly about it. Her "courts of love," however, were truly egalitarian, and she reserved most of her biting satire for medieval male chauvinists who placed women on phony pedestals. What she thought in the last years of her life as she watched the crumbling of the society she had loved, we do not know. She stopped political writing and turned toward a more contemplative life, but we do not know how she conceived of her own choice in relation to her times. Her retirement to a convent may have been a conventional choice such as many older women made; but perhaps not. Her ballad celebrating Joan of Arc, written after years of convent silence, tells us she could still hear the world.

Working Life for Women

The Manor

Because of the great diversity of life-styles in the Middle Ages, it is very difficult to give a coherent account of the physical and social spaces that women moved in as they lived and worked. The manor houses, and the homes of the stewards, *maires*, squires, and other gentry below the lords of the castles in the feudal hierarchy in England and on the continent, were an important feature of village life in a society where most people lived in villages. I will therefore begin by describing the life of women in the manor houses.[28] The mistress of the manor worked very hard indeed. She supervised a considerable domestic work force, including many women laborers, in the care of domestic animals and poultry, production of butter and cheese, butchering of livestock for table and market, care of the kitchen garden, food preparation and preservation, spinning, weaving, and sewing. (Originally, the word *spinster* referred to female spinners. Later, it came to mean an unmarried woman.) In addition to these activities, she supervised the marketing of everything produced over and above family needs and oversaw storage in the manor warehouses. She was expected to run a school for the village children, teach domestic skills to the dozen or so young women who boarded at the manor, give some supervision to the training of the young men boarders also, and provide nursing and other helping services to the peasants and cottagers associated with the estate. In addition to all of the above, she was responsible for feeding the entire household—which in an average manor house could run between 15 and 30 people and in a castle to nearly 100. As hostess, she also had to entertain all guests. When her husband was away at wars or in the city or at court on business, which could be for long periods of time, she had to be able to manage the entire estate, supervising agricultural fieldwork and handling finances. The economic productivity of these estates, as well

Figure 1.7. Woman Shearing Sheep, Middle Ages. Redrawn by HBR.

as the social welfare of the villagers, depended to a considerable extent on the skills of the lady of the manor.

Enterprising women could expand the domestic workshops of the manor houses beyond the usual dozen women and girls. In the towns of northern Europe, these manor house ladies sometimes supervised a number of workrooms where women worked at making silk and wool cloth. Such supervision usually entailed maintaining dormitories where women "of all conditions and ages" could live, although occasionally workers would come in by the day. These establishments were in fact preindustrial factories (Lacroix 1926: 667).

The young girls who worked in the manor house workshops married the peasant boys who worked in the fields, and after marriage they carried on a modest replica of the manor house activities at home. Women were usually needed in the fields alongside of husbands at

Figure 1.8. Women Preparing Flax Stalks, Sixteenth Century

SOURCE: Woodcut, *Virgiliis Solis* (Singer et al., *A History of Technology*, 1956: Vol. 2, p. 196; Imperial Chemical Industries Limited; used by permission).

plowing and harvest time and worked even longer hours than the manor house ladies, at harder manual labor. The girls who did not make it to the manor house for education were the children of cottagers—the squatters who were available for day labor who tried to grow enough food for subsistence from common land in the village. The life of a cottager's wife was very hard indeed, for she did the heaviest of outdoor work as a day laborer with her husband, taking her children along to help in the fields. Nevertheless, she usually had her own garden and was "muscular and well-nourished"; her babies were healthy, and she was of the class of women that the gentry used for wet nurses for their own babies (Clark 1919: 58). There were small children everywhere in the rural world, and all but the babies were put to tasks of some kind near their mothers.

The work was so physically exhausting that a woman's life expectancy at birth was not much beyond 25 years and shorter than male life expectancy. One effect of the move from the country to the city was the lengthening of the life expectancy of women as compared with men (Herlihy 1975: 1-22). Bad as city life was, it was easier than rural life for women.

For widows, rural life was hardest of all. They were hemmed in on all sides by feudal obligations that they had to meet if they were to retain their rights to farm, obligations that were hard enough for a husband-wife team to meet. Typical is this description of a village woman in the manor of Frocestor (1265-67):

> Margery, the widow, holds half a virgate of land which contains 24 acres and she renders 3s. every year at two terms, 12d. at Christmas and 2s. at Michaelmas. And from Michaelmas to the Feast of St Peter in Chains she must plow half an acre every week, and one day's plowing is worth 3d. And from the Feast of St John the Baptist until August she must perform manual service 3 days every week and the day is worth three farthings. The fourth day she carries on her back to Gloucester or else where at the bailiff's will and that is worth three-halfpence. She shall mow the lord's meadow for at least 4 days and the day is worth 1½d., which is counted as manual service estimated above at three farthings. And she must lift the lord's hay for at least 4 days at her expense, this not being counted as a task, and it is worth altogether 3d. She shall weed 2 days apart from the work due which is worth three-halfpence. And from the Feast of St Peter in Chains until Michaelmas she must perform manual service with a man 5 days a week and the day is worth three-halfpence.
>
> And every second week during the same period she must perform carrying service for one day, this being counted as one day's task.
>
> And furthermore she performs 8 boon works with a man in autumn which is worth altogether 12d. And she gives 2s. 2¼d. for aid. She

performs all the untaxed customs [for king and manorial lord]. And she performs a harvest boon work in autumn fed by the master which is worth, apart from the food, a halfpenny. And she must plow one day, fed by the master with half a plow. And she shall give eggs at Easter at will. (G. Duby, in O'Faolain and Martines 1973: 160-61; reprinted from *Rural Economy and Country Life in the Medieval West*, First Paperback Edition, by Georges Duby, pages 485-86, by permission of the University of South Carolina Press, Columbia SC 29208. © Edward Arnold [Publishers] Ltd. 1968)

In addition to the married women, widows, and young unmarrieds of the villages of Europe, there was another category of partnered women householders. These were the "priestesses," "the concubines who lived with the clergy, . . . a recognized class, notorious for their impertinence" (Reich 1908: 196), which we noted in the previous chapter. They continued their much-maligned and economically necessary partnerships through the Middle Ages.

The actual life situation for most couples was a more equal partnership than appears on the surface. Essentially, the woman and the man each had her or his own productive labor in or outside the home and was self-supporting, with both of them contributing resources to a common pool for the care of their children. While some women were associated with their husbands in the husbands' enterprises, the women either had additional ones of their own or contributed to the common enterprise in a way that was distinctive enough that they had independent

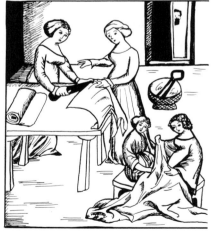

Figure 1.9. Domestic Workshops, Early Fifteenth Century: (a) Spinning and Weaving and (b) Cloth Making. Redrawn by HBR.

funds at their own disposal. One of the things Italian peasant women did for money was to sell their hair to the rich ladies of the town (Coulton 1955: 322). In England, rural women did everything from shearing sheep, to thatching roofs and mixing mortar for village building projects, to whipping dogs out of the church (Clark 1919: 60-63).

The fact that descent was often traced through women[29] is another evidence of her status. "Even where the exclusion of women continued in theory, it was soon subject in practice to many exceptions" (Bloch 1961: 201). Whatever rights and properties could be passed on to sons could also be passed on to daughters. The problem of the feudal military obligations attached to land holdings was met by women paying a substitute or sending a male relative. The widespread administration of land by women noted in the early Middle Ages continued.

The great houses of lords and merchants in the cities bore some resemblance to the rural manor house, minus agricultural activities and open spaces. Domestic crafts remained important, often with materials brought in from country estates. The activities of the ladies of the urban manors varied in the extent to which they involved supervision of women's workshops, assisting their husbands in merchandising and keeping accounts, or developing businesses of their own.

One aspect of women's economic roles in the Middle Ages that is easily overlooked is their disposition of property in wills. Wills, as Rosenthal (1972: 17) points out, were a great leveling device between the sexes. The endowment of a benefice enabled a woman to create a new chapel complete with attending clerics who would both "purchase paradise" for herself and her forebears and provide community services she thought desirable. Of interest, the prayers so purchased were always for a woman's own parents and forebears, never for those of her husband or for their children, who in law belonged more to her husband than to herself. An analysis of bequests of spouses shows that 80% of all bequests were made independently by husbands and wives and only 20% jointly. Women's wills had a different character than men's. They were longer and more detailed. They gave more attention to alms for the poor, relief of prisoners, dowries for the marriage of poor virtuous girls, and support for anchorites and hermits. It also appears that women were more apt to have libraries than men were, because much attention is given to the details of distribution of women's books in their wills (Rosenthal 1972: 118).

In short, we see upper-class women controlling the distribution of substantial amounts of capital through their wills as well as in their daily lives. The organization of the daily work routine was such that women, whether urban or rural, usually had large numbers of workers and servants of both sexes living with them. Tenement housing, providing the dark one-room apartments for city workers, came in the later Middle Ages (Mumford 1961: 284). When it did develop, it was an expression of a new demand for privacy that did not exist in early European urbanism. Many writers (Thrupp 1962: 130 ff.; Aries 1962: 391-4; Mumford 1961: 286) describe a nonfamily, public style of living as persisting well into the 1600s. People rolled out mats and slept at night wherever they could, preferably in the house of a patron or employer, sometimes in the patron's own bedroom.

As we shall see in looking at guild organization, where there were a number of workers associated with a workshop, there were often dormitories adjacent to the workshop. It is said that Michelangelo "on occasion slept with his workmen, four to a bed. As late as the seventeenth century, maidservants often slept in trundle beds (rolled under the big bed by day) at the foot of that of their masters and mistresses" (Mumford 1961: 286).

The Guilds

The guild structure of medieval society is one of the most romanticized and least understood aspects of medieval life, in particular in regard to the role of women. There is a persistent myth that women were equal with men in the original guilds and were gradually pushed out by industrialization. To trace what really happened, we will review the functions of guilds at different stages. The antecedents of guilds in antiquity and their development in medieval times out of religiously based mutual aid associations of workers in the same trade have already been mentioned. In the early stages, the emphasis was on the family units of association members, so there was good reason for an active participation of women. The brethren and the sistren helped each other's families in marriage, sickness, and death.

The guilds merchant, which were first founded in the late 1100s and continued to flourish for several centuries, were the first associations that brought the trading aspect of craft production into focus. The producers had to sell what they made. People from all kinds of crafts belonged to these early "guilds merchant," but, with expansion of demand for every kind of product, there was a later differentiation by craft, leading to the development of the craft guilds.

What was the status of women in the guilds merchant? They had membership, as they did in the old mutual aid associations, but they were not members on the same basis as were male artisans. Gross (1890: 66) points out that women, monks, and heads of religious houses were excluded within the guilds from "burgess-ship" as were foreign merchants who received trading privileges in a town through guild membership. In other words, women and clerics were treated as foreigners. They had no voting rights in town affairs, only trading rights. The guilds merchant were for a time so closely linked to local government structures that guild membership created the basis for civic rights. While it was important for women to have trading rights because they were often business partners with their husbands, voting could be taken care of by the head of the household. When widows were heads of households, we find from time to time in the coming centuries that they exercised burgess rights, but on the whole this was rare. When a legal issue was made of it, they were often disqualified. It is probable, though not certain, that the occasional references to women serving on town councils are references to widows.

When craft guilds began developing their own separate organizations, women continued to be important in them, both as business partners and as workshop helpers. The nature of their contribution to the family enterprise, however, gave them a differentiated status in the craft guilds, as it had in the guilds merchant, and the frequent references to the sistren and the brethren have been misinterpreted in regard to the status of women. For example, in a widely quoted passage from her book on English guilds, Toulmin Smith says, "scarcely five out of 500 were not formed equally of men and women. . . . Even where the affairs were managed by a company of priests, women were admitted as lay members, and they had many of the same duties and claims upon the gilds as men" (in Hill 1896: 47).

But it is clear from a careful reading of specific references to guild operations (Clark 1919; Pinchbeck 1930; Renard [1918] 1968; Staley [1906] 1967; Hauser 1927) that it was the exception for women in the mixed guilds to be trained as apprentices. The fact that they were generally excluded from training for mastery of craft meant that, unless as wives they were the business partners of guildsmen, their status was highly marginal, and they were allotted the more tedious and less skilled tasks. We do find that in the all-women guilds, of which there were 15 in Paris at the end of the thirteenth century—compared with 80 men's guilds (Renard [1918] 1968: 20)—women were regularly apprenticed and could go through the system to become guild masters (mistresses). These all-women guilds were generally in the silk, embroidery, millinery, and special garment trades. The proportion of all-women's guilds may have been somewhat higher in France than in England. It is also possible that women were taken as full apprentices more often in the mixed guilds in France than in England. Yet, even they were kept as underpaid journey-men (women) and kept from full master status, often by town law, because this status involved bur-gess rights and military duty (Renard [1918] 1968: 20, 21).[30]

In the ideal-typical fourteenth-century craft guild workshop, the guild master and his wife, in vil-lage or town, lived in a modest house with workshop attached. There was dormitory space for the live-in apprentices and journey-men and for the servant girls who helped the mistresses with do-mestic tasks so that she could be free to help in the shop, where she sold the workshop products over the counter to customers, helped in various ways in the production process itself, and supervised the training of young apprentices in certain parts of the production process. They all lived and ate to-gether as a family. The children of the master began helping in the shop by the time they were 4 years

Figure 1.10. Woman Apprentice Gold-smith, Fifteenth Century. Redrawn by HBR.

old, and the daughters frequently grew up to marry one of the journey-men, thus eventually becoming wives of guild masters and performing functions similar to those of their mothers. The interpenetration of domestic and workshop roles created considerable fluidity in the pat-terning of work roles for wife and husband, although the work of the wife was less specialized. There was also an accompanying fluidity in domestic roles. Clark, in describing the situation in the 1600s, gave a description that would be more applicable for the 1200s to 1400s:

> If women were upon the whole more actively engaged in industrial work . . . men were much more occupied with domestic affairs. . . . Men in all classes gave time and care to the education of their children, and the young unmarried men who generally occupied positions as apprentices and servants were partly employed over domestic work. . . . A considerable proportion of [domestic work] fell to the share of men. (1919: 5)

Figure 1.11. Woman Laboratory Assistant

SOURCE: Van Schriek, 1512 (Singer et al., *A History of Technology*, 1956: Vol. 2, p. 752; Imperial Chemical Industries Limited; used by permission).

Figure 1.12. Woman Potter at Kick Wheel, Fifteenth Century

SOURCE: From a Playing Card (Singer et al., *A History of Technology*, 1956: Vol. 2, p. 289; Imperial Chemical Industries Limited; used by permission).

As the workshop was home for all its members, the guild was the extended family. Guild members helped one another build their houses, and guilds provided dowries for members' daughters who married or entered a convent and sometimes also for girl apprentices. Cultural and social life was centered in the guilds, and the larger ones ran schools for the children of members.[31] Apprenticeship for girls in a mixed guild apparently often meant apprenticeship to a guild master's wife, with privileges of guild membership accompanying the girl's position in the household. Such a young woman, if she married out of the guild, would lose her membership rights. If the wife of a guild master was widowed, she could keep her guild membership if she continued to run the workshop as a widow, or if she remarried within the guild, but not if she remarried out of the guild. Confirmation of the fact that few widows who ran guild workshops were trained in the craft is found in the frequent references to their dependence on (sometimes unscrupulous) journeymen to continue the business and in records of lawsuits against widows who took in apprentices but were unable to train them.

I believe that the exclusion of the female from the skill training of the guild was responsible for her continued marginal status. She was auxiliary, if indispensable, help to the men of her family in the production process. The primacy of her childbearing and home maintenance roles contributed to the auxiliary nature of her participation in the workshop. This primacy of domestic roles was probably minimal in the small workshop, as Clark (1919) suggests. But the idealized picture of complete equality of husband and wife in the home workshop does not stand up well under scrutiny. No matter how helpful she was, the differences in their training kept appearing. In terms of salary, Hauser (1927: 158-60) reports that, in rural workshops in fourteenth-century France, women's wages

Figure 1.13. The Carpenter and His Family
SOURCE: Sean Baurdichen, c. 1500 (Singer et al., *A History of Technology*, 1956: Vol. 2, p. 391; Imperial Chemical Industries Limited; used by permission).

were set at three-quarters of the men's wages. By the fifteenth century, it was one-half, and, by the sixteenth century, still less. Hauser was not able to obtain information on wages in urban workshops but presumed that the same differentials applied there.

From Guild to Factory and the
Long Walk to Work

It was with the expansion of workshop size with increased urbanization that women's marginality became serious. As long as every daughter and female domestic apprentice could anticipate someday being a master's wife, the apprenticeship-journeyman-master system did not work so much against women. The journeyman, who as the name implies traveled around the country to gain additional skills by working in the workshops of other masters, married a guild girl when he was ready to become a master. But over time workshops grew larger. Not only were large numbers of apprentices taken in who stayed on permanently as semiskilled journeymen because they could not accumulate the resources to open their own workshops, but also large numbers of unskilled workers were hired for manual tasks and were never brought into the guild system at all. Powerful trade guilds emerged that employed thousands of laborers who had absolutely no rights as workers. This was particularly true in the cloth industry, which operated large factories in Europe well before the industrial era. The proletariat of the textile guilds were the "bluenails," the mass of workers who were employed in the manual labor of handling the heavy pieces of cloth ranging from 65 to 100 feet in length, whose fingernails turned blue from the dyestuffs (Delort 1973: 336).

This urban proletariat of dependent, unprotected workers began multiplying in the fourteenth century. The idyllic home workshop where workers of every status and sex lived as a family became rarer and rarer. Journeymen, who in an earlier era had stayed bachelor until they could become masters, now were "allowed" to marry, thus acknowledging the permanency of their journeyman status. The women of the artisan class who married the journeymen, and the women of the proletariat who married the bluenails—and the women who did not marry at all—formed a great body of female laborers in the towns and cities of the Middle Ages. They went out each morning from their one-room tenement apartments as these sprang up in Italy, in Flanders, in Paris, and in London, and they walked to the huge textile workshops built first in the middle of the towns, then on the outskirts when space came to be at a premium. Sometimes it was a long walk to work for the women, just as it was for the men.

Workers lived as near the guild warehouses and factories as they could. Women laborers brought their small children to work with them, giving them tasks that speeded up the mother's productivity. Babies were a problem. Given opiates to keep them quiet, they could be carried to work. Another solution was to give them, for the first couple of years, to a "baby farmer" who lived outside the town. The mortality rate was high for babies on baby farms, especially for the poorer women's babies because they could pay so little for their keep. Miserable as baby farms were, laboring women had few alternatives. The baby farms were the medieval equivalent of day-care centers, a 24-hour version. Another alternative was infanticide, and rates of infanticide continued to be high throughout the Middle Ages.[32] Children who survived to the age of 5 or 6 went out to work on their own or with their mothers.

Because women worked together in large groups in the textile towns, they developed a culture of their own. While the standard of living was low and the work hard, we must remember Herlihy's (1975) point about the lengthening life expectancy for urban women. This Florentine working girl's song (from Staley [1906] 1967: 235) suggests that women had their own ways of controlling an excessive pace of work:

Monday—Mondayish
Tuesday—nobody works
Wednesday—take up the distaff
Thursday—lay it down again
Friday—willy-nilly
Saturday—let us wash our heads
Sunday—well, that's the fiesta!

Women with entrepreneurial ability could make fortunes as wine merchants and innkeepers. One woman made a fortune coming into the city every day to sell cabbages from her farm. By order of the city fathers of Florence at her death, the bells of four market churches rang for her from All Saints' Day to Ash Wednesday, and she was buried with pomp in the bishop's tomb (Staley [1906] 1967: 458).

What proportion of the total population lived in towns and cities in the fourteenth century? Estimates range from one-fourth to one-third of the population for England, Italy, France, and Flanders (Clough 1951; Herlihy 1975: 1-22). This means that very substantial numbers of women led the kind of working life just described, although often in smaller workshops. Of those who lived in towns and cities, the great majority went out to work each day much as their town and city sisters of the twentieth century do. The proportion who worked by their husbands' sides in home workshops must have been very small. Even in the case of the small village workshop, it was not necessarily adjacent to the house.

The lot of women who were skilled artisans was undeniably easier because they could employ unskilled women to do their domestic work. There was a wide range of occupations available to the skilled working woman of the Middle Ages. Poll-tax returns, one source of information about working women, give the following picture for Oxford in 1380:

37 spinsters, 11 shapesters (tailors), 9 tapsters (innkeepers), 3 sutrices (shoemakers), 3 hucksters, 5 washerwomen, (and also) butchers, brewers, chandlers, ironmongers, netmakers and kepsters (woolcombers); also 148 women domestics. (Clark 1919: 155)

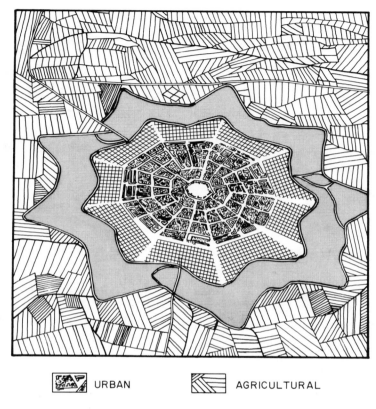

URBAN   AGRICULTURAL

Figure 1.14. Drawing of Aerial View of Palma Nova, Italy. Redrawn by KH.

On the Continent:

> From 1320 to 1500 in Frankfurt 65 lines of work are listed in which only women workers appeared, seventeen in which they predominated, 38 in which men and women were equal, and 81 in which men dominated. In other words, there were no fewer than 201 occupations in which women were engaged. (Norrenburg, quoted in McDonnell 1969: 85)

Women traders also had a broad field of operations. A citizen free-holders' list for London in the early 1400s includes 771 men and 111 women; of the women, the majority were single, conducting independent businesses; some were married, with their own business; and some were widows (Thrupp 1962: 125). English law very specifically protected the rights of married (*femme couverte*) as well as single women to do business and go to law on their own account (Cleveland 1896: 69-80).

Figure 1.15. Peasant Pushing His Wife to Work. Redrawn by HBR.

Eileen Power and M. M. Postan (1933) give a lively picture of the women overseas traders of Bristol in the mid-1400s.[33] Seven major women merchants and eight minor women shippers are mentioned and also women merchants operating from Leyden and Bordeaux. Some of them were clearly pillars of the town and subsidizers of major city enterprises. The duchess of York, the mother of Edward IV, is also mentioned as a large-scale overseas trader. Given that all this comes from the account of only one town, a complete study of the women merchants of England and the Continent would be a substantial volume.

Cities produced two very different, yet complementary, solutions to survival problems on the part of women. The first was the invention of the beguinages; the second solution was vagabondage. Much has been written about the *vagantes*, the wandering scholars so well described by Helen Waddell (1927). The book about vagabond women has yet to be written. No doubt, there are many tales to uncover about the bands of women who traveled about taking in country fairs and festivals of every kind; who trailed around after the king's court (which moved often in those days), always available as entertainers for the king and queen and their courtiers; who sometimes joined the Crusades either on their own or in a knight's party. In addition to all-women bands, many shifting man-woman partnerships were formed as people traveled the court and market routes. Women often teamed up with the vagantes (who were really unemployed clerics). Because they had to

support themselves, they always showed up on important public occasions, where their services could be required in various ways:

> In the assembling of the Imperial diet at Frankfurt in 1394 the city was visited by 800 itinerant women, temporarily increasing the adult female population by 25 percent; and at the Church Councils of Constance and Basle their number is said to have been about double this. In such cases these vagabond women had to be organized and controlled. At Basle this duty devolved on the Duke of Saxony. . . . He had the bright idea of taking a census of them, but had to give it up when halfway through as too difficult a task. (Wieth-Knudsen 1928: 223-24)

Figure 1.16. Woman Entertainer, Gothic. Redrawn by HBR.

In the wars between France and England, we meet with vagabond women by the hundreds in the baggage trains of the armies, and they were put in the charge of special bailiffs. The women's bailiff soon became a regular appointment in the armies of the time (Wieth-Knudsen 1928: 223-24). In military campaigns of any kind, it was standard to have 1,000 or 2,000 women along. Some were regular companions of the soldiers, but many were independent vagabond women. These are described as tough, hardworking women who toiled endlessly at fetching and carrying on the battlefield, at feeding the troops, and nursing the sick. They never refused a chore, were generally self-disciplined and modest, and, underneath their toughness, were gentle (Ploss, Bertels, & Bertels 1964). Probably this women's army corps was not too different in the Middle Ages than the host of women who were along on Xenophon's "March of the 10,000" in antiquity, and they were probably just as much taken for granted.

Other vagabond women worked as laborers in a variety of temporary special-purpose guilds that were formed around a specific undertaking rather than around a craft. Among such special-purpose guilds that took in women workers were cathedral-building guilds and the groups that contracted for trading voyages (Kropotkin 1972: 153-54).

A smaller class of independent women lived more settled lives and had their own houses in the towns and cities, living under the legal protection (as well as regulation) of the town council. They are frequently referred to in medieval writings as "daughters of joy," and attitudes toward them were ambivalent throughout the Middle Ages. The best organized of the residential groups were in effect entertainment guilds and, like all guilds, had strict regulations to control the competition. In some towns, as, for example, Geneva and Nuremberg, they had an elected woman leader who represented their interests to the town council (Ploss et al. 1964: 100). They were always on the lookout for illegal competition, including runaway Beguines who might be looking for work. Like the entertainers of Mediterranean lands described in Volume 1, they had status and (intermittent) respect in the community and were invited to all public functions of freemen and town councils. When royalty came to town, the council sometimes provided the women entertainers with new clothes; one lucky band all got velvet dresses when Emperor Siegmund visited in 1435 (Ploss et al. 1964: 98). And "as late as 1516 it was the custom in Zürich for the mayor, the sheriff and the women of the town to dine with the foreign ambassadors who visited the place" (Wieth-Knudsen 1928: 227).

At the French court, they were part of the Court of Ribalds. This participation was abolished by a puritanical king, but the ladies soon returned, organized under a new court-appointed officer, the "dame des filles de joie suivant la cour" (lady of the daughters of joy following the court). In 1535, Olive Sainte was paid 90 pounds by King Francis for expenses for herself and the women court followers (Lacroix 1926: 733-46). Periodically, kings issued stern orders to tone down the "joy." Orders to wear special clothes, or to wear special markings on their clothes, were frequently received by these women. This was part of the branding process that consistently has dogged the activities of working women who render sexual services. They were also repeatedly forbidden to wear jewelry and fine clothes, although this was obviously part of their professional equipment. At the worst, very punitive laws were enforced against them and, for the slightest offenses, they were jailed or fined. Typically, it was the poor among the daughters of joy who suffered the sharp edge of the law, and sentences such as the following were not infrequently imposed by the courts: hanging, being buried alive, or drowning by being placed in a cage and lowered into the river. Court records indicate such sentences were passed because of women's "demerits" (Lacroix 1926: 824-31). Those who were only pilloried were lucky.

Life was dangerous and unpredictable for the lower orders of daughters of joy; even for the wealthy and successful ones, life was not easy.

Generally, these women were segregated, taxed, and forced into city-supervised areas. Most appalling, there was a tendency to try to force all unpartnered women into these segregated houses. A little after this period, in 1493, the following ordinance was passed in Metz: "All married women living apart from their husbands and girls of evil life shall go to the brothels." Under those circumstances, it was risky to leave one's husband, risky to be single, and risky even to be a widow (Lacroix 1926: 861). The distinction between brothel and prison becomes blurred by statutes like this one: "If any girl has committed a fault and would continue to do evil," city officials shall commit her to the brothel (Lacroix 1926: 878).

A problem that we shall meet increasingly from the Middle Ages on is the habit of the authorities and the middle and upper classes to treat all poverty-level working women as prostitutes. François Villon, the vagabond scholar-poet who was hanged in the fifteenth century after a colorful life as an outlaw, wrote a famous poem to the women of his circle. Who were they? Not professional daughters of joy at all but poor working women—helmet makers, glove makers, cobblers, sausage makers, rug makers, tapestry makers, hood makers, and spur makers (Lacroix 1926: 997-98). A hardy lot and certainly independent women.

Among the daughters of joy, we find poets and ballad makers. The ancient Germanic bardic tradition flowered in delightful and much admired lyric poetry by women in the 1200s and 1300s (Wienhold 1882).

The word *prostitute*, used both by Wieth-Knudsen (1928) and by Ploss et al. (1964) to describe these women, is, as usual, an oversimplification of their status. These historians need not have been so surprised that the "women of the town" in Zürich dined with the ambassador. Zürich has one of the oldest traditions of women in public life in Europe; it is not a tradition of prostitution but of participation in public affairs. Given that public entertainments, carnivals, and fairs were such an important part of town and village life in the Middle Ages, this general delight in public recreation has to be taken into account in assessing the role of women in the entertainment sector of the medieval labor force. Both the vagabond women and the settled entertainment guild women had their places in that sector. What proportion of them were "below the poverty line" for that era it is difficult to estimate, but the evidence from art, song, and story suggests that there were many well-fed women entertainers who enjoyed their way of life. Much of the gaiety that comes through in the descriptions of fairs and street life in medieval cities is due to the colorful styles and behavior of the vagabond women. Their pride, toughness, and sense of humor were also characteristic of medieval working women generally. Their sisters in other craft guilds would not have looked or behaved very differently than the vagabonds.

The term *vagabond* covers a heterogeneous group of women. Of those who led a more mobile existence, we find at one extreme the wandering saint, on perpetual pilgrimage, and, at the other, thieves and murderers. The great bulk of women were somewhere in between—women dislodged from rural life and with no settled niche in urban life. The same was also true of the daughters of joy. Insofar as they were self-organized, they set rules and standards for their activities and tried to guard against interlopers. Some of the street fights described were probably between the wandering vagabond women and local entertainment guild members trying to protect their turf.

Prisons and Slavery

Although the term *vagabond* covers a heterogeneous set of women, as I have pointed out, in general, these women tended to be the marginal members of society. They had fewer protections than their more settled counterparts and, along with the poorest of their city sisters, were very vulnerable to being cleared off the streets and the fairgrounds and placed in jails. Jails were a new invention of the Middle Ages. Kings and lords had from ancient times had dungeons in which to put away enemies, but the concept of a prison for offenders, linked to the administration of a code of laws, was new in the Middle Ages.[34] At first, women and men were imprisoned together, but, by the thirteenth century, there are references to women's sections in English prisons at York Castle and Maidstone. In 1310, the chancellor of Oxford insisted on a separate women's section in the Oxford prison when the prison became known as a brothel. During this time, unlimited alcohol and unlimited sex were available in prisons. By the fourteenth century, separate prisons were being built for women. Punishment won out over sex (Pugh 1968: 103, 324, 352-53, 357-58).

Women were mostly imprisoned for petty theft. The most helpless of the vagabonds, rural migrants to the city who had not been able to find employment or a niche to live in and poverty-stricken unmarried mothers, were the most likely candidates for imprisonment. Every women's prison was full of babies and small children, not necessarily there with mothers: 4- and 5-year-old girls were imprisoned for "theft"—as were boys of the same age.

Jails were used very selectively. When middle- and upper-class persons were imprisoned, they had separate apartments. The poor were the ones who suffered and starved to death, for no town funds were made available for feeding prisoners in the Middle Ages. The poor depended entirely on charity. Mutilation was another punishment frequently used for the poor, and half-starved daughters of joy who were sent back into the streets minus their noses could not have lived very long. The removal of noses, ears, and hands was common punishment in Europe and Byzantium and elsewhere in the Mediterranean in the Middle Ages, for both women and men (Rusche and Kirchheimer 1968: 17).

A more serious danger that lurked for women of the working class was to be kidnapped for the slave trade. The major slave marts of Europe were in Italy, particularly in Venice and Florence. While Italian slave traders dealt primarily in captured Tartars, Circassians, Armenians, Georgians, and Bulgarians, there was also a steady movement of women from the rest of Europe to Italian slave marts.[35] Within Europe itself, after the seventh century, slavery was gradually becoming serfdom, but the evolution took a long time. It is not clear in many texts when the word *slave* means "slave" and when it means "serf," but, from the context in which either *slave* or *serf* was used in medieval Europe, it often appears that de facto slavery existed, whether it was de jure or not. In 1066, William the Conqueror supported the principle of manumission of slaves in England. The mother of Earl Godwin shipped English girls as slaves to Denmark in 1086. In 1102, the London Council passed a resolution forbidding slave trading in England, but little heed was paid to the resolution. Bristol merchants were among the worst offenders, shipping pregnant women as slaves to Ireland. In France and Germany, kings began declaring emancipation areas in the 1100s, but final abolition of serfdom in France was in 1779, in Saxony in 1832, in Denmark in 1804, in Hungary after 1850, and in Russia in 1861 (Brownlow [1892] 1969).

Considering the threats that hung over the lives of the poor, the robustness of medieval gaiety had its somber undertones. Yet that gaiety was real enough and has to be remembered when looking at the total picture of women's situation. The nuns, the anchoresses, and the Beguines would have quieter styles, but they too shared the raucous and by our standards often licentious sense of humor of the times, along with the ladies of the merchant houses and the manor houses. Miracle plays about Our Lady became so bawdy that they had to be moved out of the churches and into the squares. But they originated as celebrations in the church, and nuns, Beguines, and artisan women must have enjoyed them as much as anyone. The Virgin's sense of humor is attested to in many a bawdy medieval tale. The "Nun's Tale" in Boccaccio's *Decameron* was taken amiss by no one. This shared sense of humor between women and men had egalitarian aspects to it. When men started to creep away to tell funny stories about sex, it was a sign of something more than emerging puritanism. It was a signal that an important dimension of man-woman relationships had atrophied.

The Economic Situation of Women by the End of the Middle Ages

The idea that the decline of the craft guilds and the decline of the status of women went together, as economic enterprises moved from what Clark calls domestic and family industry to capitalistic industry, is as I have indicated partially true, but it also represents a substantial oversimplification of the actual course of events. What is true is that, before the development of greater urban concentrations, there was for rural and small town populations a pattern of domestic industry "in which the goods produced are for the exclusive use of the family and are not therefore subject to an exchange or money value." In family industry, "the family becomes the unit for the production of goods to be sold or exchanged" (Clark 1919: 6). It is also true that, in the early stages of the new urbanization, the craft guilds continued this unity of capital and labor in a kind of extended family formed on the basis of special craft skills.

The craft guilds were destroyed by the increased volume of trade, both domestic and international, which led to the development of a separate class of traders apart from producers (Renard [1918] 1968). The trade guilds grew into the vast exploitative merchant guilds (quite different than the earlier craft-based guilds merchant) that in the end turned craft workers into underpaid pieceworkers. The craft guilds belonged to the localist tradition, dealt only with municipal authorities, and had no relationship with the state. The merchant guilds derived their power from the state. The 1563 Elizabethan Statute of Artificers, which established total state control (in theory) over the movement of labor in England, was the natural outgrowth of the ordinances of 1349 and 1351, which forbade laborers to change employers and compelled every unemployed person over 12 to enter the agricultural labor force. This development, aimed at freezing the labor supply generally, in fact only froze women:

> By this Act (the Statute of Laborers) every woman free or bound, under 60, and not carrying on a trade or calling, provided she had no land, and was not in domestic or other service, was liable to be called upon to enter service in the fields or otherwise, and if she refused, she was imprisoned

until she complied; whilst all girls who for twelve years had been brought up to follow the plough, were not allowed to enter any other calling, but were forced to continue working in the fields. (Cleveland, 1896: 76)

Men continued to move where the jobs were, but village women, more directly burdened with family responsibilities, felt the full force of the compulsion to work in the fields. Beyond that, they also took piecework home, to eke out inadequate wages to maintain home and children. The more women entered into the wage labor market, the more pronounced wage differentials became. Through their relative immobility, women had no bargaining power, and so the complaints of wage discrimination began early—and they were found everywhere. The scholars of Toulouse in 1422 paid women grape pickers half of what they paid the men, who only had to carry the full baskets back to the college cellar. The monks of Paris did the same (Thrupp 1964: 240-41). The women construction workers who worked side by side with men in building the College of Toulouse were paid far less than the men who did the same kind of labor (Thrupp 1964: 244). The labor shortage resulting from the black death did not at all affect women's wages, which remained substantially the same on the Continent for nearly 100 years (Perroy 1964: 244). Neither did the supposed labor shortages from the black death help the laboring poor in England (Ziegler 1969: 240-59). Fourteenth-century workers, especially women, had to work longer and harder but were not earning more pay.

This became increasingly true as the large commercial guilds organized workers into specialties, to increase production. As early as the 1200s, there were 11 distinct process specialists in that part of the wool industry run by the commercial guilds (Renard [1918] 1968: 80-81). A family carrying out those tasks in a small household could hardly compete, and in the home workshops spinning for merchant houses increasingly replaced the earlier total production process. The division of labor was well developed so early that, as Renard says, mechanization was inevitable, and the wonder is that it did not happen sooner. The mill as a mechanical source of power had been known from the time of Alexander the Great.

The most exploitive commercial guilds developed in the major trade centers of Italy, which had the advantage of the whole Mediterranean as a trading lake. Simultaneously, the Hanseatic towns, home of the older craft guilds, went into economic decline, because there was no longer a need for the old northern trade route through Russia. But even the Hanseatic guilds had already become fairly large-scale operations, and women's subsidiary roles as auxiliary workers living in dormitory situations or as commuting day laborers already existed before the decline of the Hanse. It is important to remember that the women intellectuals and artists of Italy who flourished in the universities of Bologna and Salerno and in the courts of Florence and Venice were in a way sitting on the backs of their exploited sisters. The Venetian dogaressas, sponsoring the elegant craft work in lace and gold that their working sisters grew blind to produce, also introduced such forward-looking innovations as bullfights and eunuchs, and they certainly benefited from the flourishing slave trade. Feminism was not born in Venice.

Spinsters in Italy and elsewhere were a vast reserve labor force so totally controlled by the guilds that on holy days the bishop, instructed by the merchants, would issue a pastoral letter threatening spinsters who wasted wool with ecclesiastical censure and even with excommunication if they repeated the offense (Renard [1918] 1968: 25-26). As the older craft guilds declined, working-class women had increasingly minor roles in production.

The final squeezing out of the sisters from the guilds was a slow process. Long after guilds stopped recognizing other forms of membership and participation of women, they would still permit a widowed woman to carry on her husband's work with guild recognition, even as late as the 1600s (Clark 1919: 10). Gradually over the next couple of centuries, women were confined to a few specialties such as dressmaking, brewing, domestic service, and the street vending of food. Eventually brewing became a factory operation and women lost control of it (Clark 1919: 223-28).

While the status of working-class women was declining, the business activities of women merchants were also decreasing. The formerly productive wives of prosperous men of business in the towns of Europe increasingly transferred their activities to more strictly domestic areas and to social life and "adornment" (Clark 1919: 38-39). Only women of the upper class, and particularly those who had estates to manage, maintained economically productive roles and sometimes political roles at court. We see the beginnings of the process that led the legal commentator Blackstone later to write of the "civil death" of the married woman.

The changes that were taking place for women did not represent a sudden shift to a new and lower status. The decline was rather an acceleration of a process that began with primordial urbanization and the rise of an urban laboring class of women in antiquity. With greater population densities, improving techniques of production, and a concentration of wealth in the hands of a merchant class, an acceleration of demand for craft goods simply placed more and more women in preindustrial factory-type workshops. For working-class women, the separation of work from home led to the increased separation of mothers from their children, to baby farming, and to infanticide. At the same time, for middle-class women, there was a withdrawal from the work sites and an intensification of mothering and other social roles.

What made the guild master's wife, formerly busy in the work associated with maintaining the workshop-dormitory-school-extended family-merchandising enterprise, opt for a life of lesser mercantile involvement and more leisure? Affluence itself was the crucial factor. She was no longer needed to make the family business run, and few women had the entrepreneurial drive that would keep them in the business after necessity released them. It is a mistake, however, to exaggerate the disappearance of her work role. It did not disappear, it diminished.

It would also be a mistake to conclude that these women were choosing leisure per se. The new urban social world was a world that had to be *created*. There were no precedents for the new life patterns of a sizable and affluent middle-class urban population. Prior to the Renaissance, nearly everyone had to work hard, and the higher the status of the women, the more responsibility they had. The secluded, do-nothing middle-class women that we identified during earliest urbanization had always been a tiny sector. Now that sector was rapidly growing. In this new, expanded middle-class world, women formerly preoccupied with productive labor were confronted with the new challenges of a world in which social relationships, leisure and reflection, and cultural productivity were suddenly of primary importance. The limitations placed on women in these new spheres because of the secondary nature of their status did not become immediately evident.

The close of the Middle Ages was a period of clashing of opposite tides for middle-class women. On the one hand, some were withdrawing from mercantile involvement and exploring the dimensions of a new world of social interaction. On the other hand, there were women who were experiencing the moral and intellectual liberation of the dawning Renaissance and wished to participate more fully in the public arenas of society. Meanwhile, the lessening economic pressure for the participation of women of the middle class in family business affairs was countered by a tremendous increase in pressure from working-class women for jobs. It was in the midst of these shifting pressures that the gradual limitation of rights to hold property independently, to transact business, and to go to law took place for women. The legal

Figure 1.17. Villagers Taking "Law" Into Their Own Hands. Redrawn by HBR.

protection for women in equity law remained but was ignored. Beard (1946: 87-115) has written eloquently about the use of common law to limit women's rights (more specifically, the rights of married women)—a process that began in the late Middle Ages and was to be continued by Blackstone and his successors right up to the twentieth century.

Clark (1919: 303) reminds us that it never occurred to the writers on political philosophy who were developing a new theory of the state as composed of individuals that individuals might be women. It was simply not a question for discussion. If we ask why they did not, we are back at the concepts of public and private space, of underlife and overlife. Women never had burgess status in the medieval towns. What fluidity there was in the medieval partnership between women and men depended on the customs of the common people and on public opinion; women and men shared in the creation of that custom and opinion. With the growth of cities and large-scale commercial enterprises, local custom was increasingly replaced by common law, which, despite its plebeian sound, was actually the law of the aristocracy (Clark 1919: 236). Law is an overlife institution. Custom is not. Women did not participate in the new regulatory process whereby aristocratic law was codified, interpreted, and extended to cover the transactions of an entire population. The all-important equity law, which was developed to deal with the inadequacies and injustices of the common law, at first protected women from the consequences of the shift to national codes. But the more the legal profession specialized and expanded with the expanding economy, the more it became evident that this new public arena was a man's world. The famous (mis)statement in 1775 by Blackstone is a logical outcome of the exclusion of women from the process of developing interpretations of law in the public arena: "By marriage, the husband and wife are one person in law; that is, the very being or legal existence of the woman is suspended, during the marriage, or at least is incorporated and consolidated into that of the husband" (quoted in Beard 1946: 89).[36]

All the new clerical and administrative positions associated with the burgeoning bureaucracy of the state went, as we have already noted, to men. Many of the able, literate women were inside convents, while a whole army of wandering unemployed male clerics—the vagantes— were waiting to leap into every job opening. The beguinages, which could have provided literate women for government offices, developed a self-contained world of their own, partly—and understandably—in defense against the indiscriminate witchcraft persecutions. In strictly labor-power terms, there were plenty of literate women to fill some of the new bureaucratic jobs. In terms of functional availability, there were very few.

One could argue that there never was any overt decision to "get the women out," that it all happened by default. On the other hand, given the number of instances in which the church combined with various economic groups from doctors to lawyers to merchant guilds, not only to make pronouncements about the incapacities of women but often to accomplish the physical liquidation of women through witchcraft and heresy trials, one can hardly say that it all happened without anyone intending it. The exclusion of women was a result of a combination of impersonal and intentional forces.

Once again, we see the vulnerability of women because of their underlife roles. Even in the guilds, for all the apparently egalitarian references to the sistren and the brethren, women were relegated to the underlife of supportive and fill-in roles and rarely were apprenticed to master the full range of craft skills. Even if they were, burgess rights were denied them on the basis of the need for all burgesses to be bearers of arms in defense of the city. That same perception of civic duty kept women in secondary status in Greek city-states. The merchant bourgeoisie and the craftsmen had also belonged to the underlife at the beginning of the Middle Ages. They, however, "graduated" from feudal underlife into positions in the overlife structures that enabled them to affect public policy. It was very easy for the brethren to leave their less skilled sistren behind.

* * *

In the Middle Ages, there were queens and princesses alert to the need to defend the rights of at least some of their sisters. While the social consciousness of women royalty may leave something to be desired, they took responsibility for their sisters in convents and some responsibility for the urban poor.

> The women of the religious orders took responsibility for the education of women of all strata, within limits.
>
> The Beguines and the hermitesses took responsibility for the right of women to remain unmarried and have productive lives in the world outside the convent.
>
> The intellectuals took responsibility for knowledge. Christine de Pisan particularly spoke for the right to knowledge on the part of women, so they could act responsibly for their families and society.
>
> The vagabonds defended mobility, freedom, and the right of women to have fun.

Who is doing the work of the queens and the princesses today? Of the prophesying and fighting abbesses? Of the Beguines and the hermitesses? Of the scholars and the vagabonds?

Figure 1.18. Woman Charging Knight With Shuttle, Sixteenth Century. Redrawn by HBR.

The troubadour François Villon was already feeling nostalgic in the middle 1400s, when he wrote his famous ballad:

> Where is the virtuous Heloise . . .
> And Jeanne d'Arc, the good Lorraine . . .
> But where are the snows of yesteryear?

They are around, but they look and sound different. The idea that great women are as evanescent in history as the melting snow is a poetic statement of the fact that women are invisible to each other, as well as to men, as the makers of history. They do not know their own foremothers.

Notes

1. Gibbon thinks that Morozia, born in 880, mistress of Pope Sergius III, mother of Pope John XI, and grandmother of Pope John XII, may have been the source of the Pope Joan myth (Reich 1908: 194).

2. In Chapter 8 in Volume 1, in contrasting the educational and the military approaches to the Christianization of Europe during the early Middle Ages, I spoke of a distinct women's perspective. I may have exaggerated it there, and I may be underestimating it here. In general, the more women are drawn into positions of leadership, the more they share the perspective of the men with whom they work. The underside is a good protector of alternative perspectives. It should be noted here that the special qualities of the contributions of spiritual women to the larger society over the centuries is well documented in *Women of Spirit* (Ruether and McLaughlin 1979). This work can be turned to for information on each era until recent times.

3. Barbara Nolan's study of the *Vita Nuova* (1970) makes one aware of the commonality between Dante's work and that of the Beguine mystics, although Nolan herself does not make a point of this.

4. This mixture comes out particularly in the case histories recorded in *The Devil in Britain and America* by John Ashton ([1896] 1972).

5. See especially "L'Heresie Urbaine et Rurale en l'Italie" [Urban and Rural Heresy in Italy], by C. Violante, and "Les Flagellants du Quatorzième Siècle" [Flagellants in the Fourteenth Century], by G. S. Zekely, in Le Goff (1968).

6. For a stunning pictorial view of the many ways of life for women of the Middle Ages, and one that covers all classes of society, see Harksen (1975). See also Mosher (1976) and Baker 1978.

7. The picture of Queen Eleanor as a wealthy, spoiled aristocrat who caused Louis VII's defeat in the Crusades has been so convincingly put forth by so many historians that I had reproduced this version of her in the initial draft of this chapter. I am indebted to E. L. Hallgren (medieval historian at the University of Colorado, Boulder, personal communication, 1975) and to Charles Proctor (Department of Letters, Modern Language, and Speech, Northern State College, Aberdeen, S.D., personal communication, 1975) for pointing out that I had erroneously accepted versions of her life as told by "French chauvinist and male chauvinist historians." The rewritten account is based on Amy Kelly's *Eleanor of Aquitaine* (1950), a historical novel based on painstaking historical research.

8. One of the most interesting studies of Joan focuses on female heroism (see Marina Warner 1981).

9. The origin of the term is obscure.

10. Bücher (Wieth-Knudsen 1928: 212-13) says that, in Frankfurt in 1400, there was a 20% surplus of women in relation to the male urban population.

11. The Beguines filled a certain niche in society so successfully that they are still functioning today, albeit in a conventlike atmosphere contrary to their original function. Sacheverell Sitwell describes the modern Beguines: "They are more nunlike than the nuns and are never seen bicycling, driving cars, carrying shopping baskets or ferrying droves of school children across the traffic lights. They dwell in an inaction limpid and perfect of its kind, each Beguinage under the aegis of a Grande Demoiselle, in walled enclosures, sometimes of whitewashed walls, in little gabled houses of brick and stone with green shutters. At Courtnai the Beguinage is a huddle of little steep-roofed houses crowding together as though for company and warmth; while at Bruges and Ghent the houses are grouped together round open grassed spaces" (1965: 168-69).

12. This influx represented the convent-based wing of the women's movement.

13. Because political leaders were often themselves prey to this kind of emotionalism, and could easily rouse it in followers, a now common impression of the chiliastic movements of the Middle Ages is that they were all precursors of Hitlerism. Cohn (1970) gives that view, which seems to me a vast oversimplification.

14. A significant aspect of the Beguine movement is that it included, in addition to unmarried women and widows, married women who took more or less permanent leave from their own households.

15. Among these men were Jaques de Vitry, John of Vivelles, William of L'Olive, Ivan de Reves, and Theodore of Celles (McDonnell 1969: 20-58).

16. *The Cloud of Unknowing*, for example, one of the most widely read of these classics today, and first published anonymously in Marguerite's time, has such a warning in the introduction.

17. Except where otherwise indicated, the material in this section is based on Morris, *The Lady Was a Bishop* (1973); Eckenstein, *Women Under Monasticism* (1896); and Hilpisch, *History of Benedictine Nuns* (1958). Another book on the subject, discovered too late to use here, is Ludlow's *Woman's Work in the Church* ([1866] 1975).

18. Fontrevault owed its existence and format to the work of one of the most ardently feminist churchmen of the Middle Ages, Robert of Arbrissel (McLaughlin 1975: 323).

19. While, on the face of it, the enclosure movement was ideological, the same economic problems that weakened the subsistence base of the convents also operated to force enclosure. It was in part a measure to prevent, among upper- and middle-class women, "the return of the professed cloistered daughters to claim their share of the paternal fortunes" (Monica 1945: 320), given that, when the coming and going of professed nuns was freer, many changed their minds about convent life and tried to reenter secular life and get regular marriage dowries.

20. The Franciscan Third Order is a lay order, not conventual.

21. Sources used here are Montag (1968) and Butkovich (1969, 1972).

22. The source for material on St. Clare is *Legend and Writings of St. Claire* (Franciscan Institute 1953).

23. The terms *anchoress* and *anchorite* are interchangeable with *hermitess* and *hermit*, referring to women and men living in solitude and not in religious orders.

24. For a vivid description of life on pilgrimage for a woman, see Monica on Angela de Merici (1945: 135-45); for general descriptions of medieval pilgrimages, see Newton (1968, chap. 3). See also R. J. Mitchell (1968) on the Jerusalem Pilgrimage of 1458.

25. Rashdall tells us that "the University of London, after being empowered by royal charter to do all things that could done by any university, was legally advised that it could

not grant degrees to women without a fresh charter because no university had ever granted such degrees." He comments, "It had not heard of the women-doctors at Salerno," and footnotes further, "I have been informed by an eminent judge, who was one of the counsel on whose advice the university acted, that a knowledge of this fact would have modified his opinion" (Rashdall 1936: 460-61).

26. By the end of the Middle Ages, in the 1400s, there were still famous women professors of medicine in Italy, such as Fedele Cassandra of Venice, who lived to be 102, the mother-daughter team of the Laura Calendas in Naples, and Dorothea Bucca of Bologna. ·

27. The following books were used in this study of Christine de Pisan: Roy (1884, vols. 2 and 3); Solente (1955); Towner ([1932] 1969); Varty (1965); Kemp-Welch (1913); de Pisan ([1521], 1932, 1966, 1970); and Willard (1975). Note also the recent modern edition of de Pisan's *The Book of the City of Ladies* (1982).

28. For descriptions of life in the manor houses and their urban equivalents, see Holmes (1952), "Le Menagier de Paris" in Power (1963), and Labarge (1980).

29. For example, Joan sometimes went by her father's name, d'Arc, and sometimes by her mother's, Domremy (Bloch 1961: 138).

30. We have noted that rural women paid substitutes to fulfill military obligations. This device was apparently never used to enable women to achieve burgess status in the towns.

31. See Walsh, *The Thirteenth: Greatest of Centuries* (1970), for a glowing description of guild life in its idealized form.

32. "If sex ratios of 150 to 100 (c. C.E. 801) and 172 to 100 (C.E. 1391) are any indication of the extent of the killing of legitimate girls, and if illegitimates were usually killed regardless of sex, the real rate of infanticide could have been substantial in the Middle Ages. . . . As late as 1527, one priest (in Rome) admitted that 'the latrines resound with the cries of children who have been plunged into them' " (de Mause 1974: 29).

33. See also A. Abram, "Women Traders in Mediaeval London" (1916). Further information on women's occupations in the Middle Ages can be found in *A History of Technology* (Singer et al. 1956) and *Schaffende Arbeit* (Brandt 1928).

34. The first mention of a prison in the English law codes is in Alfred's Code, A.D. 890.

35. See Origo's "The Domestic Enemy" (1955) for a fuller discussion of the Italian slave trade.

36. It will be noted that widows and single women do not lose their rights, so the situation was never as bad for them as for their married sisters. For those who want to follow Beard's history of the misinterpretations of women's legal status beginning with Blackstone, a reading of chapters 4-6 in *Woman as a Force in History* (1946) is recommended.

References

Abram, A. 1916. "Women Traders in Mediaeval London." *Economics Journal* 28:276-85.
Adams, Henry. [1905] 1933. *Mont-Saint-Michel and Chartres*. Boston: Houghton Mifflin.
Afetinan, A. 1962. *Emancipation of the Turkish Woman*. Paris: UNESCO.
Ancelet-Hustache, Jeanne. 1963. *Gold Tried by Fire: St. Elizabeth of Hungary*, translated by Paul J. Oligny, O.F.M., and Sister Venard O'Donnell, O.S.F. Chicago: Franciscan Herald Press.
Aries, Philippe. 1962. *Centuries of Childhood: A Social History of Family Life*, translated by Robert Baldick. New York: Knopf.
Ashton, John. [1896] 1972. *The Devil in Britain and America*. Hollywood, CA: Newcastle.
Baker, Derek. 1978. *Medieval Women*. Oxford: Blackwell, for the Ecclesiastical History Society.

Baring-Gould, S. 1896. *Curious Myths of the Middle Ages.* Philadelphia: J. B. Lippincott.

Beard, Mary R. 1946. *Woman as Force in History: A Study in Traditions and Realities.* New York: Macmillan.

Bloch, Marc. 1961. *Feudal Society,* translated by F. A. Manyon. Chicago: University of Chicago Press.

Bogin, Meg. 1976. *The Women Troubadours.* London and New York: Paddington.

Bordeaux, Henry. 1937. *Au Pays des Elisabeth.* Paris: Librarie Plow.

Brandt, Paul. 1927. *Schaffende Arbeit und Bildende Kunst im Alterum und Mittelalter.* Leipzig: Alfred Kroner Verlag.

———. 1928. *Schaffende Arbeit und Bildende Kunst: Vom Mittelalter bis zur Gegenwart.* Leipzig: Alfred Kroner Verlag.

Brink, J. R. 1980. *Female Scholars: A Tradition of Learned Women Before 1800.* Montreal: Eden Press Women's Publication.

Brownlow, W. R. 1969. *Lectures on Slavery and Serfdom in Europe.* New York: Negro University Press.

Bücher, Carl. 1910. *Die Frauenfrage im Mittelalter.* Tübingen, Germany.

Buckler, Georgina. 1929. *Anna Comnena: A Study.* London: Oxford University Press.

Butkovich, Anthony. 1969. *Iconography: St. Birgitta of Sweden.* Los Angeles: Ecumenical Foundation of America.

———. 1972. *Revelations: St. Birgitta of Sweden.* Los Angeles: Ecumenical Foundation of America.

Castellani, Maria. 1939. *Italian Women Past and Present.* Rome: Societa Editrice di Novissima.

Charrier, Charlotte. 1933. *Heloise: Dans l'Histoire et dans la Légende.* Paris: Librarie Ancienne Honore Champion.

Clark, Alice. 1919. *Working Life of Women in the Seventeenth Century.* London: Routledge.

Cleveland, Arthur Rackham. 1896. *Woman Under the English Law.* London: Hurst.

Clough, Shepard B. 1951. *The Rise and Fall of Civilization: How Economic Development Affects the Culture of Nations.* New York: McGraw-Hill.

Cohn, Norman. 1970. *The Pursuit of the Millennium.* New York: Oxford University Press.

Colledge, Eric. 1961. *The Medieval Mystics of England.* New York: Scribner.

Colledge, Eric, ed. 1965. *Medieval Netherlands Religious Literature,* translated by Eric Colledge. New York: London House and Maxwell.

Coulton, G. G. 1955. *Medieval Panorama.* Cleveland: Meridian, World.

de Beaumont, Edouard. 1929. *The Sword and Womankind.* New York: Panurge.

Delort, Robert. 1973. *Life in the Middle Ages.* New York: Universe.

de Mause, Lloyd. 1974. "The Evolution of Childhood." Pp. 1-74 in *The History of Childhood,* edited by Lloyd de Mause. New York: Psychohistory.

de Pisan, Christine. [1521] 1932, 1966, 1970. *Here Beginneth the Boke of the Cyté of Ladyes,* edited by Brian Anslay. London: H. Pepwell. Film Reproduction: Edwards Brothers, no. 219.

———. 1932. *The Book of Fayttes of Armes and of Chyuarye,* edited by A. T. P. Byles; translated by William Caxton. London: Oxford University Press.

———. 1966. *The Book of the Duke of True Lovers,* edited by Laurence Binyon and Eric R. D. Maclagan; translated by Alice Kemp-Welch. New York: Cooper Square.

———. 1970. *The Epistle of Othea,* edited by Curt F. Bühler; translated by Stephen Scrope. London: Oxford University Press.

———. 1982. *The Book of the City of Ladies.* New York: Persea.

Diehl, Charles. 1963. *Byzantine Empresses.* New York: Knopf.

Eckenstein, Lina. 1896. *Women Under Monasticism.* Cambridge: Cambridge University Press.

Ehrenreich, Barbara and Deirdre English. 1973. *Witches, Midwives, and Nurses: A History of Women Healers.* 2nd ed. Old Westbury, NY: Feminist Press.

Franciscan Institute, ed. 1953. *Legend and Writings of St. Claire of Assisi.* New York: St. Bonaventure.

Gabrieli, Francesco, ed. 1969. *Arab Historians of the Crusades*, translated by E. J. Costello. Berkeley: University of California Press.

Green, Mary Anne Everett. 1850. *Lives of the Princesses of England, from the Norman Conquest*. London: H. Colburn.

Gross, Charles. 1890. *The Guild Merchant*. Oxford: Clarendon.

Guillemin, Henri. 1972. *The True History of Joan of Arc*. London: Allen and Unwin.

Harksen, Sibylle. 1975. *Women in the Middle Ages*. New York: Abner Schram.

Hauser, Henri. 1927. *Ouvriers du Temps Passé*. Paris: Librairie Felix Alian.

Herlihy, David. 1975. "Life Expectancies for Women in Medieval Society." Pp. 1-22 in *The Role of Women in the Middle Ages*, edited by Rosemarie Morewedge. Albany: State University of New York Press.

Hill, Georgiana. 1894-96. *Women in English Life*. 2 vols. London: Richard Bentley.

Hilpisch, Stephanus. 1958. *History of Benedictine Nuns*, translated by Sr. M. Joanne Muggli. Collegeville, MN: St. John's Abbey Press.

Hilton, Rodney. 1973. *Bond Men Made Free: Medieval Peasant Movements and the English Rising of 1381*. London: Temple Smith.

Holmes, Urban Tiger, Jr. 1952. *Daily Living in the Twelfth Century: Based on the Observation of Alexander Needham in London and Paris*. Madison: University of Wisconsin Press.

Hughes, Muriel Joy. 1943. *Women Healers in Medieval Life and Literature*. Morningside Heights, NY: King's Crown.

Hurd-Mead, Kate Campbell. 1933. *A History of Women in Medicine*. Haddam, CT: Haddam.

Judserand, J. J. 1890. *English Wayfaring Life in the Middle Ages (14th Century)*. London: T. Fish Urwin.

Kellog, Charlotte. 1932. *Jadwiga: Poland's Great Queen*. New York: Macmillan.

Kelly, Amy. 1950. *Eleanor of Aquitaine and the Four Kings*. Cambridge, MA: Harvard University Press.

Kemp-Welch, Alice. 1913. *Of Six Medieval Women*. London: Macmillan.

Kropotkin, Peter. 1972. *Mutual Aid: A Factor of Evolution*, edited by Paul Avrich. Albany: State University of New York Press.

Labarge, Margaret Wade. 1980. *A Baronial Household of the Thirteenth Century*. Totowa, NJ: Barnes & Noble.

Lacroix, Paul. 1926. *History of Prostitution: Among All the Peoples of the World, from the Most Remote Antiquity to the Present Day*, edited by Samuel Putnam. New York: Covici-Friede.

Laslett, Peter, ed. 1972. *Household and Family in Past Time*. Cambridge: Cambridge University Press.

Le Goff, Jacques, ed. 1968. *Heresies et Sociétés dans l'Europe preindustriale, 11-18 siècles*. Paris: Mouton.

Ludlow, John Malcolm. [1866] 1975. *Woman's Work in the Church*. New York: Strahan.

McDannell, M. Coleen. 1975. "An Examination of a Selection of Women Saints." Unpublished student paper, University of Colorado, Boulder, Department of Sociology.

McDonnell, Ernst W. 1969. *The Beguines and the Beghards in Medieval Culture*. New York: Octagon.

McLaughlin, Mary Martin. 1975. "Peter Abelard and the Dignity of Women: Twelfth Century Feminism in Theory and Practice." In *Proceedings of the International Symposium of the Centre National de la Récherche Scientifique* (July 2-9). Paris: Centre National de la Récherche Scientifique.

Mitchell, Rosamund Jocelyn. 1968. *The Spring Voyage: The Jerusalem Pilgrimage in 1458*. New York: Clarkson N. Potter.

Moncrieff, C. K. Scott, translator. 1929. *The Letters of Abelard and Heloise*. New York: Knopf.

Monica, Sister. 1945. *Angela Merici and Her Teaching Idea: 1474-1540*. Saint Martin, OH: Ursulines of Brown County.

Montag, Ulrich. 1968. *Das Werk der Heiligen Birgitta von Schweven in Ober Deutscher Lieberlieferung*. München, Germany: C. H. Beck'sche Verlagsbuchhandlung.

Morewedge, Rosemarie Thee, ed. 1975. *The Role of Women in the Middle Ages.* Albany: State University of New York Press.

Morris, Joan. 1973. *The Lady Was a Bishop.* New York: Macmillan.

Mosher, Susan. 1976. *Women in Medieval Society.* Philadelphia: University of Pennsylvania Press.

Mozans, H. J. 1913. *Women in Science.* New York: Appleton.

Mumford, Lewis. 1961. *City in History: Its Origins, Its Transformation, and Its Prospects.* New York: Harcourt Brace Jovanovich.

Newton, Arthur Percival, ed. 1968. *Travel and Travellers of the Middle Ages.* New York: Barnes & Noble.

Nolan, Barbara. 1970. "The Vita Nuova: Dante's Book of Revelation." *Dante Studies* 88:51-77.

O'Faolain, Julia and Lauro Martines, eds. 1973. *Not in God's Image: A History of Women in Europe from the Greeks to the Nineteenth Century.* New York: Harper & Row.

Origo, Iris. 1955. "The Domestic Enemy: The Eastern Slaves in Tuscany in the Fourteenth and Fifteenth Centuries." *Speculum* 30(July):321-66.

Perroy, E. 1964. "Wage Labour in France in the Later Middle Ages." Pp. 237-46 in *Change in Medieval Society,* edited by Sylvia L. Thrupp. New York: Appleton-Century-Crofts.

Pinchbeck, Ivy. 1930. *Women Workers and the Industrial Revolution: 1750-1850.* London: Frank Cass.

Ploss, Herman Heinrich, Max Bartels, and Paul Bartels. 1964. *Woman in the Sexual Relation,* revised and enlarged by Ferdinand F. von Reitzenstein. New York: Medical Press of New York.

Power, Eileen. 1963. *Medieval People.* 10th ed. New York: Barnes & Noble.

Power, Eileen and M. M. Postan. 1933. *Studies in English Trade in the Fifteenth Century.* London: Routledge.

Pugh, Ralph B. 1968. *Imprisonment in Medieval England.* Cambridge: Cambridge University Press.

Rashdall, Hastings. 1936. *The Universities of the Middle Ages.* Vol. 3. London: Oxford University Press.

Reeves, Marjorie. 1969. *The Influence of Prophecy in the Later Middle Ages: A Study in Joachimism.* Oxford, UK: Clarendon.

Reich, Emil. 1908. *Woman Through the Ages.* 2 vols. London: Methuen.

Renard, Georges. [1918] 1968. *Guilds in the Middle Ages.* New York: Augustus M. Kelley.

Rosenthal, Joel. 1972. *Purchase of Paradise.* Toronto: University of Toronto Press.

Roy, Maurice, ed. 1884. *Oeuvres Poétiques de Christine de Pisan.* Paris: Librairie de Firmin Didot et Cie.

Ruether, Rosemary and Eleanor McLaughlin, eds. 1979. *Women of Spirit: Female Leadership in the Jewish and Christian Traditions.* New York: Simon & Schuster.

Rusche, Georg and Otto Kirchheimer. 1968. *Punishment and Social Structure.* New York: Russell and Russell.

Saport, Linda. 1975. "Scientific Achievements of Nuns in the Middle Ages." Unpublished student paper, University of Colorado, Boulder, Department of Sociology.

Schomanns, Emile. 1911. *Franzosische Utopisten und Ihr Frauenideal.* Berlin: Verlag von Emil Felher.

Scudder, Vida D., translator and editor. 1905. *Saint Catherine of Sienna as Seen in Her Letters.* London: J. M. Dent.

Singer, Charles, E. J. Holmyard, and A. R. Hall. 1956. *A History of Technology.* Vol. 2. New York: Oxford University Press.

Sitwell, Dom Gerard. 1960. "Julian of Norwich." *Sponsa Regis* (September): 12-18.

Sitwell, Sacheverell. 1965. *Monks, Nuns and Monasteries.* New York: Holt, Rinehart & Winston.

Smith, Ernest Gilbrath. 1914. *St. Clare of Assisi.* New York: Dutton.

Solente, Suzanne. 1955. *Le Livre de la Mutacion de Fortune par Christine de Pisan.* Vol. 3. Paris: Editions A. et J. Picard et Cie.

Staley, Edgcumbe. [1906] 1967. *The Guilds of Florence.* New York: Benjamin Blom.

Summers, Rev. Montague, translator. 1948. *The Malleus Maleficarum of Heinrich Kramer and James Sprenger.* New York: Dover. [First published 1486.]

Thrupp, Sylvia L. 1962. *The Merchant Class of Medieval London.* Ann Arbor: University of Michigan Press.

Thrupp, Sylvia L., ed. 1964. *Change in Medieval Society: Europe North of the Alps, 1050-1500.* New York: Appleton-Century-Crofts.

Towner, Sister Mary Lewis. 1969. *Pizan's Lavison-Christine.* New York: AMS Press. (Originally a thesis, Catholic University of America, 1932.)

Underhill, Evelyn. [1911] 1961. *Mysticism: A Study in the Nature and Development of Man's Spiritual Consciousness.* New York: Dutton.

Varty, Kenneth, ed. 1965. *Christine de Pisan's Ballades, Rondeaux and Virelais: An Anthology.* Leicester, England: Leicester University Press.

Waddell, Helen. 1927. *The Wandering Scholars.* London: Constable.

Walsh, James. 1970. *The Thirteenth: Greatest of Centuries.* 12th ed. New York: AMS Press.

Warner, Marina. 1981. *Joan of Arc: The Image of Female Heroism.* New York: Knopf.

Waters, Clara (Erskine) Clement. 1904. *Women in the Fine Arts.* Boston: Houghton Mifflin.

Weinhold, Karl. 1882. *Die Deutschen Frauen in dem Mittelalter.* Wien: Druck und Verlag von Carl Geroed's Sohn.

Wieth-Knudsen, K. A. 1928. *Feminism: A Sociological Study of the Woman Question from Ancient Times to the Present Day,* translated by Arthur G. Chater. London: Constable.

Willard, Charity Cannon. 1975. "A Fifteenth-Century View of Women's Role in Medieval Society: Christine de Pisan's Livre des Trois Vertus." Pp. 90-120 in *The Roles of Woman in the Middle Ages,* edited by Rosemarie Thee Morewedge. Albany: State University of New York Press.

Worthington, Marjorie. 1962. *The Immortal Lovers: Heloise and Abelard.* London: Robert Hale.

Zeigler, Philip. 1969. *The Black Death.* London: Collins.

2

Queens, Reformers, and Revolutionaries: 1450 to 1800 C.E.

From Isabel to Elizabeth: 1450-1603

The Queens

Each of the great women monarchs in the middle centuries of the second millennium had extraordinary levels of physical energy and moral courage, coupled with high intelligence and human perceptiveness. All lived through their adolescence in great insecurity and fear for their lives. None was "groomed" for queenship, although all knew it was a possibility for them. When finally given a kingdom and a throne, each ruled with a vigor and skill that astounded the men of their courts. They could be tender or ruthless as occasion required. They all looked magnificent on horseback at the head of their armies. They all pursued expansionist policies. What did they "prove" about women? They proved that women could act on prevailing religious and cultural values and political goals as effectively as—or possibly more effectively than—men, given a chance to draw on all the resources a society has to offer. They used the conventional sociopolitical tools that men used and more. Their intellectual and social repertoire was a bit wider, perhaps, than that of most ruling men. In no way did they represent a feminine counterculture of non-militarism; they worked with the values available to them. This was one of the major reasons for their acceptance by their subjects as well as their success. Their legitimacy as rulers derived at least in part from their capacity to wield military power.[1] Even Ashoka, the great peace emperor of India, gained legitimacy first through a program of conquest.

Isabel. Isabel of Castile was plunged from a quiet life with a widowed royal mother into hectic court life at the age of 11 by the impeachment of her half-brother the king. The next ruler, her brother Alfonse, kept her close to him during his rule, and, when he died in her 17th year, she was asked to take the throne. In the years spent by her brother's side, she conceived of a mission to unite the petty kingdoms of Spain, and she spent the six years from her 17th to her 23rd year in maneuvers to accomplish this goal. She chose Ferdinand of Aragon as spouse to unite their two kingdoms, but she never let him have any regnant power in Castile. The marriage contract, concluded in 1469, was drawn as carefully as any women's rights advocate could draw it in the fifteenth century, protecting all her rights as ruler. This wounded Ferdinand's vanity, but he put up with it. In his younger days, Ferdinand never was interested in more than making Aragon strong. Only Isabel had the vision of a united Spain. Isabel was brighter, abler, stronger, and more ambitious than Ferdinand, and it is ironic that the history books tend to portray the reign as Ferdinand's.[2]

Isabel's success lay partly in the fact that she had the physical stamina to live on horseback. She frequently rode all night to be on the spot where something important would be happening by morning. She had a miscarriage during one such wild night's ride and nevertheless directed operations from horseback next morning for the reconquest of invaded territory. She had five children between 1470 and 1485 in spite of her activity level. While she took pride in her reputation as the crusading warrior queen, and personally directed major battles against the Moors as well as supervising the extermination of Jews in Spain and establishing the Inquisition, her ruthlessness was on behalf of a misguided vision of a "glorious," united, Christian Spain.

Deeply pious, spending much time in prayer, she was always soft-spoken. Her cruelty was never random. On the more peaceful side, she built a political system in the towns of Castile that enabled the inhabitants to have both local self-government and an intertown alliance that would create a new consciousness of the larger social entity of Castile and Spain. She used the power of an alliance of burgesses to destroy the older feudal powers of a rapacious nobility and thereby created a new kind of political community in Spain. She also, of course, subsidized Columbus to open up New Spain for Christianity.

Isabel died in 1504, and Ferdinand spent his remaining years trying to marry off their children in such a way as to make the most of the alliance structures Isabel had created. Much human misery was involved in these negotiations, and in the end they failed in their purpose. Political alliances kept cutting across marriage alliances. Babies died that were supposed to grow up and succeed to the throne. The marriage-alliance system crumbled. It could not withstand the complexity of the emerging new international system. Neither her husband nor her children had Isabel's skills, and the Spain she created did not really survive her, although its shadow and imperial structures seemed powerful for another couple of centuries.

Marguerite of Navarre. The French-born queen of Navarre was a minor queen, born in the year the powerful Isabel supported Columbus in his voyage to the New World. She *was* a "peace queen," acquiring the throne of Navarre by marriage (her second) at the age of 39. She spent her life as queen in protecting Catholics from Protestants and Protestants from Catholics. She drew the anger of both, inevitably, as well as charges of heresy, hypocrisy, and deceit. Nevertheless, she followed her own path all her life, and the far-seeing eyes in the kindly but determined face in a lovely painting of her as queen (Bainton 1973: 12) seem to look far into the future to a very different time:

> Marguerite was a lady of the Renaissance who read Dante in Italian, Plato possibly in Greek, and Luther to a slight degree in German. . . . Pope Paul III marveled at her saintliness and erudition. She was a poetess of distinction and originality . . . unique in French literature for her recital in verse of the Christian drama of redemption. To find a parallel in any tongue one must turn backwards to Dante and forwards to Milton. (Bainton 1973: 15-16)

Church politicians were always trying to get her on their side and, like Cardinal Pole, found her frustrating "because she was always soaring into the bosom of God" (Bainton 1973: 29). (The future Queen Elizabeth was to translate Queen Marguerite's *Miroir de l'Âme Pecheresse* [Mirror of a Sinful Soul] into English at the age of 10 and was deeply influenced by it.) Yet she also wrote a Boccaccio-style book, the *Heptameron*, showing once more what a repertoire of styles a talented woman can have. She died at 57, having witnessed more bloodshed and cruelty than most royalty have to endure and leaving behind a legacy of local welfare structures in Navarre, a model of peacemaking in the midst of the most virulent hatreds Europe had known, and a daughter, Jeanne D'Albert, who was to be the leader of the Huguenots of the next generation.

Jeanne of Navarre. Jeanne was another peace queen, who on accession to the throne of Navarre at the age of 27 in 1555 publicly announced her adherence to the reformed faith, thus turning her country into a haven for the Huguenots. (Queen Elizabeth of England sent her a message of congratulations for this.) She "is said to be the only sovereign of the sixteenth century who put no one to death for religion" (Bainton 1973: 43). Whether true or not, it indicates her reputation for tolerance. Like her mother, she led an embattled life as peacemaker and gave a lot of attention to local self-government in her little country.

Other peace queens who maintained the Protestant faith while placed by marriage alliance into Catholic settings, and who displayed great personal heroism throughout their lives, should not go unrecorded here. They were not ruling queens, but they acted as mediators, nursed both sides in wars, and continued to declare publicly their affection and loyalty to family members declared enemies and traitors for religious reasons: Catherine de Bourbon, 1559-1604; Eleanore de Roye, 1535-64; Charlotte de Bourbon, 1546-82; and Louise de Coligny, 1555-1620 (Bainton 1973).

These peace queens performed precisely the role that the diplomacy-by-marriage system was invented to further. The human cost to women of that role has always been great and, in the 1500s, became almost unbearable. The system was not to die yet—it continued to function until the French Revolution. After that, with monarchy chiefly decorative, the fact that marriage "allied" one royal house with another had less intense political interest. The banker's-daughter alliances that succeeded the royal marriage alliances had a different, although related, significance.

Catherine de Medici. Catherine de Medici was not a queen in her own right but served as regent of her principality during the years that Jeanne was queen of Navarre. She was on the other side of the religious struggle and is considered to be the author of the massacre of St. Bartholomew (which took place just after Queen Jeanne died, in 1572). Yet she was also the architect afterward of peace with the Protestants and was known equally as a skilled diplomat and a ruthless tactician. She has two major international treaties to her name and ruled in the style of an Isabel without having the latter's power or charm.

Elizabeth Tudor. Elizabeth's earliest memory was that, just before her third birthday, her father, Henry VIII, beheaded her mother, Ann Boleyn. Nevertheless, she had kind people around her while she was growing up, including her last stepmother, Catherine Parr. (It was for Catherine that Elizabeth translated Marguerite of Navarre's *Miroir.*) Formation of intellect and spirit went hand in hand: Roger Ascham, a great humanist scholar, was the tutor who prepared her for ruling. But, at 21, when her sister Mary was queen, she was sent to the tower on suspicion of plotting to overthrow her sister. She lived for four years as a prisoner, never knowing from day to day whether she might be executed, but finally she left prison to ascend the throne, having had more time and opportunity than have most rulers to think out a philosophy of life and a plan for ruling. Within her first year, she convened parliament and laid the basis for both a firm rule on her part and close collaboration with "her people" through parliament.

Marriage alliances could not serve her as they had served Isabel of Castile. Had she married, it appears that she might have had to give up her throne to her husband: "Their [her ministers'] mood was echoed in the words of the Queen's uncle Lord William Howard, who said, 'Whomsoever she shall take, we will have him and serve him to the death' " (Luke 1973). She used marriage negotiations with great skill, however, as an instrument of foreign policy. The royal families of Europe competed for years for the hand—and throne—that she so astutely kept to herself (Hume 1898; Melancon 1975).

Elizabeth threaded her way through a series of military alliances that left England much stronger when she died than it had been at her accession, and she left Spain, without an Armada, a second-rate power. She was ruthless in the way Isabel was ruthless when policy required, as in the case of the execution of Mary Queen of Scots and in the putting down of revolts within her realm and in Ireland. Her passion for a united England led to the Act of Supremacy within a year of her accession and also to the Act of Uniformity. The first act strengthened her own powers; the second outlawed religious nonconformity. Religious dissenters could only weaken England, in her view, and, after watching dissenting movements within and without the church culminate in nonconformist demonstrations in London, she pushed the anti-nonconformist legislation of 1593 that in fact made her a persecutor of religious freedom. At the same time, major legislation regarding labor and the poor was undertaken in her reign; the first poor law was passed two years before her death.

Elizabeth certainly accepted no nonsense about limitations of the woman's mind, and it is interesting to note that her women subjects caught the spirit of her independent-mindedness even to the extent of opposing her. Middle-class trading women and working-class women identified themselves strongly with the dissenting religious movements. No monarch was going to tell them how to worship, and they were the main supporters of the dissenting priests:

It was the women who occupied the front line in defense of the preachers, with the sense of emotional engagement hardly exceeded by the suffragettes of three and a half centuries later. . . . When two preachers were sent over London Bridge into exile in the country two or three hundred women feted them with exhortations and goodies. . . . There were more women than men imprisoned in Bridewell in 1569. (Bainton 1973: 245)

The determined Elizabeth set the pattern for England as "ruler of the waves" in her defeat of the Armada, in her support of high seas adventurer Sir Francis Drake, and in her successful military alliances with the Netherlands. She looked wonderful on horseback in front of her troops, although she did not herself lead them in battle. She presided over and nurtured an economically prosperous era and a great flowering of English culture, to the extent that the age has been named for her. Her critics felt that she had no views of her own and always did the expedient thing in the immediate situation. Her admirers pointed to the fantastic self-discipline she exercised all her life, the ability to keep her private wishes and needs apart in favor of the good of the realm. There are not many ways to be a successful monarch of a major world power, and, for all the depth of piety, extent of learning, and political skill that Elizabeth, like Isabel, had, her ruthlessness inevitably plays a large part in the image that has come down across the centuries.

While in this discussion of queens I have presented the "major queens" as ruthless power figures and the "minor queens" as the peacemakers, it may well be that in the long run the queens of Navarre had more to do with setting viable directions for the future than did Isabel or Elizabeth. Marguerite and Jeanne of Navarre represent new styles of overlife activity and in a sense symbolize a yet untapped potential for political leadership in nation-state systems—the potential for furthering the self-realization of national communities through creative problem solving instead of through confrontation.

Renaissance Women

Italy. Italy is the country where the term *Renaissance women* has the most meaning. While being put down elsewhere, here women flourished. Perhaps none was more dramatically honored in that era than Tarquinia Molza, who excelled both in poetry and in the fine arts, and

had a rare knowledge of astronomy, and mathematics, Latin, Greek, and Hebrew. So great was the esteem in which she was held that the senate of Rome conferred upon her the singular honor of Roman citizenship, transmissible in perpetuity to her descendents. (Potter, in Beard 1946: 261)

Italian women of the upper classes all through the 1400s and 1500s wrote and orated Latin discourses in their own circles and in public and exchanged sonnets with their friends of both sexes.[3] They also established Renaissance salons at which they acted as patrons of the arts. The court of King Robert of Anjou in Naples is given credit for being the first Renaissance setting in which women were encouraged not for their "purity" but for their wit. Boccaccio and Petrarch were both frequenters of the court at Naples and acquired their respect for women's minds there (Tornius 1929).[4] The Medici salons, on the other hand, did not feature participation of women.

The first great woman salonist is supposed to have been "the Divine Isotta" of Rimini, who died in 1450 (Burckhardt 1944). Although she was not herself learned, many poets and artists clustered around her court, and she was widely loved. Lucrezia Borgia, the duchess of Ferrara, was another major creator of a cultural center, at the court of Este. Isabella d'Este was such a compelling personality and critic that scholars and artists came to her court from all over Europe for the quality of the cultural life there. She had little money to offer her retinue, for she was relatively poor. By this time, women of the Italian nobility were competing with one another to be known for providing the best cultural milieu.

Some of the salons featured courtesans—highly educated middle-class women who "were scholars by day and lovers by night" (Tornius 1929: 97). There was Madrewa, who could recite Petrarch, Boccaccio, Virgil, Horace, and Ovid. There were Lorentina and Beatrice—when either went to church, she had a whole court of serving men and women, pages, marquises, ambassadors, and dukes in trains (Tornius 1929: 98). In the Venice of 1509, out of a population of 300,000, there were 11,654 courtesans and some of the finest salons in Italy. Some courtesans ran their own salons, such as Florentine Rullia d'Aragona, a veritable Aspasia. Her home was considered a second Academy, and she concerned herself very much with public affairs. She has been called the "priestess of humanism."

In the 1400s, contrary to trends elsewhere (except in Spain), a humanist school was established in Italy with the same basic curriculum for women and men. Latin was taught as the medium of expression and Greek as a "foreign language" for development. The Greek system of physical education and classical dancing was taught (Cannon 1916: 30-31). As might be expected, some of the first publicly recognized women composers came from Italy (Vittoria Alcotti, Francesca Baglioncella, and Orsina Vizzani). And Rome, Florence, Bologna, and Venice all had many artists, primarily of the eclectic school. In the early Renaissance period, many of the women artists were not known by name, except when they were members of the aristocracy, like Caterine de Vigri, patroness and painter of Ferrara. Canonized, she became "protectress of Academics and Art Institutions" in the Catholic world. Properzia de' Rossi, a Bolognese sculptor, who did not have the protection of being of the aristocracy, became so popular with the public that she roused the intense jealousy of her male colleagues. According to Clements, they began a crusade against her so that her commissioned work was not mounted on the public building it was prepared for, and she died at 40 of "mortification and grief" (Waters 1904: 300).

In the 1500s, the most widely renowned of the Italian artists were Anna Maria Ardoin, poet-artist-musician elected to the Academy of Arcadia; Sophonisba of Cremona (1535-1625), in demand all over Europe as a portrait painter; Lavinia Fontana of Bologna (1552-1614), one of the most prolific and most popular artists of the century;[5] and Catharina van Hemessen (1528-87), celebrated as a portraitist both in Flanders and in Spain. At the very end of this century, Artemisia Gentileschi was born (1593-1652), considered by many to be the greatest of Italian women artists. She worked in Rome, Florence, Genoa, Naples, and London and was a primary influence in the development of the Neopolitan School of painting (Tufts 1974: 59). Favorite poets in the sixteenth century, not only of Italy but of Europe, were Veronica Gambara of Padua and Vittoria Colonna, Michelangelo's great friend.

Spain.[6] Spain also encouraged learning, at least in upper-class women, Queen Isabel herself being very learned. Her companion Beatriz Galindo founded schools, hospitals, and convents all over Spain. Oliva Sabuco de Nantes at the age of 25 wrote the seven-volume *Nueva Filosofia* (1587) relating the biology, psychology, and anthropology of the day to medicine and agriculture, starting out with the abrupt statement that "the old science of medicine is in error." Her work reflects mastery of an Arab scholarship unavailable to the rest of Europe. Catalina Mendoza, a scholar with no published works, founded a Jesuit college for women.

The situation of women in Spain in the 1500s is interesting. Convents had high standards of scholarship and produced musicians and poets as well as scholars. As in Italy, there was an unbroken tradition from the earliest times of women attending universities. Such women had contact with both Italian and Arab scholars. The palace schools for the Spanish princesses provided a stimulus to women's education, in that nonroyal women were also admitted to these schools. The women's orders founded schools for laypeople as well as training schools for their own orders, so that the Augustinians, Benedictines, Franciscans, Dominicans, Tertians, and Carmelites all contributed to the education of girls in Spain. St. Teresa of Avila's writing skill came partly from her training at the Augustinian convent school in Avila, which had a teaching staff of 40 nuns.

Northern Europe. The first Renaissance schools outside of Italy and Spain were established by the Brethren of the Common Life. In 1497 in Zanten, a lay school for girls both of the nobility and of the "citizen classes" was established under Aldegundis von Horstmar, a directress trained by the Brethren of Common Life. The 84 students in this school received a Latin and classical education. The German scholar-abbess tradition produced learned women such as Margaret von Steffel, who wrote the lives of St. Bernard and St. Hildegard in verse, and Catherine of Ostheim, who abridged the *Chronicles of Limburg*. The women of the palatinate courts were poets and women of learning. Germany and the Netherlands supported many women artists, chiefly miniaturists and illuminators. One of the most renowned of these was Leonia Teerling of Flanders (1515-76), who became court painter to the British royal family. In the Netherlands, the Hapsburg Spanish traditions of learning for women were carried on, and culture and scholarship for women somehow survived the hostility of Erasmus and Luther. Visible evidence of this will be seen in the next century, when we observe the milieu out of which Dutch Anne-Marie Schurman emerges to become a world-renowned figure.

France. In France, ladies of the nobility were well educated, and some of them became writers, notably the earlier-mentioned Marguerite of Navarre, but also Anne of Beaujeu and Anne of Brittany. Outside the nobility, there seems to have been an extraordinarily adventurous lot of women in France who did not get the message that the new humanism did not apply to them. There were the poetesses of Lyons, for example, Pernette de Guillet and Louise Labé. Labé is the famous one, the gifted daughter of a Lyons rope maker who could not succeed in being a conventional housewife though she tried. *La Capitaine* Louise dressed as a soldier and tried to help rescue her city from the Spaniards, becoming the town heroine. In the end she was denounced, not for her poetry or for her soldiering, but for her love life.

One of the most significant characters in sixteenth-century France in terms of a direct confrontation with Renaissance antifeminism is Marie de Jars de Gournay. Born in 1565 and living to be 90, she actually spanned two centuries. She discovered Montesquieu, apostle of individualism, before he was generally admired, and made herself his disciple and translator. She was also a promotor of the poet Ronsard. The first of a great company of intrepid spinster intellectuals, she was ridiculed all her life; much was made of the fact that she was plain. She kept cats, which she liked better than people. She chose her own causes and supported them ardently. Her books on education and public affairs, dedicated to Henry IV and to Marie de Medici, sold well, as did her translations of Virgil, Ovid, Sallust, and Tacitus. Like Christine de Pisan, she could make a living from her writing. She also received well-earned pensions from Marie de Medici, Anne of Austria, and Richelieu. She had a passionate intellectual curiosity and mastered subjects like alchemy for fun. Her sharp retentive mind fed on everything the Renaissance had to offer, but as a sensitive human being she sometimes lashed out at the society that so scorned women—and she sometimes cast epithets at her enemies. While other women apologized for presuming to write books, Marie published two scathing documents—*Egalité des Hommes et des Femmes* and *Grief des Dames*. The latter she began with the lines:

> Lucky are you, reader, if you happen not to be of that sex to whom is forbidden all good things, to whom liberty is denied; to whom almost all virtues are denied; lucky are you if you are one of those who can be wise without its being a crime. (Schiff 1910: 89; my own translation)

In a very modern manner, Marie decried stupidity in either sex, pointed out what women had achieved in antiquity, and said the wonder was not that women had achieved so little but that they had achieved anything at all given the lack of opportunity for education and development. She even tackled the "bad theology" of the church in its treatment of God as a man instead of being beyond sex. Twentieth-century women owe a lot to Marie de Gournay, though she would not like to be thanked.

England. Returning to those in Elizabeth's England, we find the lady humanists somewhat tame there by comparison with the rest of Europe. The best education for women was found in private families, through tutors. We find three cases of fathers establishing what amounted to special schools for their daughters: Sir Thomas More for daughters Margaret, Cecilia, and Elizabeth (plus a cousin); Sir Anthony Coke for daughters Mildred, Anne, and Catherine; and the Earl of Surrey for daughters Jane, Catherine, and Margaret. (We never hear of mothers running schools for daughters.) The fact that these three "schools" are famous speaks for the general paucity of schools for women. After the closure of the convents in 1546, there were practically no schools for women. When secular grammar schools were opened later, they were only for boys. Some of the daughters of the three families mentioned wrote and published, but most of them disappeared into marriage and did not become public figures in any way. Nevertheless, a vigorous literature by English women appeared in the underside spaces of the Renaissance and has been rediscovered for today's readers (Travitsky 1981).

This may have been due in part to the considerable home tutoring of women in the upper classes, as indicated by references to how well educated women of the Elizabethan era were.[7] This home training sometimes led to a fairly active life for women. Mary Sidney, for example, was taught as a child together with her brother Sir Philip Sidney. In later life, she held the only salon I have seen mentioned in England in the 1500s. As Countess Pembroke, she entertained poets and statesmen including Spenser, Ben Jonson, Shakespeare, and John Donne. Lady Jane Grey, imprisoned and executed at 17 by the Catholic Queen Mary for having been made England's nine-day queen by enthusiastic Protestants, would surely have been a great scholar had she lived. At 14, she was corresponding with Swiss theologians and was proficient in Latin, Greek, French, and Italian. Stenton's (1957) book on English women in history describes a number of self-taught women from this period, and not all were of the nobility. How many young women of the "lower classes" taught themselves to read and write, like Anne Prowse, author of a "pious book," we shall never know. The most colorful characters among Elizabethan women were not scholars, however. The famous Bess Hardwick, who exercised control over substantial parts of England through lands and rights acquired through four marriages, was a thinker who did not get her ideas from books.

There must have been women artists and musicians in sixteenth-century England, but I have seen no references to them, except for the 1537 tombstone inscription of an Elizabeth Lucar, who died at 26 and whose grieving husband recounted with eloquence on stone her skill as artist and musician and scholar.

* * *

What this survey of Renaissance women scholars and artists indicates is that, in spite of public denial of the importance of women's mental capacities, women to a surprising extent acquired and made creative use of the new learning. Except in Spain and Italy, where women could attend universities, learning was a special class privilege of the nobility and the well-to-do and was fostered privately in homes and convent schools. It was very much an underlife activity. Also, it could only exist when tolerated—or encouraged—by men. The extent of tolerance for learning in women was certainly connected with the highly successful role played by the queens of the century, both the major and the minor queens. As far as the historical record goes, only one woman in the entire century publicly and vociferously rebelled against mere tolerance—Marie de Gournay. In the next century, many more women rebelled.

Religious Women of the
Reformation and the Counter-Reformation

Given that the Reformation was born in Germany, we think of the stocky peasant nun Katherine Von Bora, who married the ex-monk Martin Luther, as the prototype of the new Protestant woman:[8] a strong-minded materfamilias with many children; one who feeds the poor at her table, runs the family farm, and generally manages household and family affairs with little or no help from her husband yet defers to him in all things; a woman with no views on public matters. Actually, many Protestant women played precisely this role, but many also took part in community and church affairs in spite of the objections of their men (Irwin 1979). Katherine Zell, for example, who lived in Strasbourg where the peasant's war struck, was thoroughly involved in community affairs and in caring for refugees, nursing the sick, and effecting reconciliations in town conflicts. She preached in public, even at her own husband's funeral, to the great annoyance of the men of the town. She spoke out courageously and publicly against persecution wherever she found it. Another side of her life is revealed in her publication of a children's hymn book.

Men and women of the Reformation seem to have gone through an alarming number of spouses in a lifetime, an indication of the high death rate of men in war and women in childbirth. Wilbrandis Rosenblatt, after her first marriage to a tradesman, married three prominent reformers in succession, and it is said that "all her husbands loved her gentleness." Her home was a refugee center throughout her life and, even while living in this storm center, she managed to have children by each of her four husbands—10 in all.

Not all Reformation women were of the peasant and working classes. In addition to the peace queens mentioned earlier, many women of the minor nobility became involved in the Reformation controversies and often defended heretics at great risk to their own lives. Argula von Grumbach was one, Elizabeth of Brandenburg another, and her daughter Elizabeth of Braunschweig a third. They suffered persecution, physical deprivation, and banishment. On the whole, their life in Germany was perhaps even harder than the life of the Huguenots in France, although bloodshed was widespread during this period in France.

One of the early heretics among the aristocracy in England was Lady Anne Askew, great-grandmother of Margaret Fell, one of the founders of Quakerism a century later. An attendant at the court of Queen Catherine Parr, Henry VIII's last queen, she developed a reputation for preferring reading the Bible to going to mass. That Henry VIII should have sanctioned proceedings against this young court woman of 25 that included being tortured on the rack and burned at the stake for reading the Bible gives a clue to the atmosphere of suspicion and fear generated by the politics of church and state at that time. Anne was a woman of great inner strength and also a gifted writer. Letters and poems from her last days survive (see Webb 1867). Her tutor was burnt with her, for having encouraged her wicked practices, and at the stake it was *she* who encouraged and supported *him*.

The Anabaptists had the hardest time of all, partly because they were more extreme in their dissent. They also practiced complete equality of women and men in every respect, including preaching. Both Catholics and Lutherans persecuted them, and they lived hunted lives. We know little about the women except that they could never settle down to normal family life; they were always on the run. Elizabeth Dirks of Holland, an Anabaptist teacher who was imprisoned, tortured, and drowned in a sack, is one of the few we know about from the sixteenth century. That the Anabaptists had staying power in the face of extreme persecution is indicated by the fact that they were still active in the next century. Anna Marie Schurmann, born at the close of this century, became a noted Anabaptist in the next.

The homemaker wife who created a gathering place for members of the religious community was perhaps a special product of the religious struggles associated with the Reformation. It was different in every respect than the salon tradition, which was essentially antifamilial— women held salons on their own, not for or with husbands (with occasional exceptions). Protestantism was in its origin a very familistic religion, and the homemaker wife was always acting on behalf of a husband, present or absent. Partly this was a class difference, not a religious one, because familism is always stronger in the middle than in the upper classes. It was not entirely class, however. In the sixteenth century, it was Protestantism that was the more familistic religion, although in the twentieth century we think of Catholicism as the familistic religion. The homemaker-wife role was of course a Catholic one too, and at times it was a very grim role. In Protestant countries, Catholic wives and mothers were martyred for trying to bring their children up in the faith, as in the terrible story of Margaret Clitherow of York (Dessain 1971). This gay but devout young mother of perhaps half a dozen children was ordered crushed to death by the local judge for not attending the Church of England services. She and dozens, perhaps hundreds, like her accepted torture and death rather than give up their faith, although until their time of trial they were strictly domestic persons with no record of public activity. Homemaker heroines are even less likely to make the history books than are women who take community leadership roles. We know about Margaret because she was sainted afterward by the Catholic church.

In the Catholic tradition, the role of the nun has been so striking that there is danger of appearing to ignore or belittle the homemaker. The mass of peasant and artisan women, the middle-class merchant wives, and the scholars and artists we have been describing in the last several chapters were more often than not homemakers in addition to their other roles. If autonomy of nuns has been emphasized, this is not to suggest that married women with all their underlife skills did not also find spheres of autonomy. Particularly during the Reformation and the Counter-Reformation, because of the continuing high levels of conflict and violence that reached into every household, all of the homemakers' creative skills had to be drawn on daily. Peacemaking was not confined to two Protestant queens. Every woman of every faith had peacemaking tasks, although some were more skillful at them than others.

The Counter-Reformation tapped new veins of creativity in Catholic women. While all women to some degree participated in a heightened social sensitivity, women religious played a special part in the developments. The term *Counter-Reformation* is misleading and really should not be used at all; it describes developments that, in the Catholic church, began well before the Reformation, developments that had their own dynamic independent of Protestant activities. It was, of course, these developments that produced Luther. Under different circumstances, he might have completed his work inside the Catholic church. That he did not had more to do with political than religious matters.

The Dominicans, Franciscans, Beguines, and Brethren of the Common Life all played their parts in preparing for the new developments within the women's religious orders in the Catholic church. On the one hand was the emphasis on a deep inwardness, already well established by the Beguine mystics, resulting in the 1500s in the development of Illuminism, a devout orthodox movement that nevertheless hovered on the edge of heresy. Illuminati among the nuns were found particularly in Spain, home of Maria de Santo Domingo, Magdalena de la Cruz, and Maria Cazalla. In Italy, St. Catherine of Genoa helped organize such illuminati into groups called the Fraternities of Divine Love.

Paralleling this search for inwardness was another development that emphasized teaching and service. Ignatius Loyola, the soldier-founder of the Jesuits who underwent a spectacular conversion after severe wounding and disablement, was the charismatic figure in the movement. Many other forces were also pushing toward a more active service in the world, and women were particularly ready for this. In the next century, Mary Ward founded a women's counterpart of the Jesuit order, calling her group Institutes of Mary. It was too radical in conception and was dissolved by the church but was eventually reconstituted as an accepted teaching order.[9]

Angela Merici's concept of a teaching order, the Ursulines, though less threatening, also met the opposition of church authorities. Angela was a devout and conservative young Italian woman who as a dowryless orphan remained single when her friends married. She lived an austere life of service to friends and neighbors in her hometown of Brescia—a life probably duplicated by unknown thousands of spinster women in Europe whose biographies will never be known. Angela's uniqueness lay in her sense of mission. Fearful of appearing radical or hasty, she pondered her calling for years as she observed the young people of Brescia in the early decades of the 1500s. She watched inflation drive economically pressed families of the Lombard plain to pushing unwilling daughters into convents. She saw what that did to the religious life of the convents as well as to the girls. She watched ignorant teenage girls milling around the public square with nothing to do and saw them being swept away by the fads of occult, underground religions that smelled of demonism. She saw the witchcraft hysteria descend on these girls and lead them to the stake for nothing more than adolescent foolishness.

Angela knew that widows and young women with more means than she at their disposal often taught young girls in their own homes.[10] She thought something more was needed than these occasional private-enterprise widow's schools. Finally, by the age of 58, she had gained the support of some of the widows and women of means of Brescia for a bold program of establishing a nonconventional teaching order for women. Women were to take religious vows but live at home, wear no special dress or insignia, and be teachers in the community. A sympathetic bishop supported her idea to the church authorities. Thus the teaching order of the Ursulines, named after the legendary British maiden who emigrated to the Continent with a band of young women in the fifth century, was launched with the blessing of the church in

1537. Social pressures for enclosure soon limited their activities, placing them within convent walls in 1612, but a new principle had been established and was not forgotten. In 1857, the order was able to return to its original vision. In the intervening centuries, enclosure did not prevent the Ursulines from teaching in their convent-based schools; eventually they did for the education of girls what the Jesuits did for the education of boys (Daniel-Rops 1962: 25; Monica 1945).

This story has been told in some detail because it reflects the strength of the underlife of a less favored class of women—women who rarely appear in history. The self-help culture out of which Angela developed her idea for a teaching order represented a resource of initiative and quiet leadership that in the long run made greater participation in society possible for women of later generations. Angela's life also suggests that, in the 1500s, as in previous centuries, a number of women continued single and independent without being assimilated into the structures of family or church.

St. Teresa of Avila is the towering figure in the spiritual awakening of the sixteenth century. A well-educated, "society-type" convent girl, she underwent powerful religious experiences that awakened her to a very different realization of the human possibility than she had been prepared for by her own rather conventional religious formation. It says something about the attitude toward women in Spanish society that this woman was able to command the attention of the church in Spain and to carry out reforms that lifted her convents from ordinary "homes for celibate women" to centers of spiritual transformation. It happened that she was a good organizer, was an impressive speaker, and had a commanding presence. But what really carried her movement was her depth of religious insight, which stood up under every kind of test a somewhat hostile church could give it.

Teresa was well enough trained in sixteenth-century cultural patterns to preface her writings with the "I'm only a poor silly woman" routine, but her writings are among the most widely read devotional literature of the twentieth century.[11] It is sad that Teresa's counterparts have not been easily produced in the Protestant world, with its emphasis on the duties of the housewife. There is nothing in the housewife's role that prevents spiritual transformation except the legitimacy of the *intention* to place God first. The Reformation created a kind of discontinuity that had not existed earlier with regard to attitudes about religious calling in the two worlds of Catholicism and Protestantism. It is all right for Protestant women to be activists, but not contemplatives. One might say that the Reformation was incomplete in Protestantism, in not allowing for the full development of women's spirituality.

Family Life and the Situation of
Middle- and Lower-Class Women

Because the tendency for middle-class women in urban settings to withdraw from involvement in productive activities beyond strictly domestic maintenance begins in the sixteenth century, it is of some interest to look at the typical household size for the century. How many people lived in a household, and what kind of living space did families have? Recent studies (Laslett 1972) of local records in various parts of Europe indicate the surprising fact that household size has changed very little from the Middle Ages to the current time. Apart from the great manor houses of the nobility and the homes of rich merchants, most people lived in families with an average of 4.75 persons per family, plus a servant. These "servants," it turns out, were not servants in the contemporary sense of the word but children of neighboring families in the same parish. Families were in effect training each other's children. Not only were families small, but the age of marriage for women as well as men was beginning to rise. The average age at marriage for European women in the 1500s was about 21, rising in succeeding centuries as high as 25 to 28. Furthermore, multigenerational families were primarily an upper-class phenomenon. Most women were confined to small domestic spaces in small families before marriage and entered equally small domestic spaces after marriage. Although women certainly had larger households during their childbearing years, high infant death rates and the practice of older couples and widows maintaining separate living quarters created considerable domestic isolation for women as they lost freedom of movement in other spheres.

The bulk of both rural and urban women of the sixteenth century, and for several centuries to come, lived in crowded quarters. The decline in the live-in dormitory arrangements for apprentices and laborers practiced earlier in urban workshops and manor houses did not create housing pressure at first because there was plenty of housing for a plague-decimated population. With population growing again in the sixteenth century, the cottagers of the countryside could build their own little stone houses. In the cities, every kind of warehouse and other building was appropriated for family dwellings, soon giving rise to the typical city tenement. Few working-class families had more space than was needed for sleeping and eating. Other activities were carried on elsewhere in the village or town.

Middle-class families had more space, but they too lived in fairly close quarters. Women may have had more time to spend with children, but, in the compressed life spaces available, there were high tension levels and frequent expressions of physical violence. Partly this may have been a continuation of the "culture of violence" noted from time to time in the relations between parents and children. Pinchbeck and Hewitt note that in the sixteenth century the concept of "breaking the spirit of the child" still prevailed in child rearing (1969: 351).

The literature of the time contains many references to brutal child discipline, and the frequency with which mothers beat daughters is particularly noticeable. Daughter beating was often in connection with a child's resistance to parental marriage plans. Even the gentle peace queen Marguerite of Navarre beat her daughter daily for weeks on end to make her agree to a politically designed marriage choice. Lady Jane Grey's mother beat her (Bainton 1973). Agnes Paston, of the lively Paston family known for its voluminous intrafamily correspondence and numerous lawsuits, beat her daughter so badly that "her head was broke in 2 or 3 places" (O'Faolain and Martines 1973).[12] It would seem that women of this period were subject to a lot of emotional pressure that they vented by child beating. Putting daughters out to other families as servants was one of the few available means of relieving the strain, but this required reciprocity, in that such a mother must accept someone else's daughter into her home. The disappearance of convents in England and in many places in Europe, and the closing down of other occupational options for women, made marriage arrangements increasingly important and also made marriages harder to achieve.[13] Mothers bore the brunt of these problems in terms of felt pressure to get their daughters out of their small households.

The generally short life expectancy of both women and men—32 at birth in England in 1690, 27 in Breslau in the same year (Laslett 1965: 62)—contributed to this violence, because there was frequent remarriage of widows and widowers with children from earlier marriages. These children were often regarded as nuisances by their own parent as well as by the new spouse (Pinchbeck and Hewitt 1969: 12). The idea that children should be happy, and that they would respond to gentleness in a teacher or parent, was somewhat novel when it was espoused by Montaigne in the latter part of the sixteenth century (in his *Essais*, 1960). The antiwhipping movement was slow to develop.

In cities, the traditional charitable services provided by church and private charity could not keep up with urban destitution. The phenomenon of vagrant children (orphans and, also, children whose mothers were at work) is increasingly taken note of after 1500. Systems for apprenticing "idle beggars" between the ages of 5 and 14 were developed. A very few of these were humane institutions such as the model school established in Ypres in 1525. In England, roundups of "wandering beggars" began taking place, and by 1547 girl children could legally be placed in an enforced apprenticeship until the age of 15 or marriage (Pinchbeck and Hewitt 1969: 96), which amounted to de facto slavery.

In short, children were in the way. There were no family living spaces adequate for them, and it was difficult to establish enough apprentice and employment opportunities for those who were not kept by their mothers' sides as helpers in field or shop. Girls were even less welcome than were boys because of the burden of providing a marriage dowry.

The effect of limitation of opportunities for women on mother-daughter relations is a subject that needs much more attention. Obviously, not all mothers beat their daughters, nor did beatings necessarily lead to bad feelings. Rather, there was apt to be continued expression of affection between mothers and daughters throughout their lives, as in the Paston family.

That women chose to exit from confining extended-family situations and live on their own whenever possible is suggested by the fact that in the 1500s, even with all the housing shortages, 16% of all English households in 100 communities examined by Laslett (1972: 147) were headed by women: 12.9% of the heads of household were widows, 1.1% single females, and 2.3% "unspecified females." While some widows remarried, there are also many references to the joy with which women after widowhood set up their own households and to the vigor with which they resisted courting by amorous widowers. The extended-family togetherness we nostalgically refer to as part of our golden past simply did not exist in the European heritage, and there is some evidence that it never really existed anywhere, except as an upper-class phenomenon. Laslett concludes that the multigenerational household is the exception in every society.[14]

The 16% of women who headed their own households were brave women, because, in that century, at the height of the witchcraft persecutions, it was the women living alone who were the most subject to accusations of witchcraft. The majority of the witches were women, and many accusers were clergymen, although at the height of the burnings all kinds of male adventurers got into the act, collecting "bonuses" for every witch they identified. "Between 1587 and 1593 twenty-two villages in the region of Trier surrendered 368 witches to the bonfires. Two other villages survived the spasm with a female population of one each" (O'Faolain and Martines 1973: 215). In London, a Scotch witch-hunter was finally himself imprisoned: "And upon the gallows he confessed he had been the death of above 220 women in England and Scotland, for the gain of twenty-one shillings apiece, and beseeched forgiveness. And was executed" (O'Faolain and Martines 1973: 217). The last "legal" execution of a woman for witchcraft in England took place in 1716, but "witch-hunts" continued for another century.

In spite of the pressures on women of confined domestic spaces and witchcraft accusations, there is much evidence that family life "improved" in the sixteenth century.[15] The major contribution of the Reformation to family life was that priests either turned Protestant and took legal wives or stayed Catholic but stopped having exploited "priestess-concubines" in the parish household. Obviously, that practice did not stop overnight, but it could no longer be carried out as overtly as before. Whether there was a net gain for women one cannot be sure—one would have to know what happened to all the "priestesses," and there is no information on this.

Among the poor, legal marriage was a luxury, but peasant and artisan classes were also potential participants in the new familistic culture that began about this time. Contemporary chronicles describe families as playing games together, such as blind man's bluff. In countryside and town, there had always been holy days and harvest festivals that provided occasions for community recreation. Processions, dancing, and games were not new in the sixteenth century but as old as community life. What was new was that the family unit now sometimes was also the play unit, although space was too limited for this to happen except among the well-to-do.

In the sixteenth century, the lot of working women became harder, but actual starvation was the exception. Pockets of hunger in Europe and England developed from time to time, but exhaustion and overwork in field, workshop, and preindustrial factory, not simply starvation, were the killers of women, men, and children. Working hours were getting longer. Men were beginning to petition against women being given weaver's work, fearing the competition as employment became scarce (Clark 1919: 103). In better-off artisan homes, and increasingly in middle-class homes, women became the unpaid domestic servants of their husbands as they left (or lost) their own employment opportunities.

The sixteenth century was a threshold century. The great future surge of urbanization, already beginning to build up, was to be felt increasingly in the next century. By 1600, more than 75 of the world's great cities had reached the 100,000 population mark (the sociologist Sorokin's estimate in Morris 1974: 105), and humans faced a new scale of existence.

Rising Dissent: The 1600s

The seventeenth century witnessed the rapid development of colonial settlements in the Americas. It was a century of movement and a century in which women began to become more publicly articulate. The articulation came through a variety of roles, from women as intellectuals, as workers, as religious dissenters, and as overseas migrants. This was the golden age of pamphleteering, and women entered into it with zest, as we note in the 1640 pamphlet published in England, *The Woman's Sharpe Revenge*, by Mary Tattle-Well and Joan Hit-Him-Home, Spinsters, which demolished then-current antifeminist writings. When Bacon said, "Bitter and earnest writings must not be hastily condemned; for men cannot contend coldly, and without affection, about things which they hold dear and precious" (Ward 1927: xvi-xvii), few were prepared to recognize the right of women also to write earnestly and bitterly; but the boldest of the women took advantage of the new opportunities anyway.

Whether men recognized these rights of expression or not, the battle for women's rights had been joined. There were already strong male voices on behalf of women, such as the anonymous lawyer-author of *The Lawes Resolutions of Womens' Rights* (1632). In this period, the first public references to birth control appeared. The condom, first used in England in this century as a protection for men against venereal disease, began to be perceived by women as a protection against pregnancy. In France, upper-class women began to express freely their interest in limiting families (one contribution of the salon atmosphere), and, by the next century, French women had developed a technology of birth control. French birthrates began to reflect this in the 1800s.

Articulate women dissenters and militants were a small minority, but they were there—in Europe, in the Colonial Americas, and also in Asia, although another century was to go by before Europeans felt a sense of sisterhood with Asian women. The dissenting women came from all sectors of society, upper, middle, and working class. They were Catholics, Protestants, and Quakers.

Another significant dissenting group was the bluestockings,[16] who were intellectual women of the upper middle class. Much admired by the progressive men of their day, on the whole, they were no threat to anyone except their own more radical sisters. Some, like Marie de Gournay, were feminists, but many bluestockings were actively hostile to the new women's movement. Some showed great skill in privately creating public space in their own homes through the institution of the salon. While salon tradition originated in the Mediterranean, French women soon made it an institution uniquely their own.

At first, as in Italy, the salon was a mechanism by which women of the aristocracy could extend protection and patronage to artists and intellectuals. The most famous of the *salonières* were both intellectuals in their own right and patrons of intellectual men. Petted and protected by men of their own class, and courted by their protégés, from the feminist perspective they could be seen as a type of degraded courtesan. Rowbotham compares their situation with "that of the mulatto servant in slave society, aspiring only to be a sub-white, and thus enjoying the protection of the whites" (1972: 33). This judgment is unfair to the extent that it underrates the independent intellectual creativity of many salonières. However we interpret their social role, they did conform to the humanist tradition of avoiding problems of social justice while exploring intellectual frontiers.

Economic, political, and intellectual life was developing on a new scale in the seventeenth century and would be fostering new styles of dissent among women. Central to the emerging social order was the male-dominated international banking system. The banks of Hamburg, Amsterdam, and Nuremberg were all founded around 1619, the Bank of Sweden in 1658, and the Bank of England in 1694. (The Paris Bourse was not established until 1724.) Related to the rise of banking was the rise of the merchant adventurers and the establishment of the British, Dutch, and French merchant companies and crown colonies. This was also the century of the Glorious Revolution in England (1688) and of the inglorious Thirty Years War on the Continent. Not only did these developments create new economic and political structures, but they provided the intellectual background for the development of a new set of institutions, the academies. This was the century in which the Académie Française was formed (1635), the French Academy of Science (1658), the English Royal Society (1662), and the Berlin Academy of Science (1700).

In the new style of exclusion of women from economic activities, there were no women in the banks and few in the colonial enterprises except for the occasional merchant women of England and the Netherlands and the merchant widows who continued their husbands' enterprises. There were no women in the academies either, despite the power of the salons. The scholarly and scientific activities of women developed outside the academies and, for the most part, also outside the salons, in private spaces and special niches.

Women in England

Manor house militants.[17] The civil war brought the manor house aristocracy of English women into new roles. We have described them in earlier chapters as estate managers, teachers, and supervisors of village services. Now we see them as warriors.

Women, more often conservative politically than not, tended to be royalist during the civil war. Given that the prevailing trend was antiroyalist, this produced some rather unusual heroines among upper-class women who held family castles while their men were off fighting elsewhere. Lucy Apsley Hutchinson defended Nottingham when besieged, playing double duty as soldier and nurse. The countess of Derby defended Latham House for a whole year in 1643. She tore up all surrender messages and in the end was rescued by royalist troops. Lady Blanche Arundel defended her castle for nine days with 25 men against an army of 1,300, refusing to surrender; when her castle fell, she and her children were carried off to prison. Lady Mary Bankes held her castle successfully for six weeks with her daughters, women servants, and five soldiers. The baroness of Offaley, at the age of 60, successfully defended her castle against two different assaults in 1641.

Anne Howard fought for the royalist cause as a single woman and had many hair-raising escapes acting as a secret agent. Her autobiography, written after she settled down at 34 to become Lady Anne Halkett, gives an idea of how free women of daring could be in that century (Nichols [1875] 1965).[18]

A different kind of manor house militant was Lady Anne Clifford (1590-1675), who was carefully trained by her mother to battle in the courts for the right to own and administer the lands that were supposed to come to her through the will of her father, the earl of Cumberland. Her tutor was the poet-historian Samuel Daniel, and she became one of the best archivists of her era. She fought the courts and the king for 26 years for her lands and must have known *The Lawes Resolutions of Women's Rights* backward and forward. Finally, at 53, she succeeded to her lands. For the last 30 years of her life, she ran an almost legendary feudal kingdom in the old style—something no women had done for several centuries in England. While it was a step into the past, it was also a bridge into the future, in that she built model poorhouses on her lands.

Feminist scholars. Strongly feminist scholars were shaping new ways of thinking about women right through the seventeenth century, in a country that had opened no educational facilities for women since the closing of the convents in the previous century. One of the most dramatic of the feminist scholars was Margaret Lucas, duchess of Newcastle. A popular writer, in 1662 she wrote "Female Orations supposedly made by women who were deliberating on the possibility of combining to make themselves as 'free, happy and famous as men' " in a book of *Orations of Diverse Persons* (Stenton 1957: 157-58). Crowds used to go to the park in London just to see her ride by in her coach. Then there was Mary Cary, a futurist who predicted the Fifth Monarchy and the millennium. She was widely read and consulted by public figures, almost like a prophetess strayed out of the 1300s. Her millennialist predictions emphasized the role women would play in the new world (Stenton 1957: 172-75). There were also pamphleteers. The anonymous "Eugenia" attacked a "crude" wedding sermon published by John Sprint in *The Female Advocate* (1699); Lady Chudleigh wrote *The Ladies Defence* in answer to the same sermon. In 1696, an anonymous author produced a cleverly satirical *Essay in Defence of the Female Sex.*

In addition to engaging in polemics, a number of thoughtful women were developing proposals for the education of women. Lettice Cary, who died young at midcentury, made such an impression with her proposals for "places of education for gentlewomen, and for the retirement of widows (as Colleges and the Inns of Court and Chancery are for men) in several parts of the Kingdom" (Stenton 1957: 140) that she continued to be quoted much later in the century. Bathshua Makin and Hannah Woolley both published proposals on the education of women between 1670 and 1675. Both were teachers, writers, and vigorous public figures. Mary Astell, the center of a strong feminist group toward the end of the century, published *A Serious Proposal to the Ladies* (1701) including a proposal for a woman's college. Wealthy women supporters in her circle had actually put up the money for such a college, but Astell was made such fun of for appearing to propose a "nunnery" that they lost heart and retreated. Given the lack of an acceptable pattern for the education of women at the time in England, it was not unreasonable for Astell to propose the monastic model. Her intentions were completely misunderstood by many of her contemporaries. Those who came after understood better, and many of the philanthropic and educational projects begun by women in the next century were inspired by her writings. As a single woman with no income, she had had to make her own way in the world and had a strictly practical concern for helping single women live independently. She was also a political writer.

Male supporters of the education of women were certainly not absent, as witnessed by Daniel Defoe's proposal for an academy for ladies in *An Essay upon Projects* (1697). The concentration of writings on the education of women at the end of the century indicates a readiness to deal with this long-ignored issue. The militants had made an impression, both on their own sex and on men.

Working-class militants. Working-class women were in even more of a fighting mood. They sometimes literally occupied en masse the public spaces that their more educated counterparts wrote about. The civil war hit them hard, ruining their trade, imprisoning their husbands, and generally making life difficult for them. In 1643, peace proposals were before the House of Commons, which that body decided to reject. The citizenesses of London mobilized, and "two or three thousand women, but generally of the meanest sort" (Hill 1896: 195) presented a petition to parliament. Met with a smooth answer and instructions to go home, they instead stayed and increased in numbers to 5,000 women, finally to be dispersed with bullets, swords, and bloodshed.

"The meanest sort" were by no means inarticulate. The year before, they had stated in a petition: "Women are sharers in the common calamities that accompany both Church and Commonwealth, when oppression is exercised over the Church or Kingdoms, wherein they live" (Rowbotham 1972: 15). In 1647, the maids of London petitioned parliament for protection against unreasonable working conditions imposed by the "City Dames." In the same year, women petitioned for the release of Lilburne, a member of the radical Leveller movement:

> [Women] appear so despicable in your eyes as to be thought unworthy to petition or represent our grievances. . . . Can you imagine us to be so sottish or stupid, as not to perceive or not to be sensible when daily those strong defences of our Peace and Welfare are broken down and trod underfoot by arbitrary power? (Rowbotham 1972: 17)

In the 1640s, a brewer's wife, Anne Stagg, presented a petition on behalf of "Gentlewomen, Tradesmen's wives, and many others of the female sex, all inhabitants of the City of London and the Suburbs thereof" for protection against religious persecution. In 1651, the women were back again, petitioning for relief from imprisonment for debt, with cogent arguments about the oppressive nature of debt imprisonment (Hill 1896: 199, 200). While men argued that women could not possibly understand the complexities of public affairs, due to weakness of intellect, these tradeswomen showed by word and deed that they understood not only what was going on but what needed to be done about it.

Nonconformist women. A whole group of nonconforming sects was emerging in the 1640s out of the Anabaptist traditions of the previous century. In England, the nonconformists may well have been drawn from the inhabitants of that one-fifth of all English villages that had never had a resident squire: villages without manor houses.[19] Otherwise, it is difficult to account for the extent of self-sufficiency, of self-confident leadership and the total lack of deference patterns, in the behavior of both women and men of those sects. Samuel, writing of a period several centuries later, describes this same lack of dependency and deference in villages where "no sympathizing ladies made their appearance at the cottage door with words of comfort or exhortation, to bring the poor religion, to correct their spending habits, or to teach them how to work" (1975: 157).

These rough and ready artisans, with their wide repertoire of craft skills and strong self-help traditions, were a thorn in the flesh of the local representatives of church and state. They represented a form of participatory democracy alien to the feudal order. They stood for a concept of distributive justice at the opposite pole from that of manor house charity. This egalitarianism was feared wherever it emerged, in England or on the Continent.

Consistent with these egalitarian characteristics, one trait that strongly marked all Anabaptist-inspired groups in the seventeenth century and later was the strong participation of women in every aspect of the life of the group. When Winstanley issued a proclamation for the Diggers and Levellers in 1649—"Why may we not have our heaven here and Heaven hereafter too?"—it was plain that women were included in the "we." Women were equally active with men in taking over "surplus" property and redistributing it to the poor in the Leveller movement, and we will see women leaders pursuing this redistribution theme in the next century in still-newer dissenting sects. Anabaptists, Baptists, Familists (Family of Love), Levellers, and Quakers were all flourishing in the mid-1600s, and they all were noted for the activist women in their midst. When a formal structure for the Society of Friends (Quakers) evolved in 1660 out of many scattered Anabaptist groups, provision was made for separate women's and men's meetings, with separate clerks and funds, though with overlapping agendas.[20]

Militant Quaker women might seem like a contradiction in terms, but only strong and assertive women could hold their own once outside the supportive Quaker circle. Preaching in public was one of the worst things a woman could do in the 1600s, and Quaker women were continually preaching in public—in streets, in fields, wherever they could command an audience. They were in prison a great deal, often publicly whipped and always subject to having their possessions seized. The first structure developed by Quakers was an institution called "Meeting for Sufferings," which organized among other things the care of small children whose mothers were in prison. Child care seems to have been organized to free mothers for social protest even before it was organized to free them for more long-term activities, and with good reason. In 1654, "Oxford scholars so violently maltreated two Quakeresses who preached in the streets that one of them succumbed shortly after. . . . Two years later two Quakeresses were placed in the stocks at Evesham by the mayor, for visiting some prisoners" (Hill 1894: 247). The first Quaker woman to preach in London, Ann Downer, evidently fared better. London was more sophisticated than Oxford and the hinterlands.

The homes of women became the first meeting places for Quaker worship, much as the homes of Roman women became the first places for Christian worship. The organizational center for Quakerism was in the home of Margaret Fell, who worked with George Fox in the founding of the Society of Friends.[21] George Fox was a working-class charismatic whose openings (revelations) were very similar to those of the Anabaptists. His doctrine that all could be taught directly by the inner light helped to undermine reverence for traditional university-based learning and authority and encouraged the activist, self-help orientation of an already alienated countryside. Margaret Fell was a remarkable manor house lady, who as Fox's coworker built the communication networks of the new society. This phenomenon of women of wealth, education, and social position creating alliances with the artisan class on behalf of revolutionary social change will become increasingly evident from this century onward.

Margaret Fell's home, Swarthmore Hall, became (under the eye of a benign and supportive husband, Judge Fell) the world headquarters of Quakerism. Missions to all continents went out from there; all correspondence and reports were sent there. Margaret Fell was not only the organizer, however, she was also a minister and interpreter of the faith. One of her tracts is titled *Women's Speaking Justified*. Late in life, after Judge Fell's death, she and George Fox married. They used their marital partnership as an explicit testimony to the possibilities of equality in the husband-wife relationship. Some of Fox's epistles (*A Day-Book of Counsel and Comfort*, 1937) refer to this specifically.

In its beginnings, Quakerism did not create individuality in women; it attracted women who were already autonomous individuals. Some of them, like Margaret Fell, came from the manor house tradition, but the bulk of them were artisans and laborers, women who were used to a hard life. Margaret Fell herself raised her own four daughters to be economically self-sufficient. Each daughter had her own business. Three stayed at home unmarried and managed ventures such as iron smelting and sea trading (Stenton 1957: 177).

Women as colonists. A logical action for women who wanted independence was to emigrate to the Americas or travel as missionaries abroad. The Quaker servant girl Mary Fisher found her way to the court of the Sultan of Turkey and preached to him. (With what consequences we do not know, but she returned to England to tell the tale.) Others traveled to the West Indies and to Russia.

The women who came to North America found the matrilineal societies of the League of the Iroquois in New England. The Native American women, self-assured and with a powerful voice in their own tribal councils (De Pauw 1974: 4), were strong, hardworking, and kindly. We know they helped the early colonist women with food and taught them many skills. The openness of their societies, and the warmth of their family life, was such that white children in those first two centuries of settlement who were adopted into Native American families, whether by fortunes of war or for other reasons, rarely wished to return to their own families if later "rescued" (Hallowell 1972: 200-205). It has been estimated that about 70% of adults captured by Native Americans preferred not to return to white society (De Pauw 1974: 4). Native Americans were not similarly attracted to white society, largely because whites made no place for them in their society. Native Americans freely accepted whites as part of themselves; whites could be chiefs or matrons in the council of mothers, once they had been adopted into a tribe. The more complete story of how colonization affected women, particularly indigenous women, has only recently been explored (Etienne and Leacock 1980).

The Dutch and the French women who arrived in North America continued to neighbor with the Native American women, learning their languages and trading skills with them. The English women did not. They, unfortunately, felt antipathy for both Native Americans and blacks (De Pauw 1974: 9). While there must have been many exceptions to this, racial tensions seem to have developed early.

The authorities in the new colonies understood very well how important women were to the success of the settlements, and women there were not prohibited, as they often had been in Europe, from doing such things as "speaking for themselves in courts of law, running print shops and newspapers, inns and schools, practicing medicine, and supervising plantations" (Scott 1971: 4). The Virginia Assembly from the beginning gave land grants to women as well as to men.

In Maryland and New Jersey, as in Virginia, women were given a free hand according to their entrepreneurial abilities. Quaker Elizabeth Haddon persuaded her wealthy English merchant father to let her have the 500 acres of land he had bought in New Jersey. She studied medicine and agriculture, prayed a lot with her family, and set off to found what became the town of Haddonfield. Alone and single, she built her cabin in the wilderness and not until she had established a successful settlement did she take a husband (Luder 1973).

In New Amsterdam, Dutch women were crucial to the development of overseas commerce and the Indian trade. The tradition of the wife as business partner, lessening in England, remained strong in the Netherlands and in New Amsterdam. Women learned the Native American languages rapidly, and Dutch women traders competed successfully with French men for the Indian trade. They also acted as interpreters between the colonial government and the Native Americans.[22] One would like to know more about these "raucous" women traders, as Ryan (1975: 35) calls them, who were evidently as sharp as they were adventurous. One would also like to know what Native American women thought of them! De Pauw (1974) quotes a Frenchman on a Dutch woman trader in 1679:

> This woman, although not of openly godless life, is more wise than decent. . . . She is a truly worldly woman . . . and sharp in trading with wild people as well as tame ones. . . . She has a husband [who] remains at home quietly while she travels over the country to carry on the trading. In fine, she is one of the Dutch female-traders who understands the business so well. (1974: 5)

There was considerable cultural diversity in the colonies from the beginning. Women of all classes crossed the ocean from England, France, the Netherlands, and Spain and Portugal.[23] They came as young single girls, as married women with families, and as widows, alone or with children. Ladies of the manor house class might come to manorial estates of thousands of acres, like the sisters Margaret and Mary Brent of Maryland, or they might arrive with capital to establish commercial empires, like the Dutch widow Philipse, who organized the first transatlantic passenger service from New Amsterdam to Europe. From France, great ladies like Mme de Pontrincourt came with their husbands to establish estates in Acadia (later Nova Scotia). Single European women from the rural and urban poor indentured themselves to English farmers in Virginia, Maryland, and Massachusetts or to Dutch merchants in New Amsterdam. They made their fortunes according to luck and their abilities. Married peasant women sailed with their families to till new soil in New England and New France. "Vagrant" and "criminal" girls aged 5 and over were shipped, along with boys, to the English and French colonies in lieu of prison or the workhouse.[24]

In short, from Nova Scotia to Virginia, the women and children of Europe were seeking their fortunes, voluntarily or involuntarily, alone or with spouses and offspring. Everywhere they were important in the new economic order. But the early practice of giving women land grants equal to those of men stopped when settlements had "advanced" to the stage of self-government based on participation of male heads of household only.

The vast majority of immigrants to the New World were of rural background; the hard work of field and shop and bearing babies that women had known in the Old World was continued in the new. But hard as the work was, conditions were easier. Food was generally more plentiful, population densities were low, and women were able to rear to adulthood nearly all the children they bore. This situation caused a rapid population increase in all the colonies of the Americas. Griffiths points out that there was 50% mortality before the age of 21 in Europe at this time, contrasted with near zero mortality in the New World (Griffiths 1973: 14).

Acadia was a kind of "north woods paradise" during this century, oddly untouched by the turbulence in France. Catholics and Huguenots lived there side by side in peace. It was from the beginning a simpler, less urban-oriented society than its neighbor to the south, Massachusetts. The Ursulines, the order founded by Angela Merici the century before, came to Quebec in 1639 to work with the Indians. While their sisters in France had to live in enclosed convents, the Quebec band under the leadership of Sister Marie Guyard de l'Incarnation lived the pioneer life, in close contact with Indian mothers and children. In the midst of all their subsistence and service activities, they mastered the languages well enough to compose dictionaries in Algonquin and Iroquois. Their counterparts were doing the same in South America. One wonders whether relations between the English and the Native Americans would have been different if there had been Catholic sisters in puritan New England to speak the language of love that Native American women already knew. French nuns could relate to Native Americans as teachers and friends, Dutch women as traders, but English women had no culturally available role except as neighbor, which they generally rejected.

Mounting persecution of the Huguenots in France, culminating in the revocation of the Edict of Nantes, drove many Protestant families that might otherwise have settled in French Acadia to Massachusetts and Virginia. At its height, the persecution in France was so severe that many men were driven to escape alone, leaving women and children behind to devise their own escapes. One such left-behind woman was able to escape by leaving a 2-year-old child with a city guard as guarantee of her return—and never returned (Baird 1885: 102). A teenage girl escaped in a hogshead (Baird 1885: 108-9). Whenever social upheavals create large numbers of refugees, heroic altruism and selfishness both appear, and neither sex has a monopoly on one trait or the other. One of the heroic figures of the time was the Huguenot princess of Tarante. She did not flee France but for 14 years held out in her chateau, where villagers could come to Protestant worship after the church was closed by the authorities. Eventually, most Huguenots had to flee or pretend to renounce their religion. The ingenuity of mothers, widows, and young girls in finding means of escape, and tales of heroism of men in aiding such escapes, are revealed in Baird's (1885) vivid chronicles of the Huguenot migrations.

The women who came to North America were often single and young, but the colonies preferred to have the women of their communities in the married state. Local Dutch and English courts supervised the swift placement of unmarried women and men into households and marriages (Ryan 1975: 38); widows who wished to stay single had to be tough (Ryan 1975: 48). Precisely because of the importance of the women to the economic survival of the households, however, the marriages often left more freedom of action to the women than their counterparts enjoyed in Europe.

While women were appreciated as partners, they were mistrusted as intellectuals, particularly in puritan Massachusetts. The poet Anne Bradstreet complained rather gently about this:

> . . . I am obnoxious to each carping tongue
> Who sayes, my hand a needle better fits,
> A poet's pen, all scorne, I should thus wrong.
> (in Kraditor 1968: 29)

Anne Hutchinson, a few years later, gave the Calvinist church fathers an uneasy time with her self-confident heretical doctrines about grace and the role of women in the church. They told her:

> You have stepped out of your place. . . . You have rather been a husband than a wife, and a preacher than a hearer, and a magistrate than a subject, and so you have thought to carry all things in Church and Commonwealth as you would and have not been humbled for it. (Rowbotham 1972: 17)

The occasion of that quotation is in itself a historical vignette that lifts the veil on the superstructure of male dominance in the colonies. One sees underneath the terrible insecurity and fearfulness of men. Anne Hutchinson's teaching and community activities had

> upset Calvinist dogma, political differentiation, and masculine superiority. She was accordingly tried by both civil and religious authority. Pregnant and ill, at one stage while she was being questioned she almost collapsed, but they wouldn't let her sit down. The governor of the colony merely noted tersely in his record of the trial: "Her countenance disclosed some bodily infirmity." (Rowbotham 1972: 17)

While the male superstructure remained intact, the banished Anne and countless women like her found niches elsewhere and founded settlements that became refuges for independent thinkers. Nor was the Massachusetts Bay Colony left to itself. Women kept returning there to preach, particularly Quaker women, who were as regularly deported. When death was threatened for any Quaker who returned, Mary Dyer came back one more time to show that human dominance structures had no meaning in her value system. Mary, hanged on Boston Common with three Quaker men, is a continual reminder (now as a statue on that same common) of the moral frailty of a sector of politically dominant Puritan men.

The New World was not a utopia. Given that immigrants of both sexes were accustomed to political dominance roles for men, no women sat in the councils of the new village democracies. What public spaces the women occupied in the earliest years when every hand was needed soon became privatized as prosperity made narrower definitions of domestic roles possible.[25] Nevertheless, compared with Europe, it did offer expanded opportunities for women of all classes. Their hands and brains were urgently needed.

Catholic Pioneers in Europe

No pioneer women in the wilds of the Americas had harder times than the sisters in Catholic convents in regions of Europe overrun by the Thirty Years War. Some convents were evacuated and all but demolished half a dozen times or more, the sisters each time returning to rebuild. In the end, some of the convents were permanently abandoned. Another kind of war was made on the nuns when local town councils turned Lutheran and sent Protestant ministers to the convent chapels to preach. The sisters then sat helpless through long heretical sermons, although on occasion they made mass protest exits during such sermons. Sometimes a group of nuns within a convent converted to Lutheranism, and then there would be a tug of war on whether the institution was to stay Catholic or become Lutheran.

We have mentioned earlier that many French and German convents were royal convents. When a royal abbess came to be persuaded of the importance of a deeper spiritual life, in accordance with the many spiritual developments taking place within the church during the Counter-Reformation, she sometimes had a hard time persuading her royal sisters to live a more austere and devotionally oriented life. Fellow royalty might see no need for it. Peasant sisters might see it as one more whim of the aristocracy. One particularly dramatic case was in the royal convent of Urspring in Wurtemberg. The abbess, Margaret of Freiburg, wanted to introduce reforms already practiced at a neighboring convent but suspected there would be resistance to the changes. One day she arrived at her own convent door fortified by nuns from the neighboring convent,

> some abbots, several preaching friars and a number of noblemen to assist her in case she met opposition from the nuns. Some noblemen of the opposite party also appeared. Under the direction of [a sister] the group of obstinate nuns who refused the reform, had withdrawn into the isolated infirmary in the convent garden and there fortified themselves by barricading the doors with tables, benches, blocks of wood and stones. They themselves occupied the upper floor and appeared at the windows, showing their weapons: stones, sticks, whips and spears. The duchess [backing the abbess] gave her people the command to attack the house. But the noblemen objected, explaining that it would always remain a disgrace, if they fought against women. Besides, they did not wish to make enemies with their equals; after all, these were noblewomen, and nuns too.
>
> The duchess then had the alarm sounded from the nearby bell tower. This brought the common people. The simple townsmen and peasants were prepared to attack and they stormed the house. Those nuns who resisted were bound and put under arrest. (Hilpisch 1958: 52-53)

In the end, nuns who didn't want the reform were permitted to leave. Most finally returned and submitted.

As mentioned earlier, the stirrings in the religious orders led in two opposite directions: toward greater devotion in religious seclusion and toward more activity in the world. Among the activist convents, the royal abbey at Port Royal, France, underwent a complete spiritual revolution under Abbess Mère Angelique. The abbey moved from a swampy backwoods location to Paris, where it had profound and unpredictable effects on the women of the salons and became a meeting place for the major religious figures of the day. It survived embroilment in church politics and the Jansenist controversy for some time but was finally dispersed. Spirituality does not easily travel from swamps to salons. Mme de Longueville, the Pallas Athena of the salons and of the battlefields of France, was much affected by Port Royal. As a result of that influence, she spent her last days under the strict rule of the Carmelites.

The developments in the activist direction include the work of Mary Ward, the English Catholic mentioned in Chapter 1 of this volume. Her radical ideas survive in a flourishing teaching order today (Evennett 1968). Jeanne de Chantal, founder of the Visitation Sisters, was a Frenchwoman who raised a family before she responded to the religious call.[26]

She conceived, together with her friend and religious director, the mystic St. Francis de Sales, the idea of an order of nuns who would link the contemplative life with visiting the poor and the sick. This would be a kind of *devotia moderna* in action, refusing to make the separation between action and contemplation that other orders were making. It was an unusual conception, born of one of the great spiritual friendships in the history of the church. The order grew rapidly, but the sisters were not given the freedom of movement that Jeanne had intended. Once again, the unreadiness of the church to deal with the autonomy of women was made plain. Another order founded around this time, the Sisters of Charity of St. Vincent de Paul, was more successful in retaining freedom of movement, possibly because its founder, St. Vincent, was a man and could press more effectively for that freedom for his sisters. Urban Europe desperately needed the services the sisters were offering, which made the failure of male church leaders to realize the appropriateness of the service the more tragic.

Because the Lutheran church did little to promote vocations beyond wifehood for the women, most of the religious and many of the secular vocational calls that came to devout women of these centuries tended to be fostered in the Catholic church. Limited though the opportunities were, the church did provide a special public-private space within which women's abilities and contributions could develop.

The Bluestockings and the Salons

The women intellectuals of the sixteenth century were a special breed, foreshadowing the flowering of women thinkers and activists in the following century. Because the most visible and famous member of the sorority in the 1600s was Queen Christina, we will begin with her.

Queen Christina. Queen Christina (1626-89) was a bluestocking par excellence and, though she also wore a crown, she chose not to keep it. Scholars find her endlessly fascinating.[27] Her father and role model was the empire builder Gustavus Adolphus. Like the queens Isabel and Elizabeth, Christina had great physical endurance and could live on horseback for long stretches of time. As a child, however, she was often ill, at least partly because of the peculiar coffinlike existence imposed on her by an emotionally ill mother after her father's death. Brought up to reign over a Lutheran country, she found her intellectual liberation in Catholic humanism. She had read a lot as a child in her "coffin" and had examined the reflections on the human condition offered by the advanced thinkers of her day. Descartes, whom she brought to her court for a period, was crucially important in her own life, symbolizing the gift of free will to humankind. Although she fed on many ideas, she was not a deep thinker and continually frustrated people like Descartes, who expected her to be an intellectual giant.

Side by side with this intellectual emancipation, there existed in Christina what Stolpe (1966) identifies as the "Pallas Athena complex," typical of certain women of that era who thought of themselves as unique. She conceived of herself as one of the greats in history, along with Cyrus, Alexander, Caesar, and Scipio. She had counterparts among her contemporaries in France: the duchess of Montpensier, who rode to battle with Condé at the head of troops and herself fired cannon in the French religious wars, and Madame de Longueville, Condé's sister, who also rode to battle with him. The role model was entirely male. Christina consciously wished she were a man and had a horror of her own sexual urges.

She abdicated not because she did not want to be queen but because she found tiny Lutheran Sweden too confining. She abdicated, says Stolpe, because she wanted to get out into the larger world and achieve her true greatness. In support of this, he lists the long series of intrigues she engaged in after her flight to Rome to get other (presumably less confining) thrones in Naples and Poland. None of these succeeded, and in the end she had to be satisfied with creating her own court and ruling as an uncrowned queen on the outskirts of Rome. There she created not less than three academies and supported many musicians, artists, and a theater troupe. In a formal sense, she was "religious," making an abdication of conscience because she had converted to Catholicism. In fact, although living in Rome more or less under the protection of the pope, she was essentially a free thinker who turned mystical in her last years.

Christina was a "failed" great queen but a very successful bluestocking. While she was generally antifeminist and preferred the company of men, this too was a trait of many bluestockings. Typical of the Renaissance humanists, she lacked any social conscience. She scrounged shamelessly all her life to keep up the style of court she felt appropriate to her status. But she also had a great respect for "the other" major woman intellectual of Europe, Anna Marie van Schurman, and visited her in Utrecht on her abdication journey from Sweden to Rome. She was herself an idol of all the bluestockings of her century and gave them a sense of identity and belongingness in the public sphere of European culture. As Pallas Athena, she could *command* respect, while most of them wheedled it.

The salon, both a stage for gifted women and a private launching pad for aspiring and upwardly mobile artists and scholars, was eagerly adopted from Mediterranean traditions when a young Italian woman brought the custom to France. Catherine de Rambouillet was the daughter of Julia Savelli and the marquis de Pisano, ambassador to Philip II and to the Court of Rome; she married the marquis de Rambouillet at age 12. "It was a happy union of two clever young people with brains far more active than those at the French court" (Reich 1908: 70). They left court life because it bored them and created an environment where the intelligent and distinguished bourgeoisie who could *not* be received at court could mingle with the more intellectually inclined of the nobility. The salon at the Hotel Rambouillet first opened at the very beginning of the century and achieved its height under the marquise's daughter Julie during the years 1629 to 1648. While it fostered the much ridiculed *précieuses* (a style of cloying preciousness), it both welcomed the "old maid" Marie de Gournay and gave hospitality to Corneille, Boileau, Balzac, Voiture, and Molière. It was the milieu that nurtured the voluble Mme de Sévigné and made her a woman of letters. De Sévigné addressed remarkably interesting chronicles-of-the-time letters to a remarkably dull daughter—or at least this is how her fellow salonières saw it.

While the salon was primarily a man's stage, set by women, it also provided opportunities for clever women. The plain, middle-class spinster novelist Mlle de Scudery could have her own "Saturdays of Sappho" in her simple quarters and yet be favorably compared with the Rambouillets. While all but the bluestockings looked down on de Scudery, she made lots of money on her novels and held stimulating salons. Salons also helped women play at politics, and aristocratic women like Mlle de Montpensier and Mme de Longueville moved in and out of the salons between military engagements during the fighting of the Fronde, pursuing political intrigues.

Scholars and Artists

Anna Marie van Schurman. Anna Marie van Schurman (1607-78), the "Sappho of Holland," was the best known woman of her time in Europe. Her portraits, painted by admirers, hang in museums all over the Continent. In her youth, she was a disciple and friend of the older Marie de Gournay. The Holland of her childhood was the crossroads of the world. Refugees streamed there from all the wars of Europe; merchants came there to do business, and scholars came there for new learning. It was a good place for women too. We have already noted the activities of Dutch merchant women in commerce. While the University of Utrecht did not admit women, the town was proud of its lady intellectuals and artists and Anna took the leading place in that circle as a very young woman. She was installed in a special box behind a curtain at the university so she could listen to lectures. Well tutored from earliest childhood, she knew Hebrew, Syriac, Chaldean, Greek, Latin, French, German, and English. She was particularly admired for writing an Ethiopian grammar.

She was a woman of too many gifts. Having promised her father in childhood to remain single and not disperse her gifts, she was in the end unable herself to decide those on which to concentrate. Until she was 27, most of her work was in painting, etching (particularly on glass), and music; in this period, she was best known as an artist. From 27 to 46, she was the world-famous scholar, continuously visited and written to by the intellectuals of Europe and acknowledged senior critic of European literature. As we mentioned, Queen Christina made a pilgrimage to her home. This is the period in which most of her books were written, including one on the education of women. As a disciple of de Gournay, she was a firm and dignified feminist. At 46, she became a disciple of Labadie, the founder of an Anabaptist sect, and spent the last quarter-century of her life developing a utopian religious community that was visited by Quaker women and men from England. She destroyed many of her scholarly writings after her religious conversion but kept some of her artwork from her earlier days. In the eyes of the world, she was "lost" to an unfortunate religious aberration.

Van Schurman's religious conversion was not like the retirement-to-a-convent pattern we have seen for a number of other intellectual women of medieval and Renaissance times. Rather, it was to a life of difficult activism. She deliberately exposed herself to persecution and poverty by identifying herself with a despised counterculture sect with a utopian vision. It was only in the very last years that her Anabaptist community was given land and security from persecution. The Quakers who visited it from England found it inspiring. Van Schurman gave more different kinds of things to her century than any person of her time, but she is an embarrassment to the historian of thought. The pattern is too untidy. With the major public spaces of Europe at her disposal, she chose a counterculture life.

The Lowlands, Anna van Schurman's home, was a great center for women artists in the 1600s. Anna and Maria Visscher, the Dutch muses, belonged to van Schurman's circle of dedicated women who etched on glass, wrote poetry, and engaged in a variety of scholarship. Anna Breughel and Judith Leyster were gifted genre painters. Maria van Oosterwyck and Rachel Ruysch were outstanding members of the flower-painting school. There were many family workshops: Gerard

Terburg and his sisters Maria and Gezina were outstanding genre painters; Gottfried Schalkers and his sister Maria were equally famous in Europe for their scenes by candlelight. Portraitist Adriana Spilberg married portraitist Eglon van der Neer, and they painted happily ever after.

In England, the Dutch styles were popular, and Mary Beale and Anne Carlisle were its chief exponents. In Denmark, the daughters of kings Christian IV and V were talented artists along with Anna Crabbe, poet and painter of princes. In Spain, unmarried daughters, sisters, and pupils of famous artists painted side by side with the men of fame. There is no record of their contribution except the general impression that they "helped." In Italy, Elisabetta Sirani of Bologna, a prolific painter of religious subjects, whose studio in Bologna became a major tourist attraction, was poisoned (it is thought) by a jealous colleague. All Bologna mourned her early death and the city published a book of sonnets to her.

With the development of opera in the 1600s, women immediately gained a public platform as singers in every country. In some countries, they composed operas. In 1659, Barbara Strozzi, for example, had an opera performed in Venice. Most women composers in this century wrote religious music: Catterina Assandra, Mararita Cozzoloni, Cornelia Caligari, and Lucrezia Vizzana in Italy; Madelka Bariona in Germany; and Bernarda de Lacerda in Portugal.

It was not a strange thing to see women on the stage in Italy, France, or Spain, either in operas or in plays. In England, however, this was not the case for the first half of the century. On January 3, 1661, Pepys wrote in his diary that it was "the first time that ever I saw women come upon the stage" (quoted in Wilson 1958: 3). The shift came about partly because hard-up theater companies were running out of good young female impersonators, and there were many dowryless daughters of the genteel poor to be had cheaply. They were immediately a great hit. The suddenness of the innovation, and the great pressures immediately put on these women to play real-life courtesan roles for which they were totally unprepared, created much social havoc and made it difficult for several centuries for women to go on the stage who did not wish also to adopt a courtesan's way of life (Wilson 1958: 9-20). Nevertheless, the Restoration Theater provided an opportunity for women to develop a hitherto concealed talent, and there were great women actresses[28] in great and not-so-great plays on the stages of London.

Before the 1600s, most women with a scholarly bent turned to history, theology, and philosophy. In Italy, we have noted the possibility for women to be mathematicians and to study the physical and biological sciences, but each case seems like an exception. Many European women in the 1500s developed laboratory skills through the study of alchemy, the forerunner of chemistry, but the references to this are incidental to other information and we cannot identify individual women who made serious contributions to alchemical studies.[29] In the seventeenth century, we begin to find a number of reports of women in science. For each woman so identified, we may be sure there were hundreds unreported.

In France, Mme de la Sablière, part of the fashionable salon world, did her best to conceal her studies in astronomy. The word got out, however, and Boileau wrote a cutting satire on the woman who sat up nights studying the stars and ruining her complexion. Her own home was a center for scholars rather than a salon. The baroness de Beausoleil, moving perhaps in different circles, "got away with" doing a major study of French mineral resources—a work widely recognized and used in her own time.

Germany produced women naturalist-explorers of an adventurous turn of mind. Maria Sibylla Merian of Frankfurt studied birds, insects, and plants in Surinam, trained her two daughters to work with her, and published a classic volume on the subject. She might as well be listed among the artists as among the scientists, for her drawings are superb. Science has honored her by giving her name to new botanical discoveries. She was also a member of the Labadist sect that Anna van Schurman joined, and her work in Surinam was done at a Labadist colony there. Josephine Kablick of Bohemia traveled widely to make botanical and paleontological collections for all the major schools, colleges, museums, and learned societies of Europe. She was happily married to a mineralogist, and they managed 50 years of separate but coordinated fieldwork. Amalie Deutsch was another botanical collector, famous for getting specimens from hard-to-reach places where no botanist had been before; she made many new botanical finds and a number of plants bear her name. She was also happily married, to a fellow botanist.

Maria Kirch of Germany belonged to a hidden matriarchy of astronomers. Working as her husband Gottfried's astronomer assistant, along with her three sisters-in-law, she discovered a comet, which was not named after her because she was a woman; she continued research and publishing after her husband's death. She trained her daughters in astronomy, and for years they did the calculations for the almanac and other publications of the Berlin Academy of Science.

In England, Elizabeth Celleor was a noted midwife in the reigns of Charles II and James II, who designed a royal hospital and organized a corporation of midwives. She proposed the training and registration of midwives, and there is a document by her dated 1687 on this. She drew suspicion by visiting women prisoners in Newgate before prison visiting had been otherwise proposed. Having powerful enemies, she was imprisoned, pilloried, and fined 1,000 pounds for a supposed plot against Charles II.

* * *

Reviewing the 1600s, we can see a steady increase in the range of thought and activities of women, a gradual emergence from the antifeminist Renaissance, and a readiness for new fields of action. With some exceptions in the salon world, women were still not taken seriously as thinkers, yet their spheres were steadily widening. The bluestocking phenomenon was complex and served to launch the greater articulateness of eighteenth-century women.

The Century of Revolutions: The 1700s

I am told that one can provoke uproarious laughter among older-generation English party-goers when conversation lags by solemnly remarking: "Queen Anne is dead." Evidently Queen Anne was considered an absolutely no-news queen. That this joke should have survived into the late twentieth century is remarkable testimony to the enduring invisibility of women as figures in history and to the enduring attitudes that make that invisibility possible.[30] Queen Anne began her rule in the century that launched the industrial revolution in England, political revolutions in France and North America, and unrest in Russia. The eighteenth was even more a century of queens than the sixteenth—with one English queen and three Russian empresses—although it was also a century of revolution against royalty. It was the century of the turnip-generated revolution in agricultural productivity that abolished the need to keep fields fallow, yet it was also the century of food riots and increasing urban misery. It was a century that invented child-oriented education and yet shipped thousands of children overseas under the Penal Transportation Act of 1717. The steam engine was invented, the labor movement was under way, and Godwin announced in *Political Justice* that people will only have to work a half-hour a day in the society of the future (Brailsford 1913). The realities of the current time, however, were that laboring women were working up to 16 or 18 hours a day. Education for girls was still a controversial subject, and discussions on colleges for women were held in hushed tones. If there was progress, it was slow, and women by the middle of the century were showing their impatience in vigorous ways.

The Queens

Queen Anne began her reign in the year of the first daily newspaper in London in 1702. She presided over a union arrangement between England and Scotland (1707), a new set of election laws (1711) that did not exclude women (otherwise qualified under the limited franchise) from voting,[31] an abortive invasion of Canada, and the Schism Act. After her demise, the union with Scotland fell apart and the Act for Preventing Tumults had to be passed—her successor seemed to have trouble keeping things under control. Anne was a quiet queen, but she was not inept. She knew her own mind and sent other women packing from court if they played politics in a style she did not like.

In Russia, Peter the Great's widow and ex-camp follower Martha presided over Russia for two years, 1725-27, as Catherine I. Although she was ill-prepared for such responsibilities, she did it "to help out." That brief reign inaugurated a 66-year period of rule by four successive empresses, with three very brief male interregnums. Catherine I was followed by Empress Anne (1730-40), an inept ruler who left affairs of state in the hands of a foreign favorite (something a goodly number of kings have also done). Ten years of disaster were followed by the rule of two very strong women: Elizabeth, daughter of Peter the Great, and Catherine II.

Elizabeth took over at the age of 20 in a coup that ousted her not very competent aunt, and she ruled for 21 years. Raised at court and accustomed to public life from the age of 2, she was a monarch in the grand style, with lovers and all. Initially a strong, intelligent ruler, she became erratically pious, unpredictably autocratic, and unfortunately lacked her father's imagination (Longworth 1973). When she died, her daughter-in-law engineered a coup and came to the throne on horseback at the head of her own troops. She arrived no longer encumbered with her politically inept and hostile husband, Grandduke Peter,[32] and ruled from 1762 to 1796 as Catherine II, "the great."

Fighting the power of the nobility and building up a trained and specialized bureaucracy loyal to her, Catherine built the needed infrastructure for the modernization that Peter the Great had introduced. In addition to far-reaching educational reconstruction (Raeff 1972: 93-111), administrative reform was her great gift to Russia. She also fostered better services for the poor and for the bourgeoisie as well as more local elective offices (Dukes 1967). She did not pursue the emancipation of the serfs very vigorously, after a start in that direction, partly because she was frightened by revolts. Toward the end of her reign, she leaned more heavily on the nobility and the landlords. The peasant revolts made her realize what a long-term operation reform would be for a country like Russia. Also, as she got older, she lost her vigor, although to the end she carried on wars with style. She was a widely read woman and supported Diderot and the Encyclopedia project in Paris when no one else would. She wrote voluminously and corresponded with Voltaire and many European philosophers. She was much admired in Europe and generally brought Russia into European society in a way that her predecessor Peter had only dreamt about doing (Raeff 1972: 21-92).

In midreign, Catherine watched with a benevolent eye while Empress Maria Theresa of Austria and the "ruling figure" in France, King Louis XV's mistress Madame de Pompadour, created between them an alliance for their respective countries that reversed a traditional enmity. Whether this diplomacy was really a deal between women, complete with Empress Catherine's blessing, I do not know. Mary Beard (1946: 314-15) suggests that some historians think it was. Catherine also later watched the king and queen of France go to the guillotine, secure in the knowledge that her country was not ready for that kind of revolution—but not too secure. Ruling Russia was a difficult job and, given the possibilities open to a monarch, she did remarkably well. She is the last of the great absolute monarchs among women. After her, all monarchs found increasing limitations put upon their roles by national parliaments. The role she vacated is an unlamented one, but the role was there to be played, and it is to be recorded that women were among those who played it well.

England: Philanthropy Versus Radicalism

By 1700, England had been through civil wars and revolution, and "the age of conservatism" was at hand. Women of the aristocracy at Queen Anne's court were involved with politics, but it was a politics of the elite and of personality. The duchess of Marlborough was exiled from court because of her political preferences—and spent the rest of her life writing about it. Later in the century, there was a famous election campaign in Westminster in which the duchess of Devonshire rode up and down the countryside knocking on doors, rather in the style of a twentieth-century campaigner, but it was still elite politics. Salon life in England was minimal, but it did exist. According to Hill (1896), it was a dull century for women in that country and a self-centered one.

But perhaps it was not so dull after all. Lady Mary Montagu was one of the liveliest women in London, famous for eloping and marrying for love. At the age of 21, she wrote an ardent feminist letter to a bishop friend, complaining about being forbidden serious studies as a woman. Later she introduced the practice of vaccination against smallpox into England from Turkey, where she observed its use while her husband was ambassador there (Stenton 1957: 261). As a woman of learning and wit, she gathered the women and men writers of her time at assemblies (the English equivalent to salons) but finally gave up on England and fled to Italy to live 23 happy years in what was to her a more congenial environment.

Mrs. Thrale, a successful brewer's wife, threw herself with even more zest into creating assemblies—it was the only thing her merchant husband would let her do—and brought promising young women writers like Fanny Burney in contact with other intellectuals like Dr. Johnson. When her husband died, she married an Italian opera singer for love (to the horror of all her friends) and became an author. London did not beat the spirit out of everyone.

In addition to the ladies who promoted the assemblies were the philanthropists, who were beginning to respond to the problem of an expanding and uncared for population of children of the poor. The famous poor laws of Queen Elizabeth's day, set up to take over community welfare work from the convents, were increasingly useless in dealing with the problems of the laboring poor. Up to a quarter of working-class mothers were heading their own households. The growing number of children in the streets was in part due to the increased availability of food and some decline in infant mortality and in part due to the fact that the new types of factories could not absorb all the children along with their mothers. The efforts to put children in schools (particularly by the Society for the Propagation of Christian Knowledge), and to educate child factory workers, were from one point of view major developments of the age; from another point of view, they were but a drop in the bucket. By 1729, there were 1,600 English charity schools (called "the glory of the age") with 34,000 pupils (Pinchbeck and Hewitt 1969: 291). Yet between 1756 and 1862, 10,000 vagrant children were sent to sea in involuntary merchant service (Pinchbeck and Hewitt 1969: 105).

The efforts of women like Hannah More, who organized Sunday schools for factory-employed children and then day schools to give vocational training, were important, yet small in relation to need.

Hannah More and her associates were careful to provide schooling for girls as well as boys. Because no suitable schoolbooks existed, Hannah More wrote them. This work with the "wild children," as More called them, opened the eyes of educated middle-class women to a whole range of pressing urban problems.

Many manor house ladies moved to the city in this period. Some of them enjoyed a new life of leisure, others became involved in philanthropic work. Other women remained in the country to participate in the agrarian revolution, creating innovations in agricultural methods and products in response to demands for increased food production. Letters from women, describing their work, in the columns of the agricultural journals of the day reveal the extent of women's participation in this process of innovation (Pinchbeck 1930: 30-32).

In general, middle-class philanthropists were sure of themselves, secure in their position, and able, if they were strong-minded, to accomplish what they set out to do. Feminism had very different meanings for different groups of women, as Rogers (1982) shows. For the new urban group of upwardly mobile women of the artisan class, and for the moderately educated daughters of poor gentry, life was different. These were women who had to support themselves, and they found nothing but obstacles everywhere. Mary Wollstonecraft (1759-97), a weaver's daughter who had many hard knocks in trying to support her problem-ridden family, became an articulate spokeswoman for this group. She spent some years trying unsuccessfully to maintain a financially marginal school and wrote extensively on education. Her book about the education of children, written for parents, was a best seller. In other circumstances, she might have been a brilliant educator. She had a professional apprenticeship with some of the best minds of England in the Samuel Johnson circle. But mostly she had to work at hack articles and translations (from the French and German) to earn a living. She raised a child alone, not by choice, but by victimization.

When she wrote her blast against the oppression of women, *A Vindication of the Rights of Women*, the women of the salons and the philanthropists were horrified. Hannah More had no patience with feminist sentiments and said sharply, "I am sure I have as much liberty as I can make use of" (Flexner 1972). This was probably true—for her. Mary Wollstonecraft lived in an entirely different world than the philanthropists. Her struggles to make a living made her very aware of the forces operating to hold women back. She was an individual in a society that did not provide for female individualists except among the elite. A radical who identified very strongly with the ideals of the French Revolution—she lived in France during part of it—she wrote *Vindication* out of the shock of her discovery that plans for the new state-directed free educational system for France made no reference to the education of women. A plea for an education for citizenship, and for an equitable social contract for women, the book was originally intended both for France and for England. (See Flexner 1972, for a further discussion of this. See also the biography of Wollstonecraft by Tomalin 1974.) In spite of the circles in which she moved, Mary was something of a loner in her own country. Only toward the end of a rather miserable life did she and William Godwin discover each other, as she found her way into a congenial utopian-socialist milieu. She died in childbirth after a brief happy marriage to him.

Vindication was published in 1792. In 1799, the year after Mary died, Mary Anne Radcliffe published *The Female Advocate or an Attempt to Recover the Rights of Women from Male Usurpation*, an incisive work addressed specifically to the problem of single or widowed women in poverty. *Vindication* was primarily for middle-class women and *The Female Advocate*, for the poor. By the next century, a more coherent strategy was to develop, but in the 1700s women were generally working in isolation from one another, unaware of the larger picture. Women's roles were still largely privatized.

Women among the dissenters. The one striking exception to privatization was the role of women in the dissenting religious sects. The Quaker women's meetings described in the previous chapter continued to train women for community responsibility. Clarkson writes: "The Quaker women, independently of their private, have that which no other body of women have, a public character" (1806: 246). Quaker men have "given to the females of their own society their proper weight in the scale of created beings. Believing them to have adequate capacities, and to be capable of great usefulness, they have admitted them to a share in the administration of almost all the offices which belong to their religious discipline" (1806: 250). Specifically, the women carried out relief work for their own persecuted members and for the poor; went on missionary journeys sometimes for several years at a time, leaving their children in the care of their husbands and the Friends community; preached at recruitment centers against military service; and generally carried on the activities of a dissenting group in a period of rapid social change. Their main concentrations were in England and America.

Three charismatic dissenting sects, all offshoots of the Quaker-Anabaptist tradition, and all led by women, became an embarrassment to the increasingly respectable Society of Friends (Holloway [1880] 1966; Armytage 1961). The first was the Philadelphians, a community founded by the disciples of the visionary millennialist Mrs. Leade in 1696. Mrs. Leade's teachings about the imminent new age were so powerful that many of the utopia-founding movements of the late 1600s and early 1700s were influenced by her. She was also an important influence on the Moravians. Numerous colonists from Europe and England came to see Mrs. Leade first for advice. She wrote many books, some of them dictated after she went blind, and conducted a correspondence reminiscent of the prophetess-abbesses of the Middle Ages. The Philadelphians did not long survive her death at the age of 81, and her writings seem very obscure today, but she spoke a language that was meaningful to the communitarians of her day. Another dissenting sect was led by Jane Wardley. Mother Jane, as she was called, preached with great tremblings and broke into dancing under the power of the holy spirit, so that her group became known as the "shaking Quakers," or Shakers. The Shaker movement really developed under her disciple Ann Lee. Ann emigrated to America as the result of a vision, to organize a network of Shaker communities on the eastern seaboard in the 1770s. These were among the few sex-egalitarian communities of the next century, and that egalitarianism was in part achieved through celibacy. The third Quaker offshoot centered on Joanna Southcott, a less well known prophetess, who in 1802 took a house in Paddington and issued certificates for the millennium—14,000 in all. None of these women acted on the kind of political analysis of production and distribution problems that we find among women leaders in the next century. This was strictly a vision-building era.

The only massing of women in public in this century, apart from millennialist demonstrations, was in connection with the food riots that took place with increasing frequency from 1765 to 1800. Large numbers of bad harvests occurred in that period, and the employment situation became increasingly difficult with displacement of workers by machines. The studies of food riots do not usually focus on women, so we only know by chance the extent to which women were involved. We do know that "housewives" in Essex rioted in 1709-10. Because students of food riots have concluded that this is a form of social protest used to deal with other than food issues alone, and is in fact a kind of "strike," we can assume that the Essex housewives had some issues on their minds other than food shortages, but we are not told what they were (Rudé 1964).

Food riots seem to have been undertaken by occupational groups, so, whenever a guild or occupational group rioted en masse in a district, we can be sure there were women involved. The city riots that took place during this century were more apt to be machinery smashing than food riots. Again, women would be involved to the extent that their occupational groups supported the riots. At least one-fourth of all rioters must have been women. One-half is a more likely figure. Women would be more motivated to riot than men because their situation, especially that of husbandless women with children to support, would be more desperate. That old problem word *men* in the historical record conceals the facts.

Women in field and factory. The situation of laboring women in this century was very hard, as the references to rioting suggest. Tilly and Scott (1978) present the most complete information available on work, women, and families for this period. In the countryside, women were pushed more and more into competing with men for the heaviest and hardest jobs because of dwindling employment opportunities except at harvest time. The family work gangs, migrant and local, continued. Opportunities for craft work at home had dwindled substantially, although some village factories, such as pin factories, gave out piecework to be done at home. Cottage industry never totally disappeared, even by the twentieth century, because there were always women willing to add extra hours to their working day at home to increase meager incomes, and there was always some demand for products that could be produced in this way. Women cottagers who could get at land to raise food were lucky; many could not because of the reduced amount of common land. Women who had regular skilled work such as dairying were not much better off than the irregularly employed, because the working conditions were so bad. Working on cheeses that weighed up to 140 pounds destroyed the health of dairymaids and made plowing look like easy work (Pinchbeck 1930: 13-14).

The hardest hit by unemployment were widows, partnerless women with children, and young singles. Parish records frequently refer to "vagrant women"; these helpless unemployed women, along with vagrant children, were put in institutions that were increasingly indistinguishable as poorhouse, workhouse, or penal institution. In the labor force, women got half or less of male earnings and children much less than that.

Many of these women emigrated to the city, but ignorant and ill-fed as they were, they had few employment opportunities there. The women already in the cities were being pushed out of occupations they formerly had through pressures from male unemployment—a process that had already been happening for a long time. What apprenticeship and skill-training opportunities they had were similarly dwindling through pressure from male workers. The new immigrants from the countryside took anything they could get, usually odd jobs at starvation wages. If they were lucky, they might get jobs as maids to upwardly mobile women who were leaving the labor force, but the latter shrank from taking in rough laboring types of women as domestics.

Shallow-pit mining, working in blast furnaces for 24-hour spells at a time, and other types of industry-related heavy labor gave rise to inhuman working conditions and high casualty rates for women. A hard day's work was not new for women. Rather, the severe suffering of laboring women in the eighteenth and nineteenth centuries was due to the lengthening workday, the low wages, and the complete dependence of poor women on shops for food. The bit of food grown or scrounged in the country, a standby for centuries for the poorest of rural day laborers, was totally unavailable for urban women. It was increasingly so for poor villagers as well. Workdays of 16 to 18 hours left no energy for home or child care, obviously, and contributed further to the problems of the children.

Public exposés of these working conditions began in 1793, but it took another 50 years for governmental notice to be taken. There were easier occupations for women at this time, such as jobs in village smithies and metal shops, making nails, locks, and tools as well as relatively "light" work in the new industrial textile factories. Even in these factories, however, the work load was heavy and the hours long.

The women most vulnerable of all to the evils of industrialism were the urban unemployed. Many sold sexual services for food under the grimmest of conditions. Prostitution in this century changed character with the increase in poverty. I have noted earlier that there was a vast difference between the wealthy courtesan and the underemployed proletarian prostitute. The development of urban destitution vastly widened that gap and created the class of streetwalkers that represent the very bottom of the pit of social suffering for women. The poorer women were, the more liable they were to be picked up and imprisoned, and they made up a goodly number of the 10,000 convicts that were shipped from the Old Bailey alone to the North American colonies between 1717 and 1775. This practice of dumping prisoners in the colonies, increasingly protested against by the colonists themselves, was only brought to a halt by the American Revolution (Rusche and Kirchheimer [1939] 1968: 58).

Yet, for all the suffering experienced by workers in England, the situation only led to riots, not to revolutions. For a revolutionary situation, we must turn to France.

Revolutions in France

In France, the eighteenth century started with the last large-scale nationwide famine that country was to have. The revolt of peasantry and proletariat in 1700 against long-continuing persecution of the Huguenots by the Catholic regime was probably not unrelated to famine conditions. After an amnesty was declared, warfare and riots stopped (Whitworth 1975: 13) and things settled down to relative quiet. There were periodic epidemics of bread riots in the 63 years between 1725 and 1788, which meant women were out in public laying siege to bakeries or seizing supplies, but these were all locally inspired, spontaneous occasions and apparently not linked to any continuing movement. To understand the regular coupling of poor harvests with bread riots, one must understand that bread was the food staple of both the rural and the urban poor and it accounted for 50% of their expenditures (Rudé 1964). Furthermore, the rural poor were not able to grow grain or even to bake bread (because of a lack of fuel for ovens), so they had to buy bread like their city sisters.

In the cities, crowds would gather in protest against specific injustices, but again there was no overall program of protest. That 5,000 Parisian women and men would mass in protest in 1721 against the whipping and putting in stocks of a nobleman's coachman certainly indicates a high level of awareness of social injustice. In 1770, there was a major riot protesting the rounding up of vagrant children to be shipped overseas as labor for the colonies (Rudé 1964: 49), a practice England had been engaging in for some time, apparently unchallenged. The mothers of the "vagrant children," for the most part poor single or widowed working women, joined in a mass exodus from their places of work to the ensuing protest demonstrations. For the moment, the protest was effective and the children were not deported—but neither was the situation that gave rise to the "vagrancy" remedied. Guilds and artisan groups struck with increasing frequency from 1724 on, and went right on striking through the revolution, but the revolutionary government paid little attention to them. By and large, the revolution was not interested in the poor.

It is difficult to estimate the extent of poverty in this century. From 1733 to 1778, incomes were generally rising and more peasants were able to buy small pieces of land. Yet, general prosperity rarely reaches the very poor, and working women probably benefited little from chances to buy land. The fact that in 1780 there were 7,000 to 8,000 abandoned babies out of 30,000 births in Paris does not suggest increasing prosperity for the poor; neither does the fact that 4,000 persons a year were dying in the poorhouses of Paris (Braudel 1973: 380).

The situation for upper-class and upwardly mobile middle-class women was very different. This was a great period for the salon movement; by the middle of the century, these intellectual hothouses were at their height.[33] We do not really know how scholarly or gifted the women who ran the salons were. We do know that they nursed along scholarly and gifted men. Many of the major male writers of the day had salonières as critics and editors of their work, and this was general knowledge. Abbé Galiani had Mme d'Epinay; D'Alembert had Mlle d'Espinasse; Voltaire had Mme du Châtelet; and Diderot had Marmontel.

The women were the entrepreneurs of the Encyclopedia project, the first "modern" attempt at assembling knowledge. Much of the work for it was planned in salons, and Mme de Geoffrin's place was famous as the Encyclopedists' headquarters. Mme de Geoffrin was quite a character: She laid out her life plan at 20 and followed it; before 30, she began dressing like an old woman "to be beforehand with a difficult period" (Reich 1908: 124).

Mme du Châtelet was exceptional among the salonières in being independently creative, but she chose to hide her brilliance and subordinate herself to Voltaire, with whom she lived for 20 years. She died young. A mathematician, she wrote in the manner of Pascal, prepared commentaries on Newton, and translated Leibniz.

Each salonière had her own specialty. One went to Mme Hudson for conversation; to the duchess de Maine for clever entertainment; to the marquise de Lambert, Mme de Tencin, Mme de Geoffrin, and the maréchale de Luxembourg to meet famous people; to Mlle Pleneuf for music; to the duchess of Gramont for politics; and so on. The only dull place in Paris was the court itself. There one would find a queen, some mistresses of the king, and boredom (so it was said).

The romanticism of Rousseau and the wit of Voltaire, the two dominant century-spanning male intellects, did little to ground these salon women in problems of social justice. Rousseau fostered the worst kind of image of the mental domestication of women:

> To please, to be useful to us, to make us love and esteem them, to educate us when young, to take care of us when grown up, to advise, to console us, to render our lives easy and agreeable. These are duties of women at all times, and what they should be taught in their infancy. (Rowbotham 1972: 36)

This passage very straightforwardly tells women to educate men from childhood to oppress them. It was somehow not interpreted that way by the delighted saloniéres. Yet, if some of them were very confused bluestockings, there were others who were much involved with the politics of revolution, as we shall see.

The long period of relative prosperity in France came to an end by 1778, with falling prices and unemployment, and strikes and riots increased in frequency and intensity. The issues of the French Revolution are far too complex to be explicated here, but by the 1770s all the unsolved issues of the previous century exploded at once for the monarchy. The administrative divisions of France no longer reflected social, economic, and political realities. The fiscal system was an absurdity and the country was bankrupt. The king and queen, and the 4,000 families of the Great Nobility who controlled one-fourth of the national budget, were trying to hang on to the old absolute monarchy. The minor nobility and the bankers (who had money) were trying for a limited monarchy. The middle class and the artisans were more or less manipulated by the minor nobility and the bankers, and the poor peasants and unskilled workers (the 3 million illiterate poor of France) were squeezed out entirely. Women fought hard in the first, second, and third groups during the revolution (and fought against each other too), but in the end all but the nobility and the bankers' daughters were dumped and disqualified from every kind of participation, sharing the lot of the poorest of the men. Whoever "won" the revolution, the women of France lost it.

What was the role of women in the time of the revolution? Starting at the top, Queen Marie Antoinette by the early 1780s was busy mobilizing the resources available to the French monarchy through the alliance Empress Maria Theresa had created back in 1756. Poor Queen Marie—she is not usually thought of as a victim of the social expectation that women should remain quiet and demure, but she was. Her well-meaning husband was a do-nothing, so her efforts came to nothing. By 1792, she was writing to a friend:

> As for myself I could do anything, and appear on horseback were it needed; but that would be furnishing weapons to the king's enemies: throughout all France a cry against the Austrian and the rule of a woman would be raised instantly. By coming forward I should, moreover, reduce the king to a humiliating and inferior position. A queen who, like me, is nothing in her own right—who is not even regent, has but one part to act—to wait the event silently, and prepare to die. (Kavanagh 1893: 94)

She died with dignity. In fact, all the women who went to the guillotine, nobility, middle class, and working class, died with such quiet bravery that Kavanagh (1893) suggests this alone prolonged the Reign of Terror. A few hysterical scenes by women at the scaffold might have shocked the men of the Terror sooner into realizing what they were doing. Only poor old Madame DuBarry, the king's former mistress, gave way to hysterics on the scaffold—embarrassing everyone terribly.

The bankers' daughters went scot-free. They moved right through every phase of the revolution without being touched. Madame de Pompadour was the first banker's daughter to play politics, well before the revolutionary decade. As a young girl, she had been adopted by one banker, later married another, and, as Louis XV's mistress, ruled France (according to one school of historical thought) for the bankers. She was the coarchitect, with Maria Theresa, of the French-Austrian alliance. Her foreign policy was terrible for France, and her secret police were everywhere. She died before the revolution.

Madame Necker, the wife of a Swiss banker, and her daughter Germaine, who became Madame de Staël, ran salons that brought together bankers, literati, and political leaders in clever conversation in an atmosphere of "liberalism." They closed down their salons in the Reign of Terror, but not their activities. Mme de Staël ran a newspaper chain and survived not only the revolution but also the enmity of Napoleon. Another banker's daughter, Therése de Fontenay, re-created a court atmosphere in her Paris home after the revolution and was acknowledged as "uncrowned queen of Paris." Her friend Rose de Beauharnais, not a banker's daughter but a bourgeois adventuress friend of bankers' daughters, survived the revolution by her wits and then, as Josephine, married Napoleon.

Not all salons were run by bankers' daughters, and not all women of the upper class insulated themselves from concern for the deeper issues of the revolution and from the poverty of the masses. Madame de Condorcet and her husband, one of the few genuine husband-wife teams in the salon world, championed the equality of women and the rights of the working class when very few of their social class were interested in these subjects. Their salon has been called "the command center for thinking Europe." It was the most international of all the salons, anticipating by a century the internationalism of later political movements. Condorcet was the only Frenchman who spoke out strongly in the National Assembly for the political participation of women.[34] He lived in hiding, protected and supported by his wife for the last months of his life, only to be discovered in the end and guillotined. Mme de Condorcet, a former canoness and a pupil of Rousseau, survived and brought up their only child in retirement.

Mme Roland was another woman who did not insulate herself from the issues of the revolution, though she was strictly a "limited monarchy" advocate. An engraver's daughter who married into the upper class, she never moved in salon circles. Because of her own keen interest in the liberal politics of the upper-middle-class/minor-nobility alliance, however, she created a kind of political salon under the cover of helping her husband (at one point finance minister to the king) in his work. She appears as a kind of *eminence grise*, for she never spoke in public, hardly spoke even to the political visitors in her own house, and yet was generally recognized in her time as the authoress both of the ideas and of the documents that issued from the gatherings of highly placed political personages that took place in her modest home. She was both hated and admired in her day, and both positive and negative pictures of her have come down to us through the history books. She wrote many letters to political leaders, and both her style and her sentiments today seem sententious. She had courage, however, and went to the guillotine (sedately) for continuing to support the limited monarchy idea after the revolution had swept past that point.

The heroines of the French Revolution were other kinds of women entirely. Shop workers, fish vendors, laundresses, seamstresses, journalists, actresses, street women—they were a real medley of lower-middle-class and laboring women. Their participation in the revolution is somewhat unique in the annals of European history, both because they were so visible and well mobilized during certain crucial events and because they were so completely excluded from all civic participation even before the revolution was over. (For an account of the activities of French women during this period, see Levy, Applewhite, & Johnson 1979.)

Their effectiveness was founded in the preceding decades of experience with bread riots and protest demonstrations. Although each of the previous demonstrations had been spontaneous, the women who participated in them gained a certain sense of the patterning of demonstrations, and of their value, on which they could now draw. Women on the whole succeeded in keeping the price of bread within bounds; because the authorities could not afford to be continually dealing with riots, they sometimes went to great lengths to control the price of bread. The women who were present at the storming of the Bastille were not neophytes. They had been there before.

The decision of women to march to Versailles three months after the storming of the Bastille, and to bring the king to Paris, was also a direct outcome of their previous experience. When bread prices were lowered, it was usually done in the name of the king, so in their view the king was the source of rectification of injustice. If he could be brought to Paris to see how bad things were, he would do something about it. Members of the bourgeoisie-minor-nobility alliance were not hungry, so this item was not on their political agenda. But the unemployed women of Paris, and the poorest of the employed, *were* hungry. And their children were hungry. Their slogan reflected their concerns: "Bring back the Baker, and the Baker's wife, and the Baker's little boy, to Paris."

The women who marched to Versailles (it is a fairly long walk—20 miles) were of all kinds, and historians have described the crowd differently depending on their political sympathies. "Poor but honest" working women led the way. Women like Madelaine ("Louison") Chabray, a 17-year-old unemployed sculptress who was now making a living as a flower girl, walked side by side with the market women and porteresses of the city. The unemployed who picked up what pennies they could by prostitution followed. These poverty-stricken women are the ones who have been described as an obscene drunken mob. Well-wishers (and there were many) gave them wine on the road, not thinking what wine would do to malnourished women with empty stomachs. Some of the walkers were reeling by the time they got to Versailles, but the reeling was as much from hiking 20 miles on empty stomachs as from the wine. Louison, the flower girl, was appointed spokesperson. When she stood before the king, she was so overcome with emotion and hunger that she fainted. The king picked her up and embraced her, and she came stumbling out crying *"Vive le roi!"* Much fun has been made of this scene, but the women did march back to Paris with grain decrees from the king and with the Declaration of Rights from the National Assembly. They had used the tactics familiar to them, and they had gotten results.

Théroigne de Mericourt, ex-courtesan and opera singer, was a colorful person with a degree of worldly experience who injected some leadership into the situation at Versailles. Dressed flamboyantly in a huge hat, bright red coat, with a sword at her side, she protected the massed women from being fired on outside the king's palace by throwing herself on the soldiers and persuading them to desist. It was at this point that people began bringing food to the famished women, so they did not have to march back with empty stomachs. Théroigne led what appeared to be a well-organized crowd of about 100 fish vendors into the gallery of the National Assembly on a mission to get the assembly to turn its attention to the basic business of bread. An observer of this scene reported that the women seemed to know many of the deputies and shouted to them by name. Théroigne led the group, and they shouted or stayed quiet at her signal. This vignette (Michelet [1885] 1960: 64) indicates considerable political know-how on the part of some of the worker women.[35]

A postscript to this story of the women's march to Versailles is that, after the main body of women had started back to Paris, a small group of women and men broke into the queen's apartment with the intention of seizing her bodily and bringing her back to Paris. The upshot of that incident was that the "Baker and the Baker's wife and the Baker's little boy" did indeed come to Paris, escorted by triumphant crowds of women and men. Thus the women won twice over, in bringing back both the grain decrees and the whole royal family.

Much was hoped for from the National Assembly, in which the third estate for the first time took an active part. Activated women worked to mobilize rural France in support of the assembly, organizing festivals and persuading local village and department officials to write "love letters" to their new government. Urban middle-class women realized increasingly that a more sophisticated type of support of the revolution was required, and Jacobin societies for men and women were formed. The first such "Friends of the Revolution" club was organized by a merchant's widow, a printer, and two surgeons. Sex-integrated fraternal societies of working men and working women were also formed, and the aristocrats came and lectured to them on the issues of the revolution. Condorcet, Abbé Fauchet, and a Dutch woman, Mme Palm Aelder, spoke before the National Assembly on the recognition of the political participation of women in the revolution, but the assembly turned a deaf ear. A group of bourgeois women presented a petition: "You are about to abolish all privileges, abolish also the privileges of the male sex. . . . Thirteen million slaves are shamefully dragging the chains of thirteen million despots" (Sokolnikova [1932] 1969: 147). The assembly remained deaf.

While Jacobin "Brotherly Societies of the Patriots of Both Sexes" continued, Olympe de Gouges, an actress and pamphleteer, felt that a stronger woman's voice was needed. She founded all-women's societies in 1790 and 1791 and prepared a Declaration of the Rights of Women. Unfortunately, Olympe herself did not have enough political experience—how could women gain political experience in this Rousseau-mesmerized society? She lost her sense of direction, finally turning proroyalist out of confusion.

In 1793, another former actress, Claire Lacombe, and a laundress, Pauline Léon, organized a club specifically for working women, the Republican Revolutionary Society. Its members were tailoresses, dishwashers, laundresses, ragpickers, artisans, and laborers, and the society quickly allied itself with the "Enraged," a group concentrating its attention on the food difficulties. Unfortunately, there was considerable political dissension within the Revolutionary Society, and the radicals who identified with the Enraged came to be in the minority. In addition, the royalist fish-market women who felt that the revolution was ruining their business developed a strong hatred of the radical women. It was these tough fish-market women who are supposed to have been the implacable revolutionaries who counted with such fierce satisfaction the heads that fell into the basket from the guillotine. In reality, according to Sokolnikova ([1932] 1969: 176-77), they were compelled to attend the executions and only rejoiced when, during the Reign of Terror, former prominent revolutionaries took their turn at the guillotine.

In any case, tensions between the radicals and the moderates rose until finally there was a great free-for-all in the streets of Paris in October 1973. The minority radicals were caught between the angry moderate members of their own club and the furious fish women. The word having gotten out at dawn that there would be trouble that day, the market women were well prepared. They let loose with rotten fruit and vegetables, stones, sticks, and fists, attacking the radicals when they were evicted from their clubroom. The equally hostile men from the neighborhood also joined the fray, and the radical women barely escaped with their lives. The National Assembly self-righteously forbade women to hold any kind of meeting in the future—took away their right to organize, in fact—and that was the end of the role of citizenesses in the revolution. At first, the radical women tried to fight the ban, invading the assembly itself to get a hearing, but public opinion was against them, including the public opinion of most women.

The failure of women to become politicized to the point of sustained and effective participation in the activities of the revolution is one of the tragedies of that era. In one sense, the radical women were more sophisticated than the bulk of their sisters or the National Assembly itself, in that they were trying to promote attention to economic issues that the assembly preferred to ignore. In another sense, they were too unskilled in political analysis to deal with the very issues they were trying to promote. It is painful to read their declarations before the assembly on the occasions when they got a hearing. Olympe de Gouges and Claire Lacombe both sound like bad ham actresses doing a stilted morality play (Sokolnikova [1932] 1969: 155, 165-68, 248-51). Yet the men were speaking in the same style and operating at an even cruder level of analysis.

Where would the women have learned what they needed to know? Two centuries of intellectual exercises in the salons had done little for the capacity of women to engage in economic and political analysis. Except for the bankers' daughters, the women who had the mental training had no sense of the relevance of economic issues. For all the importance of the salon movement in playing nursemaid to the men of the Enlightenment and to the project of the Encyclopedia, with respect to the revolution, the salonières contributed little.

The position of women during the revolution was further weakened by the attack on the church and its "nationalization," which, as in England earlier, emptied convents and deprived rural and urban areas of convent-rendered education and welfare services. The Goddess of Reason parades in which the prettiest woman of the town was dressed up like Minerva were a poor substitute for what the women had lost.

Nevertheless, there was a long-run gain to women in their exposure to issues that they had not before confronted. Romanticized histories of the revolution obscure this fact. Bemused writers like to feature women like Charlotte Corday, who "killed for peace."[36] When Robespierre, the architect of the Terror, was finally himself executed, women of every class and sector turned out in a huge carnival of celebration. But, after that, there was apparent silence. This suggests a response level of unthinking emotionalism on the part of women activists that does them an injustice. Thoughtful women among the discredited radicals, in fact, began at this time the long, slow process of thinking out the situation of women and of society that was to bear fruit in the socialist movements of the next century.

Women and Salons in German Lands

The peculiar mixture of romanticism and hothouse intellectualism that characterized the salon movement of France was not confined to France. The palatinate castles on the Rhine also had their salons, although these were to a far greater extent male organized and male dominated. The salon in Frederick's castle at Rheimsberg could be taken as typical. There were women present but as a kind of intellectual adornment. When Frederick became emperor, he stopped entertaining even the women-as-adornment idea, and his court became actively antifeminist. His shift in attitude gives a clue as to how dependent on male benevolence the women of the German salons were.

At Darmstadt, a group of middle-class women attached to the minor courts of the upper classes developed the extreme of the romantic outlook and life-style, which included playing at being shepherds and shepherdesses. Three of these women, intimates of Goethe, were known as the three muses: Psyche, Lila, and Urania. Marck, the man whose home was the salon center for this group, alternated between entering fully into the chorus of Wertherian[37] sighs and making it the butt of his very keen wit. Later, in Weimer, Ann Amelie's salon became the last home of the Minnesinger Court of Love tradition, with Goethe, Herder, Schiller, and Wieland all gathering there. In Berlin, Rahel Levin presided over the last of the Goethe salons, 1796-1806, but also lived to introduce another salon of the Heine era, 1819-33.

The French tradition of display of incisive wit and of intellectual entrepreneurship in bringing together male brilliance of different hues never developed in the same way for German women. There were scholar-nuns in the convents, but these were a world apart. Between them and the shepherdesses, no middle ground appears in the general intellectual histories of the time. This is probably an artifact of the way the history is written but also suggests that intellectual entrepreneurship was not valued in German women.

Women Adventurers

Working-class women not only appear in this century as oppressed laborers and as determined demonstrators and rioters, they also appear as adventurers who leave behind the humdrum, edge-of-poverty existence of their sisters to enter armies, navies, and pirate bands. In general, their lives were probably not very different than those of the vagabond women of the Middle Ages, but in this period some of them begin appearing as individuals in the historical record, probably because record-keeping systems became better organized (Hargreanes 1930). The very fact that some of these women caught the fancy of the public suggests that many a working-class woman was a potential adventuress who never made it out of her urban—or rural—captivity.

Christian Ross (1667-1739) served through many battles and was a trooper of the Scot's Greys, a 10-year seasoned soldier, before her sex was discovered. Because army life was the only life she wanted, after her discovery, she was allowed to stay on as army cook, and soldier Ross became known as "Mother Ross." How the fighter role was transformed into the nurturant role by a simple act of relabeling would make a fascinating sociological study. Mary Read and Anne Bonney had briefly successful careers as pirates, and their exploits from 1718 to 1720 were widely recounted.

Flora MacDonald is perhaps the most famous of the eighteenth-century adventuresses. She was the young Scotswoman who engineered the escape of Bonnie Prince Charlie to France after the rebellion of 1745. In the story of that escape, she moves like a lightning-quick, steely-strong superbrain through and around the laborious maneuvers of the ponderous Scots and English (MacGregor 1932). Imprisoned after the escape had been successfully carried out, she was released by popular demand and became even in her life a legend. Flora the real-life woman, however, married and bore many children, living a long hard life of poverty after her great adventure. No one thought to draw on her talents in the public sphere again or history might have been different.

Hannah Snell (1723-92) was an infantry fighter with English troops in India. Mary Anne Talbot (1778-1808) is one of the puzzles among fighting women. She lived a rough life as a sailor but always under the whip of an exploiting man. The best known of U.S. women fighters is Mollie Pitcher, who fought in the American Revolution. For all these women, the battlefield, whether on land or at sea, was for longer or shorter periods their home and their way of life. Like the women who emigrated to become pioneers, and the women who stayed behind to fight for life in the cities of Europe, they exhibited the basic toughness and resiliency that has been part of the survival equipment of women at the bottom of the social ladder in all periods of history.

Colonists

Most women colonists of North America had less exciting lives than the adventurers, but they too were living through rapid changes. During the eighteenth century, the small towns of North America became urban centers—Quebec, Boston, Philadelphia, New York. Commercial agriculture and urbanism developed together, and enterprising women in the colonies as in Europe participated in agricultural and commercial innovation. Eliza Lucas of South Carolina, for example, pioneered the indigo trade. As in Europe, village workshops hummed with the labor of women and children. Ryan notes that "a twelve-year-old girl devised a method of making straw braid for bonnets in 1798 and generated an industry that employed hundreds of women in her hometown of Dedham" (Ryan 1975: 103). The difference between European and colonist labor was that in the colonies working hours were shorter and standards of living higher in terms of food and environmental conditions.

For slave women, this was not so, and the eighteenth century witnessed a steady increase in the number of women slaves in both the northern and the southern colonies. The eighteenth century was also the century of the great slave writers and poets, however. It was not until the nineteenth century that it was forbidden to teach blacks to read and write. Phyllis Wheatley, brought to Boston as a slave from Africa at the age of 7, was taught to read and write by the invalid wife of her owner and became a widely read poet among New Englanders (Bontemps 1969: 44).

In Boston in this century, 10% of the merchants advertising locally were women, although many of these were widows carrying on their husbands' businesses. With the shift of emphasis away from subsistence farming, women began to limit family size, in some areas as early as 1700 (Ryan 1975: 121). Large families were not such an asset in a more commercial economy. The same trend was taking place in France and northern Europe.

A major event of the century for North America was the American Revolution, a war in which matrons of the Iroquois League played an important and little recognized part. Mary Brant, Mohawk head of a society of Six Nations matrons and widow of an important pro-British chief, was an important force in keeping the western tribes of the Six Nations allied with the British even though the league itself had decided to stay neutral. The minority of tribes that sided with the colonists were influenced by Englishwoman Jerusha Bingham Kirkland, considered a "mother" of the Oneida nation and leader among tribal women (De Pauw 1974: 17-18). Apparently, white women living with the Indians and accepted as "mothers" could intervene diplomatically, and one loyalist white widow thus prevented the Cayuga from making peace with the Continental Congress (De Pauw 1974: 27). A story of the American Revolution written from the point of view of the Iroquois matrons, and of the white sisters who functioned in their councils, would provide an interesting perspective on that war. With the defeat of the British, the Mohawks emigrated to Canada and the other nations moved farther West; "Iroquois matrons retreated with their tribes and never again influenced the mainstream of American history" (De Pauw 1974: 35).

A little-known fact is that white women became involved in revolutionary terrorist organizations in the period just prior to the revolution. "There were Daughters of Liberty just as there were Sons" (Riegel, quoted in Maine 1975: 15). "Once, when a group of loyalists disguised as Indians was arrested for robbing . . . and terrorizing the inhabitants, it was found that five of them were women, and three of those were a woman and her two daughters" (Evans, quoted in Maine 1975: 15).

In general, terrorists apart, white women were not listened to by their men, either in the councils of war or in the councils of peace. They performed typical underside roles in spite of Abigail Adams's warning to her Continental congressman husband John Adams: "If particular care and attention is not paid to the ladies, we are determined to instigate a rebellion, and will not hold ourselves bound by any laws in which we have no voice or representation" (quoted in Ryan 1975: 85). But after many wars of liberation in which women fought side by side with men, nothing changed for women after the American Revolution. "Neither the Declaration of Independence nor the Constitution of the United States elevated women to the status of political beings" (Ryan 1975: 85).[38]

The upheavals associated with the aftermath of the revolution brought many women to the Shakers, the Quaker-offshoot sect that, under the leadership of Ann Lee, traveled from England to America in 1774. Newly independent Americans flocked to this millennialist, celibate sect that preached the essential duality of God as mother and father as well as the equality of women. The communitarian organization of the Shaker church after 1788 offered attractive living conditions for proletarian women, and, after the great revival in Kentucky in 1799, large numbers of women and men became Shakers (Whitworth 1975: chap. 2). The conditions of life that made this and other communitarian sects of the next century attractive to women will be discussed in the next chapter. These movements sparked a continuing commitment to pioneering in the New World.

Women artists and scholars could not flourish easily in these wilderness and pioneer town settings, where hard physical labor was required for survival. For developments in the cultural sphere, we must turn to some of the more leisured settings in Europe.

Scholars and Artists

As in earlier periods, Italy continued to produce the outstanding women scholars and scientists of the century. Three extraordinary women were born within 18 years of each other in Bologna and Milan: Laura Bassi, physicist (1700-1778), Anna Manzolini, anatomist (1716-74); and Maria Agnesi, mathematician (1718-99). Bassi, professor of physics at Bologna, was already famous at 21. Her public disputations drew scholars from all over Europe and she was an active public figure in the academic world until her death. Bologna's favorite daughter, with a medal struck in her honor, she was also a very beautiful woman. It is a little surprising to learn that she also had 12 children, an unusually happy family life, was deeply religious, and wrote and published poetry. She did not publish very much in physics—her fame came from her teaching. Holding a professorship of anatomy at Bologna in the same years was Manzolini, noted both for her anatomical discoveries and for her creation of wax anatomical models that were copied and widely used around Europe after her time. Universities and courts all over the Continent tried to lure her away from Bologna, but she would not leave. She was probably aware that she lived in the most nurturant milieu in Europe for women scholars. Why leave it?

Maria Agnesi was a different case altogether. She started out like the others, only more brilliantly, if possible. She gave learned discourses in Latin to the city fathers of Milan at the age of 9 and could work in seven languages in her teens. The work that ensured her fame in mathematics, *Le Instituzioni Analitiche,* was begun when she was 20 and took her 10 years to complete. During that 10 years, her absorption in mathematical problems was total. She used to bound from her bed during the night while sound asleep and, like a somnambulist, make her way through a long suite of rooms to her study, where she wrote out the solution of the problem and then returned to her bed. The following morning, on returning to her desk, she found to her great surprise that while asleep she had fully solved the problem which had been the subject of her meditations during the day and of her dreams during the night. (Mozans 1913: 144-45)

The opus was an international scientific sensation when published. The French Academy of Science wrote congratulating her on the work (unfortunately, they could not elect her to their body because she was a woman). It was translated into French at once, into English somewhat later. She was immediately appointed to the chair of higher mathematics at Bologna. Bassi, Manzolini, and Agnesi would have made a remarkable trio there. But she did not accept the chair. Instead, to the amazement of her contemporaries and even more to the amazement of twentieth-century historians, she retired from the world and devoted the rest of her life to the care of the "poor, the sick and the helpless in her native city" (Mozans 1913: 148). It seems that she had written the *Instituzioni* "primarily for the benefit of one of her brothers who had a taste for mathematics." From the age of 30, when she finished the magnum opus, to the age of 80, when she died, she lived a retired life as a single woman in her own home (she did not become a nun), going out to care for the poor. From the moment of her retirement, she cut her ties completely with the scientific world and never attended a scholarly gathering again.

What was the meaning of that retirement? Catholic scholars have proposed that she be canonized as a saint, although this has never been done. Because she did not take religious vows, she cannot be typed into any "retirement-to-a-convent" pattern. She was in fact very active in social welfare work and directed a home for the aged poor for the last 15 years of her life. She never explained her own actions, and legend makers have had a field day. One possible interpretation that I have not seen proposed is that she found the life of the intellectual somewhat hollow. In her own time, with a breadth of social vision, a brilliant mind, and a deeply religious nature, what were her alternatives? No one today can know the full meaning of her choice, but she was as much of a deviant in her own time as she would be in ours. She is one of the few known examples in history of a woman who had the "world," as defined by men, at her disposal and simply said, "No thank you."

Agnesi had a host of sister-mathematicians in the 1700s and 1800s in Italy, including Diamante Medaglia, who wrote on the importance of

mathematical training for women as part of their mental development—a very revolutionary concept. In France, a woman chemist important in the historical record of her century is Madame Lavoisier. She
was not only a coworker with her chemist husband in his laboratory,
doing the drawings for his textbooks, and editing his memoirs on
chemistry after his death by guillotine, but she was also a painter,
trained by the classicist David. Another century passes before we hear
of another woman in chemistry in France. Emilie du Châtelet, mentioned in the section on salons as Voltaire's companion, was the mathematician who translated Newton's *Principia* into French. She herself
wrote *Institutions de Physique* and also a philosophical work, *Reflections
on Happiness*.[39] The salonières, who evidently hated the idea of a disciplined scholar in their midst, could not say enough nasty things about
her. Among her chief persecutors in the salon world were Mme de Staël
and Mme du Deffand.

Catherine Macaulay (1731-91) was the *first* major English historian to
bear the name Macaulay, although Thomas Macaulay of the next century
is usually thought of as "the" Macaulay. Her eight-volume *History of
England*, considered the best offering of the then new "radical school of
history," was written as a "history of the love of freedom." Catherine was
also a lady of high fashion and a salonière, achieving in England a kind of
recognition that du Châtelet in France neither could nor wanted to achieve.
She was a major public figure of her time and the center of a circle of the
most influential politicians of the day. Her 46th birthday was the nearest
thing to an Italian-style celebration of a woman ever carried out by the
skeptical English male, complete with parades and public jollity. Her
disciples and admirers all melted away, however, when at 47, having been
widowed for some years, she married a young man of 21. It was bad
enough that she married the young man. What was worse was that this
turned out to be a very happy marriage. Fond of America, and a great
supporter of the American Revolution, Catherine Macaulay and her new
young husband were great friends of George Washington—who was
evidently more broad-minded than her British friends.

We do not hear of English women scientists, but Jane Marcet, who
took as her task the popularizing of contemporary science for children,
began a tradition of rewriting science for the layperson, which won
great respect from scientists among her own contemporaries and had
many imitators in later periods.

In the world of art, as in the world of scholarship, Italy continued
in the lead in this century. Waters (1904) says there were no less than 40
good women artists in northern Italy in this period, whose works are
all to be found in known private collections. Rosalba Carriera of Venice

was among the best loved, most renowned, and prolific painters of the century. Two others who received a great deal of public recognition were Matilda Festa, professor in the Academy of St. Luke in Rome, and the princess of Parma, who was elected to the Academy of Vienna in 1789 (and married the archduke of Austria).

In France, there are many names of women artists but little is known about them. Elizabeth Vigée Le Brun is a notable exception. She was the salonière who invented the famous "Greek supper," bringing flair to the serving of small intimate suppers among the aristocracy of art in the salon world. It is an accident that she is more famous for her suppers than for her art, for she was a very popular artist in her day and a member of the French Academy. She painted in the style of Watteau, and her pictures were very much in demand.

In Germany, most women painters were associated with the court and painted for the royal families and for aristocracy. In addition to their work on large canvasses, they were miniaturists, makers of medals, and, increasingly, gem cutters. Susannah Dorsch became famous as a gem cutter. Angelica Kauffman was perhaps the most famous European painter of her time. Born in Switzerland, claimed by the Austrians as their own to the extent of their placing her image on their 100-schilling bank note, having lived and painted many years in both England and Italy, her work was everywhere in demand. During her residence in England, she and her fellow-painter Mary Moser actually became founding members of the British Royal Academy.

Many of the women we have noted were daughters of artists, trained in their fathers' workshops. Countless more women worked unrecognized in family workshops with fathers and brothers.

In music, the 1700s continued the development of the opera, and, in England, Italy, France, and Germany, women were composing operas as well as symphonies and ballets. Cécile-Louise Chaminade of France, Carlotta Ferrari of Italy, and Emilie Mayer of Germany were the outstanding women composers of the century. Given that women of the middle and upper classes were encouraged to cultivate musical skills as part of the "finishing process," women with talent could blossom in the domestic sphere with relative ease. Few were encouraged to work at music seriously, however.

Although the movement was so slight as to be scarcely noticeable, there seems to have been some tendency in this century for women in the rest of Europe who were scholastically or artistically gifted to join their Italian sisters in moving outside the family circle to exercise their gifts. Compared with Italy, the movement was slight indeed. It must be seen in the context of the conflicting pressures of (a) a gradual increase in educational opportunities for girls as well as boys; (b) the final phasing out of the old craft guilds, particularly the women's guilds; (c) a steady increase in the amount of urban housing available; and (d) the rise in importance of the home as a center for child rearing, living, and recreation. We will close this survey of the 1700s with an examination of family life in the century.

Family Life

In the eighteenth century, the household as *home base* steadily attained more importance. This new home base was different than the craft workshop of the Middle Ages,[40] and it was only available to the middle and upper classes. The working classes continued to have tiny houses and apartments in which they could do little but eat and sleep.[41] For the middle and upper classes, however, the disappearance of the custom of boarding apprentices and shop workers, already beginning in the sixteenth century, may have had some kind of effect on the privatization of family interaction. Because we know that household size did not change appreciably over these centuries (Laslett 1972), we must conclude that apprentices were replaced by domestic servants. Possibly domestics required less interaction with family members than apprentices did. The other change affecting the household was the decline in participation of middle- and upper-artisan-class women in the labor force, either in or out of the home. This gave women free time, the consequences of which were being noted in print by 1799: "This leisure, however, has one good effect, it makes the mothers better and more wholesome nurses, and induces them to keep themselves and children clean and tight, and contributes greatly to the healthy and good looks universally met with" (quoted in Pinchbeck 1930: 239).

Two parallel developments include an increase in the number of school places generally available to children all over Europe and the appearance of literature on "child development." De Mause (1974) notes a shift in attitudes regarding discipline by physical punishment in this century and the beginning of concepts of molding the child by nonphysical means. These developments meant a decrease in compulsory labor force activity for children and an increase, however slight, in the amount of autonomous space available to children in society.[42] This slight increase in autonomy was accompanied by an increase in the time mothers had for children in sectors above the working class. It could be argued that women of these classes were now in a position to do more in the mother role than perhaps had been done since the Roman matrons devoted themselves to the education of their children.

How important the differentiation of space in middle-class homes was to this development we cannot be sure. Mumford (1961: 383-84) makes a good deal of the differentiation of household space, as does Aries:

> Domesticity, privacy and isolation were born together: There were no longer beds all over the house. The beds were confined to the bedrooms, which were furnished on either side of the alcove with cupboards and nooks fitted out with new toilette and hygienic equipment. In France and Italy the word chambre began to be used in opposition to the word salle . . . the chambre denoted the room in which one slept, the salle the room in which one received visitors and ate. . . . in England . . . a prefix was added [to *room*] the dining room, the bedroom, etc. (1962: 399)

It is important to remember that this all applied to a very small sector of the urban population in any European country. For this sector, family life may have developed as a new art of living privately. Certainly this was the period when calling cards and the institution of receiving hours were invented. Family conversation and family letter writing became an art. If there was in fact a change in the character of family life in the eighteenth century, it was toward an affluence-generated "liberation" for non-task-oriented familial interaction. Thus, when it is noted that health and the weather had become major topics of family conversation and correspondence, what is really being noted is that more families had time to talk about the weather, a phenomenon closely tied to individual health and well-being.

As standards of housing improved, even better-off workers' families could afford a separation of sleeping and living quarters, and the family living room became an increasingly general institution. There was development of the arts of indoor recreation and parlor games and of reading aloud. The family became a *play* group, not just a subsistence enterprise.[43] Quakers are a notable example of this. Clarkson, a contemporary chronicler of Quaker ways, was particularly enthusiastic about their "domestic bliss":

> In consequence of denying themselves the pleasures of the world [they] have been obliged to cherish those which are found in domestic life. . . . The husband and wife are not . . . easily separable. They visit generally together. They are remarked as affectionate. . . . They are long in each others society at a time, and they are more at home than almost any other people. (1806: 257-58)

The delights of family life were all very well for Quaker women, who had other spheres of action too. For other women, the domestic

delights were all there was. One could argue that, in general, outside
the dissenting sects, the rise of domesticity meant a decline in status
and opportunities for women. The focus on the child and the home
resulted in progressively more restrictive legislation concerning the
right of the woman to make decisions concerning children and property
and produced a peculiar inversion of de facto and de jure responsibility.
As suggested earlier, it may well be that very few women *felt* themselves deprived. They probably felt that the leisure for domesticity and
social life represented a far better way of life than had the earlier
pressure of work roles. Women's rights were far more an issue for the
genteelly poor, the widowed, and the unmarried mothers as well as for
the philanthropists who saw the relationship between these women's
economic plight and their secondary social status.

It is important to remember what crowded spaces most women with
families lived in to realize that the "pleasures of domesticity" were a
scarce commodity in most households. Whether the household aver-
aged five, as in Europe, or six to eight, as in colonial North America,
where fewer children died at birth, most families had to carry out
daytime activities within one room. Demos (1972), reviewing family life
in colonial America, asks how these cramped households avoided
quarreling all the time. The answer is that they did not. Family and
neighborhood quarrelsomeness is ancient, as court records of antiquity
show. Certainly in North America, there was a high degree of conten-
tiousness. Demos points out: "The men and women of these communities went to court again and again, to do battle over land titles, property
losses, wayward cattle, rundown fences, unringed pigs—not to mention slander, and witchcraft, and assault and battery" (1972: 563). The
reference to witchcraft is particularly illuminating. While witchcraft
accusations may have started as primarily political maneuvers for
power, by the 1600s, many accusations of witchcraft were from women
against their own neighbors. I have no frequency counts on this, but
many of the accounts in Ashton's *The Devil in Britain and America* (1972)
are of such neighbor-to-neighbor accusations. The Salem witchcraft
madness of 1692 was initiated by a group of hysterical teenagers acting
out the grudges and hostilities against neighbors prevalent in their own
families or in the families where they were servants (Ryan 1975: 78-79).
By the 1700s, these accusations became so totally absurd that no one
believed them any more, but they kept on being made right through the
eighteenth century.[44]

What triggered the accusations? Unneighborly behavior, such as
failing to lend a bit of yeast, figured in more than one story. Social
historians often describe the contentment and security of a society in

which the women reign as queens over the domestic hearth. As far as I know, no one has investigated the possible relationship between community quarrelsomeness and the extent to which women are confined to this domestic queenship.

This is not to suggest that quarrelsomeness is particularly a feminine trait. I do not know the proportion of male- and female-initiated suits against neighbors to be found in court records over time, but the chances are that men are better represented in such suits than women. Morgan (in Samuel 1975: 36-37) notes the high level of quarrelsomeness in the English countryside in the eighteenth century, especially under the pressures of harvest time. Both sexes reflected the constraints of confined spaces and a heavy work load. When women became more confined than men were, as seemed to be happening in this century, then we might expect them to feel the consequences of that confinement more keenly, but only to the extent that confinement is felt as deprivation.

If frustration is one accompaniment of a rise in domesticity for women, a rise in the level of unused skill reservoirs is another. The general increase in schooling for women in this century, paralleling the decline in women's labor force participation, left a lot of untapped competence and free time in the social pool. It was this accumulation of competence and free energy that helped produce the explosion of civic activity on the part of women in the next century.

We have seen women moving through three and a half centuries of eventful developments that have left the status of women less changed than we might have expected. The effect of the developments leading up to the industrial revolution has been to widen the gap between the condition of rich and poor women, even while creating a general rise in societal levels of affluence. Increased leisure and education for the well-to-do have been accompanied by longer working hours for the laboring women. The increase in life expectancy for urban women tells us that rural life was even harder and, at the same time, masks the suffering of urban widows, unpartnered mothers, and children. Children of the poor had an especially hard lot, with no choice except to be in the labor force from the age of 3 or 4 on or being picked up as vagrants and shipped overseas as labor for the colonies.

The picture is not all dark, for we have seen utopian religious movements coming out of the proletariat. Utopian communities, as such, rarely promoted redefinition of women's roles, only a lessening of their labor. The Anabaptist tradition, however, seems to have freed women for greater participation in the larger society. Among middle- and upper-class women, there was increasing awareness of the meanings of inequality and social injustice, both for the poor and for themselves, although not always where one would expect to find it. Little such awareness was to be found among the women of the French salons. On the other hand, awareness takes many forms, and women's increased productivity as intellectuals, as artists, writers, religious leaders, and social activists could be seen as manifestations of that awareness. So could the activities of women colonists and adventurers. We have all but seen the last of the great queens and witnessed the first of the "modern" revolutionaries. In Part II, we shall see the closing in grand style of the scenario of the queens and the ascendance of new types of women shaping new scenarios for the twentieth century.

Notes

1. A number of "peace queens" have been described in previous chapters, but they were consorts, not regnant queens, and sometimes, for brief periods, regents. As far as I know, no major regnant queen in history has pursued an active no-war policy, although some minor ones have, as we shall see in this chapter. The politics of dominance as exercised over the last 4,000 years does not readily produce peacemakers at the ruling level.

2. As, for example, in *The Rise of the West* (McNeill 1963: 579-80). See the *Queens of Old Spain* (Hume 1906) for the view of Isabel given here.

3. An important and usually ignored aspect of the Renaissance was a new cultural emphasis on women-to-women relationships; see Lillian Faderman (1981).

4. Discussions of Renaissance women rarely include mention of such traits as business acumen, but Chojnacki (1974: 176-203) makes it clear that they also had a sharp eye for profit and managed considerable business enterprises independently of the men of their families. Other interesting information about women of this era and later who thought for themselves may be found in Labalme (1980).

5. Fontana had a portrait medal cast in her honor. In addition to having produced 135 documented works, she also had 11 babies (Tufts 1974: 31-34).

6. The information on Spain comes from Cannon (1916).

7. It is very probable that literate women of the middle class opened up their homes for schools for the "displaced girls" of that class, a practice common in Europe for several centuries and referred to in the discussion of Angela Merici later in this chapter.

8. Information on Protestant women, unless otherwise indicated, comes from Bainton (1973).

9. Mary Ward was born in York just the year before St. Margaret Clitherow was martyred, in 1585. She grew up knowing intimately the story of St. Margaret, and in a way the martyred Catholic homemaker was the founder of the Institutes of Mary. The nuns of the order have a very special tradition of veneration for St. Margaret that continues to this day (Dessain 1971: 109-10).

10. Sister Monica's biography of St. Angela (1945: 337-38) cites instances of this voluntary establishment of schools by the women of a town in France, Italy, and Geneva for Angela's own time, and one reference dates back to the thirteenth century.

11. *The Interior Castle* is a major classic of spiritual growth. The three-volume compilation of her complete works (St. Teresa of Avila 1958) is continuously kept in print. Also see Elizabeth Hamilton's *The Great Teresa* (1963) for an interesting biography.

12. The records all refer to mothers, not fathers, beating their daughters. Leigh Minturn (University of Colorado, Boulder, Department of Psychology, personal communication, 1975), on the basis of cross-cultural psychological studies of women's roles, suggests that fathers would never beat daughters; that was the mother's job.

13. The pressure on mothers to get rid of daughters also existed in the Middle Ages at the height of convent life, and many daughters were beaten half to death by mothers who were trying to force them into convents against their will. There are interesting records of lawsuits of nuns who claim having been forced by parents to take vows (O'Faolain and Martines 1973: 270-75).

14. Maher, examining Moroccan society for evidences of the extended-family household, comes to the same conclusion (1974: 70-71).

15. For further discussion of the problems of women as wives and mothers in this period, see chapter 4 of Laslett (1965).

16. While the term *bluestocking* was used only in England, the phenomenon is generally identifiable on the Continent.

17. This section is based on chapter 7 of Georgiana Hill, *Women in English Life* (1896).

18. Lady Halkett in her *Autobiography* (edited by Nichols [1875] 1965) gives a poignant account of maternal cruelty in describing her youth at home. She was so severely treated by her mother that in desperation she got an uncle to intervene on her behalf. There is no suggestion that Anne was crushed by maternal cruelty—rather, she accepted it as part of the conditions of her life.

19. Laslett (1965: 62) points out the special characteristics of these villages but makes no connection with the dissenting sects. It may be worth exploring.

20. I attended one of the last of these separate but concurrent women's/men's meetings at an American Yearly Meeting of the Society of Friends in rural Ohio, in 1942, the practice having died out almost everywhere else in Quakerdom before then. I can testify to the impact even in my own youth of seeing women clerks presiding over Meeting for Business and being consulted by the men through the little door set in the partition between the two meetings in the big, old meetinghouse. There has been discussion among Quakers about whether the separate meetings really fostered the participation of women or whether they were another way of keeping women out of significant decision making. The dignity and self-assurance that I saw in the rural Ohio women in 1942 suggests that it was not a way of excluding women.

21. Among Friends, the term *Quaker* is used interchangeably with the official label, *Society of Friends*.

22. Governor Peter Stuyvesant used a woman as his interpreter in making the original treaty with the Six Nations in the middle of the century (De Pauw 1974: 5).

23. The story of the Spanish women is included, much too briefly, in the "Two-Thirds World" overview in Chapter 4 of this volume.

24. In 1619, 100 vagrant London children were shipped to the colonists of Virginia and a second lot followed the next year. This form of cheap labor became so popular that, by 1627, 1,400 or 1,500 children of both sexes had been sent out (Pinchbeck and Hewitt 1969: 105-7).

25. In addition to Ryan's *Womanhood in America* (1975), there are a number of studies of the varieties of roles performed by women in colonial America that are referred to in the excellent "Women in American Society" by Ann Gordon, Mari Jo Buhle, and Nancy Schrom (1971).

26. The story of the day the widow took leave of her husband's family and her 14-year-old son to enter the religious life is a famous one. Her son, who did not want her to go, threw himself across the threshold and cried out: "I'm not strong enough to hold you back, but at least it shall be said that you trampled your own child underfoot!" (quoted in Stopp 1962: 110). The story has been quoted often, sometimes in condemnation of her callousness, sometimes in support of her fortitude.

27. Most of my material is drawn from the study by a Swedish scholar, Sven Stolpe (1966), who used new documentation not available to previous writers. See also the biography by Georgina Masson (1968).

28. Examples are the tragedians Elizabeth Barry and Rebecca Marshall, the comedienne Elinor Leigh, and the irrepressible Nell Gwynn.

29. The whole issue of women alchemists needs careful study, given that so many different types of roles intersected with the alchemical one. Some women alchemists were primarily prechemists, as suggested in the text. Others were herbalists and healers; some were students of philosophy and religion; and some were practicing ancient druidic and Greco-Egyptian mystery cults, which had enjoyed a "revival" in the fifteenth century. All ran some danger of being accused of witchcraft.

30. Mary Astell, at least, did not let the good queen down. She writes of "that Great Queen who has subdu'd the Proud, and made the pretended Invincible more than once fly before her; who has rescu'd an Empire, Reduc'd a Kingdom, Conquered Provinces in as little time almost as one can Travel them, and seems to have Chain'd Victory to her Standard" (Smith 1916: 246). Furthermore, a historian colleague points out that the last few months of Anne's life, when she was obviously dying, were perhaps the most politically suspenseful in English history. When she died, a coup by the Jacobites (Catholics) was just barely avoided (Susan Armitage, University of Colorado, Boulder, Department of History, personal communication, 1975).

31. In short, in Queen Anne's reign, women held the same franchise as men, could vote, and did.

32. Historians disagree as to whether she was personally responsible for his death.

33. S. G. Tallentyre calls the salons "forcing-houses of the revolution, the nursery of the Encyclopedia, the antechamber of the Academie" (1926: 1). I would not give them that much credit, but I could be wrong.

34. Condorcet is the author of the essay "The Admission of Women to Civic Rights" (Reich 1908), which has never received the attention that John Stuart Mill's *Essays on Women* has received.

35. To what extent the women of the Camisard movement—a band of male and female prophets who arose during a proletarian-triggered guerrilla war in the Cevennes region between 1702 and 1705—were still active and supplying leadership for the women of Paris I do not know, but this seems to me a possibility that should be investigated.

36. Corday has been accused of founding the "religion of the poignard," but men have functioned for a long time as political assassins with and without the help of women.

37. Goethe's *The Sorrows of the Young Werther* became a kind of theme song for this group. Read Tornius's (1929) "Sensibility" to get the flavor of this circle.

38. Women had sporadic voting rights in the colonies until a few years after the Revolution, when the right of franchise was specifically denied (De Pauw 1974: 36).

39. For more about women scientists in this fertile era, see Margaret Alic (1986).

40. In fact, by 1800, the last of the guilds were gone. Shorter (1973) makes a strong case in *Work and Community in the West* for the relationship between the decline of the guilds and the privatization of the family.

41. In Italy, the poor lived under bridges, on old boats, and in holes in the ground. In winter, the men sold themselves as galley slaves for the season (Braudel 1973: 205).

42. Pinchbeck and Hewitt (1973) make a strong case for the school as a setting that fostered autonomy and personhood for children in this century. I believe they overstate the case, but nevertheless school was an improvement over existing conditions for the child.

43. The playing of games is an ancient occupation; no civilization has been without evidence of children's and adult's games. Rabelais's *Gargantua*, published in 1542, included a list of 217 parlor, table, and open-air games that his young hero played after

dinner. As far as I can tell, however, these games were not played in family groups of adults and children until the eighteenth century (Bakhtin 1968).

44. The year 1727 was the last year for the hanging of a woman for witchcraft in England. From then on, the judges either dismissed cases or went to some trouble to disprove the charges.

References

Alic, Margaret. 1986. *Hypatia's Heritage: A History of Women in Science from Antiquity Through the Nineteenth Century.* Boston: Beacon.

Aries, Philippe. 1962. *Centuries of Childhood: A Social History of Family Life*, translated by Robert Baldick. New York: Knopf.

Armytage, W. H. G. 1961. *Heavens Below: Utopian Experiments in England 1560-1960.* London: Routledge & Kegan Paul.

Ashton, John. 1972. *The Devil in Britain and America.* Hollywood, CA: Newcastle.

Bainton, Roland H. 1973. *Women of the Reformation in France and England.* Minneapolis, MN: Augsburg.

Baird, Charles W. 1885. *History of the Huguenot Emigration to America.* Vol. 2. New York: Dodd Mead.

Bakhtin, Mikhail. 1968. "The Role of Games in Rabelais." Pp. 124-32 in *Game, Play, Literature*, edited by Jacques Ehrmann. Boston: Beacon.

Beard, Mary R. 1946. *Woman as Force in History: A Study in Traditions and Realities.* New York: Macmillan.

Bontemps, Arna, ed. 1969. *Great Slave Narratives.* Boston: Beacon.

Brailsford, H. N. 1913. *Shelley, Godwin, and Their Circle.* New York: Holt.

Braudel, Fernand. 1973. *Capitalism and Material Life: 1400-1800*, translated by Mirian Kochan. New York: Harper & Row.

Burckhardt, Jacob. 1944. *Civilization of the Renaissance in Italy.* Gloucester, MA: Peter Smith.

Cannon, Mary Agnes. 1916. *The Education of Women During the Renaissance.* Washington, DC: Catholic Education Press.

Chojnacki, Stanley. 1974. "Patrician Women in Early Renaissance Venice." *Studies in the Renaissance* 21:176-203.

Clark, Alice. 1919. *Working Life of Women in the Seventeenth Century.* London: Routledge.

Clarkson, Thomas. 1806. *A Portraiture of Quakerism.* 3 vols. New York: Samuel Stansbury.

Daniel-Rops, Henry. 1962. *The Catholic Reformation*, translated by John Warrington. London: J. M. Dent.

de Mause, Lloyd. 1974. "The Evolution of Childhood." Pp. 1-74 in *The History of Childhood*, edited by Lloyd de Mause. New York: Psychohistory Press.

Demos, John. 1972. "Demography and Psychology in the Historical Studies of Family Life." Pp. 561-70 in *Household and Family in Past Time*, edited by Peter Laslett. Cambridge: Cambridge University Press.

De Pauw, Linda Grant. 1974. *Four Traditions: Women of New York During the American Revolution.* Albany: New York State American Revolution Bicentennial Commission.

Dessain, Mary Joanna. 1971. *St. Margaret Clitherow.* Slough, England: St. Paul.

Dukes, Paul. 1967. *Catherine the Great and the Russian Nobility.* London: Cambridge University Press.

Etienne, Mona and Eleanor Leacock, eds. 1980. *Women and Colonization: Anthropological Perspectives.* New York: Praeger Scientific.

Evennett, H. Outram. 1968. *The Spirit of the Counterreformation*, edited by John Bossy. London: Cambridge University Press.

Faderman, Lillian. 1981. *Surpassing the Love of Men: Romantic Friendship and Love Between Women from the Renaissance to the Present*. New York: Morrow.

Flexner, Eleanor. 1972. *Mary Wollstonecraft: A Biography*. New York: Coward, McCann, and Goeghegan.

Fox, George. 1937. *A Day-Book of Counsel and Comfort from the Epistles of George Fox*, compiled by L. V. Hodgkin. London: Macmillan.

Gordon, Ann D., Mari Jo Buhle, and Nancy E. Schrom. 1971. "Women in American Society: An Historical Contribution." *Radical America* 5:3-74.

Griffiths, Naomi. 1973. *The Acadians: Creation of a People*. Toronto: McGraw-Hill-Ryerson.

Hallowell, A. Irving. 1972. "American Indians, White and Black: The Phenomenon of Transculturalization." Pp. 200-224 in *Native Americans Today: Sociological Perspectives*, edited by Howard Bahr, Bruce Chadwick, and Robert Day. New York: Harper & Row.

Hamilton, Elizabeth. 1963. *The Great Teresa*. London: Burns and Oates.

Hargreanes, Reginald. 1930. *Women-at-Arms: Their Famous Exploits Throughout the Ages*. London: Hutchinson.

Hill, Georgiana. 1894. *Women in English Life*. Vol. 1. London: Richard Bentley.

————. 1896. *Women in English Life*. Vol. 2. London: Richard Bentley.

Hilpisch, Stephanus. 1958. *History of Benedictine Nuns*, translated by Sr. M. Joanne Muffli. Collegeville, MN: St. John's Abbey.

Holloway, Mark. [1880] 1966. *Heavens on Earth: Utopian Communities in America 1680-1880*. Rev. ed. New York: Dover.

Hume, Martin A. S. 1898. *The Courtship of Queen Elizabeth*. London: Unwin.

————. 1906. *Queens of Old Spain*. New York: McClure Phillips.

Irwin, Joyce L. 1979. *Womanhood in Radical Protestantism 1525-1675*. New York: Edwin Mellen.

Kavanagh, Julia. 1893. *Women in France During the Eighteenth Century*. 2 vols. New York: Putnam.

Kraditor, Aileen S., ed. 1968. *Up from the Pedestal*. Chicago: Quadrangle.

Labalme, Patricia H. 1980. *Beyond Their Sex: Learned Women of the European Past*. New York: New York University Press.

Laslett, Peter. 1965. *The World We Have Lost*. London: Methuen.

Laslett, Peter, ed. 1972. *Household and Family in Past Time*. Cambridge: Cambridge University Press.

Levy, Darline Gay, Harriet Branson Applewhite, and Mary Durham Johnson. 1979. *Women in Revolutionary Paris, 1789-1795: Selected Documents Translated with Notes and Commentary*. Urbana: University of Illinois Press.

Longworth, Philip. 1973. *The Three Empresses: Catherine I, Anne, and Elizabeth of Russia*. New York: Holt, Rinehart & Winston.

Luder, Hope Elizabeth. 1973. *Women and Quakerism*. Pendle Hill Pamphlet 196. Wallingford, PA: Pendle Hill.

Luke, Mary. 1973. *Gloriana: The Years of Elizabeth I*. New York: Coward, McCann and Geoghegan.

MacGregor, Alexander. 1932. *The Life of Flora MacDonald; also, Flora MacDonald in Uist, by William Jolly*. Stirling, England: E. MacKay.

Maher, Vanessa. 1974. *Women and Property in Morocco: Their Changing Relation to the Process of Social Stratification in the Middle Atlas*. London: Cambridge University Press.

Maine, Mary E. 1975. "Women's Political Roles in Colonial America." Unpublished student paper, University of Colorado, Boulder, Department of Sociology.

Masson, Georgina. 1968. *Queen Christina*. New York: Farrar, Straus and Giroux.

McNeill, William H. 1963. *The Rise of the West: A History of the Human Community*. Chicago: University of Chicago Press.

Melancon, Diane. 1975. "A Queen as a Role Model: Elizabeth I of England." Unpublished student paper, University of Colorado, Boulder, Department of Sociology.

Michelet, Jules. [1885] 1960. *Les Femmes de la Révolution.* Paris: Hachette.

Monica, Sister. 1945. *Angela Merici and Her Teaching Idea: 1474-1540.* Saint Martin, OH: Ursulines of Brown County.

Montaigne, Michel de. 1960. *Essais.* Introduction by Henri Benac. Paris: Hachette.

Morris, E. J. 1974. *History of Urban Form: Prehistory to the Renaissance.* New York: John Wiley.

Mozans, R. J. 1913. *Woman in Science.* New York: Appleton.

Mumford, Lewis. 1961. *City in History: Its Origins, Its Transformations, and Its Prospects.* New York: Harcourt Brace Jovanovich.

Nichols, John Gough, ed. [1875] 1965. *The Autobiography of Anne Lady Halkett.* New York: Johnson Reprint Corporation.

O'Faolain, Julia and Lauro Martines, ed. 1973. *Not in God's Image: A History of Women in Europe from the Greeks to the Nineteenth Century.* New York: Harper & Row.

Pinchbeck, Ivy. 1930. *Women Workers and the Industrial Revolution: 1750-1850.* London: Frank Cass.

Pinchbeck, Ivy and Margaret Hewitt. 1969. *Children in English Society. Vol. 1. From Tudor Times to the Eighteenth Century.* London: Routledge & Kegan Paul.

————. 1973. *Children in English Society. Vol. 2. From the Eighteenth Century to the Children Act 1948.* London: Routledge & Kegan Paul.

Raeff, Marc, ed. 1972. *Catherine the Great: A Profile.* New York: Hill and Wang.

Reich, Emil. 1908. *Woman Through the Ages.* 2 vols. London: Methuen.

Rogers, Katharine. 1982. *Feminism in Eighteenth-Century England.* Urbana: University of Illinois Press.

Rowbotham, Sheila. 1972. *Women, Resistance, and Revolution: A History of Women and Revolution in the Modern World.* New York: Pantheon.

Rudé, George. 1964. *The Crowd in History, 1730-1884.* New York: John Wiley.

Rusche, Georg and Otto Kirchheimer. [1939] 1968. *Punishment and Social Structure.* New York: Russell and Russell.

Ryan, Mary P. 1975. *Womanhood in America: From Colonial Times to the Present.* New York: New Viewpoints.

Samuel, Raphael. 1975. *Village Life and Labor.* London: Routledge & Kegan Paul.

Schiff, Mario. 1910. *Marie de Gournay: La Fille D'Alliance de Montaigne.* Paris: Libraire Honore Champion.

Scott, Anne Firor, ed. 1971. *The American Woman: Who Was She?* Englewood Cliffs, NJ: Prentice-Hall.

Shorter, Edward, ed. 1973. *Work and Community in the West.* New York: Harper & Row.

Smith, Florence. 1916. *Mary Astell: 1666-1739.* New York: Columbia University Press.

Sokolnikova, Galina Osipovna. [1932] 1969. *Nine Women: Drawn from the Epoch of the French Revolution,* translated by H. C. Stevens. Freeport, NY: Books for Libraries Press.

Stenton, Doris Mary. 1957. *The English Woman in History.* London: Allen and Unwin.

Stolpe, Sven. 1966. *Christina of Sweden,* edited by Sir Alec Randall; translated by Sir Alec Randall and Ruth Mary Bethell. New York: Macmillan.

Stopp, Elisabeth. 1962. *Madame de Chantal: Portrait of a Saint.* London: Faber and Faber.

Tallentyre, S. G. (Evelyn Hall). 1926. *The Women of the Salons.* New York: Putnam.

Teresa of Avila, St. 1958. *The Interior Castle, or the Mansions,* edited by H. Martin. Naperville, IL: Allenson.

Tilly, Louise and Joan W. Scott. 1978. *Women, Work, and Family.* New York: Holt, Rinehart & Winston.

Tomalin, Claire. 1974. *The Life and Death of Mary Wollstonecraft.* New York: Harcourt Brace Jovanovich.

Tornius, Valerian. 1929. *Salons: Pictures of Society Through Five Centuries,* translated by Agnes Platt and Lilian Wonderley. New York: Cosmopolitan.

Travitsky, Betty, ed. 1981. *The Paradise of Women: Writings by Englishwomen of the Renaissance*. New York: Columbia University Press.
Tufts, Eleanor. 1974. *Our Hidden Heritage: Five Centuries of Women Artists*. New York: Paddington.
Ward, A. C., ed. 1927. *A Miscellany of Tracts and Pamphlets*. London: Oxford University Press.
Waters, Clara (Erskine) Clement. 1904. *Women in the Fine Arts*. Boston: Houghton Mifflin.
Webb, Maria. 1867. *The Fells of Swarthmoor Hall and Their Friends*. London: F. Kitto.
Whitworth, John McKelvie. 1975. *God's Blueprints: A Sociological Study of Three Utopian Sects*. London: Routledge & Kegan Paul.
Wilson, John Harold. 1958. *All the King's Ladies: Actresses of the Restoration*. Chicago: University of Chicago Press.

The pictures on the following pages show women in many and varied underlife spaces. On pages 175-177 we find them as workers in field and factory; on page 178, as writers and artists; on page 179 as scientists. On page 180 and 181, we see women warriors and revolutionaries from antiquity to the present. The last pictures, on page 182, show women in one of their rare overlife spaces; here are some of the great queens of recent centuries.

Women Typesetters

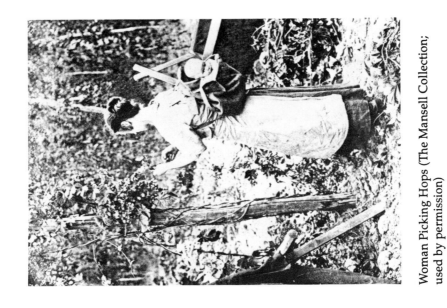

Woman Picking Hops (The Mansell Collection; used by permission)

Women Harvesters in Norfolk (Colman & Rye Libraries of Local History, Norfolk County Library; used by permission)

Max Liebermann, *Flax Barn in Laren* (Berlin National Gallery)

George Sand (International Museum of Photography, Rochester, New York; used by permission)

Rosa Bonheur (Museeé du Louvre; used by permission)

Edmonia Lewis (Southern Methodist University, Fine Arts Division; used by permission)

Harriet Martineau (National Portrait Gallery, London; used by permission)

Witch of Agnesi (MIT Press; used by permission)

Beatrice Webb (A. Watkins, Inc., New York; used by permission)

Sonja Cowin-Kovalesky (MIT Press; used by permission)

Madame Curie (Historical Picture Service)

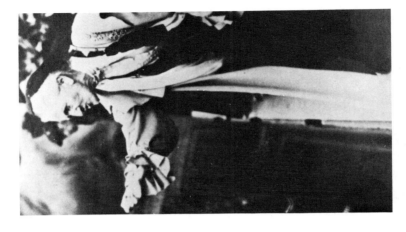

Charlotte Despard (The Press Association Limited, London; used by permission)

Tania (Babylon Brigade, Inc., New York; used by permission)

Deborah

Dahoman Woman Warrior (From *A Mission to Gelele, King of Dahome*, by Richard Burton, Routledge & Kegan Paul; used by permission)

Vietnamese Woman Learning to Shoot (Josef Breitenbach photographer, Thomas Y. Crowell, Inc.; used by permission)

Goya, *What Courage* (The Hispanic Society of America; used by permission)

Isabella

Elizabeth I (by kind permission of
Lord Brooke, Warwick Castle)

Catherine II

Victoria

The Transition Centuries: The 1800s and 1900s

Introduction

We move to the century of the last strong ruling woman monarch, Victoria. Much of the traditional monarchic power is gone. The salons are gone. The power the great landed families and their women had in the affairs of state is gone. By 1800, the state has passed "to the control of parliament composed of men and elected by men" (Beard 1946: 317).

Because most of this introduction will be dealing with social change triggered by new types of social movements, perhaps we should begin by discussing the changes triggered by the last major exercise of traditional monarchic power. When Queen Victoria ascended the throne at the age of 18 in 1837, she had outlived a weak father and entered public life in an atmosphere characterized by the immoralities of her "four wicked uncles." "I will be good," she is supposed to have said when she took the throne. And she was. Although the political significance of royal alliance structures had declined substantially, Queen Victoria created a set of interlocking alliances with almost every royal house in Europe through the judicious marrying off of each of her nine children. She was the matriarch of Europe, every king's mother-in-law, and it has been said that, had she still been alive, World War I would never have happened. She would simply have told Kaiser Wilhelm, one of her sons-in-law, to stop misbehaving.

Victoria extended the empire on other continents but kept peace in Europe—give or take a few revolutions over which she had no control. She also maintained an anti-slave trade patrol on the high seas, which eventually brought that practice to a halt, although not before another 2 million slaves had been shipped to the Americas. She kept track of kings and political leaders everywhere through a voluminous correspondence. A strong-minded queen, she made many decisions herself and never let go of the reins even during the years she lived in widow's retirement after the death of her husband, Prince Consort Albert. She happened to choose a husband whose thoughts were in tune with an age yet to come. In designing the first world's fair, the London Exposition of 1851, Prince Albert inaugurated the postcolonial age of internationalism. One might say that Victoria, who became empress of India in 1876, presided over the era of imperial nationalism while Albert opened the door to the successor era of internationalism.

Because she lived for so long, having reigned for 63 years when she died, people tended to remember the sorrowing widow and forget the lively, fun-loving young queen. While her reputation for driving vice underground in England was well deserved, she was far from gloomy. She was gay and determined. What brought her out of her retirement after Albert's death was a love affair (quite probably platonic) with her highland ghillie John Brown, who appears in her delightful book *Life in the Highlands*. This gave her renewed zest for life and made her decide to take the crown of India. She was the despair of the women of her century, being one of those strong-minded women who could not let anyone else be strong. Her contribution to the suffrage movement at the time that the women's suffrage bill was before parliament in 1870 was the word that

> the Queen is most anxious to enlist everyone who can speak or write to join in checking this mad, wicked folly of "Woman's Rights" with all its attendant horrors, on which her poor feeble sex is bent, forgetting every sense of womanly feeling and propriety. Lady Amberley [an advocate] ought to get a *good whipping*. (Langford 1964: 208)

The fact that women were remarkably active (and remarkably un-Victorian, like Victoria herself) all through the Victorian age is evidence that women learned to model themselves on her deeds rather than on her words. It is also evidence that they were clever, because none of the new scripts had parts written for women. The new nationalism was not a salon game but serious business, carried on by men (Queen Victoria always excepted). Although women contributed energy and personpower for the revolutions of 1848 in Germany, Austria, and Italy, this created no places for them in the new parliaments. Women helped liberate the Latin American colonies beginning with Paraguay and Venezuela in

1811, ending with Brazil and Central America in 1822-25, but there was no place for them in these parliaments either.

Was there to be any place for women in the overlife of this new world, or were they to remain forever in the underlife, building necessary support structures for men to manipulate and destroy? There is a certain urgency to asking this question at the beginning of the nineteenth century, with so many possibilities coming together for humankind. This is the century in which the modern transport and communication systems developed, with the telegraph, the universal postal union, and the fast steamship making it possible to move about rapidly and make decisions in consultation with on-the-spot "experts" anywhere on the globe. A new international system was emerging, even while the nation-state system was still in the making. Where would women fit?

The implications of the trends that began in the nineteenth century have yet to be worked out in the closing years of the twentieth century. In the nineteenth century, alliance structures were formed between aware groups of women and the men who shared their social perceptions on behalf of common social goals. We will examine these alliance structures, their goals and their possibilities. One major alliance structure was that of middle- and upper-class women with the liberals among industrialists and political leaders. This alliance was to create a new set of welfare institutions to deal with the social problems generated by increasing urbanism and industrialization. In 1801, 26% of the population of England lived in cities of 5,000 or more (21% in cities of 10,000 or more). By 1861, 55% of the total population of England lived in urban areas, and, by 1891, 72% were living in urban districts (Cook 1951: 115). The employment situation was serious, particularly for proletarian women. Insufficient earnings increasingly had to be supplemented by prostitution.

In the mid-1800s, it is estimated that there were between 20,000 and 80,000 prostitutes in major cities like London and Paris. The practice of police registration of prostitutes makes it possible for us to see that many women preferred other means of employment when available. In Paris, women were struck from the records when they could demonstrate that they had other employment, and, between 1817 and 1827, 1,680 women had their names thus removed. Notations about the employment they entered ranged from laundress to shoemaker to a music mistress in a boarding school (O'Faolain and Martines 1973: 301). Middle-class prostitutes, at the professional courtesan level, had a very different situation. They lived well and were not entered on police rolls. But the poor lived constantly under the double threat of hunger and police regulation, and so did their children. Increasingly, alcohol, the anodyne of poverty, heightened violence levels on the streets and in the homes of the poor.

The tradition out of which middle- and upper-class women allied themselves with men in power to alleviate these problems is that of the aristocracy and of the manor house lady. The women who looked to those traditions, however, were many of them middle-class women who in an earlier generation would have been shopkeepers and skilled workers of various kinds. They shared with their upper-class sisters increased education, exposure to new ideas, and a general restlessness about the limitations of their lives. In a way, these women were again facing the situation women faced in the Renaissance. There were new discoveries about the nature of "man" from which they were excluded. The political theories of the seventeenth century led to a conception of the state as an organization of individual men or groups of men rather than as a commonwealth of families. This led to an emphasis on individual thinking and action. "*None* of the associations which were formed during this period for public purposes, either educational, economic, scientific, or political, include women in their membership," however (Hill 1896: 286). Theories of social evolution referred to men only.

This time, however, women did not accept exclusion. More of them were reading, more of them were traveling, observing, thinking, writing, more of them were going off to pioneer in new lands. Would there finally be a reversal of the situation that had obtained in the first agricultural villages after 12,000 B.C.E. when women lost out for failing to see the larger scene? In the 1800s, men of affairs were overburdened with the tasks of industrialization. More and more, it was middle- and upper-class women who were realizing the larger picture. They were developing new approaches to the problems of urban poverty. For the first time, middle-class women were in a position to make the kinds of judgments possible earlier only for royal women, and this produced tensions. On the one hand, the women were developing their analytic capacities and developing confidence in their own abilities as they got reality feedback from their efforts. On the other hand, they were repeatedly confronted with absurdities: the absurdity of the conventional limitations on their role, the absurdity that men controlled the resources women needed to do their work, and the absurdity that these same men held a definition of women that implied that women could not possibly understand the issues with which they were dealing.

In the end, women found that task-oriented cooperative relationships with men in social welfare work could not be carried out as long as women and men were not equal partners in political decision making. The detour that women took on behalf of women's suffrage was in the context of overcoming obstacles to work to be done. It was not at first primarily a consciousness-raising phenomenon. The consciousness-raising came as a consequence of the violence of the reactions of the men to the very pragmatic course the women chose. Neither was there any grand theory of history involved—just a simple conviction that the rights of man were also the rights of woman.[1]

The men of the gradualist liberal tradition who allied themselves with the gradualist liberal women reformers were not entirely comfortable with the alliance. They all belonged to the same social class, but there was an uneasiness there, and it has remained to this day. This is why the issue of the need for separate women's organizations, first tried by the Quakers in the 1600s, is still a live one in the twentieth century. The bloodiness of some of the later suffrage battles can only be understood if one perceives the underlying sense of threat to the foundations of the social order felt by men over the issue of equality of women. Because there was no accepted liberal theory of institutional change that could explain new structural relationships between family and society, and between women and men, any change that was threatened must be bad. Although it may seem absurd to suggest that a *theory* of the role of women in society might have helped the male liberal of the past two centuries, the lack of one made it harder to envisage alternative future male-female relationships.

Socialist societies have a long way to go before women are equal partners with men, but the fact that they have a theory that (imperfectly) accounts for the possibility of equality and an ideology that supports it shows up in a variety of practical ways, including the fact that women have tended to be better represented in the political bodies of socialist countries than in nonsocialist countries.[2]

A second type of alliance made by women in the nineteenth century was the alliance of different sectors of middle-class women, and some of their working-class sisters, with middle- and working-class men of the socialist movement to build a classless society. These women were responding to the same set of social problems the reformist women were responding to, but their analysis was different. They had no confidence that a "hidden hand" (with a little help from the reformers) would see to the optimal distribution of goods in a free market, as Adam Smith theorized (*The Wealth of Nations* [1776] 1939). Before the midcentury, thinkers like Flora Tristan Moscosa and Louise Michel among women, and Marx and Engels among men, saw a basic block to optimal distribution of goods in the loss of control by the worker over both the instruments and the products of labor. The social relations of production had become pathological through failure to adapt to the changing character of the forces of production. The capitalist system that permitted individual owners of means of production to exploit their workers by appropriating all surplus productivity beyond bare subsistence requirements was an institutional anachronism that created poverty for the masses in the very age in which technological advance made abundance for all possible. The concept of "social relations of production" as developed by Marx and Engels had included the concept of husband-wife relations in the production of children. The first producers whose product was appropriated were mothers, whose children and domestic work were appropriated by fathers in oppressive monogamous family structures. It is interesting that none of the socialist theories of the time (at least to my knowledge) seems to have explored fully the meaning of the social relations of production inside the family in terms of men's responsibility for fathering and domestic maintenance work. Rather, they turned immediately to the liberation of women from family roles through (a) entry into the nondomestic labor force and (b) the provision of child care and all domestic chores through state facilities. Because it happens that these state facilities tend to be operated by women, not all that much has changed for women. Nowhere is the production of children conceived as a joint process. The "protection of motherhood" theme that was the theme of the nonsocialist women's movement in Europe after midcentury also lingers in socialist theory. Mothers must be protected in bearing children, protected in their domestic responsibilities, and protected in their right to participate in the labor force, but nowhere is there any mention of fatherhood, or parenthood, or a redefinition of the reproductive process. There is in fact no sociology of reproduction.

As is well known, the Russian socialist state at first thought it could do without the family in the new society. Divorce was available on request, and the state intended to provide public facilities for human maintenance. It turned out that the state was not rich enough to do this. Given the resources available, it was cheaper to get the maintenance work done within individual families by women. And so, while the ideology of state facilities and of the participation of women in the labor force continued, the underlying reality was that most children still had to be cared for outside of state facilities. Within the home, women still carried on the traditional tasks of marketing, cooking, laundering, cleaning, and child care in addition to working outside the home.

The basic issue of the future of private family life in a society that promotes the participation of women in the public sphere will be further examined in the last chapter in this volume. The record of the nineteenth century in this matter is that some groups experimented with communes, and there was a certain amount of urban boarding house living,[3] but that, in general, family units took individual housing when available, along with the tasks that went with individual housing. The question of permanent versus temporary pairing was hardly an issue in earlier centuries when there were large numbers of unmarried "vagabond" women and married women were for the most part working partners with their husbands. In the nineteenth century, that issue became linked, appropriately, to the phenomenon of increasing numbers of wives isolated in household settings where they had very little to do.

The chief contribution of the socialists to the problem of women's roles was to acknowledge that productive life for women was problematic in the industrial era. Fourier was one of the first to articulate clearly that the status of women could be used as an indicator of the progress of society:

> The change in a historical epoch can always be determined by the progress of women towards freedom, because in the relation of woman to man, of the weak to the strong, the victory of human nature over brutality is most evident. The degree of emancipation of women is the natural measure of general emancipation. (quoted in Rowbotham 1972: 51)

Marxist theory vastly overrated the productivity inherent in technology per se and assumed that machines would mean abundance of food and material goods for all. It also vastly underrated the difficulty of developing a redistribution system that would regularly redistribute away from the advantaged and toward the disadvantaged at any moment in time. The classless society was supposed to have no distribution problems. The concept of classlessness itself did not take account of the shifting advantage and disadvantage for individuals in various social situations, particularly for women.

The painstaking task of developing figures on women in the labor force, on wage levels, and other relevant data on the conditions of women was all undertaken by socialists: Engels, Marx, and Bebel in Germany and Harriet Martineau and (in the next century) Beatrice Webb in England. We shall see that women came to play an increasingly important role in the science of measurement of states of the social system and in providing the inputs for social planning and the evaluation of planning outcomes. In the early days of the workers' movement, this was not so. Then it was a question of getting firsthand experience in the field, of mobilizing women and men and getting them to work separately and together. Radical women had to face the same problem reformist women faced—that the alliance with men even of the same class interests was an uneasy one. Not all radical men supported the ideology of the equality of women, and many who supported the ideology did not practice it. The issue of separate radical women's organizations therefore developed very early, and some women worked in segregated organizations while others worked with men. On the whole, I have the impression that more radical women stayed in the mainstream radical movement than reformist women stayed in the mainstream reform movements. The alliance process went on, whether from separatist or integrated stances, but under difficulties and with periodic revolts of women against inappropriate male dominance behavior.

Whether separatists or integrationists, reformers or radicals, activist women were in a sense exposed to a more complex set of stimuli in the nineteenth century than men were. This was due to the fact that they entered the public sphere when nationalism was at its height but in the same century that internationalism was born. While mastering the problems of participation in their own society, they were also seeing these problems in a world context that was completely new. The development of rapid communication and transportation facilities mentioned earlier was one reason for this. The very capitalism that fostered colonialism and the organization of world market networks also fostered an alternative set of perceptions about the world itself. The new internationalism was very different than the old international marriage-alliance system that women aristocrats knew. In this new arena, women participated as individuals, although marriage alliances were still to continue.[4]

The very newness of this double exposure to nationalism and internationalism enhanced women's social perceptions in ways that led to an extraordinary flowering of their creativity in the public sphere in the latter part of the century. It also led to sophisticated perceptions of the general social contract that few men of either liberal or radical groups were prepared to accept. Women increasingly understood the character of their underlife position and were no longer willing to work at social reconstruction from that position.

Because so much of the focus in Part I of this volume was on women in the West, it becomes necessary in this closing part to stop and take a look, however superficial, into the movement of time as experienced by women of the *Two-Thirds World* (a term I use rather than the pejorative *Third World*), many of whom live in societies with such ancient traditions that the culture of the European West appears as a hastily constructed hodgepodge by contrast. The feeling of Western women that their history began yesterday is part of a general Western pathology that has had its effect on Two-Thirds World women and robbed them of their own history. Who did the most harm in the eighteenth and nineteenth centuries: the colonial administrators and merchants who obliterated the indigenous women's traditional positions of responsibility by ignoring them or the wives of these men, who too often served as role models for a life of unproductive glamour in Two-Thirds World countries? Some combination of these two forces erased a considerable part of women's history from public consciousness in the Two-Thirds World. Yet, that is not the whole story. Many Western women who came to Africa and Asia in the nineteenth century as missionaries, as teachers, as feminists, allied with their sisters to create a global women's community that has survived all the disastrous wars of the twentieth century. To understand that global community, not well known to the younger women of the West, even after the International Women's Decade, the historical experience of Two-Thirds World women with "modernization" must be noted.

Islamic modernizers came to north and sub-Saharan Africa, Persia, and India in the eighth to tenth centuries. By the thirteenth century, they had spread to much of Southeast Asia, establishing coexistence and Hinduism and Buddhism. By 1450, when Islam had great empires in Persia and India, and had reached the Philippines, the tides were shifting; the first Portuguese boats were reaching Africa, and Christian Europeans were driving the Moslems out of Spain. In an all-too-brief note, we will try to touch base with some developments in recent centuries in Africa, West Asia, China, and Latin America. Then we move on to developments worldwide in women's movements in the twentieth century. We will see how the nineteenth-century beginnings of women's transcontinental networks blossom into strong women's INGOs (international nongovernmental organizations), substantially aided in the second half of the twentieth century by the international platform and communication structures that became available to them with the birth of the United Nations and its agencies.

Notes

1. The men who shared that conviction—Condorcet at the time of the French Revolution, Fourier and William Thompson in the early 1800s, John Stuart Mill, and Marx and Engels in the middle 1800s—all went considerably beyond the gradualist evolutionary doctrines of the rights of man in their perspectives on society. They were also more radical than most women reformers.

2. Whether the quality of male-female relationships is better there is another question.

3. Read Frances Trollope's horrified account of married couples living in boarding houses in *Domestic Manners of the Americans* ([1932] 1949: 280-285).

4. In fact, marriage alliances continue to be important to this day both in the international business community and among royalty.

References

Beard, Mary R. 1946. *Woman as Force in History: A Study in Traditions and Realities.* New York: Macmillan.

Cook, Robert, ed. 1951. "The Great World Cities." *Population Bulletin*, September.

Hill, Georgiana. 1896. *Women in English Life.* Vol. 2. London: Richard Bentley.

Langford, Elizabeth. 1964. *Victoria R. I.* New York: Harper & Row.

O'Faolain, Julia and Lauro Martines, eds. 1973. *Not in God's Image: A History of Women in Europe from the Greeks to the Nineteenth Century.* New York: Harper & Row.

Rowbotham, Sheila. 1972. *Women, Resistance and Revolution: A History of Women and Revolution in the Modern World.* New York: Pantheon.

Smith, Adam. [1776] 1939. *The Wealth of Nations.* New York: Random House.

Trollope, Frances. [1932] 1949. *Domestic Manners of the Americans*, edited by Donald Smalley. New York: Random House.

3

Preparing the Modern World: The 1800s

The Revolutionaries and the Workers

The working women of the nineteenth century were not in a situation very different than their eighteenth-century sisters, except that there were more of them, towns and cities were more crowded, and sanitation and housing were even more of a problem than before. Women worked in village, town, and city at an amazing variety of jobs. Appendix Table 3A.1 gives an occupational census for women in England in 1841, which is probably not unrepresentative of the occupations of women elsewhere in Europe, although other countries were not as far along in industrialization. Lewenhak (1980) provides an integrated picture of the effects of industrialization, trade, and colonization on the women of this period, as do Tilly and Scott (1978). The employment of children also continued through this century. Even by 1901, the reporting of the employment of women is stated in terms of females age 10 and over (Richards 1974: 350). Appendix Table 3B.1 gives an idea of the range of employment for children outside the cities. If we added city employment and factory work, the list would be much longer.

The working life of proletarian women, as that of men, began in early childhood and lasted throughout life. Whether there was time off for childbearing in the working class depended on the level of earnings of a partner, if there was a partner, and of the children already born, and on the possibilities of the woman getting piecework to do at home. There were many never-married working women. In England, 42% of women in the age group 20 through 40 were spinsters (Richards 1974: 349); we shall see that figures were equally high on the Continent. We do not know how many of these women had stable, unregistered partnerships. While schooling facilities for children were steadily increasing, they were not keeping up with population growth. There was often resistance on the part of parents to putting children in school, even when this option was available, because their earnings helped out at home. Vagrant children continued to fill the workhouses throughout this century and to be shipped overseas to Australia and Canada to meet various fates.

The disproportion between the number of women seeking jobs and the jobs available continued to grow. The same phenomenon that has been noticed in the twentieth century in the Two-Thirds World, that of a faster contraction of traditional-sector jobs than an expansion of modernizing-sector jobs,[1] was taking place in England over the eighteenth and nineteenth centuries. As Eric Richards points out, there was "a clear shrinkage of opportunities in many of the metal trades and in agriculture after 1815" (1974: 345). Factory opportunities were very limited. Those who did enter factory employment, whether in England or New England, were at least 50% children under 14 (Richards 1974: 346). The fact that only 27% of factory women were married was not because they did not wish to go on working but because factories found it cheaper to let them go as they grew older and replace them with children. With traditional employment declining, women swarmed into domestic services—another phenomenon paralleling the experience of women in Two-Thirds World countries today. Those who could not get domestic employment were forced into a variety of pittance-paying odd jobs and prostitution. Richards asks where this large surplus army of employable women came from and suggests rhetorically but disbelievingly that they may always have existed (1974: 348). In the view of history I am giving, they certainly always existed and became visible only because of the shrinking employment opportunities accompanying industrialization. Their visibility helped the cause of feminism, as numerous publications on the problem attest.[2] Although exact figures are not available, it is probable that not until World War II did employment opportunities for women begin to approach the preindustrialization levels of 1700 (Richards 1974: 354).

Urban working women bore the brunt of an industrialization that outpaced every kind of facility for human welfare, and it is among the urban proletarian women that we find the revolutionaries of the nine-teenth century. In France, these women revolutionaries were the grand-children and great-grandchildren of the bread rioters of the eighteenth century. When Louise Michel broke into the bakeries of Lyons in 1882 to distribute bread to the unemployed, she was following an old tradi-tion. But the movement she represented was a different kind of move-ment. A schoolteacher who had had her baptism in the Paris Commune of 1871, Michel became a leading exponent of anarchist communism. Her *Memoirs* (1886) and *Le Monde Nouveau* (written in 1888) show what a long way women have come from the rhetoric of Olympe de Gouges and Claire Lacombe in the days of the French Revolution. The theme of bread, however, remained a constant. When the women of Paris were faced with endless queuing at the bakeshops during the revolution of 1871, they started remembering "how things were a hundred years ago when the women of Paris had gone to Versailles to carry off the baker and the baker's little boy" (Rowbotham 1972: 104). In France, men and women fought, and women searched for bread in 1789, in 1848, in 1871, and in 1882—and countless other times.

The triple responsibility that women faced in each of the revolution-ary uprisings had the cumulative effect of radically politicizing one group of French women. The triple role involved (a) helping the men to arm, (b) taking arms themselves, and (c) finding bread for the children, the men, and themselves. In some cases, as in the uprising of the Paris Commune in 1871, they organized nonviolent brigades to disarm the government soldiers.[3] The role they were not permitted was participation in the political decision making of the male revolutionar-ies. Their very flexibility and capacity for multiple approaches to prob-lem solving made them a threat to the single-minded male leaders. The 1871 Declaration of the Commune, like all previous declarations that were to inaugurate a new society, said not one word about the partici-pation of women.

To present a clear picture of the many aspects of the revolutionary movements of the nineteenth century is an impossible task. There were many separate lines of development, they often crisscrossed, and women were involved in them all. The socialist movement born of the ideas of Saint-Simon, Robert Owen, and Charles Fourier came to encompass two essentially contradictory developments: the cooperative move-ment, which represented a voluntary effort to improve the condition of the working class, involving cooperation with capitalist structures; and the revolutionary movement, which aimed at destruction of capitalist institutions and their replacement by worker-controlled institutions. Many of the utopian socialist experiments of the 1800s came under the category of cooperation with capitalist structures. Revolutionary socialism, involving replacement of structures, was itself divided into factions. One group tended toward decentralist anarchistic socialism and emphasized the democracy of the masses, continued participation by the masses in decision making, and continued involvement in the education of the masses. Another group tended toward the conspiratorial elite view, a centralist planning perspective that involved a small group of highly trained persons acting on behalf of the masses. For a fuller picture of socialist feminism in the nineteenth and early twentieth century, see Boxer and Quataert (1978).

In general, the mass-participation socialists were committed to internationalism and opposed the nationalistic tendencies of increasing numbers of socialists in the communist movement after the 1880s. They also tended to oppose all wars. The centralists on the other hand tended to be nationalists and were more inclined to support national wars as tools for communism. Most of the groups, whether cooperative socialist, or centralist, or decentralist revolutionary socialist, supported equal participation of women in the movement and in society *in theory*. Few did so in practice.

Marx himself played a relatively unimportant role in the evolution of these movements. His 1848 manifesto, as Cole (1953-60: vol. 2, chap. 1) points out, was almost unnoticed at the time. The revolutions of 1848 collapsed, and the predicted fall of capitalism did not take place. It was "back to the drawing boards." The Paris Commune of 1871 also collapsed and with it the First International. It was back to the drawing boards again. In terms of actual organizing activities, there were whole sets of actors too numerous to mention here. We will instead pick out some of the women who worked in these movements. Most of these women can be found in the popular chronicles of revolutionary history if one searches carefully for them, but their role has rarely been emphasized except by revolutionary women themselves. Until their role has been more carefully scrutinized, I suggest that our understanding of the meaning of the socialist and later communist movements of the nineteenth century cannot be properly understood, nor can their successes and failures.

The women who appear to have stood out in terms of articulateness and leadership all supported the decentralist, democratic, mass-education, nonelite approach to revolution. They also represented internationalism and opposed war. In short, they represented all the features of socialism that lost out in the European communist revolutions of the next century. Had their leadership been more acceptable to the men of the movements, the story of European socialism might have been different.

Flora Tristan Moscosa (1803-44) is the first representative of women's contribution to revolutionary socialism. She was one of the first to draw up a plan for a worldwide workers' international (*L'Union Ouvrière*, 1843). She not only devised a theoretical underpinning and a practical organizational scheme for the workers' movement, but she also spent her short life in traveling about the world arousing the consciousness of workers and recruiting them for the *internationale*. French born, half Peruvian, she was a revolutionary heroine on both sides of the Atlantic. She was a strong supporter of women's rights and linked the emancipation of women to the emancipation of the worker. (Her *Emancipation of Women* was published posthumously.) Pretty and talented, she was herself a typical victim of the life situation of the woman worker. The master of her workshop first married and then abused her. After three pregnancies and continual abuse, she ran away, then was shot by her husband and yet survived. Divorce was not an option for women at that time. When she entered the socialist movement, she gave herself completely to it and drove herself so hard through writing, traveling, and organizing that she died, worn out, at 41. A laundress coworker cared for her at the end. Exposed to much ridicule, she felt very much alone toward the end of her life. "I have nearly the whole world against me. Men because I demand the emancipation of women, the owners because I demand the emancipation of wage-earners" (Rowbotham 1972: 55).

Jeanne Deroin was a self-taught working woman who became a schoolteacher and a journalist. She also linked the liberation of women and the liberation of the working class and together with Pauline Roland worked with a group of trade union men on a plan for the federation of all existing unions—a simpler version of the Tristan Moscosa plan. She was the thinker and organizer for the group. Nevertheless, when she and her male associates were arrested for illegal political association, the court preferred to record her as a prostitute. The political issues were fastened on the men alone. The difficulties of a woman revolutionary working with men is seen in the trial record (O'Faolain and Martines 1973: 312, 315; Rowbotham 1972: 110). Apparently, the union men were as eager as the judge for their case to be dissociated from that of Jeanne Deroin. Rowbotham tells us the men begged her before the trial to pretend she knew nothing about the federation she had designed.

Side by side with these more radical women were the "moderates" such as Mme Poutret de Mauchamps. Her form of action was the publishing of a women's rights journal, *Gazette des Femmes* (1836-38). She took the position that the Constitution of 1830, proclaiming the political emancipation of Frenchmen, had used *man* generically "so that the new charter of liberties necessarily included Frenchwomen in its provisions" (Stanton [1884] 1970: 240). Mme de Mauchamps was a good politician. Every issue of the *Gazette* was introduced by a new petition to the king and parliament, making specific requests for reforms in the code relating to women. She always took care to associate prominent public personages with her declarations and petitions. Many decades were to pass before any of them were attended to, but this represented the start of a new kind of women's campaign: well thought out, sophisticated, coolly rational—and insistent.

Mme de Mauchamps's way of working with men caused no problems; she could assume the style of a *salonière* when it suited her. For women like Tristan Moscosa and Deroin, committed to living the revolution as if it were now, things were harder. The women who tried to work with men had to be strong-minded to endure the disapproval of both the public and their own coworkers. The women who worked in all-women's groups dealt with a smaller segment of the same set of problems—how to increase control over their own lives. Women in government workshops—dressmakers, laundresses, midwives—sought that control by forming associations to increase their pay. Their 12-hour-plus workdays for low wages were forced by competition with women in prisons and convents who worked for even less. The situation of the women in the workshops is a good illustration of the problems of antagonistic class interests among women's groups. From the upper-middle class came the lady philanthropists convinced that they knew how to improve the lot of poor working women. These same upper classes were helping to support the convents and the beguinages, which had by now in some cases become sweatshop perversions of the earlier cooperative workshops for women.[4] In these shops, stunted girls bent over fine embroidery all day in the name of "education."

The women in government workshops suffered more heavily from this competition because most of them had children to support, and they were often without legal partners. In 1882, one-third of the babies born in Paris were "illegitimate." Not all the mothers of these babies were ready to become political radicals, but some were. They came to increasingly realistic perceptions about the conditions of their lives. They knew that they needed not only higher wages but also help with child care. Their children needed human care as well as food while their mothers were at work. In 1848, the year of revolutions and declarations, the first petition from women workers for crèches went to a government. Working-class neighborhoods with gardens, reading rooms, and communal dining rooms as well as crèches and a school were proposed. Almost 150 years later, such plans still seem utopian for most working women in any country—north, south, west, or east. We will see later how the need for child care merged with the Froebel kindergarten movement but in the process moved away from the proletarian women who needed it most and toward the middle class.

The most important thing about the 1840s movements was that proletarian women were beginning to define their own problems and organize to solve them. Self-educated working women and middle-class teachers and journalists united in associations and in producing journals to provide a forum for their new ideas. *La Voix des Femmes* and *La Politique des Femmes* (later, *L'Opinion des Femmes*) both began as socialist papers, voicing the opinions of dressmakers and midwives as well as of socialist women teachers. The journals became the focus also for organizing women to improve workshop conditions and to discuss other social problems. These clubs frightened men, and not just the conservatives among them. Who knows what the women might be hatching to disturb the social order? Within the associations, the radicals soon frightened the middle-of-the-roaders, who usually did not have such urgent personal economic problems to handle.

One arena in which the alliance of middle- and working-class women was very important was that of prostitution. The euphemism *fallen women* used by philanthropists masked an increasingly desperate situation for many of the working poor as well as the unemployed poor. The combination of increased numbers of young women in urban areas and the fact that the age of consent for girls in a country like England was still 12 in the 1870s was a recipe for disaster. The use of children 12 years and younger for prostitution was extremely widespread. They were there, and they were unemployed. This meant, as Rowbotham (1973: 53) points out, that there were many very young unmarried mothers who, to feed their children, had to choose between the prisonlike workhouse or the dreary streetwalker's routine. Associations organized to help these young women, often mere children themselves, were somewhat misdirected in their preoccupation with the morality rather than the economics of prostitution. Nevertheless, the efforts of middle-class women did succeed in bringing about a substantial reduction in the white slave traffic in little girls, particularly the international traffic.

An important person in these efforts was Josephine Butler, a courageous British woman who devoted her life to the abolition of government regulation of prostitution, the abolition of the international white slave trade, and a fundamental transformation in the character of institutions for "fallen women." Butler was responsible for the creation of the British and Continental Federation for the Abolition of Government Regulation of Prostitution in 1875, and she fought corrupt police and male class privilege in every country in Europe as well as in England and the United States (Petrie 1971).

The situation of working women in Paris who lived at the margins of subsistence was such that they lived under a reign of terror administered by the dreaded *Police des Moeurs*. The police had an arrest quota to fill each month. Any woman obviously belonging to the working class, or living alone in furnished rooms, could be arrested by the police on no other evidence than their lack of affluence or a partner to protect them and forcibly inspected and licensed. Inevitably, many nonprostitutes were picked up in this way. If they refused to submit to registration, they were kept in the prison of St. Lazare until they gave in or died. Butler's investigations of such situations are graphically described in Petrie (1971: 155 ff.). Her discovery of child abuse in London brothels, and of a regular traffic in children and young girls shipped to the brothels of Europe from London, did not make her popular with "enlightened" British liberal men, many of whom patronized the very institutions she exposed.

The middle level of prostitutes and the well-to-do courtesans were not subject to imprisonment, but their own protection was bought at a price. They shared their earnings liberally with the police, whether in London, Brussels, Paris, or New York. *The Women of New York* (Ellington [1869] 1972) gives some fascinating sketches of women of the New York "underworld." The well-to-do salonière types among them gave liberally to charity, particularly for their hard-up sisters in the profession and for children, and they seem to have introduced some wider perspectives into an otherwise dull social scene. The poor young prostitutes with younger siblings, aged dependents, and children of their own to support, who walked the streets of New York in the middle 1800s, were the same young girls who walked the streets of Europe— only the language was different.

Another very vulnerable group in the nineteenth-century city was the servants. The habit from slavery days of men considering women household workers as being at their disposal for sexual service continued after slavery. If a servant girl became pregnant, there was no recourse when the mistress of the household turned her out. Many prostitutes were forced into the profession via that route, other employment being barred. As soon as other employment was available, women left domestic service in droves and went to the factories. The slavelike character of domestic service made it unattractive when there were alternatives, so the "servant problem" began early. Salmon (1897) gives an interesting description both of the character of domestic service toward the end of the century in the United States and of the efforts of innovative women to organize cooperative housekeeping services to solve the needs created by the exodus of servants. The development of specialized services through women's exchanges and of cooperative housekeeping associations were in the best utopian tradition of the eighteenth century. Some of these ventures were inspired by Edward Bellamy's utopia, *Looking Backward* ([1887] 1967). There were certainly similar developments in Europe, although I lack details on this.

* * *

It is impossible to give an adequate description of the overall situation of women in this century because the social climate was so different in each country. In Germany, August Bebel's *Women Under Socialism,* which appeared around 1880, introduced the women's question to a highly resistant German population. The book is a lengthy indictment of the situation of women in the current society, brings up the glories of her matriarchal past, and proposes a working partnership between women and men in the future (Bebel [reprinted in the United States in 1904] 1971). The objections to the participation of women in society were perhaps stronger in Germany than anywhere else in Europe. The German culture was domestically oriented, and the fact that women made up at least a fifth of the industrial work force was not allowed to intrude on the image of domesticity. Women like Adelheid Popp, who in the 1880s became trade union militants, did not even know there was a women's question when they were young. It was not written about, not discussed.

Yet we find major leaders of the international socialist women's movement coming out of Germany. Bebel's work certainly helped, but the women who were mobilized in Germany and Austria in the 1880s went considerably beyond him in their analysis of the economic situation of women. Clara Zetkin (1857-1933) was a major figure on the European scene after 1890. She was the leader of the women's section of German Social Democracy. After 1892, she edited the journal *Gleichheit* (Equality), the voice of socialist feminism for many years. Like her sisters in the movement, she was a strong exponent of the international emphasis of socialism as against nationalistic developments. She and Rosa Luxemburg teamed up again and again to defend internationalism before their more chauvinist (in the original, nationalistic, meaning of the word) male colleagues. She was also a pacifist.[5]

Polish-born Rosa Luxemburg (1871-1918) was a towering figure whose work spanned the close of the nineteenth and the beginning of the twentieth centuries. Not only did she write more than 700 books, pamphlets, and articles (Whitman 1970: 16), she was one of the most skilled educators and organizers in the international socialist movement. She fought against elitism and on behalf of more democratic participation of the masses in revolutionary activity and was an antinationalist and a pacifist. In short, she represented all the best contributions of women to the concepts of revolutionary action. She did much more than that, however. She rethought the theory of capital accumulation as contained in the second volume of Marx's *Das Kapital* and produced what Joan Robinson, a leading woman economist in Britain, suggested was a major theoretical contribution to economics not recognized at the time or since. Robinson says that Luxemburg's work, while incomplete in its analysis, is a "remarkable anticipation" of concepts that were only to be generally understood by economists in the 1930s (Cole 1953: Vol. 3, pp. 517-18). The first volume of her two-volume book, *The Accumulation of Capital*, has just recently been translated into English.

Luxemburg and Zetkin worked closely with their Austrian counterpart, Luisa Kautsky, who was also a writer and editor for the movement. In Russia, Alexandra Kollontai was beginning the groundwork of political activity among working-class women that was to result, at the time of the Russian Revolution, in the Zhenodtl, an organized effort to redefine and restructure women's roles in society. Kollontai was a novelist as well as an activist and a "distinguished official," an ambassador, in the later Bolshevik government. Her novels give sociological insight into the dilemmas of the woman revolutionary.[6]

Krupskaya, who married Lenin and shared his Siberian exile, was one of the few revolutionaries to have a happy personal life. She began teaching classes for workers in her teens and spent her life building the institutional structures that would strengthen a socialist society: children's homes, nurseries, youth organizations such as the Young Pioneers, and related community facilities (Bohrovskaya 1940).

Another link in the chain of international women socialists[7] is Anzhelika Balabanov, Italian feminist socialist and Lenin's wartime secretary (Balabanov 1938). Zetkin, Kollontai, Kautsky, Balabanov, and Luxemburg all worked together, and their closest English collaborator was Eleanor Marx, daughter of Karl Marx. In addition to working with the women's socialist international, Eleanor Marx was an active trade union organizer, writer, and translator of Ibsen. Her *Woman Question: A Socialist Point of View* brought into focus for English socialists the need to pay attention to the economic basis of women's oppression and the need for change in the sexual relations between women and men.

The story of the Karl Marx daughters is a sad one and points up the dilemmas faced by many revolutionary women. Eleanor committed suicide with poison provided for her by her husband, Edward Aveling. Her sister Laura committed suicide jointly with her husband, Paul Lafargue. Their mother Jenny, by being a good German *hausfrau,* had not provided an adequate role model for her revolutionary daughters.[8] Both women had married active socialists and were deeply involved with the movement. Marriage was disastrous for both. Many revolutionary women have given poignant accounts of their desire for love and for children. Some have achieved love; some have achieved children; few have achieved both. Intellectual allegiance to the concept of love without lifetime commitment is at war inside these women with personal needs for continuing relationships. The conflict creates dark threads of tragedy in the lives of many of them. Emma Goldman, Russian emigré and American anarchist, put the hopes and dreams of her generation most beautifully in "Love Among the Free," an essay in her *Anarchism and Other Essays* (1910), suggesting that in some future society, where people have not been misshaped by material conditions, people will be able to give and receive love freely.[9]

* * *

While England was very much linked to the international socialist women's movement, it also had its own indigenous revolutionary experience. In that country, working-class women worked side by side with men in the workers' rights movement (the Chartist movement) to a greater extent than happened in other countries. Possibly this was a holdover from earlier traditions of husband-wife cooperation in the guilds. The role of working women in these movements is somewhat overshadowed in the social histories of the time by the tremendous initiatives taken on their behalf by the upper classes.

The Nottingham bread riots of 1812 were led by women, but these preceded the development of a sustained working-women's movement. Visible female leadership in the trade union movement began in the 1830s. In an account of the part that women played in the 1843-44 strikes in Lancashire, Staffordshire, and Yorkshire, Rowbotham notes:

> It is a singular fact that women were in many instances the directors of the strike—women held their meetings, sent their delegates and drew up their terms—and women accompanied the turnouts in immense numbers, in all their marchings and counter marchings throughout the manufacturing districts. . . . At Halifax these women headed the mob, on

some occasions seizing the soldier's bayonets and turning them aside with the words "We want not bayonets but bread." (1972: 112)

Because men workers for several centuries had been bending their efforts to keeping women out of certain trades, women organized to protect their rights in a dwindling occupational arena. Here alliances with middle-class women were important. Clergyman's daughter Emily Faithfull is legendary in English women's history for her success in holding open certain occupational fields for women. Among other activities, Faithfull opened and successfully ran a printing press in the teeth of male insistence that this work was too heavy for women.

The women in the Fabian movement and in the Independent Labour Party in England during the 1890s and 1900s were one important group in the cross-class alliance process. Beatrice Webb, the leading woman Fabian, will be discussed later. Charlotte Wilson, the Fabian anarchist who was Kropotkin's close collaborator after his final settlement in England as a refugee in 1886; Katherine St. John Conway, who was a leader of the Independent Labour Party in the 1890s; Emmaline Pankhurst, leading Labour Party suffragette; Maud Pember Reeves, who wrote tracts for the Fabian society; and Annie Besant, who headed the London match girls' strike in 1888—all brought a breadth of perspective, social status, and human energy to the working-women's cause. Among these women, Annie Besant was one of the most colorful. She edited *The Link,* a journal that was to bring together the moderate socialists and the radicals, and was a major writer and activist in the Fabian movement before she turned to mysticism and theosophy. (Madame Blavatsky was another prominent socialist-turned-theosophist, and Christabel Pankhurst also later turned to religion.) Besant supported the Indian nationalist movement in the 1870s before anyone else was ready for that cause. Even after her shift to mysticism, during her long residence in India, she was an active Indian nationalist and served in the first Indian government.

A special study of the women who have been secular activists and also have become mystics and religious leaders would be interesting. Anna van Schurman is an outstanding example from the seventeenth century; Elise Van Calcar, reformer of women's education in Holland in the mid-1800s, and then editor of a spiritualist monthly *On the Banks of Two Worlds,* is another. Olive Schreiner, British author of *Women and Labour* (1911), is still another. A member of the Fabian women's circle, Schreiner studied the conditions of women in South Africa and in various parts of England and provided a cogent comparative analysis of the situation of the employed woman in society.[10] Yet she is probably better known for her mystical writings. Beatrice Webb, dean of the Fabians, was another person for whom the religious impulse was powerful and basic, as comes out in her autobiographical *Our Partnership* on her life with Sidney Webb (1948: vii).

Side by side with the Fabians were the Tolstoyans, another visionary band with active women members. Still a third approach is represented by a group of women who were active in the Voluntary Cooperative Commonwealth, which was intended to interpenetrate the capitalist system and "shame it" to decay: Mary Grover, Mary Boole, Eliza Pickard, Miss Dunn, Nellie Shaw, and Miss S. A. Miller, principal of the Diocesan Training College at Oxford, worked at community experiments and contributed to *The New Order*, a journal reporting on communitarian experiments in America and elsewhere.

The worker-middle-class alliance of women did not survive the turn of the century. The proletarian women of East London embarrassed most of their upper-middle-class sisters, and, in the minutes of the East London Federation of suffragettes, we find that the mainstream group felt that the East Londoners

> had more faith in what could be done by stirring up working women than was felt at headquarters, where they had most faith in what could be done for the vote by people of means and influence. In other words they said that they were working from the top downward and we from the bottom up. (Rowbotham 1972: 131)

* * *

A very different sector of women involved in revolutionary movements in the 1880s and 1890s were the peasant women of Italy and Spain. These were caught up in a revolutionary millennialism that was essentially anarchist but that in Italy became joined with the communist movement. The peasant women of Italy in particular took a leading part in the development of the peasant leagues, called the *fasci*, and adapted the religious beliefs of centuries to the necessities of political reform: " 'We don't go to church any more,' said a peasant woman from Piana dei Greci, 'but to the fascio. There we must learn, there we must organize for the conquest of our rights' " (Hobsbawm 1963: 99). Women and men treated visiting socialist leaders "as though they were bishops . . . throwing themselves on the ground and strewing flowers in their path" (Hobsbawm 1963: 98). They were not confused about religion, however. They had their own understanding of the conflict between the teachings and the practice of the church.

From an interview with a peasant woman of Palermo:

> *How do you stand with your priests?*
> Jesus was a true Socialist and he wanted precisely what the Fasci are asking for, but the priests do not represent him well, especially when they are usurers. When the Fascio was founded our priests were against it and in the confessional they said that the Socialists are excommunicated. But we answered that they were mistaken, and in June we protested against the war they made upon the Fascio, none of us went to the procession of the Corpus Domini. That was the first time such a thing ever happened.
> *Do you admit people convicted of crimes to the Fascio?*
> Yes. But there are only three or four out of thousands and we have accepted them to make them better men, because if they have stolen a bit of grain they have only done so out of poverty. . . . Society should thank us for taking them into the Fascio. We are for mercy, as Christ was. (Hobsbawm 1963: 183)

The woman who spoke these words could not read, but she could think. The movement she was part of was completely wiped out by the military force of an alarmed government before it could reconstruct the rural life of Italy. Danilo Dolci has been able to build on these older traditions in his nonviolent work of reconstructing the peasant society of Sicily (Dolci 1970) in recent years. His work shows that, while militarism may crush movements, it does not crush the social memory.

* * *

U.S. women had available neither the revolutionary traditions of French working women nor the history of bread riots or peasant anarchist traditions of Europe. Not even the lady-of-the-manor pattern of assistance to the poor was known to them. But the same giant-toothed comb of the industrial revolution that was drawn across the lives of European women left its furrows in the lives of U.S. women too. If the industrial revolution had a beginning in the United States, it began in 1798 when Samuel Slater opened the first U.S. textile factory in Pawtucket, with a labor force of nine children, girls and boys all under the age of 12 (Greenway 1953: 122). By 1820, half of all textile workers were girls and boys 10 years of age and younger, and the other half were young girls from nearby farms. By 1870, 14.7% of the female population 16 years of age and over were in the labor force and, by 1900, the percentage was 20.6 (Scott 1971: 13). One-quarter of these women were in factories. While they were admitted into a wide variety of occupations (women were reported as employed in all but 9 out of 369 manufacturing and mechanical industries [Scott 1971: 17]), their working hours, low pay, and (often) heavy family responsibilities[11] made life as hard for them as for women anywhere. Living conditions for women heads of household in Boston, New York, and Philadelphia were as bad as in any European city, and the descriptions of slum housing in Boston in 1849 might well have come from Octavia Hill in London (Ware [1924] 1958: 13).

In the 1830s, conditions worsened considerably for working women in the United States. After many farmers were wiped out in the panic of 1837, a new phenomenon developed: a group of women who were part of a permanent mill-dependent labor force. During this era, the "Lowell Factory Girls" entered labor and folk song history. "The Lowell Factory Girl," composed about 1830, was still being sung by a wandering woman minstrel at a Texas cattle fair in the early 1900s (Greenway 1953: 125). The New England mill town was originally considered an "industrial utopia." The Lowell girls were publishing their own magazine, *The Operatives,* and, later, *The Offering.* The first generation of operatives from Lowell produced a poet, an editor, a suffragist, a sculptor, and a labor leader (Josephson 1949). Lowell was a microcosm of the industrialization process as experienced in all parts of the world, because, as working hours lengthened and wages declined, the poets were replaced by pale-faced undernourished daughters of poverty. But the leadership generated in Lowell did not die out. In 1845, the activities of women labor leaders broadened to cover the whole region of New England with the Female Labor Reform Association. By the 1850s, women were organizing their own branches within unions organized by men and drawing up their own demands as in the case of the Shoemaker's Union in 1851.

Already by the 1850s, however, the leadership in the labor movement was almost entirely male. The textile industry labor force became 50% male and the leadership almost 100% male. Hence the need for women's branches, or auxiliaries, as they were sometimes called, to articulate the needs of women workers usually not noticed by men. (The term *auxiliary* did not at this time mean "wives of members" as it often does today.)

During the 1890s, when European women were active in the women's socialist international, U.S. women were evolving their own style of participation in the social change movements of the time. The nearest thing to an international elite among U.S. women, the circle around Jane Addams, was not at all socialist. It was rather liberal reformist, in a more conservative sense than its counterpart circles in England.

The working class produced its own women leaders in America. Their names are immortalized not in the labor histories but in the protest songs and ballads of the labor movement. In the songs, and in the notes of explanation that accompany them when folklorists record these songs, we see fleetingly the faces of the faceless—the hundreds of thousands of women, with or without partners, who were raising children and working 12-hour (or longer) days without earning enough in the end to support their families: Ella Mae Wheeler, mother of five and a mill hand so talented in song and speech that she was singled out to be shot and killed in a demonstration, and Ella May Wiggins, mother of nine, four of whom died of whooping cough because her supervisor would not let her shift from night work to day work at the mill so she could nurse the children through the worst of their coughing spells. She was a talented leader, best known for her song, "The Mill Mother's Lament":

> We leave our homes in the morning,
> We kiss our children good bye
> While we slave for the bosses
> Our children scream and cry.
>
> And when we draw our money
> Our grocery bills to pay,
> Not a cent to spend for clothing,
> Not a cent to lay away.
>
> And on that very evening,
> Our little son will say:
> "I need some shoes, Mother,
> And so does sister May."
>
> How it grieves the heart of a mother,
> You everyone must know,
> But we can't buy for our children
> Our wages are too low.
>
> It is for our little children,
> That seem to us so dear,
> But for us nor them, dear workers,
> The bosses do not care.

But understand, all workers,
Our union they do fear;
Let's stand together, workers,
And have a union here.
(from Greenway 1953: 251-52;
People's Songs Library,
used by permission)

Mother Jones was the best known of all, an active organizer among the miners for 50 years, still organizing strikes at 89. She died at the age of 100. Aunt Molly Jackson was another famous organizer among the miners, trained to union leadership by her father from the age of 5. So was Sarah Organ, the most powerful of the women singers. "Which Side Are You On?"—one of the best known of U.S. labor songs—was written by Mrs. Sam Reece after her home had been ransacked by men looking for her labor-organizer husband. All these women could sing as well as organize.

This combination in women of charismatic leadership qualities, organizing abilities, and the gift of song is not unique to the U.S. labor movement although most easily documented there. Protest ballads are as old as urban concentrations, but most folksingers are not recorded in history. (Remember the Sumerian women who sang to the public assemblies.) There were women singers at fairs back in the earliest Middle Ages, and we have mentioned their contribution to ballad lore at that time. As they moved into factories around the world, they certainly lifted their voices in song about their conditions. A study of references to women in ballads through history would provide valuable insight into women's lives as workers.

The women described above did not consider themselves radical and were very angry when in the 1900s they were increasingly described as "commies." There was an unusual group of women in the Industrial Workers of the World (the IWW): Katie Phar, Elizabeth Gurley Flynn, and Vera Moller. John Greenway (1953) calls them amazons. They were young at the end of the last century and did most of their work in the twentieth century. These women were of the same fiber as their European sisters in the international socialist movement. They had some contacts with Europe but fewer than their male colleagues.

Emma Goldman, an anarchist-socialist and therefore more extreme than the IWW, was part of an even smaller and even more embattled group. Her nickname, "Red Emma," still conjures up images of a horned she-devil, though in fact she was a warm-hearted, sensitive woman with incredible energy (Goldman 1931).

For all their charisma and organizing ability, women never achieved major leadership in the trade union movement. Where they had it initially, as in the textile industry, they soon lost it (see Maupin 1974: 5-11). The extra burden of child care and home maintenance that women carried and men were free from partly accounts for this, particularly because many of these women had no men in their homes to help. The greats among the women leaders, however, carried out their organizing in spite of five, nine, or more children (the two Ella Mays, for example).

The trade union movement could never have gotten off the ground without substantial support from women, both those in the factories and the homebound wives. Nevertheless, the prevailing working-class culture, as well as the middle-class culture, was such that women had to accept typical underlife roles just when they should have been operating in the public spaces. The privatization of their union roles was the mirror image of the privatization of their factory jobs. Somehow they were not really in the labor force—working on the assembly line was just another way of standing at the kitchen sink.

* * *

In general, radical movements fared considerably less well in the United States than in Europe. At the same time, the United States was a hotbed of experimental communities. While Europe had room for radical thought, it was America that had land to spare for radical experiments. Nordhoff's ([1875] 1965) study of communistic societies in the United States, which documents eight groups of communities with 72 settlements in all, focuses primarily on religiously or humanistically oriented communities[12] and does not include the Fourier and Owenite and other more politically oriented experiments. Holloway's (1966) study includes another 14 of the socialist type of utopian communities plus 40 Fourierist phalanxes, all founded in the 1840s. There were probably twice as many experiments as those recorded and hundreds more that died as gleams in someone's eye. If we add the Mormons, who also were in the utopian community business, we add many hundreds of communities.

What is particularly interesting about these experiments of the 1800s is that two completely different types of utopian ventures were going on simultaneously, drawing on different classes of people. One drew on intellectuals, the other on workers. Women did much better in the working-class communities. The humanists, transcendentalists, and socialists for the most part had very short-lived communities and gave no explicit recognition to women in spite of socialist theory about the role of women.[13] The religious communities that recruited farmers and laborers, many of them immigrants, were longer lasting. Some have persisted into the current time. Except for the Shakers, founded by Ann Lee and with a continuing tradition of women's leadership, most were and are led by men. The tradition of women's leadership among the Shakers is not unconnected with their practice of celibacy, which leaves them as free for leadership as are men.

Women thrived in the conservative, working-class, religious utopias because these communities dealt very directly with the hardest problems faced by working women. For single women, this was finding an economically secure niche and a respectable social status. For married women, it was protection from a crushing burden of household responsibilities on top of outside employment. The organization of work, housing, and communal facilities in the 72 communes listed by Nordhoff was such that women's working hours were considerably shorter than those of their noncommune sisters, their children were better cared for, and meals were provided with far less effort; except for the Perfectionists, all were monogamous. Whitworth (1975) calls the religious utopias "God's Blueprints," thus emphasizing the dynamism inherent in these experiments.

The polygamous Mormon communities also offered "improved working conditions" and drew women by the thousands because of the attractiveness of economic security and shared work loads. Plural marriage did not put them off—they were more interested in the conditions of life than in the number of cospouses. In some religious communities, women sat as elders on the community council, but there was no particular emphasis on political participation of women. Rather, there was an emphasis on sharing the general work load as evenly as possible among all.

In the socialist utopias, there seems to have been no equivalent of women elders. Many community entrepreneurs among the socialists obviously had competent, hardworking wives who did a lot of the work of community maintenance, but these wives remain nameless. The only woman's name that surfaces in accounts of the Owenite communities was Marie Louise Duclos Fretageot (Armytage 1961), a pupil of Pestalozzi who conducted schools in Paris and Philadelphia and then developed the educational system at New Harmony. All references to community schooling seem to indicate that girls were taught traditional women's work. The daughters of utopists frequently married utopists and continued as wives the role they played as daughters, doing the "dirty work" for communities. Evidently they never caught on to the advantages of celibacy—the secret of the Shakers, who replenished their numbers by adoption and conversion.

In spite of crowding in Europe, there were some communal experiments there too. When these were led by men, women played the usual maintenance role. A few "esoteric," nonsocialist ventures were led by women, however, and are particularly interesting because they were directed to the usually ignored problems of working women. Armytage (1961) calls them esoteric because their leaders were charismatics. There was Mary Ann Girling, who at the age of 45 had a divine call and founded a community of 160 people (the Abode of Love); many unemployed women were included, and 50% of the members were children. Clarissa Rodgers was a Paolo Solerian a century ahead of her time. Her whole community lived in a tower in the countryside where the family needs of working women were met. Katherine Tingley in the 1890s founded a Universal Brotherhood Organization. All of these women were hounded by men and their organizations destroyed. Because their practical economic and social programs were put in a cultic context rather than a political one, they are rarely described in the history of social experiments of their time.

One of the few experiments in Europe that succeeded in creating a sex-egalitarian community was the Familistère at Guise, France. It began in the 1850s as a patriarchal community based on a hardware industry. By 1880, it had evolved into a workers' cooperative. It was a "social palace" organized with complete political equality for women in governance, and it provided a range of public and family services for its members. There were similar experiments outside France. In the 1860s and 1870s, young women in Russia organized associations and communes, and Chernychevsky's What Is to Be Done? had a great influence in this direction.

> In St. Petersburg workshops and communes appeared. . . . [They were] important in providing homes and shelter for women workers and students who had left parents and husbands. It was believed too that it was necessary to create alternative cultural forms of association before the revolution. (Rowbotham 1972: 124)

The communes not only solved economic problems but provided educational and support settings for women breaking away from families and traditional modes of life, trying to learn new skills and be self-supporting. Few of these Russian women were working class—they were, rather, middle and upper class. Many of them converged on the

University of Zurich to work out their revolutionary ideas in the context of the study of philosophy, history, and economics. Zurich was one of the few European universities in the 1850s that admitted women.

* * *

After the 1850s, the bulk of workers, male and female, moved toward the (apparently) simpler goal of better pay. The revolutionaries, committed to more sweeping social changes, became increasingly isolated and operated from increasingly precarious niches in the larger society. One of the few who could offer security and a place to meet for the revolutionaries was Christine Trivulzio (1808-71), the Milanese princess of Bolgiojose. She was an adventurous soul who became a Parisian emigré after leading an army to defeat against Austria. She ran a St. Simonian salon in Paris.

In the 1870s, after the failure of the Paris Commune, there was a period of collapsed morale among the revolutionaries and a feeling of isolation. Out of this situation of "alienation from alienation," the women leaders' continuing commitment to working with the masses was finally picked up again as a way out of the isolation they had experienced. A major campaign was mounted "to go among the people and prepare the revolution." That campaign aroused such fear in the authorities, who thought they had crushed the revolutionaries for good, that a countercampaign of mass arrest and deportation of revolutionaries ensued. It was this countercampaign, Cole (1953-60: Vol. 2, p. 318) suggests, that drove many moderates among the revolutionaries, and particularly those committed to nonviolence, to terrorism, the "propaganda of the deed."

The scenario was not unlike the one to unfold 50 years later in the nationalist movement in India, and in both cases we see women playing key roles in terrorist activity. (See Chapter 4 of this volume for an account of Indian women terrorists.) There was Sophia Pervoskaya (former aristocrat), who headed the 1881 bombing mission that killed Czar Alexander. She was directly involved in three separate attempts before the one that succeeded. She and her coconspirators of the Narodnaya Volya were publicly hanged (Cole 1953-60: Vol. 2, pp. 319-21). Vera Figner was arrested in the process of reorganizing the Narodnaya Volya after the hanging of most of its leaders and survived 21 years of imprisonment to be released by the revolution of 1905 (Cole 1953-60: Vol. 2, pp. 320-21). Vera Zasulich, the anarchist who translated the

Communist Manifesto into Russian and later became a prominent socialist, shot the chief of the czarist police but was acquitted because of his
unpopularity! (Cole 1953-60: Vol. 2, pp. 317-18) A particularly vivid
picture of five leading women in this revolutionary group is found in
Engel and Rosenthal (1975). A broader account of Russian women is
given in Atkinson, Dallin, and Lapidus (1977).

The resort to terrorism on the part of revolutionaries is one way of
entering the public spaces of society after the privatization (and delegiti-
mation) of all other revolutionary activity. Many of those who practiced
terrorism were opposed to all war. Even Kropotkin supported the
strategic necessity of terrorism at this juncture as the only possible
course of *public* action, although he did not personally approve of it. It
is of particular interest that women, members of the most privatized
sector of all, should be able to perform strategic terrorism competently
and with cool heads.

The majority, though by no means all, of the women revolutionaries
were aristocrats or of the middle class. The intensity of their struggle
was not the less for their privileged background. It is a great cost to a
woman to throw away a ready-made identity and put herself on the line
for revolution and change when she has no assurance that the men she
is working with will accept her as a comrade. It follows that the women
we have been describing were all women of extraordinary caliber. (See
Woman as Revolutionary, Giffin 1973, for more about women in these
roles.)

Every once in a while, the male conspiracy of silence about the
importance of women in revolution is broken. Trotsky was one of the
few who publicly acknowledged the comradeship so many men refused
to see. Here, from his *History of the Russian Revolution*, is a rare passage
that gives women a key role in the start of the Russian Revolution:

> In spite of all directives the women textile workers in several factories
> went on strike, and sent delegates to the metal workers with an appeal
> for support. . . .
>
> It had not occurred to anyone that it might become the first day of
> the revolution. . . .
>
> The February revolution was begun from below, overcoming the
> resistance of its own revolutionary organization, the initiative being
> taken of their own accord by the women textile workers, among them no
> doubt many soldiers' wives. The overgrown bread-lines had provided
> the last stimulus. About 90,000 workers, men and women, were on strike
> that day. The righting mood expressed itself in demonstrations, meet-
> ings, and encounters with the police. A mass of women, not all of them
> workers, flocked to the municipal Duma demanding bread. It was like

demanding milk from a he-goat. Red banners appeared in different parts of the city, and inscriptions on them showed that the workers wanted bread, but neither autocracy or war. Women's Day passed successfully with enthusiasm and without victims. But what it concealed in itself, no one had even guessed by nightfall. (quoted in Rowbotham 1972: 134)

From bread riots in France in 1620 to bread demonstrations in front of the Russian duma in 1917 is a long way. Women had learned a lot in the meantime.

The Activists and the Middle Class

Middle-class reformers made less dramatic choices than their revolutionary sisters but did not necessarily lead less dramatic lives. Women's activism of the nineteenth century—middle class or proletarian, radical or reformist—was a new phenomenon on the world scene and deserves more attention than it has received. In this section, we will look at the reformers.

We saw in the eighteenth century the birth of the movement to deal with poverty by working with the poor in terms of their own needs. The nineteenth century witnessed an enormous extension of urban welfare activities on the part of women. Like the radicals, the middle-class women were more sophisticated about industrialism. We find the science called "political economy"—the forerunner of the later separate sciences of economics, sociology, and political science—being developed and used by women to analyze problems of the industrial society. We also find these same tools being turned to an analysis of the situation of the woman herself.

Ideas about the perfectibility of the individual and of society were implemented by increasing attention to education at all levels. If Rousseau's educational theories were something of a setback to women in denying them nondomestic roles in society, Froebel provided a powerful counterforce that released women all over Europe into the schoolroom. Froebel's developmental approach to children and the educational model he developed for the kindergarten began in a traditional all-male context; it was young men he was training to work with children. More memorable perhaps than all the revolutions and declarations of 1848 is the decision Froebel made that year to train women rather than men to work with children. While today we may deplore the fact that women are shunted aside into the role of primary school teacher, this role nearly became one more male specialty. Strategically, training large numbers of young men in child development might have brought about more rapid change in male roles than the women's emancipation movement has achieved, so to a degree it is hard to know whether to celebrate or deplore Froebel's choice. Nevertheless, in the world of the future, primary school teaching will not be a sex-linked role, and in 1848 Froebel's decision to train women instead of men opened up the opportunity for postelementary education for women in the new teacher-training centers that sprang up everywhere. It also opened up the almost limitless job market in elementary education.

From the point of view of women philanthropists, here was a chance to improve the situation of the poor and of women of all classes. In addition to opening model private schools, women pushed the governments of Europe in the direction of universal elementary education. They pushed simultaneously for government-sponsored industrial schools to give skill training to workers' children. Because hardly any governments sponsored girls' industrial schools, women founded private associations to support both industrial and normal schools for girls. (See Stanton [1884] 1970, for a country-by-country account of this.) It is not too much to say that women's voluntary associations undertook the bulk of the responsibility for agricultural production. In Italy and Sweden, the women's associations took note of this and established agricultural training centers for women, thus reversing a centuries-long trend of keeping women as ignorant farmhands rather than as knowledgeable agriculturalists (Stanton [1884] 1970).

The demand for higher education for middle- and upper-class women was an inevitable accompaniment of the educational efforts on behalf of working women. Higher education for women turned out to be a much more controversial issue than elementary or industrial education. Men said publicly and plainly that women were already getting out of hand and would be impossible to manage if they had more education. The famous Edinburgh medical school riots in 1869 after a small group of women had been admitted as students are a clue to the intensity of male fears of competition from professionally trained women. The University of Zurich, which had no sex barriers, became the mecca for women seeking higher education in midcentury. In 1866, the University of Paris, which only permitted women at lectures, abolished differential status between women and men students. Italian universities had no sex barriers. Whatever the country, however, only women of the elite could afford to be students. They also had to be strong enough to withstand general public ridicule. It was not until the 1880s that England

and other European countries provided regular admission to women at universities. In the meantime, women formed associations to establish their own colleges. In the United States, this began as early as the 1820s and, in England, in the 1840s. (U.S. male medical students were apparently less insecure than their British counterparts, because they accepted Elizabeth Blackwell as a fellow student as early as 1847. Geneva, New York, opened the first women's medical college in 1865, three years before the Edinburgh riots.)

The very widespread resistance on the part of men to providing anything beyond elementary education for women sharpened the awareness of women about their status in society. On the one hand, they were shocked that they were not supposed to thirst for knowledge. On the other hand, they became increasingly aware of the growing band of women in the labor market who, lacking skills, were unable to get employment. The genteel starving spinster looking for a post as governess became a marked feature of the social landscape. With domestic craft production removed from the urban middle-class household, families could no longer afford to feed spinster aunts, sisters, and daughters. The spinsters went job hunting, but class feeling kept them out of domestic service and the factory. What were they to do?

New social sensitivities considerably broadened the action agenda of women philanthropists. They turned to the establishment of more intermediate and normal schools for women and also formed women's employment associations. One set of employment associations specialized in helping women to emigrate overseas.

These activities had a consciousness-raising effect on women of the philanthropic classes. For some, this consciousness-raising was channeled toward an identification with problems of poverty, and the energies released went into the formation of associations like the Women's Christian Temperance Union and the Salvation Army. For other women, it led to an identification with the larger world community and the problems of slavery, oppression, and war in far-off colonial territories. The energies released in that direction went into the formation of international antislavery and peace associations. For still others, it led to a specific awareness of the anachronism that the women providing solutions to problems that governments of men were unable to handle were classified legally with children and idiots. This glaring inconsistency built up support for the suffrage movement, which was from the beginning both national and international in scope. Because the newly emerging group of women social scientists were in close alliance with the activists, we will begin by describing the social scientists.

The Social Scientists

The social sciences were still in a formative stage in the 1800s. Political science had developed along certain lines with Hobbes and Locke in the preceding century. The mercantilists of the 1600s and the physiocrats of the 1700s had developed a well-defined, though narrow, approach to a subject that in France was being pursued by people called *économistes*. In England, the tradition of political economy as developed by Adam Smith was much broader in scope than the work of the économistes and encompassed significant aspects of political science. It also encompassed what was later to become the discipline of sociology. Adam Smith can equally be called the father of sociology and of modern economics. In *The Wealth of Nations* ([1776] 1939) and the *Theory of Moral Sentiments* ([1759] 1976), he mapped the economic and political infrastructure of the modern world and analyzed the dynamics of social interaction.

Women of the 1800s to a significant extent participated in the shaping of the new social science disciplines. Given that there were no institutionalized public roles for individuals professing these sciences, there was nothing to bar women from them. The situation in England was particularly fluid. The need for information about the working of social structures was great, so knowledge and competence (even if self-taught, as in the case of women) could gain a hearing. The Social Science Association, founded in London in 1857, played a particularly important role in bringing the expertise of women to the information seekers in the government (Kamm 1966: 34, 45, 53-54 ff., 102 ff., 130). Every important issue before parliament was discussed there, on the basis of carefully researched papers prepared by women and men. For women, that platform was the more important because they had no other. The association also provided the basis for a working partnership between women social scientists and women activists. The activists also collected data but in the main relied on their scientist sisters for more basic analyses.

The action research concept was taken for granted by nineteenth-century reformers. Thus we find that Mary Carpenter, who worked with children in prisons, gave a paper at the Social Science Association that shaped parliamentary legislation establishing reformatories for juvenile delinquents. Louisa Twining, active in dealing with the plight of workhouse inmates, presented a paper at the association that formed the basis for substantial workhouse reforms. Anne Jameson's paper on the employment of women, Emily Davies's session on university examinations for women, and Barbara Bodichon's paper on women's suffrage all had direct consequences in parliament or among relevant authorities. (Of course, Bodichon did not see quick results—suffrage was long in coming.)

The other women we will be discussing in this section were primarily scientists, but they were usually in close touch with activists. Several of them became major public figures, both nationally and internationally. Because they could offer new kinds of mappings of social systems, their special knowledge was needed for public policy. Here at last was a time of surfacing of the particular kinds of infrastructures that women had worked on for centuries in the special spaces allotted to them. This was not a "family life specialty" that was being offered but an expertise about the institutional matrix within which family life takes place.

Harriet Martineau (1802-76), the first major woman social scientist of the century, had a great gift for translating abstract concepts into vivid scenes and stories that stay in the mind of the reader. Not primarily a theorist, she was a translator who made the problems of industrial England understandable alike to members of parliament and to factory hands. Martineau had been a timid, unhappy child full of religious fears in her early years; with frail health and early deafness, she might have been just another member of the army of employment-seeking spinster governesses. Her health and timidity precluded teaching, and she tried writing with trepidation. Only the instantaneous success of each of her efforts gave her the courage to recognize her own talents and use them.

What tuned her in to the social problems of her day? It is hard to tell from her autobiography (1877a, 1877b), but at some point her omnivorous reading and the finding of a religious home in radical Unitarianism gave her a sense of mission. She had been writing little stories on issues she read about in the newspapers, such as the machine-breaking riots. Her piece on "The Rioters" was such a success that "some hosiers and lace-makers of Derby and Nottingham sent me a request to write a tale on the subject of Wages, which I did, calling it 'The Turn Out.' " This was such a success that from then on she received a steady influx of requests to deal with workers' issues—from the workers themselves. While some of the pieces sounded abstract, like "Principles and Practice," in each case, there was a story setting and an underlying analysis of a social problem. After she had been writing these "stories" for several years, a neighbor lent her Mrs. Marcet's *Conversations on Political Economy*. She discovered to her amazement that she had been teaching the subject of political economy unaware in her stories about machinery and wages. It was then that she conceived the plan for what she considered her major work—a series of stories that would provide a complete exposition of political economy in a form that would speak to the major issues of contemporary British industrial society and deal squarely with controversial policy problems, including population control. She undertook the ambitious *Illustrations of Political Economy* (1832, 1833, 1834), convinced that it would ruin her reputation and destroy all future possibilities for her as a writer but also knowing that workers wanted it and legislators needed it. The quality of sociological imagination that comes through in Martineau's stories is suggested by the fact that workers in any category that became the subject of a story—such as cotton mill hands, inmates of workhouses, domestic servants—were all convinced that she was one of them and wrote out of personal experience. Because her works were also quoted in parliament, no greater audience-reaching capacity has ever been achieved by a social scientist.

Her powers of observation and comparative analysis of social structures come out in another, better known work, *Society in America* ([1837] 1968), which, like Tocqueville's *Democracy in America* ([1835-40] 1944), is a major work on American society by a European, as relevant today as when it was written. Her outspoken support of abolitionism while in America led to lynch threats that left her in daily fear for her life for the remainder of her stay in America—but neither shortened that stay nor softened her outspokenness.

Martineau inevitably became concerned about the situation of women as a result of her studies. She made cogent observations on the similarity of the position of the slave and the woman. To call her a feminist, however, would be to exaggerate a limited aspect of her work. Her powers of observation and analysis were put at the service of all disadvantaged groups. She had a capacity for social listening, and for a creative mirroring back to people of many conditions, that made her a unique contributor to the social change movements of the nineteenth century. All women activists consulted her (except the ones she refused to see because she thought they were phony—she was merciless with phonies), and so did leading men of affairs.[14]

Martineau wrote a gently appreciative sketch of the woman who "taught" her political economy, Mrs. Marcet (Martineau 1877a: 386-92). Mrs. Marcet was a self-effacing housewife with a high-powered mental engine that could only be quieted by being used. Apologetically, she set to writing textbooks on political economy that were adopted in schools all over England. She humbly served social causes whenever social evils were brought to her attention and would do the "homework" on the problems activists encountered. There were probably a great many housewifely Mrs. Marcets doing the intellectual homework for the activists in her century.

An unusual wife-husband team who were publishing in political economy toward the end of Harriet Martineau's life were Mary Paley and Alfred Marshall. Alfred Marshall is the great figure in the neoclassical school, but much of his work was written jointly with his wife, and *The Economics of Industry* (1879) bears both their names. Mary Paley Marshall was widely known in the 1880s as the international clearinghouse for the neoclassical school, and after her husband's death she edited all his works.

Other intellectual women who were doing productive scholarly work independently or with male collaborators sometimes did not attach their names to their work for family reasons. In the literary world, we know that women often used male pseudonyms to "protect" their families. An unusual case of unlabeled intellectual partnership involves Harriet Martineau's contemporary, Harriet Taylor (1807-58). (The two Harriets knew one another and belonged to the same social circle of Unitarian radicals.) Harriet Taylor was a self-taught political economist who worked as John Stuart Mill's collaborator on his *Principles of Political Economy*. Rossi (1973: 34-41) reports that Harriet's husband, John Taylor, refused permission for her name to appear with Mill's as coauthor of the book. The Rossi study gives the details of the unusual collaboration between Harriet Taylor and John Stuart Mill, which led to their marriage after the death of Taylor's husband. Their long and intimate relationship during the lifetime of her first husband suggests that there were more "open marriages" in the Victorian era than is generally supposed. Taylor and Mill also collaborated on essays on marriage and divorce, and Taylor is the author of "The Enfranchisement of Women." Mill's "The Subjection of Women," written after Taylor's death, was one of the major suffrage documents of the second half of the nineteenth century and has been translated into many languages.

Close to the intellectuals who coded and analyzed social conditions for the printed page were young women like Octavia Hill, who in the 1870s belonged to the employment-seeking army of middle-class women. While teaching in a school for girls at the edge of a London slum, she got acquainted with her poor neighbors and discovered living conditions she had never imagined. She became a leader in the development of what was then a brand-new concept—the settlement house—and was a founder of the Charity Organization Society in 1869. The women and men who began making their homes in the London slums, some of them university students like Arnold Toynbee, were fired by the idea that the moral philosophy taught at the university should be translated into practice in the new industrial city. They were creating what was later to become the profession of social work.[15] The first "social work-ers" in Octavia Hill's tenement house organization were specially trained rent collectors. It was their job to help poor women with whatever problems surfaced on rent collection visits, including finding the jobs from which to produce rent money. Hill's equivalent in the United States, working in the very same decades, was Jane Addams.

Beatrice Potter Webb, the first social investigator to develop modern survey research methods, based her life work on what she learned from Octavia Hill and her associates in the London slums. She was not one of those drawn into the labor force by economic need. In her well-to-do home, Herbert Spencer, the "father of sociology," had been a frequent visitor when Beatrice was a child; she grew up familiar with the lan-guage of "the law of increasing heterogeneity." She had Martineau's intellect and moral determination as well as a passion for firsthand investigation of social facts. After completing a history of the coopera-tive movement, she married Sidney Webb. Their union became one of the most productive and affectionate social science partnerships in modern times. Together they documented trade unionism, industrial democracy, and English local government in seven massive volumes.

Sidney and Beatrice had very different abilities, temperaments, and even social philosophies (within the broad framework of socialism) and exerted separate as well as joint leadership roles in the Fabian socialist movement. It was Beatrice who developed for the Fabians the theme of a "national minimum standard of civilized life." Cole (1953-60: Vol. 3, p. 210) suggests that she was more a sociologist than she was a socialist. She was very critical of economics as it was developing by the late 1800s—a narrow abstract science that ignored noneconomic factors in human behavior. She promoted a general social science that could deal with a broad range of social and economic issues, such as her predeces-sor Harriet Martineau had practiced. She was also a decentralist con-cerned with local and nongovernmental action—seeing the state as one huge consumers' cooperative. One of her major contributions to En-glish society was her work on poor-law reform, which in time led to the abolition of the pauper concept and to the provision of a broad range of social services to the poor. Her book *My Apprenticeship* (Webb 1926) is a vivid documentary of the making of a social scientist, and *Our Partnership* (1948) is an autobiographical account of how researchers can affect policymaking.

Beatrice Webb occupied the center of the public policy arena in Britain for 30 years, from the 1880s to the 1920s, but she never served the government except in an advisory capacity on government commit-tees. She rejected positions of official power when they were offered her and also refused the social hostess role that went with her husband's government position. With the privileges of the aristocratic tradition to back her, she remained a completely autonomous person all her life.

The young women trained under people like Octavia Hill and Beatrice Potter Webb should logically have moved into government civil service in the 1890s. Except for poor-law supervision, however, trained women were in general not dealing with women's labor and other issues in government offices until some time after the turn of the century. Instead, these women either stayed in the private sector as volunteers or became paid staff of voluntary associations.

Many of Webb's apprentices were fired with an intellectual curiosity that led them to further training and to a life of scholarship at the London School of Economics and Political Science, which Beatrice herself founded. The university atmosphere in London was very encouraging to women, and, with Harriet Martineau and Beatrice Potter Webb as role models, many women took up the study of economics.

Women made particularly distinguished contributions as economic historians, and a significant part of our insight into the complex nature of the economic transition from the Middle Ages to the twentieth century comes from women. Alice Clark and Ivy Pinchbeck focused on the particular role of the woman worker before and during the industrial revolution. Ada Lonfield, Margaret James, Eileen Power, Carus Wilson, and Doris Leech all became specialists on various aspects of economic history. Eileen Power was one of the most prolific, and one of the most versatile, of these historians. The American Sylvia Thrupp, who as a young woman studied in this stimulating environment of British historians, carried on that same tradition as one of America's outstanding social historians.[16]

In France, roughly contemporaneous with Harriet Martineau, Clemence Augustine Royer published a book on political economy that led to her sharing a prize with Proudhon. She was a generalist, publishing studies of Comte's positivism and an attack on the Laplace theory of the origin of the universe, translating the *Origin of the Species* into French and writing her own book, *L'Origine de l'Homme et des Sociétés*. Her work created many storms, and she was so controversial that, although her election to the French Academy was often discussed, it was never carried out. Renan's praise of her is probably typical of the attitudes of her day: "She is *almost* a man of genius" (italics mine). There were a number of women Saint Simonians in France at this time, but the references to them are so brief (and so hostile) that it is hard to tell whether they were trained économistes or simply enthusiastic advocates of free love.

There must have been many other women doing original social science work in Europe in the second half of the nineteenth century, but their work has gone largely unrecorded. A few stand out by the sheer force of their achievements. One such woman is Conception Arenal, born in 1820 in Spain; she was a self-taught specialist in "penitentiary science," international law, and public education. She entered the public arena with an essay on philanthropy that won the Madrid Academy of Moral and Political Sciences first prize; her manual on visiting the poor has been translated into five languages; her essay on law is the only work by a woman ever printed in the *Biblioteca Juridica;* and she wrote a two-volume work *The Social Question* as well as two books on women.

Rosalie Olivecrona, a graduate of the first girls' school in Sweden, also made herself into a generalist social scientist of broad scope. She helped found a magazine to discuss social questions for women (1870), did a number of surveys of women's work in Sweden, and contributed papers at international social science congresses, including studies of the work of women reformers.

In the United States, social science also attracted women during the latter part of the nineteenth century. Only a few are visible in social history, among them Charlotte Perkins Gilman (1860-1935). An evolutionist whose main work lay in expounding sociological theories of social progress (as in *The Man-Made World*, 1911), her best seller was *Women and Economics* (1970), which, as Rossi (1973: 567) points out, had much the same impact in her day that psychologist Betty Friedan's book, *The Feminine Mystique* (1963), had in the 1960s. Gilman addressed herself directly to the situation of the working woman and the need for institutional change to deal with the problems of home maintenance and child rearing. As an evolutionist, she saw the reabsorption of women into the economic life of society on the basis of more holistic roles for both women and men and more equitable support services for both. She also pointed to the effects of socialization processes in maintaining obsolete role structures and wrote a book, *Concerning Children* (1900), that dealt with rearing both girls and boys for autonomy, independence, and greater social responsibility. The story of her life may be found in her autobiography, *The Living of Charlotte Perkins Gilman* (1935).

As in England, U.S. women were beginning to study economics in increasing numbers toward the end of the nineteenth century. Most of their publications are not well known, but Helen Laura Sumner's major work, the *History of Women in Industry in the United States* ([1910] 1974), has been reprinted.

Ida Turnbell, the social historian, had quite an impact on public opinion through her antitrust writings, including the *History of Standard Oil,* and recruited many Americans to socialism through her work.

Mary Marcy, editor of the *International Socialist Review,* wrote a best seller that had the same effect—*Letters of a Pork Packer's Stenographer,* based on her own experience in working in a slaughterhouse.

There was a whole group of U.S. intellectual women, half scholars, half activists and reformers, who worked together in the latter part of the nineteenth and through the early twentieth century. Jane Addams (1860-1935) founder of Women's International League for Peace and Freedom, is the best known internationally of these women. She played a special role in the group because of her commitment to linking urban neighborhood reform with the broader question of women in society and the still broader question of international peace. She belonged to that growing community of international women who helped conceptualize global society at the turn of the century; they saw women's roles in terms of community and world housekeeping. The economists Emily Green Balch of Wellesley and Julia Grace Wales of Wisconsin University—whose work in the early twentieth century on international peace and mediation plans has come down through records of the peace movement—and Sonia Baber—the geography professor whose research on public peace monuments around the world was an early contribution to peace research (Baber 1948)—were her colleagues in the peace movement. *Peace and Bread in Time of War* (1972) is Addams's major theoretical contribution to the linking of the local and the global. Lillian Wald, a founder of the Children's Bureau; Florence Kelley, organizer of the National Consumers' League; Alice Hamilton, founder of the field of industrial medicine; Edith and Grace Abbott, founders of the profession of social work; and Mrs. Warbasse, a founder of the New School for Social Research and organizer of the American Women's Peace Party, all worked with Jane Addams in the development of social services in the United States.

Mary Ellen Richmond, working somewhat outside the Jane Addams circle, was another major figure in the development of social work in the United States. Richmond has disappeared from sociology textbooks because of her social work orientation. A study of her research work as director of the Charity Organization Department of the Russell Sage Foundation shows that she was one of the first U.S. researchers to develop the theory and methodology of indicators to measure states of social welfare (see her *Social Diagnosis,* 1917). She is said to have invented the casework method of teaching (her *What Is Social Case Work?,* 1922, was translated into Dutch and French and has had seven reprintings). Her discussion of social policy issues in relation to welfare administration at the time when social work was first becoming a profession could be reprinted as a contribution to current discussions (*Friendly Visiting Among the Poor,* 1903). It can now be seen that she was anticipating many of the problems that have since developed in the profession.[17] Most important of all, she understood the new phenomenon of social activism that was appearing on the turn-of-the-century scene and perceived that the future of social work lay in the capacity of social workers to operate at the point of intersection with other services and social activities in a community (see "The Interrelationship of Social Movements" in *The Long View: Papers and Addresses,* 1930: 285). *The Long View,* published posthumously, makes excellent reading today.

It is hard to arrive at a balanced discussion of the contributions of women to social history at the turn of the century. There was the Jane Addams circle. There were the radicals. There were the suffragettes. There were also women social scientists who were not part of any circle and who have dropped out of the social record. The radical thinkers are now being rediscovered and reprinted by various feminist presses.[18] Others are not so lucky. One not-yet-rediscovered thinker is the political scientist Mary Follett, whose *The New State* (1920) will sound more relevant to readers in the 1970s than it did to her own contemporaries. Follett saw the significance of what she called the "group organization movement"[19] when it was receiving little attention. Her book spelled out the significance of the increase in voluntary associations and provided a new view of social progress as interpenetration. She developed concepts of the beyond-contract society that are in my view some of the very concepts needed to solve the power and dominance dilemmas discussed in Chapter 2 of Volume 1 of this book. She was also an early peace researcher. While some of her thinking is obviously limited and outdated, a reprinting of her best work is overdue.

There were other women social scientists who must go unmentioned here for lack of space. A book-length study of women social scientists of the nineteenth and early twentieth centuries is badly needed. It is striking to compare the intellectual climate for women scholars and activists today with the period we have just been discussing, particularly with regard to the interfaces between domestic and international issues. There are few women scholars today working at those interfaces, and most of the activists who concern themselves with them are women who work in organizations founded before 1920. These organizations remain small.

The Philanthropists: England and Europe

In discussing social scientists, I emphasized the collaboration between scholars and activists. The scholars were the theorists, and the activists the practitioners, both drawing on a common stock of knowledge of the workings of the social structure. Both groups were concerned with social change. The philanthropists were more often of the upper class, although not uniformly so.

The development of the transport and communication facilities in the nineteenth century that made international collaboration possible had, as already noted, a special effect on women. They acquired new public spheres of action simultaneously in the national and international communities, and each reinforced the other. Thus we can hardly speak of national philanthropic activity without mentioning the series of international congresses that took place between 1851 and 1893. These were four forums at which elite women for the first time came together from Europe, the Americas, and the Orient (but not yet Africa) to scan and compare social landscapes, thereby much enlarging their comprehension of the problems with which they were dealing. Only in the twentieth century do "ordinary" middle-class women participate in this kind of international event, and working-class and rural women are still by and large excluded.[20]

The first international exhibition was held in London in 1851, the second and third in Paris, in 1855 and 1867, respectively, and the fourth in Chicago in 1893. The Chicago Exhibition was the first that formally organized a section devoted to the work of women, but the three previous congresses had prepared the groundwork for that. Princess Christian of Schleswig-Holstein commissioned a report on the philanthropic work of women in England (Burdett-Coutts 1893) for the Chicago occasion. Mary Kavanaugh Oldham Eagle collected reports from U.S. women for the same occasion (Eagle [1895] 1974). I regret that I do not have similar reports available from other countries. As an overview of activities of interest to the international community of women in 1893, the Burdett-Coutts document in particular gives us some valuable clues to the accomplishments of women philanthropists in the preceding half-century. The woman who compiled the report, Baroness Burdett-Coutts, was the richest woman in England, stayed single all her life and devoted herself full-time to the development and administration of a series of welfare ventures. In 1893, she was certainly the world's leading female philanthropist.

The introduction to the Burdett-Coutts volume on England points out what must have been true for all countries, that is, that much of the philanthropic work carried out in the nineteenth century was not new in substance but only in form. The antecedents of all these currently urban-centered activities had been carried out in rural areas by the lady of the manor house before industrialization. We observed in a previous chapter that the manor house was a training school for young girls and boys of the village in agriculture, crafts, and domestic skills. The manor house kitchen provided food in times of distress; the manor house chapel, religious services; and the manor house library, reading matter for literate villagers. The manor house tradition was still very much alive in the nineteenth century. In towns and villages, there were women carrying on such services as a matter of course, usually under the patronage of the "first lady" of the community. These groups of women were often not dignified by "association" labels yet did the work formal associations carried out in more urban areas.[21] With urbanism, the shift from individual to collective helping efforts became essential, and the manor house lady modernized and collectivized.

All the English activities discussed here come from the 1893 Burdett-Coutts report, with activities from the rest of Europe added from Stanton ([1884] 1970). The Stanton essays, although collected at the same time as the Burdett-Coutts report, do not seem to have been collected in connection with the Chicago Exhibition.

Work for Children

In Europe, Catholic religious orders had long provided orphanages and crèches for babies and small children. The Froebel kindergarten movement spread to the Protestant areas of Europe from 1848 forward but was also found in Catholic areas. Froebel Associations for women were widely established. In the larger cities, such as London, these associations not only provided orphanages and crèches but also developed "houses of industry," which were industrial schools for younger children. They also started special houses for crippled children and children of prisoners. Early (1840) forms of schools for poor children were called "ragged schools"; but this label was soon dropped. In England in the second half of the century, a boarding-out program for workhouse children was developed in an attempt to remove children from a crime-breeding atmosphere. Societies for the "prevention of cruelty to animals" were started in several countries beginning in 1824 in England, but societies for the "prevention of cruelty to children" were much later in starting, an interesting commentary on the sensibilities of the 1800s. Women were among the first workers, although not the titular founders, in both.

Work for Women

In England in the 1850s, the Friends of Workhouse Girls was formed to follow the careers of workhouse graduates as servants and help them in their adjustment problems. A Society for the Promotion of the Employment of Women was also founded in 1859. In 1856, urban family-style residency centers for working girls began in England, which developed later into the international YWCA with residences for working girls in 81 countries. Many independent residence and training centers for working girls developed throughout Europe in the 1880s. The French and the English were the most active in this, because they had the largest cities. In Germany, the Lette-Verein and the Alice-Verein (*Verein* means association) were formed about 1866 to further the employment of women. Also, nurses' training centers were established. Holland approached the employment issue through associations based on the kindergarten movement, providing training for women to be teachers. In Denmark, women concentrated on government legislation to promote the employment of women and, in 1857, achieved significant enabling legislation. Women in Sweden founded a number of institutions to provide services for working girls and also formed associations to promote rural and village handicrafts. In Italy and Spain, women's associations established industrial training centers for girls.

Dutch women at this time were very limited in the activities allowed them and could only form associations around direct charitable purposes such as aid to "fallen women." (They could not aid "falling" ones, the *rapporteur* for Holland says!) In Russia and Poland in 1880, women's associations as such were not permitted. Women could only work in association with men. During this same period, organized nursing services for the urban poor began to develop in England and elsewhere in Europe. Florence Nightingale was a leader in this movement.

Emigration societies were formed in England about 1850, aimed at regulating emigration so that migrating women would be prepared for employment at the other end. The societies also provided aid and reception services at the destination points. (I have not been able to find out whether other countries had emigration societies for women.) This service became important in helping relieve the unemployment of middle-class English women, because many thousands of women were to emigrate to jobs outside of England between 1850 and 1900.

Migrant families, specializing in tunnel, deck, and canal building, known as "navvies" and consisting chiefly of Italians, Norwegians, and English families (about 100,000 in 1880), began receiving special services in 1870. It was to be almost 100 years more before Gypsies were to receive similar attention, in the 1960s.

In this same century, Anglican and Protestant sisterhoods for service to the urban poor were formed. The distrust of celibate sisterhoods that was a legacy of Reformation anti-Catholicism had finally been overcome.

Most of the services and institutions described above were organized by local women's associations in each country. There were also some women who traveled around and spread the word, which meant that the model effect operated rapidly when a particularly valuable program, such as the Froebel kindergartens or services for working girls, was started. An area in which I do not have comparative information from country to country is that of the role of women in improving and innovating in poor-law administration. Judging from publications by the women social reformers mentioned earlier, it is likely that there were women active in this regard in every country in Europe. We know that in England in 1834 women began organizing local volunteer commissions to visit workhouses. The suggestions for improvement they made to local authorities were so useful that by 1853 a regular system of workhouse inspection had been developed based on their recommendations. By 1850, women were publishing a journal on workhouse visiting. This remained an unofficial though recognized activity until 1870, when legislation finally permitted the election of women to the boards of guardians of the poor. It took nearly 40 years, in other words, for women's activities on behalf of the poor in workhouses to move from the privatized volunteer space to the public spaces of the local community. In 1875, the acme of public legitimacy was reached when the first woman government inspector of workhouses was appointed.

The Philanthropists: The United States

In the United States, the development of women's activities was not so urban centered. Until 1900, the United States was still a country of small towns. These small towns were very different than the European villages, with their centuries of tradition. Rather, each town had its pioneer memories. Women could recollect the way of life of mothers and grandmothers who had helped clear land and build homes. They remembered the agriculture and domestic crafts that were no longer necessary to the average small-town household by the mid-1800s. There were no manor house models to look to, just a do-it-yourself tradition.

On the East Coast, there were the cosmopolitan cities of Boston, Philadelphia, and New York from which women traveled abroad and engaged in "exotic" intellectual and radical movements. Margaret Fuller (1810-50), the New England transcendentalist, part of the Brook Farm group and editor of *The Dial*, who finally went abroad to discover new horizons and identify herself with the Italian independence movement, was not comprehensible to the small-town American activist. Neither was Frances Wright (1795-1852), a Scotswoman and Owenite identified with the major European movements of her day, including the movement for women's rights. Wright first traveled to the United States with Lafayette and later returned to found an Owenite colony, Nashoba, in the swamps of Tennessee. This was to be a utopian community with complete racial and sexual equality. Disease ridden, it lasted for four sad years, 1825 to 1829. Wright spent considerable time in the United States trying to organize urban reform on the British model, with a focus on working-class problems. Because her free thinking shocked the small-town U.S. women, however, her energy and reform instincts never connected with the perspectives of U.S. "organization" women.

In Europe, the lady of the manor house bridged the rural-urban gap for women. In the United States, there were no gap bridgers. Out of the need that gap represented, however, was born a social invention of profound significance for America and for the world community of women: the women's club movement. Neither philanthropic nor suffragist, it rather asserted the right to a social and intellectual identity for women apart from service roles. It was born in New York and first spread to Boston, Philadelphia, and Chicago. It soon took root in small towns across the United States and provided a sphere of autonomy for women and a protected place to develop civic understanding.

Sorosis, the first women's club, was born in New York in 1868. It was created out of the indignation of a group of women journalists who had been denied the right to purchase tickets for a Press Club dinner to hear Charles Dickens speak. "The (male) club" was a very special kind of private public space in American society, and women were completely excluded from the intellectual life that went on in such organizations. After the Dickens affair, the New York women journalists formed their own club, to the jeers of their male colleagues (who said it would not last a year). When later condescendingly invited by the Press Club to a tea at which they were only allowed to listen, not speak, they retaliated by inviting the Press Club to a tea at which the men were not allowed to speak. The men got the message, and a historic dinner was jointly sponsored by the two groups, with women and men participating equally in planning and speaking.

There were many efforts to steer women to service activities, but they resisted successfully. They wanted to *think*, observe the social scene, develop perspectives on society. That this was a strongly felt need is best evidenced by the fact that in 1898, when the first history of the women's club movement was written (Croly 1898), there were already 934 affiliated clubs in 42 states and the District of Columbia as well as affiliates in India, England, Australia, East Africa, Chile, and Mexico. From Sorosis to the nearly 1,000-branched Federated Women's Clubs was quite a leap, and it all happened in about 25 years.

The clubs took on a great variety of names locally. In Hypatia and Shakespeare clubs, historical and scientific societies, civic clubs, social science associations, village improvement clubs, business and professional women's groups, the members were all ardent generalists, discovering their individual and societal identities in the late nineteenth century. The movement was one of the most impressive self-education ventures in history, and out of it subsequently came many specialized women's professional associations and special-purpose organizations. The suffragette movement was greatly strengthened by it, and the League of Women Voters was one of its many offspring. The federation itself continues today as a generalist organization and has played an important part in the development of international associations for women. By the 1950s, women's clubs were an object of fun in the United States, affectionately but not very flatteringly immortalized in the Helen Hokinson cartoons in *The New Yorker*. That they were a vehicle invented by pioneer society to further the creation of civic culture in the absence of lady of the manor traditions has not been adequately recognized.

The U.S. women who paralleled in their work that of European women in the settlement house movement, and in protective legislation for women and children in factories, who created reformatories and juvenile courts, and who humanized police stations by introducing police matrons, for the most part sharpened their skills in the women's clubs. A major consequence of the proliferation of clubs for women in the United States was the development of organizing skills. To this day, the U.S. woman's ability to "organize a meetin'" at the drop of a hat awes her European sisters.

Small-town activism at its most creative can be seen in states like Michigan, which played a key role in the operation of the Underground Railway, the pre-Civil War social invention that expedited the movement of escaped slaves from the South to Canada. Laura Haviland, an intrepid Quaker of Michigan, was in her day known as the Superintendent of the Underground Railway.

Haviland is the prototype of the competent American small-town activist, although it should be pointed out that, coming from a Quaker tradition, she possibly had more encouragement to speak up in public than some of her neighbors. She also had an unusually sharp mind and a quality of Christian faith that carried her serenely through physical dangers from which most men and women would shrink. She was not afraid of physical confrontation with furious slave owners, yet she was smart enough to escape from the kidnap traps they set for her. She not only traveled freely through the South, where she was Public Enemy Number 1, where there were "WANTED" signs up for her everywhere, she also moved freely through the military bureaucracy once the war was on, to clean up scandalous prisons and hospitals and to get malevolent or simply incompetent administrators removed.

Laura Haviland was a self-taught operations research analyst. Her technique was simple, brilliant, and effective. She would collect supplies of clothing and food on her own initiative in Michigan and surrounding states, then travel with her shipment from one army station to another. At each place, she presented herself to the commanding officer as one who had supplies to distribute, asking for a letter that would admit her to all the installations under his command. Because supplies were always needed, she always got the letter. In the course of allocating her medical supplies, she would incidentally improve hospital sanitation systems and reorganize ward medical services and administration of supplies. Haviland did all this with one hand while with the other she took the excuse of providing food supplies to clean up the kitchens and teach the cooks how to prepare and serve food properly. She did the same in prisons. When army administrative personnel protested, she had her magic letter from the commanding officer. She could make one shipment of food and clothing from the North carry her through a whole series of battle stations. At every hospital through which she moved with her reforming "magic," she always had time to sit at the bedside of dying soldiers.

Her trips to the battle stations did not interfere with her continued superintendence of the Underground Railway or with running the school she had founded in Michigan for black and white children. If Laura Haviland had not toward the end of her life taken time out to write her autobiography as a device to raise money for the chain of schools she was then organizing, there would be no way of knowing the part she played in the Civil War era. Today, a lucky reader may, as I did, come across a crumbling dusty copy of that autobiography (Haviland 1882) in an old midwest Quaker meetinghouse library. This gentle, iron-willed Quaker lady has a significance beyond her time and place as an example of how an ingenious woman can preempt public spaces and authority to serve the public good, successfully rejecting the underlife spaces allotted her by society.

The reports from which the above accounts of women's activities have been taken were written with pride. They represent substantial achievements, mostly in urban settings. It was in these same urban settings, however, as noted earlier, that the class interests of bourgeois and proletarian women often conflicted. Certainly perceptions of program priorities might conflict. To the extent that the voluntary associations confined themselves to specific services such as identifying employment opportunities, providing skill training, and creating alter-

TABLE 3.1 Date of Founding of a Sample of 116 Women's Religious Orders

Pre-1200	2
1200-1399	5
1400-1799	13
1800-49	28
1850-99	47
1900+	20
Not ascertainable	1
Total	116

SOURCE: Data are from the *Guide to the Catholic Sisterhoods in the United States* (McCarthy 1955), which describes more than 300 sisterhoods in detail.
NOTE: The countries of origin of these orders are Algeria, Belgium, Brazil, Canada, England, France, Germany, Italy, Mexico, the Netherlands, Spain, Switzerland, South Africa, and the United States.

natives to the workhouse for women and children, the conflict was minimal. But, when the philanthropists were insensitive to the underlying economic issues and focused on morality and life-styles, the potential conflict was great. Because poor women were not in a position to argue with their benefactors, the conflict was rarely overt. Many of the social attitudes (particularly of condescension) with which benefactors carried out their activities would be totally unacceptable today. These attitudes were a cultural product of their time and should not obscure the really remarkable amount of social problem solving that went on in this privatized women's sector. For a whole century, women were in effect tutoring male civil servants and government officials in how to deal with social welfare problems.

Religious Philanthropies and Women's
Religious Orders

The religious counterpart to the secular developments described above is to be found in the explosion of new teaching and service sisterhoods within the Catholic church and in new Protestant religious service organizations. It was in this century that the Catholic sisterhoods were finally able to break the cultural barriers within the church that kept earlier efforts to develop missionary teaching and service activities from coming to full fruition.

Counting only those orders that developed branches in the United States, almost 500 new Catholic women's orders were founded between 1800 and 1899. The tabulation in Table 3.1, based on a sample of 116 of these orders, puts this development in the context of the entire history of women religious.

It is of interest to know to what extent these orders were founded *for* women or *by* women. Because a male religious superior must put through the "founding" request in every case, it is not always easy to tell whether the original initiative came from a church dignitary or a woman. Relying on the way the historian of the order describes the founding, and listing as "founded by women" each order where a woman initiator is mentioned by name, I conclude that, of the 116 orders studied, 67 were initiated by women and 44 by men, with 5 unclear. "Man-initiated" means that a parish priest or a bishop specifically asked for women to come and organize under his auspices a teaching or social service program. "Woman-initiated" means that a woman or several women gathered together, decided on a service, then found church backing to do it. Given the prolonged emphasis on enclosure for women, the figure of 67 women-initiated service orders is impressive. While many of the orders began with one specific mission such as conducting an elementary school in a certain parish, by the twentieth century, they are nearly all administering a great variety of institutions and services. Their activities can be summarized under the following headings: (a) *teaching and administering schools*—elementary, secondary, college, university, nursing school, normal school; (b) *social service and administering health and welfare institutions*—orphanages; institutions for the handicapped; homes for unwed mothers; residence homes for working girls; urban settlement houses; schools and community centers for Native Americans, blacks, Mexican Americans; centers for juvenile delinquents; hospitals; nursing homes; and (c) *community ministry*—home and community service to the categories of people listed above, outside institutional settings. I was not able to find how many countries each order serves, but no order is confined to only one country, and some may serve up to a dozen or more.

Cita-Malard (1964) estimates that there were about 1 million women in Catholic orders at the time she was writing. Only 6% of these orders are contemplatives; the other 94% are service orders. That new contemplative orders should continue to be founded in the 1800s is a clue to the continued perception of the relevance of the contemplative life on the part of women in the contemporary world; there are between 1,500 and 1,800 contemplative convents around the world today. If secular institutes and sisterhoods from Anglican and other Protestant groups and sisterhoods from Buddhist, Moslem, and Hindu traditions were considered together with the Catholic orders, there would probably be more than 2 million women living a life vowed to celibacy, poverty, and service. How many women religious there were in earlier centuries we do not know, but the million figure for the Catholics was probably reached in the nineteenth century. Women religious tend to be long-lived, so many founder-sisters were personally known to the current generation of sisters of their order.

Most of the sisterhoods were founded in Europe at the height of the emigration era, and sisters sailed to new lands right along with the migrant women seeking their fortunes. Whether their destination was North America, Australia, Africa, or Asia, when they landed they had to fend for themselves just as their immigrant job-seeking sisters did. They, too, cleared land and built buildings, but not for themselves. They contributed to the earliest beginnings of schools and hospitals wherever they went. They took their chances with hunger and privation along with everyone else and sometimes had the added burden of mistrust and persecution. The Catholic church did not always know how to respond to this new brand of pioneering nuns, so different than the quiet cloistered sisters priests were used to—and neither did the Protestant community. The sisters earned the right to teach and nurse and serve by winning the respect and friendship of the communities to which they came. Humor, ingenuity, courage, and faith opened doors for them.

In the United States, for example, German sisters emigrated to German settlements in the Midwest and provided a transition educational experience for the children of German immigrants. In fact, every emigrating national group brought its ministers and priests along, and this national enclave effect caused problems at first. Those who held to a strong melting-pot ideology wanted to bypass this transitional period entirely. In the end, the sisterhoods were probably the most effective facilitators of immigrant adjustment. They provided a broader matrix of services than priests and ministers could offer. Their teachings encompassed the nationalisms left behind, as well as the nationalisms entered into, and set them in the context of the more universal sisterhood that the church in its original intention represented.

Some of the most radical developments in the contemporary Catholic church have come from the twentieth-century inheritors of these sisterhood traditions. By breaking out of the cloister and away from the motherland, the sisters gained many new perspectives at once. Their relative freedom to move about in the new terrains they entered, given their freedom from marital obligations, made them available for innovations that are still being worked out today.

The Protestant sisterhoods soon found their way abroad too. The nineteenth century was the great missionary century. Every church established its "mission field" and sent women and men abroad to teach, to care for the sick, to farm—and to proselytize. The missionary movement was sparked by the dawning internationalism of the century, in which concepts of a family of humankind as a world Christian family played an important part. There were a lot of limitations to that concept. The rhetoric about the "little brown brothers" ("little brown sisters" were rarely mentioned) was a rhetoric of condescension. But the missionary travels sparked new learnings both for the missionaries and for those among whom they settled.

The popular image of the nineteenth-century missionary is of a narrow-minded preacher dressed in black, traveling with a Bible under his arm to preach fierce sermons to uncomprehending natives. In the first place, more than half of the "he's" were "she's." In the second place, many of them were of working-class origin themselves and had a more practical approach to relating to "the heathen" than they have been given credit for having.

Their endeavors were in part an outcome of a humanitarian impulse to try to undo the harm of the slave trade. Assistance to resettled colonies of ex-slaves was part of the new missionary thrust. The European governments' policy of "Christianity, Commerce, and Colonization" was intended to introduce trading with ex-slaves as "equals," and to replace the earlier trading in slaves,[22] and many of the early missionaries were carriers of the new intentions. But the new style of trade did not suit the colonial situation, in which centuries of violence and exploitation had set up quite other expectations. In the end, "merely to keep order," European governments found themselves intervening more and more in the affairs of local peoples. Furthermore, the slave trade was hard to stop, and another 2 million slaves were shipped across the Atlantic even while the "new" type of European-African relations were being established.

The missionaries were by no means always an arm of these intervening governments. They had their own agendas. While they made many mistakes, and learned the hard way to take account of differing social values, they often gave a type of aid that in the twentieth century we would label "intermediate technology." They may in fact have done less harm and more good than twentieth-century aid experts.

There is a whole literature on the activities of women missionaries, both Protestant and Catholic, in Africa, Asia, and the Americas in the nineteenth century that deserves special study. The encounter of women of other continents with the missionary women of Europe should properly be written as an encounter between two sets of women's cultures. The scramble to carve up Africa and establish imperial control over Asia was a male enterprise, carried out by the men of Europe with the enforced cooperation of the men of Africa and Asia. Traditional political and trading roles of indigenous women were ignored in the process. It is possible that valuable information on women's activities in colonized areas can be recovered from accounts of women missionaries, who would be far more likely than men to have entered into the women's spaces.

In addition to the church-based missions, there were the broad nondenominational movements such as the Young Women's Christian Association (YWCA), the Salvation Army, and the Women's Christian Temperance Union (WCTU). The YWCA addressed itself particularly to the problems of young working women. The Salvation Army and the WCTU worked with everyone—young, old, in families, and particularly with deserted, widowed, and single women with children.

Because these organizations were born in the cities of Europe and North America, when they expanded to Africa and Asia, it was in the cities of these continents that they took root. Tokyo, Peking, Bangkok, Delhi, Lagos, and Cape Town were among the first settings where women of the West worked with their Two-Thirds World sisters. Often, it was the elites of one society meeting the elites of another, as wives of businessmen and diplomats from Europe brought their organizational habits with them to the Two-Thirds World and entertained their indigenous counterparts in ways they thought appropriate. Nevertheless, it was a beginning. The missionary-trained women doing the everyday work of the YWCA and the WCTU abroad were not elites; they belonged to the middle and upper working classes.

All three of these international movements had in common a twin commitment to spiritual and economic welfare. All three movements emphasized moral purity and practical hard work, all were urban based, and all contributed to some degree to the growing world consciousness of the nineteenth century. The YWCA and the WCTU were for women only; the Salvation Army worked with both women and men. The parts of their programs that twentieth-century observers find easiest to understand are those relating to social welfare and the "Puritan work ethic." The spiritual welfare concept is to some degree intelligible, but the moral purity concept seems hopelessly out of tune with "liberal" contemporary understandings of human beings. To appreciate the significance of the moral purity concept for organizations working with women, one has to remember how vulnerable the 50% or so of urban women who lived as singles were to venereal disease. The more men a woman provided sexual services for, the greater the likelihood of her being infected. At the same time, the Malthusian problem, which we tend to think was first taken seriously in this century, was in fact taken seriously in the last. It was perfectly obvious that poor single women with children suffered. Contraceptive technology existed but was largely unavailable to the poor. The Mensinga diaphragm, invented in 1870 in Holland, was only for the well-to-do. Margaret Sanger had to go to France to find techniques to help urban working women in the United States. Abortions were risky to women's health. Infanticide, the poor women's abortion, was abhorred. The best protection for women was abstention, and the concept of moral purity put the practice of abstention into a context of self-development of the personality and the will. It was not a cramping, inhibiting concept; it was a releasing one. Moral purity was one aspect of a holistic development of the person, a development that included spiritual and social awareness. Young women trained in the educational programs of missionary reform movements were often able to deal very practically with their own life problems.

The Salvation Army was founded by Catherine Booth and her husband, William (Bolton 1895). Coming out of the dissenting traditions that encouraged the participation of women, both the Booths were drawn to the revivalist movement and went to London out of a fervent desire to save the poor. The difference between the Booths' and some other evangelical movements was that the Booths shared the way of life of slum people. The Salvation Army centers that dot the world today developed at that time out of the practical need to find food, clothes, shelter, and jobs for the unemployed of the slums. While Salvation Army workers acted on the premise that there were two hungers, they did not confuse physical and spiritual hunger. Their spiritual message was the better heard because they had a practical approach to economic problems: a network of city centers connected to self-supporting agricultural communities. There has always been equality between women and men at all levels of the organization.

The Salvation Army phenomenon could never be explained by practical problem-solving skills alone, however. Catherine Booth in particular had a quality of joyfulness that infected the movement. English folk over 50 who remember bands of Salvation Army lassies singing on the streets remember happy faces. People loved the lassies. In their overseas expansion, they have kept to the same practical simplicity of organization and to the same cheerfulness.

The Women's Christian Temperance Union has many of the qualities of the Salvation Army, although it is an all-women's group and does more social work and less preaching. An offshoot of an earlier all-male group, it became a national organization in 1873 and an international one in 1891. The WCTU's strength is that it has aimed directly at the problems that face both single and married urban working women—skill training, employment, and decent housing. It has also confronted in a constructive way the associated problems of alcoholism and unwanted babies. Today's more sophisticated generation may smile at the

WCTU rhetoric on the evils of alcohol, but urban WCTU centers around the world have provided significant "new start" opportunities for women. They have seen personal problems in social contexts and local and national welfare problems in the international context. Their literature on the problems of world peace can hold its own with that of the more "intellectual" peace organizations. Their triple program of "temperance, moral purity, and world peace" has taken shape in centers that create environments for young women in which they can reach their full potentials. The WCTU has sections in 61 countries, and one of the finest of these is in Japan. The programs for young working women in Tokyo rival or surpass the best urban facilities for women in Europe or North America.

There is a long roster of women who have made the WCTU what it is. In the United States, Frances Willard, its founder, is its best known member. Her words describe the quality of the organization very well:

> We are a world republic of women—without distinction of race or color—who recognize no sectarianism in religion, no sectionalism in politics, no sex in citizenship. Each of us is as much a part of the world's union as is any other woman; it is our great, growing, beautiful home. The white ribbon includes all reforms; whatever touches humanity, touches us. (Gordon 1924: 69)

It is interesting to speculate on why the two nineteenth-century organizations that dealt most directly and honestly with the special problems of poor urban women are looked at with condescension today, yet most liberal middle-class American women are not comfortable with the idea of sitting in a meeting with a group of prostitutes. Why not? Perhaps because the latter are trying to shift into the public spaces of society issues that the middle class would prefer to keep privatized.

The International Peace Movement

One issue that seriously troubled the suffragette section of the nineteenth-century women's movement was that of international peace. All the other social problems that the century's women's organizations dealt with had to do with improving conditions for women, even if they did not directly contribute to her gaining political rights. World peace, however, was problematic and has remained so for many feminists right up to the current time. And yet, as I have suggested, there was a pervasive internationalism in many women's activities. Some women really did feel, even if they would not have put it into just those words, an identification with Frances Willard's "world of community of women."

The double socialization process into national and world public spaces was noticeable as early as 1802, when a young Englishwoman published *A Vision Concerning Peace and War* at the time of the Peace of Amiens between Britain and France (Posthumus-van der Goot 1961: 11). Between 1816 and 1828, national peace societies were founded in England and America. In 1820, the first all-women's peace societies were active in England and, by the 1830s, they were active in America. *An Examination of the Principles Considered to Support the Practices of War*, published by an Englishwoman in 1823, was repeatedly reprinted and translated into French, Dutch, German, Spanish, and Hebrew. A steady stream of publications came from the British women's peace societies in the 1830s, with women beginning to sign their names to their writings.

In 1848, the first international peace congress was held in Brussels. One of the most remarkable events of that congress was the unprecedented behavior of the chairman, who addressed the assembled delegates as "mesdames et messieurs." The International Anti-Slavery Congress in London several years previously had refused even to seat women. The peace congress seated women, saluted them, and had them speak.

By 1852, the Anglo-American women's peace societies (the Olive Leaf Circles) were issuing the first women's international publication, *Sisterly Voices*. Fredrika Bremer of Sweden proposed an international association of women for peace, and the leaders of this little international community of women were Bremer, a distinguished writer; two French Saint-Simonians, Elise Grimault and Julie Toussaints; Marie Goegg, a leading humanist of Geneva; Julia Ward Howe of the United States, writer; Priscilla Peckover, English Quaker activist and editor of the journal *Peace and Goodwill*; and Bertha Suttner of Austria, author of a major work on disarmament, *Die Waffen Nieder* (published as *Down with Arms* in 1894). All of them except Peckover worked both with all-women's groups and with mixed groups. Peckover was adamant about keeping out men. She single-handedly built up the first major women's international network, with members in England, France, the Rhineland, Hannover, Rome, Warsaw, Constantinople, Russia, Japan, Polynesia, Portugal, and the United States. The Peckover international network has probably been used by many women's groups since, to the third generation. Suttner was the most public figure of all these women. Her first book was *The Machine Age* and her second was the documentary on disarmament. She played a leading role in the Interparliamentary

Union and was responsible for persuading Alfred Nobel to establish the Nobel peace prize. An Austrian aristocrat and a powerful and imperious woman, she had been educated in the scholar-aristocrat tradition still extant in Europe. Her biographer Ursula Jorfald tells us how excited she was at 12 finally to have a playmate after a solitary childhood; the playmate was versed in Hegel, Fichte, and Kant (Jorfald 1962: 7)! Suttner brought to the international peace movement both the strengths and the weaknesses of elitist traditions.

By 1891, after a century of activity, there was an International Peace Bureau in Berne (100 years old in 1991), which coordinated the activities of 200 different peace societies. Women were active in most of these, and some were all-women's organizations. If we look at women who were attracted to the women's peace movement in the beginning of the twentieth century such as the Womens International League for Peace and Freedom, many of them had been active since 1880, and we are struck with the extent of their professionalism and commitment to public life (see Table 3.2 and also the earlier section in this chapter on women social scientists). It was clearly a task-oriented group, directing its attention to problems that today, more than a century later, still defy definition and precision. It seemed to be a challenge whose time had come, but, for lack of specific approaches to meeting the challenge, much of this concentrated effort of women has since been diverted from international peace to other problems closer at hand.

The Women's Rights Movement

In my descriptions of women's activities during the nineteenth century, I have made only slight reference to the attitudes and values of the male-dominated societies of which they were a part. For every word or deed I have described as directed to public ends by women in this century, I could reprint pages of male abuse aimed at each word and at each deed. While in some ways it seems unproductive and unduly depressing to pay too much attention to the barrage of male abuse poured on women through the nineteenth and all preceding centuries, that ongoing phenomenon must be recalled at this time to understand the intensity of the women's rights movement when it came into full swing. Women were fighting to throw off legal disabilities that hindered their full command over their own persons, limited their share in societal resources including employment and protection from illness and poverty, and blocked their role in societal decision making. They were also fighting for the right to be

TABLE 3.2 Occupations of Professional Women in the 1915 International Peace Movement

Occupation	Number
Doctor	2
Judge	1
Trade union movement	3
Lawyer	3
Social worker	1
Economist	4
International relations	1
Government official	2
Member of parliament	8
Physical scientist	2
Educator	6
Social scientist	1
Suffragette, public figure	5
Total	39

SOURCE: Data from Bussey and Tims (1965).

treated as adult persons worthy of consideration and respect rather than as children or idiots vulnerable to any abuse.

Many different currents came together to trigger the women's rights movement in the nineteenth century, and this chapter focuses on some of the less frequently recorded ones. I am suggesting that the sheer amount of frustration built up by the fact of women being active in a wide variety of problem-solving activities, without accompanying political rights and responsibilities, was one force for suffrage. At the same time, it should be pointed out that a number of activist women stayed outside the suffrage struggle, even at its height, because they felt it inappropriate or unnecessary to include suffrage among the causes for which they worked. They did not see themselves as part of the victimization system. Among the successful elites, there was often blindness to the class-based nature of their own privilege and freedom as well as failure to recognize that others with equal abilities from other classes could not do what they had done.

Because the suffrage movement is the best-documented part of women's history, no attempt will be made here to detail that history. Rather, I will point out some cultural differences in origin and program emphasis among different national movements. Each country has dealt better with some of the issues associated with women's rights than with others.

The Anglo-American women's rights movement has its roots in the stream of thought that can be picked up in Christine de Pisan in the 1400s, in Marie de Jars Gournay in the 1600s, and in Mary Wollstonecraft in the 1700s. In the colonial United States, the thinking of Abigail Adams (C. F. Adams 1975) and Anne Hutchinson (Abramowitz 1946:

307-42) belong in the feminist stream, but neither woman wrote for publication, so their ideas never became part of the international women's culture.

One milestone on the road to removal of women's civil and legal disabilities was the publication in England in 1825 of the *Appeal of One Half the Human Race, Women Against the Pretensions of the Other Half, Men to Restrain Them in Political and Thence in Civil and Domestic Slavery,* by William Thompson and Anna Wheeler. Thompson alone appears as author, but his dedication makes it clear that this was a joint product (Pankhurst 1954: 26). Anna Wheeler (born 1785) was one of the most advanced thinkers of her time. Victim of a terrible marriage from which she finally escaped with her two surviving daughters, she was for a time the center of a Saint-Simonian circle in France and close to the young Fourier. Returning to England, she worked with Robert Owen in Jeremy Bentham's circle. She and William Thompson are often linked in the records of the cooperative movement, and their friendship of "mutual opinions and ideals" had something of the flavor of the Taylor-Mill friendship of the next generation, described earlier (Pankhurst 1954: 65-78). The occasion of the *Appeal* was the publication of James Mill's famous "Article on Government" (1824 supplement to the *Encyclopedia Britannica*), which expounded the doctrine of "included interest" for women, stating that women did not need independent political representation because their interests were included in those of their fathers and husbands. The Wheeler-Thompson book dealt not only with the subjection of married women but with the casually ignored one-fourth of the female population with neither father nor husband.

The Wheeler-Thompson appeal profoundly affected the position of the cooperative movement and the thinking of Marx and Engels, becoming a historical landmark in thought about the position of women in society. The appeal was also incorporated into the original draft of the People's Charter of Rights and Liberties framed by the Chartist movement in 1838. Women began at this time to form associations to promote the Wheeler-Thompson suffrage clause, with Birmingham as the center of the movement. The clause was soon removed from the Chartist declaration as being "premature," but the women's associations stayed alive.

In the preceding decade, women had started writing articles advocating the vote for women. In 1832, a Yorkshire woman, Mary Smith, petitioned parliament for the right of unmarried women to vote. Four different groups converged in the 1830s to form the first major suffrage movement: (a) the previously mentioned political associations formed in connection with the Chartist declaration; (b) the women's "auxiliaries" in the Anti-Corn Law League, which were giving women direct political experience in lobbying on economic issues; (c) a broad mass of women whose consciousness was raised by the Caroline Norton divorce case, which remained a major public issue from 1836 when it first went to court until 1856 when the Marriage and Divorce Reform Law was passed; and (d) the social scientist-activist alliance engaged in the welfare and education reform movements described in the preceding pages. The Chartist-inspired women's political associations kept issuing leaflets and statements for several decades after their initial proclamation in 1838.

In 1851, the Sheffield Women's Political Association was formed, and, in 1865, the Kensington Society, composed of outstanding women leaders, was formed and began attracting considerable attention. Their first activity was to campaign (successfully) for John Stuart Mill's election to parliament. Next, all the women's political associations mobilized to get signatures for the petition Mill presented to parliament in 1866 for the enfranchisement of women. In 1867, the London National Society for Women's Suffrage was formed. While most people date the British women's movement from that time, there had already been more than 30 years of activity on behalf of suffrage.

The famous incident in London in 1840, when U.S. women delegates were refused seats at the International Anti-Slavery Congress held there, did not play the decisive role in the English suffrage movement that it played in the U.S. movement. It was fury over that event that brought Elizabeth Cady Stanton and Lucretia Mott back to the United States to organize the Seneca Falls Convention of 1848 that launched the U.S. suffrage movement. One reason the antislavery congress incident is not part of the public history of the English movement is that English women already had a fairly high level of activity and awareness at the time. The congress event was not their first shock and therefore did not have the same dramatic mobilizing effects on them that it had on the Americans.

In the course of the three decades of buildup of the suffrage movement before 1867, two different kinds of emphasis became clear: Enfranchisement to overcome *economic disadvantage* was the theme of the working-class women, the Chartists, who were suffering severely from economic setbacks during this period; enfranchisement for *political decision making* was the theme of the middle-class women, the suffragettes, who had personally secure situations but wanted a freer hand to set things straight for society at large. Economic issues were not entirely lacking among the suffragettes—large numbers of unemployed single women seeking nonexistent positions put some added pressure on their suffrage activities—but, in the main, the suffrage movement stayed middle class, and trade union women worked for their rights separately. When the suffragettes went radical, with the formation of the Women's Social and Political Union in 1903, there was a conscious effort to make an alliance with working-class women, but this only lasted three years. The styles were too different.

For all the class feelings of confidence and superiority with which suffragettes carried on their campaigns, strategically they were not very successful. The sweet reasonableness of the nineteenth century was followed by campaigns of fire and fury in the early twentieth century with women chaining themselves to the gates of parliament. The fire-and-fury period was one of real martyrdom for many English suffragette leaders. Elite women who had always been able to exert authority and control by virtue of their class status were thrown into prison for months at a time and, when they went on hunger strikes, they were brutally force-fed. Some women had their health permanently damaged as a result of the force-feeding. This was a new experience for such women, and they might in the end have been politicized in a new way and rediscovered the alliance with their worker sisters had not the war intervened and set another dynamic in motion.

It is interesting to reflect on the course of the British suffrage movement. Neither reason nor fury got the suffragettes the vote, and many volumes have been written on why a group of women as sophisticated and useful to the national welfare as the British suffragettes could not succeed in their own enfranchisement. In the end, it was political convenience that got them the vote—after the war (Pugh 1974). The suspension of suffragette activity and identification with the war effort on the part of many suffragettes showed that many women were more nationalist than feminist. Those who adhered to international allegiances became pariahs among their former sisters. This split was felt inside the Pankhurst family, England's "First Family" in the suffrage movement. Mother Emmaline and daughter Christobel threw themselves wholeheartedly into the war effort. Daughter Sylvia remained stubbornly socialist and pacifist.[23]

In general, the suffragettes stayed a one-issue group, and this meant that they backed away from the very issues that became central to the German and Scandinavian women's rights movements: protection of single women and their illegitimate children and protection from abusive prostitution-control laws. Josephine Butler was actively disliked by many suffragettes who felt that her campaign for the abolition of police regulation of prostitution deflected attention from feminist issues as they saw them.

While I have used the term *Anglo-American* for one style of suffrage work, there really was no Anglo-American entity. The U.S. women who came into the women's rights movement were not inexperienced— some of the leaders had participated in the temperance and abolition movements and the moral crusades of the early 1800s—but they were on the whole conservative, small-town activists concerned with the protection of society as they knew it and with a modest extension of their freedom into the political arena.[24] Only a few U.S. suffragettes were interested in international movements. The fact that the U.S. suffrage movement was born out of indignation over the exclusion of U.S. women from an international antislavery congress in London was not calculated to sharpen interest in international activities! The movement's strength lay in the middle classes of the small towns. There were no alliances with working women and little concern with the protection of single women and illegitimate children. Such phenomena were handled under the category of "fallen women."

There was a link between one wing of the U.S. suffragettes and the peace movement, which led to the formation of the Woman's Peace party in the early twentieth century. That group was led by the same Addams-Wald-Kelley-Hamilton-type coalition of women leaders noted earlier; they seem to have been a democratic version of England's leading elites. In the end, however, U.S. women, like their English sisters, earned their suffrage in the eyes of men through vigorous support of the war. The pacifist women were as isolated from their sisters in the United States as they had been in England. In terms of outcomes, U.S. women were slightly more successful than their British sisters were. English women over 30 voted by 1918, but not until 1928 could they vote at the same age as men—21. American women voted by 1920, and everyone over the age of 21 was enfranchised at once.

In northern Europe, the vote itself never took center stage in the women's rights movement. Rather, the *Mutterschutz* idea became the overriding goal for the movement. "Protection of motherhood" is not an adequate translation of the concept, which is not directly translatable into Anglo-American values. It has to do with a different approach to the role of women, involving the reform (or, in extreme versions, the abolition) of marriage so that every woman may enter and leave marital relationships freely and at will and may bear children independently of marriage status. The care and responsibility for the welfare of children was not to be linked to marriage. Social security legislation that protects mothers and their children, assures educational and employment opportunities, and guarantees equal pay for equal work was part of the program as was a reform in sexual ethics. The vote was considered important too but was not necessarily the top priority in the program.

The Mutterschutz concept does not represent a drive to send women back into the home but a drive to protect women wherever they are, including the factory, and to protect their right to bear children without harassment. Why this focus on the single woman, ignored in most women's rights programs? As in England, about 40% of German women of childbearing age were unmarried in the 1880s, and this situation persisted into the 1900s. In 1905, 1 out of every 12 German babies was born out of wedlock. As Katharine Anthony summarizes it, "Owing to emigration and colonial expansion, industrial accident and war, the women find themselves in the unsought position of the majority" (1915: 85). The result was that half the adult female population were heading a household. Many of these women might wish children even though only temporary unions with men were possible. Many illegitimate children were in fact wanted children, in spite of the opprobrium associated with illegitimacy—not all, of course. For women who did not wish children, said the women's rightists, abortion must be possible.

Ellen Key, the Swedish feminist, took a rather deviant stand on Mutterschutz. She was for the complete abolition of marriage and the return to what she visualized as an original matriarchal system, in which all women would live surrounded by their children and men would support them but have no marriage rights. Public affairs and the vote would be left to men, the lesser beings. This line of thought went so contrary to emerging conceptions of both proletarian and middle-class women that in the end she modified her position and supported suffrage.

Such extremes of the Mutterschutz movement sound like a Nazi program for master race eugenics. The main body of the movement, however, kept its eyes unwaveringly on the issues that AngloAmerican women's rights movements generally ignored: the plight of the unpartnered woman with children, wanted or unwanted. Only relatively recently has the "new" women's liberation movement begun to deal with this issue in the United States.

The Mutterschutz movement has to be seen side by side with the movement to expand education and employment opportunities for women. This became formally organized on a national basis in Germany in 1865, about the same time that the British women's suffrage movement was formalized. A bimonthly journal, New Paths, was started. Legislative reforms for women came slowly, but they did get the vote at the end of the war—paid off, like their sisters everywhere, for loyalty.

None of the high-activity suffrage movements gained the vote before World War I was over. But there were some countries in which suffrage was granted to women *before* the end of World War I: Australia, in 1902; Denmark, 1915; Finland, 1906; Iceland, 1915; New Zealand, 1893; Norway, 1913; and the former Soviet Union, 1917 (United Nations 1964). These dates all refer to the right to vote in national elections on the same basis as the men. Some countries, such as Sweden, had limited municipal suffrage as far back as 1863, so the date of universal suffrage does not reflect previous levels of political involvement of women. Scandinavia and parts of the British Commonwealth did best on early achievement of enfranchisement, but these were not areas of high suffrage activity. Political convenience and chance may have more to do with the date of suffrage than anything else. It was clear from the 1840s on that it had to come, but no known strategy hastened the day of the vote.

Giving women the vote may in some countries have seemed like a power issue, but it was not in fact. When women had the vote, they used it conservatively, to support existing power structures. They did not use it to elect women to office or to promote radical reforms (Duverger 1955).

Adventurers

Not everyone in the nineteenth century was involved in social movements. The great bulk of women were laboring unadventurously at their places of employment. There was also that other breed of women—the migrants, the adventurers, the pioneers. *New Horizons* (Women's Migration and Overseas Appointments Society 1963), the story of British women's migration societies, tells harrowing tales of women's adjustments to new life in places as far apart as Canada, New Zealand, Nigeria, Kenya, and Jamaica. The women who organized the migration schemes were as intrepid as the ones who migrated, and often the organizers traveled over the migrant terrain themselves to make sure their planning was relevant. In the early years, the societies had to deal with many genteel ladies who shipped overseas only to return immediately to England because they could not cope with pioneer conditions. Migration organizers soon learned to select for the ability to cope.

U.S. women who headed west were another category of migrants. *The Gentle Tamers*[25] (Brown 1958) describes U.S. pioneer women who built claim shacks to dig for gold, who took land and developed it alone. In 1885, Mary Meegher owned the largest ranch on the Pacific slope.

Arizona Mary drove a 16-yoke ox team and made a fortune. "Charlie" Pankhurst was a stagecoach driver from 1860 to 1879. In 1850, eastern seaboard teachers began the trek westward to open schools. Brown suggests that pioneer women did so well because they had more optimism than men did in the face of hardship, more flexibility, and more physical and psychological endurance at the farthest reaches of suffering on the covered wagon treks. (There were cases where all the men died on a trek, and only the women survived.) All types of women made it: college girls, "fancy women," middle-aged ladies, bloomer girls, teachers, missionaries, ordinary middle-class wives, and tough army women. It is perhaps no accident that the first states to give women the vote at the state level in the United States were the western states. There was no private space-public space issue for women in the West in the middle and late 1800s. The women were simply *present*, wherever there was anything to be done.

Another category of adventurers in addition to the settler-pioneers are the travelers who traveled for the sake of seeing the world. *Celebrated Women Travellers of the Nineteenth Century* (W. H. D. Adams 1903) tells us about the princess of Bologna, the radical who ran an expatriate salon in Paris. Her other activities included equipping a 200-horse army and leading it against Austria—to defeat. She went to Turkey to live when she got bored with Paris. Mme Hommaire de Hell wandered over Russia and Turkey and found a number of European women living "as lonely exiles" in the Crimea. (Some of them may have been happier than she thought.) Fredrika Bremer, the Swedish novelist mentioned earlier as an international peace movement activist, traveled around the world to get background for her novels. Alexandra Tinne of the Hague explored Africa. Ida Pfeiffer was a globe-trotting scientist. Lady Hester Stanhope left high society England to establish a "petty kingdom" in Lebanon. Lady Brassey sailed around the world in the yacht *Sunbeam* in 1876. The list goes on and on. Some traveled out of curiosity, some as scientists, some to write. Isabella Bird, the Englishwoman who explored the Rocky Mountains in 1878, was one of those who seems to have sought the extremes of hardship for adventure's sake. She is a legend today in Colorado.

Women soldiers flourished in the nineteenth century. The Austrian and Italian armies regularly commissioned women soldiers who saw action, received the highest decorations soldiers could receive, and often married and had children. Augusta Krüger of the Ninth Prussian Regiment was decorated both with the Iron Cross and the Russian Order of St. George and had the pleasure of seeing her grandson commissioned to her own regiment. In France, Angélique Brulon, sub-lieutenant of the infantry, was decorated with the Legion of Honor. Dragoon Thérèse Figuer had four horses killed under her in action but died in her bed at 87. The American Civil War brought out a whole collection of midwestern "Joan of Arcs," mostly schoolteachers and sometimes wives who preferred fighting by their husbands' sides to sitting at home: Mary Ellen Wise of the Indiana Volunteers, Mary Hancock of Illinois, Anny Lillybridge and LaBelle Morgan of Michigan, Mary Dennis (a six-foot-two-inch commissioned soldier in a Minnesota regiment), and others.

Lurking behind the midwestern schoolmarm soldiers is the shadowy figure of Anna Ella Carroll, a southern lady of the antebellum aristocracy. She served in Lincoln's "kitchen cabinet" and supposedly formulated the Tennessee River campaign, which is considered the decisive action that gave victory to the North in the war (Greenbie 1940).

Scientists

Records of women scientists became more frequent in this century. Many of them were married and had children but tended now to practice their science independently rather than in a husband's laboratory. Self-taught Sophie Germain of France, one of the founders of mathematical physics, won a prize from the French National Academy of Science for the solution of an "unsolvable" problem and did a major work on vibrating surfaces in 1816. Mary Somerville, also a self-taught mathematician, wrote *The Mechanism of the Heavens*, which became a University of Cambridge textbook and brought her election to the Royal Astronomical Society and a government pension. (She was also a mother of two who tutored her own children, ran a home famous for hospitality, and was actively writing at her death at the age of 92.) Sonya Kovalevsky of Russia held the chair of higher mathematics at a Swedish university, also won a French National Academy prize for the solution of an "unsolvable" problem, and unfortunately died young while planning her major work. Italy, France, and the United States all produced world-famous women doctors in this century. Mme La Chapelle revolutionized midwifery in France; Maria dalle Bonne, a peasant's daughter, became professor of obstetrics at Bologna; and Elizabeth Blackwell pioneered medical training for women in England and America. Caroline Herschel, astronomer, was the first Englishwoman to receive a government scientific appointment. She discovered eight comets and several nebulae and received gold medals from all the crowned heads of Europe. She and Somerville were the first two women members of the British Royal Society.

Ida Pfeiffer, Mary Kingsley, Mme Coudreau, and Eleanor Ormerod were all natural scientists who traveled to difficult and dangerous places for exploration and specimen collection. They published widely, were much honored and paid little. Ormerod was perhaps the most exploited as well as the most bemedaled. She became the "world pest expert" and ran an unpaid international consulting service on how to deal with pests.

The ingenuity of these natural scientists suggests another category of ingenious women who were not scholars but inventors. This is as appropriate a place as any to point out the role of women inventors in providing some of the major devices we associate with the industrial revolution. The following passage comes from Russell H. Conwell's *Acres of Diamonds*, written in 1890. He has some startling remarks about who the "real" inventors were in the nineteenth-century United States:

> When you say a woman doesn't invent anything, I ask, Who invented the Jacquard loom that wove every stitch you wear? Mrs. Jacquard. The printer's roller, the printing press, were invented by farmers' wives. Who invented the cotton-gin of the South that enriched our country so amazingly? Mrs. General Greene invented the cotton-gin and showed the idea to Mr. Whitney, and he, like a man, seized it. Who was it that invented the sewing-machine? If I would go to school tomorrow and ask your children they would say, "Elias Howe."
>
> He was in the Civil War with me, and often in my tent, and I often heard him say that he worked fourteen years to get up that sewing machine. But his wife made up her mind one day that they would starve to death if there wasn't something or other invented pretty soon, and so in two hours she invented the sewing machine. Of course he took out the patent in his name. Men always do that. Who was it that invented the mower and the reaper? According to Mr. McCormick's confidential communication, so recently published, it was a West Virginia woman, who, after his father and he had failed altogether in making a reaper and gave it up, took a lot of shears and nailed them together on the edge of a board, with one shaft of each pair loose, and then wired them so that when she pulled the other way, it opened them, and there she had the principle of the mowing-machine. If you look at a mowing-machine, you will see that it is nothing but a lot of shears. (quoted in Robins 1975: 255)

For some reason, it was easier to honor women scientists than women inventors.

The women scientists mentioned above, and many others not mentioned, all made contributions to their respective fields that were widely honored in the international community (Alic 1986). In that sense, they were public figures. A few had government appointments, but most of them supported themselves on private incomes or from publications. They lived privatized lives in the sense of rarely having official niches yet moved in the public arena as far as expectations of their performance went. A good example of the moral and social climate in which they worked can be found in the essay written by the Swedish dramatist Strindberg about Sonya Kovalevsky after she had been appointed to the chair of higher mathematics in Sweden, proving "as decidedly as that two and two make four, what a monstrosity is a woman who is a professor of mathematics, and how unnecessary, injurious and out of place she is" (quoted in Mozans 1913: 163).

Artists and Writers

The nineteenth century produced so many writers that it becomes impossible to survey them in brief. The Georges—George Sand in France and George Eliot in England—demonstrated something important to women about holding to artistic integrity and personal autonomy under conditions of great public success. This was also the century of the great expressive artists in literature: Jane Austen, Mary Shelley, Elizabeth Barrett Browning, Emily and Charlotte Brontë—and robust Maria Edgeworth. (See Vineta Colby, *The Singular Anomaly,* 1971; Ellen Moers, *Literary Women,* 1976; and Martha Vicinus, *Suffer and Be Still,* 1972. These sources aren't exhaustive; specialized literary-historical study of women writers of the nineteenth—or any—century is just beginning in earnest.)

Because so much was happening in art, again more than can be conveyed in brief, I will mention only two particularly unusual women artists here. One is the great French animal painter, Rosa Bonheur, daughter of an impoverished Saint-Simonian. She was one of the first painters to consciously assume a women's rights stance and to avoid marriage explicitly to maintain her freedom and integrity as an artist. She was also the first woman artist to be named an officer of the French Legion of Honor. She had every honor that the world could bestow and died with 77 years of extraordinarily productive life behind her. The other artist, Edmonia Lewis, was half Native American, and half black, raised by her mother as a Chippewa. She went to Oberlin on an Abolition Scholarship and became a sculptress who won fame in America and Europe for her sculpture on themes of emancipation of the Negro and on native Chippewa themes. She was last seen working in Rome in 1886 and then disappeared from the record. Both these women were creative in settings of initial poverty and great hardship, unlike the great bulk of women artists mentioned in previous centuries who were born into families of artists and given oils with their mother's milk, so to speak. These two women represent the new woman who chooses her métier independently of family circumstances.

This may be the place to reflect briefly on the women artists we have glanced at from the fifteenth through nineteenth centuries. In spite of the general impression in the twentieth century that there have been no great women artists,[26] the women we have described in each of these centuries achieved great fame in their own lifetimes. They were on the whole long-lived; most of them married, but they married late; some of them even had large numbers of children. They were for the most part daughters of artists and trained by an artist-parent. What was characteristic of all of them (except the early family-workshop painters) was an independence that was hard to come by for women in their time, even for the elite. It is an interesting commentary on the strength of the creative drive in women that some of these artists should have been both biologically and artistically prolific and so long-lived.

Overview: Women, the
Family, and the World

The situation of women in the nineteenth century was one of contrasts. The most rigid expectations of domesticity and obedience stood in confrontation with extraordinary initiatives in mapping and shaping new social realities. It was *not* a century of superwomen. Rather, it was a period in which the talents women had were given freer play because among women an inner confidence was developing. The practical background experience for the new roles had been there for a long time. Georgiana Hill, in her insightful book on Englishwomen, writes:

> It is one of the peculiar characteristics of women that they are able to attend to so many things at one time. Their lives are so usually encumbered with detail that they have acquired the faculty of passing rapidly from one subject to another, added to which their sympathies and their perceptive powers are quicker than those of men, so that they are both stirred to action and able to grasp their object more readily. (1896: 233)

This "faculty of passing rapidly from one subject to another" is the only possible explanation of the intellectual productivity of women with heavy responsibilities and of the social productivity of women who have become involved in many spheres.

A variety of special studies are needed of women's activities in the nineteenth century to get the full picture of the beginning of their entry into the public spaces of society. No one has ever looked at the total social science output of women in this century. When this is done, I believe it will be found that a number of significant conceptual break-throughs, as well as techniques of observation and measurement, came from women. Much of this is lost in our social histories. No one has looked systematically at the institution building women did to meet the problems of industrial urbanism or examined in detail the attendant misery of family living conditions. No one has yet studied adequately the real-life situation of the unpartnered woman in the context of a pervasive social ideology of familism or analyzed in adequate historical perspective the structural and behavioral adaptations for survival made by poverty-class women. The ideology of familism has drawn a curtain over many of these adaptations.

Understanding the ideology of familism is essential to an under-standing of the century. For all the negative things that can be said about the Victorian age, it did indeed promote family delights for the middle class:

> The prettiest sight in Paris . . . was the crowds of children with their parents in the Tuileries or Luxembourg gardens on Sundays or holidays, and the extraordinary kindness and attentiveness of both parents. . . . [I]n the French family every soul is open to the day. (Robertson 1974: 425)

Similar descriptions could be written for the public parks of any major city of Europe or North America.[27] A new style of family life in which parents and children spend much time together began to receive liter-ary attention. The Taylors of Ongar popularized the idea of reading aloud in the family and of letting children help in family decision making (Robertson 1974: 442-43). Mrs. Beeton, author of the bible of home management, *Mrs. Beeton's Cookery and Household Management*, wrote, "It ought to enter into the domestic policy of every parent to make her child feel that home is the happiest place in the world" (Robertson 1974: 423). This was the era of rich family play life, and *The Girls' Own Book* of 1848 records 130 games to play at home with people of all ages. Families built puppet theaters together, put on shows together, played charades together.

Yet there was family cruelty too. Robertson writes of the two attitudes running in counterpoint through the nineteenth century: "Those who like children against those who do not . . . the Age of Reason confronting the Puritan Ethic" (1974: 422). There were the gentles, like Maria Edgeworth, author of *Practical Education* (1801), who "was once asked how she knew so much about children. 'Why, I don't know,' she said. 'I lie down and let them crawl all over me' " (in Robertson 1974: 420). There were also the stern disciplinarians who believed in total control of the child's mind, like the German doctor Daniel Schreber, who believed that "a well-trained child could be controlled by the eye of the parent, since a good child would not want to behave differently from what the parent wished" (Robertson 1974: 429, n. 27). Schreber's son became a famous psychiatric case and was analyzed by Freud.

For all the emphasis on the traditional family, the fact remains that in this century between 40% and 50% of women were not partnered with men in most countries of Europe. Single, widowed, or separated are the categories provided for nearly half the women of Europe. Alva Myrdal tells us that, as far back as 1750, 35% of the population of Sweden was single and that, in the 1860s, the average age of marriage for women was 26.92, and for men 30.57, years. In the mid-twentieth century, 20% of Swedish women had never taken male partners (Myrdal 1945). Where did the idea come from that "everyone" lived in traditional families?

The percentage of unmarried women who stayed in their parental households we do not know, but, among the proletariat, few women would have stayed in overcrowded parental households after reaching their teens. Many of them lived as domestic servants, others took rooms or lived in boarding houses. We do not know how many of them took women partners. We know that widows often chose to live alone. If we estimate 20 years as the average length of married life in these centuries, widows may have quite a few years alone. Because women not partnered with men are not usually considered a significant social category, their living circumstances have not been adequately studied. When they are, I believe we are in for some surprises.

A historical picture is beginning to emerge of a society organized "as if": *as if* every household consisted of a husband, wife, and children; *as if* every household must have a woman home at all times; *as if* there were no lesbian households; *as if* there were no single women, no illegitimate children; *as if* all productive labor were carried out by men and all significant civic arrangements created by men.

Reality has always belied the "as if," but it was never challenged. The changes in economic conditions, rising population densities, and particularly the steady growth of urbanism from the seventeenth century on finally brought some women to examine the reality and to challenge the "as if," the myth of total familism.

By the nineteenth century, many women were no longer willing to support the old fictions of male guardianship of the female, which included the concept of women's intellectual, social, and legal minority. They had knowledge and skills often unavailable to men, talents that were crucial to the task of making urban society workable. Activists began to insist on partnership roles with men and a social, economic, and legal status commensurate with the functions they were performing. The doctrine of "included interest" was exploded forever.

The assertion process for women was slow and painful. They were, and still are, caught in a set of conflicting loyalties and conflicting perceptions of reality. Many are frightened at the thought of having rights instead of protection. Others feel no need for more autonomy than they already have. Counterfeminist movements evolved in the nineteenth century and continue in the twentieth, representing women who are content with traditional patterns and who fear that feminism will destroy the family life they cherish. Women who have lived in private spaces do not see the social whole objectively. It is hard for them to see the broad spectrum of social arrangements that can enhance the lives of women, men, and children, both inside and outside of traditional family households. The absurdity of the privatization of a women's world within the larger society is by no means evident to Western women generally.

In the next chapter, we will gain a broader perspective on women's roles in the household and the public sphere by reviewing briefly the developments for women in Africa, Asia, and Latin America over the past millennium. We will see that the problems women face in the "Two-Thirds World" are different than "First World" problems. We will also see that expectations and achievements have been different. This leads us to an overview of the situation of women as they begin moving into some of the public spaces of the twentieth century, and provides the springboard for a look at the possibilities for women in the twenty-first century, in the last chapter.

Appendix 3A

TABLE 3A.1 Occupations of Women in 1841

	Females 20 Years and Upward	Under 20 Years		Females 20 Years and Upward	Under 20 Years
Accoutrement maker	39	4	Brick and tile maker	261	169
Actor (play)	310	71	Broker (branch not specified)	256	3
Agent and factor (branch not specified)	40		Broker, furniture	84	5
			Brush and broom maker	535	157
Agricultural implement maker	40	18	Buckle maker	31	12
			Builder	74	—
Anchor smith and chain maker	54	49	Burnisher	168	48
Artist (fine arts)	261	17	Butcher	1,047	26
Auctioneer, appraiser, and house agent	37	1	Butcher, pork	85	—
			Butter dealer, merchant, factor	39	1
Author	15	—	Button dealer and merchant	13	—
Baby linen dealer and maker	68	8	Button maker	1,031	607
Bacon and ham dealer and factor	23	1	Cabinet maker and upholsterer	1,846	181
Baker	3,144	79	Cap maker and dealer	837	237
Banker	7	—	Card maker	488	362
Basket maker	262	51	Carpenter and joiner	389	—
Bath keeper and attendant	77	—	Carpet and rug manufacturer	87	158
Bazaar keeper	26	2	Carrier, carter, and wagoner	464	14
Bead maker	26	10	Carver and guilder	68	10
Bed and mattress maker	90	7	Cattle and sheep dealer and salesman	13	—
Blacking maker and dealer	26	4	Chair maker	237	43
Blacksmith	469	—	Charwoman	18,019	265
Bleacher (branch not specified)	185	164	Chaser	46	3
Boat and barge builder	19	—	Cheese monger and factor	115	1
Boat woman	117	13	Chemist and druggist	148	4
Boat and barge owner	19	—	Chemist, manufacturing	11	1
Bobbin maker and turner	19	10	Chimney sweeper	125	—
Bonnet maker	3,331	976	China, earthenware, and glass dealer	602	84
Bookseller, bookbinder, publisher	1,561	458	Clerk (commercial)	137	22
Boot and shoemaker	8,611	1,953	Clock and watchmaker	164	21
Brace and belt maker	322	80	Clothes dealer and outfitter	206	11
Braid maker	34	10	Coach maker (all branches)	108	8
Brass founder and molder	39	4	Coal laborer, heaver, porter	184	187
Brazier, brass finisher, tinker	100	10	Coal merchant and dealer	371	18
Brewer	172	5	Coffeehouse keeper	178	4

continued

TABLE 3A.1 Continued

	Females 20 Years and Upward	Under 20 Years		Females 20 Years and Upward	Under 20 Years
Comb maker	97	33	Hatter and hat		
Cooper	113	6	manufacturer	1,711	544
Corn merchant, dealer,			Hawker, huckster, and		
factor	114	10	peddlar	3,177	214
Corn cutter (chiropodist)	12	—	Hook and eye maker	33	34
Cotton manufacturer			Hose manufacturer (all		
(all branches)	65,839	49,586	branches)	5,934	2,371
Cupper and dentist	23	—	Iron monger	259	9
Currier and leather seller	140	5	Jappaner	328	165
Cutler	129	30	Jeweller, goldsmith, and		
Die engraver and sinker	6	2	silversmith	296	69
Draper	1,596	377	Keeper, lunatic asylum	157	6
Draper, linen	529	100	Keeper, or head of public		
Dressmaker, milliner	70,518	18,561	institution	1,427	—
Dyer, calenderer, and			Knitter	814	274
scourer	417	74	Laborer	9,398	1,757
Eating house keeper	173	1	—agricultural	26,815	8,447
Embroiderer	593	209	Lace agent	15	1
Engine and machine maker	45	8	Lace dealer and laceman	100	25
Engineer and engine worker	45	57	—manufacturer		
Factory worker (manu-			(all branches)	14,394	5,651
facturer not specified)	4,338	4,449	Lamp and lantern maker	10	—
Farmer and grasser	13,398	—	Lapidary	21	10
Farmer, cattle doctor, and			Laundry keeper, washer		
veterinary surgeon	78	—	and mangler	43,497	1,522
Feather maker, dealer, dresser	97	13	Lead manufacturer	47	21
File maker (all branches)	92	31	Leech bleeder and dealer	51	1
Fish monger and dealer	614	42	Librarian	106	3
Fisherwoman	277	29	Lime burner	54	7
Flax and linen manufacturer			Lint manufacturer	84	28
(all branches)	2,746	3,625	Livery stable keeper	107	—
Flour dealer and mealman	207	5	Locksmith and bell hanger	35	7
Flower (artificial) maker	475	380	Lodging and boarding		
Fork maker	32	10	house keeper	6,073	33
French polisher	81	23	Maltster	121	5
Fringe manufacture	207	106	Map maker and publisher	34	5
Furrier	664	134	Marine store dealer	90	1
Fustian manufacture	918	354	Mason, paviour, and statuary	146	4
Gardener	891	75	Mat maker	89	7
Gas fitter	2	—	Match maker and seller	58	14
Glass and bottle			Mathematical instrument		
manufacture	209	70	maker	2	—
Glove maker	4,249	1,600	Medicine vendor	23	2
Glove manufacture, silk	106	81	Merchant	77	—
Government post office	449	11	Metal manufacturer	89	74
Greengrocer and fruiterer	2,629	70	Midwife	676	—
Grocer and tea dealer	7,005	127	Milk seller and cow keeper	1,622	52
Gun maker and gunsmith	67	12	Miller	410	47
Haberdasher and hosier	779	109	Millwright	25	3
Hairdresser and barber	231	15	Miner (branch not specified)	334	364

continued

TABLE 3A.1 Continued

	Females 20 Years and Upward	Under 20 Years		Females 20 Years and Upward	Under 20 Years
—copper	903	1,200	Pottery, china, and earthen-		
—iron	363	36	ware manufacturer		
—lead	25	18	(all branches)	3,843	3,253
—tin	68	82	Poulterer and game dealer	196	7
Mop maker	33	4	Press worker	32	32
Molder	12	5	Print seller	36	9
Music seller and publisher	33	—	Printer	114	43
Musical instrument maker	23	—	Printer, copper plate	10	2
Musician and organist	199	51	—cotton and calico	239	384
Muslin manufacturer	35	11	Provision dealer	217	12
Nail manufacturer	2,673	1,366	Pump maker	17	4
Needle manufacturer	505	243	Quarrier (branch not		
Net maker	106	26	specified)	15	4
News agent and vendor	67	3	—stone	15	18
Nurse	12,476	517	Quill cutter	11	4
Nurseryman and florist	183	49	Quilter and quilt maker	92	18
Oil and colorman	62	9	Rag cutter dealer and		
Optician	17	—	gatherer	446	93
Painter, plumber, and glazier	349	25	Reed maker	26	8
Paper hanger	10	1	Register office (servants')		
—manufacturer (all			keeper	19	—
branches)	857	370	Ribbon manufacturer	2,394	636
—stainer	60	32	Roller maker and turner	114	27
—box maker	42	38	Rope and cord spinner		
Parochial church and			and maker	401	85
corporation officer			Rush dealer and		
(exclusive of those			manufacturer	21	4
returned in trade)	359	5	Sack and bag dealer		
Pastry cook and			and maker	187	31
confectioner	1,681	158	Saddle, harness, and		
Pattern and clog maker	65	10	collar maker	272	36
Pawnbroker	242	14	Sail, sail cloth, and tarpaulin		
Pearl cutter and worker	60	41	manufacturer	99	22
Pen maker and dealer	66	27	Saleswoman	117	5
Pen (steel) maker	128	104	Sand merchant	37	1
Percussion cap maker	17	8	Sawyer	12	—
Perfumer	86	11	Schoolmistress, governess		
Pewterer and pewter pot			(see also teacher)	27,754	1,499
maker	17	1	Scissors maker	101	47
Pig dealer and merchant	11	1	Silk manufacturer (all		
Pin manufacturer (all			branches)	18,038	11,795
branches)	472	356	—mercer	118	—
Pipe maker	343	98	—merchant	13	1
—tobacco maker	18	3	Skinner and skin dresser	49	9
Plasterer	69	2	Slater	11	—
Plater	20	5	Slop maker and seller	261	39
Polisher	151	40	Small ware dealer	92	4
Porter, messenger	165	36	Small ware manufacturer		
Potato dealer and merchant	33	—	(all branches)	122	75

continued

TABLE 3A.1 Continued

	Females 20 Years and Upward	Under 20 Years		Females 20 Years and Upward	Under 20 Years
Smelter (ore not specified)	118	204	Teacher (see also school-		
Snuffer maker	16	2	mistress)		
Spectacle maker	8	3	—dancing and gymnastics	60	1
Spinner (branch not			—languages	62	6
specified)	3,458	1,906	—miscellaneous	36	6
Spoon maker	87	48	—music and singing	629	91
Spring maker	16	—	Thimble maker	18	11
Stationer	387	30	Thread manufacturer		
Stay and corset maker	4,149	666	(all branches)	172	181
Steelworkers	18	13	Timber merchant and dealer	33	4
Stewardess (ship)	27	2	Tin manufacturer		
Stock (men's) maker	318	103	(all branches)	125	149
Straw bonnet and hat			Tinplate worker	72	31
maker	6,457	2,021	Tobacconist and tobacco		
—plait dealer, factor,			and snuff manufacturer		
merchant	64	19	(all branches)	1,683	89
—plait manufacturer			Toll collector	426	20
(all branches)	5,686	3,161	Tool dealer and maker		
Stuff manufacturer			(all branches)	58	13
(all branches)	2,028	1,144	Toy dealer and maker	386	76
Sugar baker, boiler,			Tray maker	47	10
and refiner	12	—	Trimming maker	162	72
Surgical instrument maker	9	—	Tripe dealer and dresser	71	6
Tailor and breeches maker	5,155	954	Trunk and box maker	226	84
Screen maker	88	75	Truss maker	22	5
Screw cutter and maker	279	122	Turner	74	20
Screw (wood) maker	22	7	Typefounder	3	3
Seamstress	15,680	2,266	Umbrella, parasol, and		
Seedsman and seed			walking-stick maker	423	118
merchant	52	3	Undertaker	69	3
Servant, domestic	447,606	264,887	Warehouse woman	567	202
Shawl manufacturer			Weaver (branch not		
(all branches)	107	60	specified)	17,728	8,583
Ship and smack owner	48	—	Wheelwright	141	5
Shopkeeper and			Whip maker	41	8
general dealer	9,316	266	Whitesmith	23	—
Shroud maker	14	4	Willow weaver and worker	56	20
Sieve maker	72	24	Wire agent and merchant	79	1
Tallow and wax chandler	71	7	Wire drawer and maker	9	1
Tanner	38	4	—worker and weaver	88	56
Tape manufacturer			Wood cutter and woodman	61	12
(all branches)	258	131	—merchant and dealer	33	—
Tassel maker	62	17	Wool, agent, merchant, and		
Tavern keeper, namely			stapler	34	5
beershop keeper	1,471	15	Wool (Berlin), dealer and		
—hotel and innkeeper	2,941	34	worker	22	2
—publican and victualler	5,574	51	Woollen and cloth manu-		
—spirit merchant	114	4	facturer (all branches)	13,196	7,742
—tea broker and merchant	3	—	—draper	57	3

continued

TABLE 3A.1 Continued

	Females 20 Years and Upward	Under 20 Years		Females 20 Years and Upward	Under 20 Years
Worsted dealer and merchant —manufacturer (all branches)	26 6,016	6 6,126	Yarn manufacturer (all branches) Yeast dealer and merchant	118 51	48 1

SOURCE: Appendix in Pinchbeck and Hewitt (1969: 317-21; used by permission).
NOTE: These dates are from the *Occupational Abstract of the Census Returns* 1841 (P.P. 1844, xxvii, pp. 31-44). While not altogether accurate, the figures are interesting in showing the distribution of women in industry at this time. The numbers given are for England alone, and trades employing only very few women have for the most part been omitted.

Appendix 3B

TABLE 3B.1 Employment of Village Children in Nineteenth-Century England

acorning	laundry work
bait girls	mangold wurzel pulling
band making	mangold wurzel trimming
bark stripping	manure spreading
bean dropping	net braiding
bean picking	onion peeling
bean tying	osier peeling
binding and stooking	pea picking
bird scaring	pig minding
brickmaking	poaching
cattle minding	rag cutting
cockling	shallot pulling
cow minding	sheep minding
dinner carrying	shrimping
door-to-door selling	singling and thinning root
flax pullers	crop
fruit pickers	stone picking
gang labor	straw plaiting
gloving	turnip pulling
hoeing	turnip singling
hop picking	vegetable cleaning
hop pole shaving	vegetable pulling
hop tying	walnut bashing
lace making	water drawing
laundry carrying	weeding

SOURCE: Constructed from the index entries under "Children's Employment" (Samuel 1975: 266-67).

Notes

1. See the discussion of this in Boulding (1972: 13-14), also the detailed analysis in Weller (1968) and Collver and Langlois (1962).

2. Richards illustrates the "surge of sympathetic writing" with titles like "How to Provide for Superfluous Ladies" and "Why Are Women Redundant" (1974: 350).

3. Edith Thomas (1966), who was at the barricades of 1944 against the Vichy government, had a very vivid sense of the continuity of women's participation in revolutions and has written a striking account of women's participation in the Paris Commune of 1871.

4. It would be a great mistake to conclude that this pathological development applied to convents and beguinages generally. They were, however, susceptible to prevailing economic conditions.

5. See Thönnessen (1973) for more on the women's movement in Germany.

6. The recent unexpurgated edition of her autobiography (Kollontai 1971) gives a poignant picture of those dilemmas as we read what she herself censored before publication in 1926.

7. Other women of that international socialist circle who published on socialism were Clara Meyer-Weichman, *Mensch en Maatschappij* (1923); Lydie Pissarjevskij, *Socialisme et Féminisme* (1910); Ethel Snowdon, *The Woman Socialist* (1907); Marguerite Thibert, *Le Féminisme dans le Socialisme Français 1830-1850* (1926); Lily Gair Wilkinson, "Revolutionary Socialism and the Women's Movement" (1910); and Dora Russell, *Hypatia, or Woman and Knowledge* (1925).

8. Neither had their father Karl provided a good role model for a revolutionary spouse, because, while devoted to his family, he also exploited Jenny's house-wifeliness.

9. There were many ways for a revolutionary to handle the "love" component of life, and some chose Kollontai's approach, putting the revolutionary movement first: "Love, marriage, family, all were secondary, transient matters. They were there, they intertwine with my life over and over again. But as great as was my love for my husband, immediately it transgressed a certain limit in relation to my feminine proneness to make sacrifice, rebellion flared in me anew. I had to go away, I had to break with the man of my choice. . . . It must also be said that not a single one of the men who were close to me has ever had a direction-giving influence on my inclinations, strivings, or my world-view" (Kollontai 1971: 13). This type of solution is of course not limited to revolutionaries. Gifted women and men of a certain temperament have always chosen this solution.

10. It was Olive Schreiner who called the fine lady "the most deadly microbe which can make its appearance on the surface of any social organism" (1911: 81).

11. The tradition that factory workers were single girls with nothing to spend their money on but clothes, and only worked until marriage, stems from the early days when farmers' daughters went to the mills for a brief interlude in their lives. Later in the century, there were widows and other unpartnered mothers in the factories and daughters who supported widowed mothers and younger brothers and sisters.

12. Five nonreligious communities are mentioned.

13. Brook Farm was perhaps a little better than the others, due to its articulate women transcendentalists, Elizabeth Peabody Palmer and Margaret Fuller, and to its ardent commitment to the abolition of domestic servitude (meaning, however, domestic servants, not the domestic labor of women).

14. A sense of the versatility of Martineau can be gained from reading Alice Rossi's description of her in *The Feminist Papers from Adams to de Beauvoir* (1973: 118-43). Rossi's essay deals with a different set of Martineau's attributes than those discussed here. Two major sociological contributions of Martineau's not mentioned above are her abridged

translation of Comte's *Positive Philosophy* (1853) and a treatise on social science method-ology, *How to Observe Manners and Morals* (1838).

15. See *Women in Social Work* (Walton 1975) for a more complete account of the development of this profession in England.

16. Thrupp founded and edited the journal *Comparative Studies in Society and History.*

17. She was not all-wise. She never realized the dimensions of the single-woman head-of-household problem and tended to treat widows as special cases, therefore not assisting women as a class.

18. An example is the Feminist Press, City University of New York, 311 East 94th Street, New York, NY 10128.

19. I find it striking that both Mary Ellen Richmond, from the social work perspective, and Mary Follett, from the political science perspective, saw the significance of new patterns of association before these phenomena became general subjects of study.

20. One notable exception is the Associated Country Women of the World.

21. That this village manor house service tradition can even today be identified in an old urban area like Birmingham, England, I can testify from personal observation. There is no counterpart institution in the United States, because we never had manor houses.

22. See Collins, *Europeans in Africa* (1971), for a discussion of this.

23. Jo Newberry (University of Edinburgh Institute for Advanced Studies in the Humanities, personal communication, 1975), a Canadian historian working on the life of Catherine Marshall, another suffragette who was actively pacifist, points out that far more women continued to oppose the war throughout its duration than suffragette histories suggest.

24. See Rossi (1973: 241-81) for an excellent characterization of the U.S. movement.

25. *Pioneer Mothers of the West* (Frost 1972) contains similar records.

26. See, for example, Linda Nochlin's "Why Have There Been No Famous Women Artists?" (1971).

27. There was one group of women and men in the nineteenth century for whom the ideology of familism was not generally considered relevant: the slaves in the antebellum South. An interesting study of slave family records (Blassingame 1972: 90) between 1864 and 1866 in the South shows only 13.6% unbroken families during that period. Of the 86.3% of broken families, 32.4% were broken by the master, 39.9% by death, 3.3% by war, and 10.7% by personal choice. Given the setting for slave family life on plantations, probably worse than the worst rural poverty in England, the 13.6% of families that stayed together represent a triumph for the ideals of family partnership.

References

Abramowitz, Isidore. 1946. *The Great Prisoners.* New York: E. P. Dutton.

Adams, Charles Francis, ed. 1975. *Familiar Letters of John Adams and His Wife Abigail Adams During the Revolution.* New York: Houghton Mifflin.

Adams, W. H. Davenport. 1903. *Celebrated Women Travellers of the Nineteenth Century.* New York: E. P. Dutton.

Addams, Jane. 1972. *Peace and Bread in Time of War.* New York: Garland.

Alic, Margaret. 1986. *Hypatia's Heritage: A History of Women in Science from Antiquity Through the Nineteenth Century.* Boston: Beacon.

Anthony, Katharine. 1915. *Feminism in Germany and Scandinavia.* New York: Holt.

Armytage, W. H. G. 1961. *Heavens Below: Utopian Experiments in England, 1560-1960.* London: Routledge & Kegan Paul.

Atkinson, D., A. Dallin, and G. Lapidus, eds. 1977. *Women in Russia.* Stanford, CA: Stanford University Press.

Baber, Zonia. 1948. *Peace Symbols.* Philadelphia: Women's International League for Peace and Freedom.

Balabanov, Anzhelika. 1938. *My Life as a Rebel.* New York: Harper.

Bebel, August. 1971. *Women Under Socialism,* translated by Daniel de Leon. New York: Schocken. (Reprint of 1904 New York Labor News Press edition.)

Bellamy, Edward. [1887] 1967. *Looking Backward: 2000-1887,* edited by John L. Thomas. Cambridge, MA: Harvard University Press.

Blassingame, John W. 1972. *The Slave Community: Plantation Life in the Antebellum South.* New York: Oxford University Press.

Bohrovskaya, C. 1940. *Lenin and Krupskaya.* New York: Workers Library.

Bolton, Sarah Knowles. 1895. *Famous Leaders Among Women.* New York: Crowell.

Boulding, Elise. 1972. "Women as Role Models in Industrializing Societies: A Macrosystem Model of Socialization for Civic Competence." Pp. 11-34 in *Cross-National Family Research,* edited by Marvin Sussman and Betty Cogswell. Leiden: E. J. Brill.

Boxer, Marilyn and Jean Quataert. 1978. *Socialist Women: European Socialist Feminism in the Nineteenth and Early Twentieth Century.* New York: Elsevier North Holland.

Brown, Dee. 1958. *The Gentle Tamers: Women of the Old Wild West.* New York: Putnam.

Burdett-Coutts, The Baroness. 1893. *Woman's Mission.* New York: Scribner.

Bussey, Gertrude and Margaret Tims. 1965. *Women's International League for Peace and Freedom, 1915-1965: A Record of Fifty Years' Work.* London: Allen & Unwin.

Cita-Malard, Suzanne. 1964. *Religious Orders of Women,* translated by George J. Robinson. New York: Hawthorn.

Colby, Vineta. 1971. *The Singular Anomaly: Women Novelists of the Nineteenth Century.* New York: New York University Press.

Cole, G. D. H. 1953-60. *A History of Socialist Thought.* 5 vols. New York: St. Martin's.

Collins, Robert O. 1971. *Europeans in Africa.* New York: Knopf.

Collver, Andrew and Eleanor Langlois. 1962. "The Female Labor Force in Metropolitan Areas: An International Comparison." *Journal of Economic Development and Cultural Change* 10:367-85.

Croly, J. C. 1898. *The History of the Woman's Club Movement in America.* New York: Henry G. Allen.

Dolci, Danilo. 1970. *Report from Palermo,* translated by P. D. Cummins. New York: Viking.

Duverger, Maurice. 1955. *La Participation des Femmes à la Vie Politique.* Paris: UNESCO.

Eagle, Mary Kavanaugh Oldham, ed. [1895] 1974. *The Congress of Women, Held in the Woman's Building, World's Columbian Exposition, Chicago, 1893.* New York: Arno.

Ellington, George. [1869] 1972. *The Women of New York or the Under-World of a Great City.* New York: Arno.

Engel, Barbara Alpern and Clifford N. Rosenthal, eds. 1975. *Five Sisters: Women Against the Tsar.* New York: Knopf.

Follett, M. P. 1920. *The New State.* New York: Longmans Green.

Friedan, Betty. 1963. *The Feminine Mystique.* New York: Norton.

Frost, John. [1869] 1972. *Pioneer Mothers of the West, or Daring and Heroic Deeds of American Women, Comprising Thrilling Examples of Courage, Fortitude, and Self Sacrifice.* New York: Arno.

Giffin, Frederick C., ed. 1973. *Woman as Revolutionary.* New York: New American Library, Mentor.

Gilman, Charlotte Perkins. 1900. *Concerning Children.* Boston: Small, Maynard.

―――. 1911. *The Man-Made World or Our Androcentric Culture.* New York: Charlton.

―――. 1935. *The Living of Charlotte Perkins Gilman.* New York: Appleton-Century.

―――. 1970. *Women and Economics: A Study of the Economic Relations Between Men and Women as a Factor in Social Evolution,* edited by Carl N. Degler. Gloucester, MA: Peter Smith.

Goldman, Emma. 1910. *Anarchism and Other Essays*. New York: Mother Earth.

———. 1931. *Living My Life*. New York: Knopf.

Gordon, Elizabeth Putnam. 1924. *Women Torch-Bearers: The Story of the Woman's Christian Temperance Union*. Evanston, IL: National WCTU Publishing House.

Greenbie, Marjorie Lotta. 1940. *My Dear Lady: The Story of Anna Ella Carroll, the Great Unrecognized Member of Lincoln's Cabinet*. New York: McGraw-Hill.

Greenway, John. 1953. *American Folksongs of Protest*. Philadelphia: University of Pennsylvania Press.

Haviland, Laura S. 1882. *A Woman's Life-Work: Labors and Experiences*. Cincinnati, OH: Walden and Stowe.

Hill, Georgiana. 1894. *Women in English Life*. Vol. 1. London: Richard Bentley.

———. 1896. *Women in English Life*. Vol. 2. London: Richard Bentley.

Hobsbawm, E. J. 1963. *Primitive Rebels: Studies in Archaic Forms of Social Movement in the Nineteenth and Twentieth Centuries*. 2nd ed. New York: Praeger.

Holloway, Mark. 1966. *Heavens on Earth: Utopian Communities in America, 1680-1880*. Rev. ed. New York: Dover.

Jorfald, Ursala. 1962. *Bertha Von Suttner: Og Nobels Fredspris*. Oslo: Forum Boktrykkeri.

Josephson, Hannah. 1949. *Golden Threads: New England's Mill Girls and Magnates*. New York: Russell and Russell.

Kamm, Josephine. 1966. *Rapiers and Battleaxes: The Women's Movement and Its Aftermath*. London: Allen & Unwin.

Kollontai, Alexandra. 1971. *The Autobiography of a Sexually Emancipated Communist Woman*, translated by Salvator Attanasio. New York: Herder and Herder.

Lewenhak, Sheila. 1980. *Women and Work*. New York: St. Martin.

Marshall, Alfred and Mary Paley Marshall. 1879. *The Economics of Industry*. London: Macmillan.

Martineau, Harriet. 1832-34. *Illustrations of Political Economy*. 9 vols. London: C. Fox.

———. [1837] 1968. *Society in America*, edited and abridged by Seymour Martin Lipset. Gloucester, MA: Peter Smith.

———. 1838. *How to Observe Manners and Morals*. London: Charles Knight.

———. 1877a. *Autobiography*. 3 vols. London: Smith Elder.

———. 1877b. *Biographical Sketches: 1852-1875*. London: Macmillan.

Maupin, Joyce. 1974. *Working Women and Their Organizations: 150 Years of Struggle*. Berkeley, CA: Union WAGE Educational Committee.

McCarthy, Thomas P., C. S. V. 1955. *Guide to the Catholic Sisterhoods in the United States*. 3rd ed. Washington, DC: Catholic University of America Press.

Meyer-Weichman, Clara. 1923. *Mensch en Maatschappij* [Persons in society]. Arnhem, the Netherlands: Loghum, Slaterus and Vesser.

Michel, Louise. 1886. *Memoires*. (In English, *The Red Virgin: The Memoirs of Louise Michel*, edited and translated by Bullitt Lowry and Elizabeth Ellington Gunter. University: University of Alabama Press.)

Moers, Ellen. 1976. *Literary Women*. Garden City, NY: Doubleday.

Mozans, H. J. 1913. *Woman in Science*. New York: Appleton.

Myrdal, Alva. 1945. *Nation and Family: The Swedish Experiment in Democratic Family and Population Policy*. Cambridge: MIT Press.

Nochlin, Linda. 1971. "Why Have There Been No Great Women Artists?" *Art News* 69(January):23-25, 32-33, 36-39, 69-71.

Nordhoff, Charles. [1875] 1965. *The Communistic Societies of the United States*. New York: Schocken.

O'Faolain, Julia and Lauro Martines, eds. 1973. *Not in God's Image: A History of Women in Europe from the Greeks to the Nineteenth Century*. New York: Harper & Row.

Pankhurst, Richard K. P. 1954. *William Thompson (1775-1833): Britain's Pioneer Socialist, Feminist and Co-operator*. London: Watts.

Petrie, Glen. 1971. *A Singular Iniquity: The Campaigns of Josephine Butler.* New York: Viking.

Pinchbeck, Ivy and Margaret Hewitt. 1969. *Children in English Society. Vol. 1. From Tudor Times to the Eighteenth Century.* London: Routledge & Kegan Paul.

Pissarjevsky, Lydie. 1910. *Socialisme et Féminisme.* Paris: Congrès International Permanent Féministe.

Posthumus-van der Goot, W. H. 1961. *Vrouwen Vochten Voor de Vrede.* Arnhem, the Netherlands: Van Loghum Slaterus.

Pugh, Martin D. 1974. "Politicians and the Woman's Vote, 1914-1918." *History* 59(October):368-74.

Richards, Eric. 1974. "Women in the British Economy Since About 1700: An Interpretation." *History* 59(October):337-57.

Richmond, Mary E. 1903. *Friendly Visiting Among the Poor.* New York: Macmillan.

———. 1907. *The Good Neighbor.* Philadelphia: J. B. Lippincott.

———. 1917. *Social Diagnosis.* New York: Russell Sage.

———. 1922. *What Is Social Case Work?* New York: Russell Sage.

———. 1925. *Child Marriages.* New York: Russell Sage.

———. 1930. *The Long View: Papers and Addresses.* New York: Russell Sage.

Robertson, Priscilla. 1974. "Home as a Quest: Middle Class Childhood in Nineteenth Century Europe." Pp. 407-31 in *The History of Childhood,* edited by Lloyd de Mause. New York: Psychohistory Press.

Robins, Elizabeth. 1975. "Ancilla's Share." Pp. 250-65 in *Unsung Champions of Women,* edited by Mary Cohart. Albuquerque: University of New Mexico Press.

Rossi, Alice S. 1973. *The Feminist Papers from Adams to de Beauvoir.* New York: Columbia University Press.

Rowbotham, Sheila. 1972. *Women, Resistance, and Revolution: A History of Women and Revolution in the Modern World.* New York: Pantheon.

———. 1973. *Hidden from History.* London: Pluto.

Russell, Dora. 1925. *Hypatia, or Woman and Knowledge.* New York: E. P. Dutton.

Salmon, Lucy Maynard. 1897. *Domestic Service.* New York: Macmillan.

Samuel, Raphael, ed. 1975. *Village Life and Labor.* London: Routledge & Kegan Paul.

Schreiner, Olive. 1911. *Woman and Labour.* New York: Frederick A. Stokes.

Scott, Anne Firor, ed. 1971. *The American Woman: Who Was She?* Englewood Cliffs, NJ: Prentice-Hall.

Scott, G. R. 1936. *History of Prostitution from Antiquity to the Present Day.* New York: Greenberg.

Smith, Adam. [1759] 1976. *Theory of Moral Sentiments,* edited by D. Raphael and A. L. Macfie. Oxford: Clarendon.

———. [1776] 1939. *The Wealth of Nations.* New York: Random House.

Snowdon, Ethel. 1907. *The Woman Socialist.* London: George Allen.

Stanton, Theodore, ed. [1884] 1970. *The Woman Question in Europe.* New York: Source Book.

Sumner, Helen L. [1910] 1974. *History of Women in Industry in the United States* (Report on Conditions of Woman and Child Wage-Earners in the United States, Vol. 9; 61st Congress, 2nd Session, Senate Document no. 645, Washington, DC). New York: Arno. (Reprint.)

Thibert, Marguerite. 1926. *Le Féminisme dans le Socialisme Français, 1830-1850.* Paris: Marcel Gerard.

Thomas, Edith. 1966. *The Women Incendiaries,* translated by James and Starr Atkinson. New York: George Braziller.

Thönnessen, Werner. 1973. *The Emancipation of Women: The Rise and Decline of the Women's Movement in German Social Democracy, 1863-1933,* translated by Joris de Bres. Bristol, England: Pluto.

Tilly, Louise and Joan W. Scott. 1978. *Women, Work, and Family.* New York: Holt, Rinehart & Winston.

Tocqueville, Alexis de. [1835-40] 1944. *Democracy in America*, translated by Philipps Bradley. New York: Knopf.

United Nations. 1964. *Civic and Political Education of Women*. New York: United Nations Department of Economics and Social Affairs.

Vicinus, Martha. 1972. *Suffer and Be Still: Women in the Victorian Age*. Bloomington: University of Indiana Press.

Walton, Ronald. 1975. *Women in Social Work*. Boston: Routledge & Kegan Paul.

Ware, Norman. [1924] 1958. *The Industrial Worker: 1840-1860*. Magnolia, MA: Peter Smith.

Webb, Beatrice. 1926. *My Apprenticeship*. New York: Longmans Green.

————. 1948. *Our Partnership*, edited by Barbara Drake and Margaret I. Cole. New York: Longmans Green.

Weller, R. H. 1968. "A Historical Analysis of Female Labor Force Participation in Puerto Rico." *Journal of Social and Economic Studies* 17(March):60-69.

Whitman, Karen. 1970. "Our Sister Rosa Luxemburg." *Women: A Journal of Liberation* 1(Summer):16-21.

Whitworth, John McKelvie. 1975. *God's Blueprints: A Sociological Study of Three Utopian Sects*. London: Routledge & Kegan Paul.

Wilkinson, Lily Gair. (circa) 1910. "Revolutionary Socialism and the Women's Movement." Glasgow: Social Labour Party. (Pamphlet.)

Women's Migration and Overseas Appointments Society. 1963. *New Horizons: A Hundred Years of Women's Migration*. London: Her Majesty's Stationery Office.

4

An Historical Note on the Underside of the "Two-Thirds World"

Introduction

In writing elsewhere about Two-Thirds World women in the twentieth century (Boulding 1977, 1980), I have referred to these sisters of the less industrialized continents as a marginalized "fifth world." Historically, that is hardly appropriate, because they were the cobuilders of great civilizations as well as the coarchitects of viable, peaceful small-scale societies for centuries before "the West" erupted on the world scene. Their partnership was carried out, as has been shown, from the underside, but coshapers of their world they nevertheless were. We will now pick up a little of the more recent history of each continent, to follow how women have dealt with the impacts of colonization and industrialization, intrusive forces that have had creative aspects but have also been destructive of cultures, life-styles, and ancient understandings of how to live on the planet. Helpful references in considering the similarities and differences in the situation of women on each continent include Jean O'Barr's *Perspectives of Power: Women in Africa, Asia and Latin America* (1982) and Haleh Afshar's *Women, Work and Ideology in the Third World* (1985).

Africa

The Portuguese set sail for Africa during a period when several great African kingdoms were at their height. Ancient Axum (Ethiopia) had stayed outside the Moslem world, keeping its Coptic Christian ruling traditions intact. The kingdom of Ghana, already flourishing in the eighth century, had been absorbed by the kingdom of Mali in the thirteenth century, which in turn was absorbed by the kingdom of Songhai in the fifteenth. In the meantime, another great kingdom developed in the Lake Chad region, Kanem. The kingdom of Benin and the city-states of Yoruba, the Congo, Kilwa, and Zimbabwe—the forest states that wove together many tribal groupings below the Sudan—also flourished at this time. By 1450, when Prince Henry's navigators arrived, all these kingdoms and other groups of stateless tribes were solidly interpenetrated by Moslem merchants and their ever-present holy men. The merchants had created a network of trade, culture, and mosques linking sub-Saharan Africa with the Islamic world centered on the Mediterranean as well as linking states internally on the African continent (Levtzion 1968). Unlike the North African states of present-day Algeria, Morocco, and Tunisia, which were directly under Moslem rule, these sub-Saharan kingdoms were independent and used Islamic trade and culture as tools for their own internal development. Roland Oliver, writing about "The African Achievement," comments that "Islam's African fringe can bear comparison with Christendom's northern European fringe at any time up to the late sixteenth century. It was in the seventeenth and eighteenth centuries that Europe, and especially northern Europe, drew ahead" (1968: 97). In terms of the standard of living for the average person, "an easier life was lived in the round houses of Africa than in the cottages of medieval Europe's serfs and free peasants. Certainly the African peasant enjoyed more leisure" (1968: 98). It was in the great concentrations of wealth that Europe and Africa differed. African chiefs never amassed personal wealth in the style of the European nobility. Although they often had plural wives, their life-styles remained *relatively* simple.

The slave trade, long practiced in Africa, increased gradually through the activities of Arab and Jewish[1] merchants between the eleventh and sixteenth centuries but did not reach a substantial volume until the demand from Europe and the Americas developed. The sixteenth century was the turning point. The activities of European Christian "modernizers" resulted in the shipping of 1 million slaves to Europe in that century. In the seventeenth century, 3 million and, in the eighteenth century, 6 million slaves were exported (Collins 1971: chap. 2). By the nineteenth century, the slave trade slowed. The story of the impact of slavery on African women is told in Robertson and Klein (1983).

What was the status of women in the African kingdoms, and what were the relative effects on them of the activities of Moslem and Christian modernizers? First, one has to distinguish the nonstate tribal groups that lived scattered across the whole of Africa from the kingdoms. The local tribes varied greatly, from stratified chiefdoms with nobility at the top and serfs at the bottom, to acephalous egalitarian bands (see Tuden and Plotnicov 1970). The latter were perhaps the most victimized by the slave trade, although no one, including sons and daughters of chiefs, was safe from kidnapping by fellow African slavers for the European trade. The small egalitarian bands will not be further discussed because this type of structure has already been examined in this work in several other settings. This chapter will, however, offer a glimpse into the great variety of occupational roles of tribal African women.

The stratified chiefdoms had varying degrees of matrilineality. There was usually a hierarchy of women in ruling positions paralleling those of men. The mother, wife, and sister of the chief, and a council of matrons, usually played an important role in each society. The tribal organization was often such that women administered the affairs of women, including economic affairs, and also had a general input into overall tribal business. In the Great Lakes kingdoms, the sister of the chief, or *kabaka*, was also a kabaka, as was his mother, and they shared the rule. There were women as well as men in the priesthood. Sometimes the corulership turned into primary rulership for a woman, as in the eastern Transvaal. In the nineteenth century, there were three successive reigning queens in one Transvaal tribe, Mujaji I, II, and III. Mujaji I, an outstanding ruler, set a regular fashion of ruling queens in neighboring tribes.

It is not clear how often women succeeded to the primary chief's role. There are legends of various queens that filter through the history of the major "slaving" centuries:

> In the Niger and Chad regions and in Hausa territory, women founded cities, led migrations, conquered kingdoms. Songhai groups still remember the names of celebrated ancestresses who governed them: in Katsina, Queen Amina became famous during the first half of the fifteenth century through her widespread conquests. She extended her influence as far as the Nupe, built many cities, received tribute from powerful chiefs, and is still held to have been responsible for introducing the kola nut to the region. In a neighboring state, south of Zaria, another woman called Bazao-Turunku appears in the tradition at the head of a group of warriors

who established themselves in a town, the ruins of which are still extant. In the myths concerning the establishment of the So in North Cameroon it was also often a woman who chose the site of a city, held the insignia of power, or governed the district. (Lebeuf 1963: 94-95)

One famous warrior queen well documented in history was Queen Nzinga (1582-1663) of the Mbundu peoples in what is now Angola. She successfully defended her people from the Portuguese for years. In spite of a life of continuous hardship, she lived to the ripe old age of 82 (Sweetman 1971). Legends of women founders of states are found among patrilineal as well as matrilineal tribes. The Congo, Cameroon, and Transvaal tribes mentioned above are all patrilineal. It is less surprising to find women as founders of states in matrilineal West Africa, as in the small states of Mampong, Wenchi, and Juaben. Sweetman (1984) has written an arresting account of women leaders in African history.

There are also traditions of all-women's armies. The king of Dahomey's well-muscled women warriors, and the system of parallel women and men officials in his court, seem to be a later version of an ancient tradition: Sir Richard Burton witnessed an attack by the king on a neighboring principality and reports that the women's army was better disciplined and fought better than the men's army, although neither performed very creditably (R. Burton 1966: 254-67).

Lebeuf provides ample documentation of very widespread political participation of women in the political life of traditional Africa. The participation varied greatly according to whether the society was primarily kin structured or class based and according to the economic base of the society, but nearly always the historical participation patterns have been better defined than current political roles for women.[2] As Lebeuf says, "There are no valid historical grounds for explaining the present lack of interest in political matters so often found among African women as being a heritage of the past" (1963: 96).

Because there are so many Africas, it is difficult to make meaningful statements in a summary as condensed as this one. The vast majority of Africa's population through the centuries has been rural. What proportion have practiced agriculture and what proportion have been nomadic is not clear, but the settlement of nomadic peoples has been going on for a long time. Up to 75% of the population of certain countries like Somalia remain seminomadic today. We have already seen that in nomadic societies women are freer than in settled societies.[3] Yet, according to Germaine Tillion, it was the urbanization of former nomads that was responsible for the extremes of veiling and seclusion of women in North Africa, as the men tried to protect their women from the dangerous environment of the city: "The Bedouin-become-bourgeois, deprived of the protection of the vast desert emptinesses and the unconditional support of his cousin-brothers, falls back on all the artifices and means that come to his mind: iron bars on windows, complicated locks, mean dogs, eunuchs . . . and the veil" (quoted in Gordon 1968: 8).

The nomad woman, and the farm woman with her digging stick, retained substantial independence. Although marriage was nearly universal, marriage and dowry practices were such that women usually supported themselves and their children after marriage, with the dowry serving as "venture capital" for the trading activities associated with farming. The woman-as-economic-partner model applied whether marriages were monogamous or polygamous. While women of Moslem North Africa were restricted in their movements, working-class women had to work, whatever the religious or political ideology. In some areas, the poorest women worked veiled in the fields, but they worked.

The women of sub-Saharan Africa largely moved in the same spaces of society as the men, although their political roles tended to be of a subsidiary character. In West Africa, and to a lesser extent elsewhere, the marketing roles of women developed apace with pre-European Moslem-stimulated urbanization. The traditional prerogative of women to sell surplus produce from their land, and to sell the products of home craft work, led to larger-scale ventures as urban densities increased. In West Africa, women administered the market system and the protolegal systems associated with it. European colonial administrators eventually came to forbid administrative market roles for women, because they were considered inappropriate for the female sex by European standards.

Among the Africans with the longest contact with Europeans were the Akans, who traded successively with Portuguese, Dutch, English, French, Danish, and Swedish merchants on the coast of what is now Ghana. A class of wealthy Africans, women and men, developed out of this trade. (African men quickly adapted to the trader role earlier associated with women, once they discovered how lucrative it was.) These wealthy Africans sent their children to the schools built by the Christian missionaries who followed the European traders as the Moslem holy men had followed the Arab traders. The Christian schools educated both sexes. This is one of the rare instances where traditional African values coincided with a set of congruent European values, in this case, values carried by feminist Christian missionaries. The resulting African professional class, strongly marked by European culture, from the beginning included African women. This created a new class of women, distinct both from the traditional African and from the traditional European. These women were the primary initiators of coco farming. They also became successful businesswomen in the new international trading arena as well as successful professionals. In various ways, women's traditional roles translated into modern ones, although always in the face of resistance from European men and Europeanized African men. The most Western-oriented women might face the greatest status deprivations, pushed to accept dependent roles by virtue of their adoption of Western life-styles as the wives of professional men (Oppong 1974: 118). The less Westernized ones succeeded in expanding their commercial domain. The Nigerian Omu Okwei, the "merchant queen" of Ossonari (1872-1943), is an example of the success women could obtain who did not permit themselves to be placed in dependent Western-style sex roles. Omu Okwei amassed a large fortune and was elected the last market queen of Ossonari, chairwoman of the Council of Mothers (Ekejiuba 1967). During her lifetime, however, the supervision of markets was transferred from the Council of Mothers to the city council under pressure from the British. African women's struggle for economic independence is described by Obbo (1980).

A culture as rich in active roles for women as the African market culture does not simply disappear in the face of an alien intrusion. The women's councils kept meeting and, when the occupying colonial government appeared to threaten their economic welfare, as in the case of the famous taxation issue in Owerri Province of Nigeria in 1929, the women's council network could bring thousands of women to the colonial administrative headquarters for demonstrations. Sylvia Leith-Ross's study of Ibo women gives a sensitive picture both of the 1929 uprising of women and of the women's councils as they carried on their traditional responsibilities in the face of increasing European constraints. In describing a council meeting, she refers to "that curious sense one so often had among Ibo women of private and independent lives, an existence of their own lived quite apart from home and husband and children" (1939: 118), which she finds herself powerless to understand in spite of the common bond of sex. If an empathic Britishwoman could not understand it, we must not be surprised that European men could not understand it. She also mentions the large number of women who lived alone, whether married or widowed, and finds it difficult to understand that this is taken for granted by African women, who simply assume that women living alone can manage their own lives (1939: 94). Two studies of sex and gender roles in Africa that will be helpful to the interested reader are Amadiume (1987) and Oppong (1983).

By the end of the nineteenth century, rural women in all parts of Africa were having serious problems that they did not have 200 years before. Soil depletion, deforestation, and the introduction of cash cropping laid heavy additional work burdens on women. They had to work harder to grow food, walk further for fuel, and carry more water for the larger cash-crop fields that were increasingly managed by men, making the profits unavailable to the women (Boulding 1977; White, Bradley, & White 1972; Boserup 1970). At the same time, economic conditions were pushing the men to work sites far away, to cities, to mines, to plantations, making them unavailable for any kind of help on the farm. The separation of rural and urban women's associations has meant that only recently are these problems being tackled on a scale that may bring some relief.

Today, the women's councils are taking a new lease on life as women realize these councils are a useful tool in dealing with their economic problems. At the same time, because these councils in no way parallel the modern male governing councils in function, women also are seeking and gaining positions in male political bodies at every level. Some aberrant things are happening in the process, however. Thus we find the shadow of the *kabaka* pattern without the accompanying legitimacy of supporting community consensus, in the tendency of rulers to place their wives, sisters, and daughters in positions of political power in a "dynastic family" approach that is neither traditional nor modern. The "Kenyatta dynasty" in Kenya and the "Bandareika dynasty" in Sri Lanka have both placed a number of women in positions of family-derived power. This pattern enhances the position of elite women at the expense of the participation of other classes of society. On the other hand, it does also use available skills. Active leadership by wives of traditional leaders is another commonly found pattern, and it provides a more direct link between traditional and modern practices. An example of this type of leadership at its best, one of many such examples, is that of Mrs. Anna Angwafo of West Cameroon. The daughter of a priest and the wife of a *fon* (traditional ruler), she became a key agent in rural development programs in West Cameroon (Matheson 1970).

The trading women in African towns may be the most effective modernizers in Africa. They are translating a whole range of traditional women's associations into modern organizations that provide them with capital, social insurance, and outlets for their social and religious needs (Little 1973). A variety of women's cooperatives handle both rural and urban needs. Links between rural and urban women's associations are still weak, but urban women have discovered how to link their traditional organizations with the international world of the women's INGOs (international nongovernmental associations), thus tapping both economic and political opportunities in a wider arena.

North Africa has a substantially different character and racial composition than the rest of Africa. Algeria, Morocco, and Tunisia are the sites of the trading cities of ancient Phoenicia, a terrain well worked over by all the trading civilizations of the Mediterranean for at least a millennium before Roman times and then ruled by Rome after the defeat of Carthage. Egypt and the kingdoms of the Sudan and Axum (Ethiopia) belong to the most ancient of civilizations. By the time Moslem rule came to North Africa, these societies were already experienced in many types of political and economic organization.

Because the North African coast has been the scene of so many migrations and conquests, almost every kind of tradition of the participation of women has at one time or another been found there. The Berber tradition contains many variations from tribe to tribe, and these include the possibility of women rising to power and influence as magicians, saints, and mystics. The Berber Kabyles still have shrines to their holy women Lalla Imma Tifellut, Lalla Tawritt, Lalla Imma Mr'ita, Lalla Imma Wachaa, and Lalla Imma Mimen (Gordon 1968: 10). All-women's religious orders arose in this context. Berber women of the Aures and Shawia women had a great deal of freedom, and a Shawia woman, widowed or divorced, could adopt a special position as *azriya* (free woman), which enabled her to live independently more or less as a courtesan. The Tuareg were the freest of all; women were the writers, musicians, and administrators of community wealth. Nail women have been professional prostitutes in the cities of the Sahara for centuries and were women of wealth, dignity, and status before European tourists came on the scene.

The interaction of tribal and urban ways—while it may have intensified the Moslem practices of seclusion beyond what obtained elsewhere, as Tillion (in Gordon 1968) suggests—also brought powerful women into the politics of Islam. Queens and princesses thread their way through the politics of the North as well as in sub-Saharan Africa. Nevertheless, as the veil spread everywhere, middle-class urban women were increasingly secluded. The gradual elaboration of more extreme seclusion practices in parts of the Moslem world after the eleventh century, coinciding with a period of economic development and prosperity, led to an urban purdah culture for the middle and upper classes, in North Africa and elsewhere. Purdah foreshadowed the withdrawal of women from the labor force that industrialization brought about much later for Western women of the same classes.[4]

Nevertheless, women's communication networks brought news of the world into their underlife spaces. Elizabeth Cooper (1915), writing at the beginning of this century, describes what a strong women's culture can develop even under the most confining conditions. It is clear that there was a great deal of visiting between houses. Pilgrimages to the tombs of saints, going to the women's section of the local mosque, frequent visits to the baths, trips to market on special days for women, and going on all-women's expeditions to nearby parks or woods, all provided additional opportunities for communication.

The fact that women played a crucial part in the liberation struggles of a number of countries with strong seclusionary practices indicates that women do participate in the ongoing life of a society, even from purdah. The underlife is strong. The two Algerian revolutionary heroines, Djamila Bouhired and Djamila Boupacha, were not mutants. They were only more articulate representatives of thousands of women who became coolheaded terrorists carrying bombs under their *burkas*, women who withstood torture without a word when caught, women who identified completely with the cause of liberation. Repeated raping did not break them. They were tough (see the account of Algerian women in the revolution in Gordon 1968). The fact that after the revolution women were forced back into purdah indicates that it takes extraordinary physical and moral energy to overcome the barriers to public participation and that such energy cannot be easily sustained after a revolution. During a revolution, participation is made easy by the men of a society because they need their women on the battlefield. Afterward, doors that were opened for women may be shut again.

West Asia

In West Asia, the heartland of Islam, there are traditions of male-female economic partnership as strong as those of any African country, side by side with the practice of seclusion of women. From 981 to 1278, there were a series of decrees progressively limiting women's public appearances and dictating how they could dress. In 1030, Abbasid Qadir b'Ullah banned women from public ceremonies. Nevertheless, there was a great variety in the patterning of women's life from one country to another depending on the mix of pre-Islamic traditions and the character of the Moslem colonial occupiers. The Turks retained some of the earlier freedom for women from their nomadic days. The princesses of the Seljuk Turks in the tenth to thirteenth centuries built hospitals and schools in the tradition of urban princesses everywhere (Afetinan 1962: 23). The tombs of the princesses may be visited on pilgrimage today. Upperclass women were ladies of learning, like Muneccime Hatun, a lady astronomer at the Seljuk court.

The sixteenth-century Mongol invasions were hard on the succeeding Ottoman Empire (1299-1918) and contributed to the seclusion practices that increasingly affected the status of Turkish women. Middle-class families copied upper-class practices of having separate women's quarters in the homes. It was stylish, and it was safer. Queens remained active, however. Bibi Khanam, Tamerlane's queen, did much to rebuild what her Mongol husband ruthlessly destroyed, and her tomb at Samarkand was still an object of veneration at the beginning of this century. Gouhan Shad, the wife of Timur's son and successor, was also of Bibi's caliber, and many of the mosques and colleges destroyed by the Mongols were restored with her help (Ali 1899: 766). Such women were in no way secluded from the realities of their societies.

Segregation was hardest for middle-class women. Working-class women continued to go about their traditional labor. One new occupation for women was that of vaccinator. The practice of vaccination against smallpox spread to England when Lady Montagu reported it in her travel letters. There was also a class of trading women, in the Mediterranean woman-merchant tradition. Among the upper classes, there were writers, poets, and musicians: Zeynep Hatun (d. 1474), Fahrinusa Mihri Hatun (d. 1522), and a series of women in a great lyric tradition, the Divan, that lasted until the mid-nineteenth century. Some of these women lived in Dervish convents that may have paralleled the convents of Europe as centers for gifted women, although in the West little is known about them.

The status of women was not high in the Ottoman court, however, and the royal harem was filled with slave concubines. No sultan raised any woman in his harem to the status of queen between 1403 and 1541. At that date, the Russian slave Roxelana persuaded the sultan to marry her and received the title "Sultan Valide." Roxelana began what Penzer calls "the rule of women" in the empire, and he suggests that, for the next 150 years, women had the major political power. One such woman ruler, Safieh, is supposed to have corresponded with Catherine de Medici to keep the Turks from war with Venice (Penzer 1935: 187).

The freedom of women in Constantinople, much envied by women elsewhere in the Moslem world in the nineteenth century (Ali 1899: 773), is hard to relate to the practice of rigid purdah and is more evidence that women found ways to be active in spite of sequestration customs. The fact, mentioned before, that boys were reared in the women's quarters at least until the age of 7 meant that women had a chance to train boys to respect them and that boys saw women as autonomous actors in the harem world, the only world the boys knew, during their most formative years. An account of the education of boys in the Ottoman Empire in 1604 mentions that boys stayed in the harem until they were 11, although a male tutor came in from outside for their fifth to eleventh years. Eleven years is a long time to live in the women's world (Penzer 1935: 128). It was essentially through their harem tutelage of boy rulers that women seized political power in the period ushered in by Roxelana.

European colonization of some West Asian countries on the one hand spurred an intensification of purdah practices to protect native women from Westerners and on the other hand set countercurrents in motion as women missionaries from Europe arrived to open schools for Asian girls. An indigenous reform movement in many Asian countries also began in the mid-nineteenth century. Attention focused on cases like the Constantinople factory girls with working hours from 4 a.m. to 8 p.m.—a replication of the European story (M. E. Burton 1918: 46). This reform movement also involved providing schools for women. Turkey began a major program for women in 1869. Many extraordinary women entered public life in the latter part of the nineteenth century, demonstrating once again what a high level of readiness can exist in a purdah society. Among many distinguished women, one of the best known and most widely read outside Turkey is Halide Edib, fighter in the revolution, active in international diplomacy, leader in developing a national education system for women, social philosopher, innovator of social services, and novelist. The *Memoirs* (Edib 1926) of this outstanding "peace heroine" of the turbulent turn of the century make moving reading. She describes reading bloody martial histories of her people as a child and wondering what children did in those times. Did they go out to play? The roster of activist women visionaries like Edib is far longer than we shall ever know.

There is a series of photographs in Woodsmall (1960) of the women leaders who have been active since the turn of the century in Turkey and other West Asian countries. Looking at those intent, self-confident faces, it would be hard to believe that these are women who have emerged from centuries of purdah if we did not know that purdah involves an active underlife.[5] The bathhouse alone probably fomented more than one revolution.

Persia (now Iran), traditionally one of the more seclusionary of the West Asian societies, has its share of stories of women's activism. In 1861, government officials were profiteering during a famine, keeping food prices astronomically high. The word went out through the women's networks, and thousands of women came out of seclusion to surround the carriage of the shah when he was returning from a hunting trip one day, to demand action in the food crisis. The thoroughly startled shah promised to meet the demands the women made—and did (Cooper 1915: 35-36). Another story that lifts the tip of the purdah veil to give a glimpse of the life underneath comes from 1911, when Russia threatened Persia's sovereignty in an ultimatum to the National Assembly. A group of 300 veiled women marched out from the harems of Teheran to the assembly and demanded admittance. They confronted the president, "tore aside their veils, and confessed their decision to kill their own husbands and sons and add their own bodies to the sacrifice, if the deputies should waver in their duty to uphold the liberty and dignity of the Persian people and nation" (M. E. Burton 1918: 171). Many of the women held pistols under their skirts or in the folds of their sleeves, says Burton.

Persia was also the scene of the persecution of thousands of women followers of the sect of Baha Ullah in the same century. Cooper tells the story of one fragile-looking woman who was forced to witness the beheading of her 14-year-old son and then had the son's head thrown in her lap by the executioner. After holding the head for a long moment in prayer, the mother flung it back to the executioner, saying "I do not take back what I give my God" (Cooper 1915: 37). Women who lived in purdah were not necessarily sheltered, not necessarily timid, and certainly not necessarily ignorant.

India, like Turkey, developed a rigidly seclusionary set of institutions that overlaid ancient traditions of public participation of women in society. The freer Vedic traditions were not totally abrogated by the Laws of Manu, composed in the early centuries C.E., nor were the laws in themselves entirely destructive toward women. As Romila Tharpar says, the laws were originally written to preserve some of the finer values of Hindu society, and "the rigid application of ill-digested ideas, taken from this book, led to the emergence of a society which . . . ended up by becoming a minor hell for some of its members" (Tharpar 1963: 473). The customs of child marriage and *suttee*, self-immolation of the widow on her husband's funeral pyre, became some of the features of this "minor hell." If anything, the modernizing elite of Islam that took over in the 800s somewhat improved the status of women, in that Islam provided property rights for women that they had not had before. On the other hand, they also introduced purdah (the women's quarters are called *zenana* in India), which added to Indian women's other disabilities the handicap of total sequestration for some castes.

That elite women suffered relatively little from the sequestration is suggested by the activities in the early 1600s of the Persian woman Mehr un-Nissa. She came as a refugee to the court of the Mongol emperor Akbar in India with her parents and, after many adventures, married Akbar's successor, Jehangir. Known in history as Nur Jehan, Mehr un-Nissa was the virtual ruler of India and was responsible for reforms including the forbidding of some Hindu practices of mutilation (Akbar, her father-in-law, had forbidden suttee). Ali describes a number of daughters and wives of emperors who were gifted in the arts, and as political leaders, and lived active public lives (1899: 770-72).

Although India had several sets of colonizers through the centuries, each imposing their own patterns, the Indian working-class woman labored changelessly, with a veil handy to pull over her face if men were nearby. Working women crushed stones for road making, labored in the rice fields, tended the silkworms, and later worked long hours in the textile factories. Children worked with their mothers, in field and factory. After 1600, the last wave of occupiers, the British, steadily encroached on the country, laying a London-based administrative system on the ancient empire they did not understand. Maharanis and maharajahs kept what control they could. Warrior Maratha princesses rode against the British with their armies, but to no avail. The eighteenth century saw a succession of very able Maratha queens: Tarabai of Kolhapur, Anubai of Ichalkaranji, and 24-year-old Ahalyabai (Altekar 1978: 189).

> An Anglo Indian officer of long standing had observed to J. S. Mill that if a Hindu principality was vigilantly and economically governed, if order was preserved without oppression, if cultivation was extending and people prosperous, in three cases out of four he found it to be under a woman's rule. (Altekar 1978: 189)

Indian girls of the upper classes had always been tutored at home. When Christian mission schools for girls were started by the British, an indigenous schooling movement also developed that gave Indian girls education without the background pressure of conversion. This movement spread rapidly across India, and many home-tutored Indian ladies found an outlet for their talents as teachers. By the 1800s, schools and new types of social services of every kind were being formed at a very rapid rate, as worldwide stirrings of women and men were translated into Indian needs. The unsuccessful revolt of 1857 was followed by the formation of the Indian National Congress in 1885, events that brought women increasingly into public life. There were violent and nonviolent branches of the independence movement, and women were active in both. By the 1930s, the nonviolent movement was clearly identified with Gandhi. He is given credit for "mobilizing the women of India" because they played such an active role in his *satyagraha* campaigns. They often were in the very front row in protest demonstrations and were shot down by the British on more than one occasion. While Gandhi deserves full credit for recognizing the part that women could play and encouraging this, more account should be taken of the readiness of the women themselves. Gandhi did not simply "drag the women folk of India from their kitchens into the public life of India" (Guba 1973: 18), he provided an opportunity for women to carry their concerns from the underlife to the overlife of society.

The women who chose the terrorist route had no protective spokesmen, only their own commitment. Like their European, African, and Asian sisters who chose that route, they were coolheaded. The district magistrate of Comilla was assassinated by two young women, and there were numerous other attacks by women including one on the governor of Bengal in the senate hall of Calcutta and a second on the same governor on the polo grounds in Darjeeling (Guba 1973: 22). Many women went underground to continue their activities, unhindered by the jail terms regularly meted out to Gandhi and his followers. Among those who went underground were some who continued in leadership of the radical wing of the women's movement in India in recent decades, like Asaf Ali. She belongs to that generation of older women revolutionaries found on all continents, trained in the demanding turn-of-the-century struggles, working at a pace in the closing decades of the century that few younger women could manage.

When Gandhi went to jail in 1939 in the civil disobedience involving breaking the salt laws, Sarojini Naidu took the leadership of the movement. Poet Sarojini, "the nightingale of India," was one of the four women presidents of the Indian National Congress. Annie Besant, the English labor leader turned mystic who settled in India, was the first, in 1917; Naidu was the second, in 1925; Nellie Sengupta was the third, in 1933; and Indira Gandhi the fourth, in 1959. (She became prime minister in the late 1960s.) Women have served as state governors, as foreign ambassadors to major powers, as ministers in the national cabinet, as justices of the supreme court, and generally have had a distinguished record of public service. Some of them have combined government service with a long record of revolutionary activity and international work in the peace movement. Sushila Nayar, Gandhi's disciple as a teenager and his physician as a young woman, served later as minister of health for independent India and as international vice president of the Women's International League for Peace and Freedom. A special combination of gentleness and toughness, and a commanding physical presence, characterized all these women.

Some of the women associated with Gandhi, such as Kamaladehvi, came from the matrilineal societies of South India, where even today women are more active and visible than elsewhere. Kamaladevi, a national leader in the promotion of craft enterprises in the Gandhian tradition, reminisces about her grandmother who used to hold a salon every afternoon for the intellectual enlightenment of the men of the community. The women of her family were traditionally educated at home, and Kamaladevi grew up taking women's dignity and civic responsibility for granted (Kamaladevi, personal interview, Varanasi, India, 1974, also see her memoirs, Kamaladevi 1986).

Another important and not yet evaluated contribution to the general activism of Indian women is coming from the tribal sector, which, in a category referred to as "the scheduled tribes, the scheduled castes, and other backward classes," represents about 25% of India's population (Pritam Singh, Varanasi, India, personal communication, 1974). The tribal women, who have much more personal freedom than other Indian women do, are considered "immoral and backward." Their freer, more outspoken ways often cause havoc when they enter the university, as they are being encouraged to do currently. University administrators are sometimes hard-pressed to know how to deal with them. Many middle-class women's organizations in India see them as a problem, not a resource.[6]

Another set of traditional castes that are now insisting on recognition in modern India are the castes whose traditional occupation has been prostitution. The Nautch women, courtesans traditionally under the special protection of the ruling class, and temple dancing girls all had an accepted social status. These women were well educated and had a great deal of personal freedom. In 1961, when the Allahabad city police tried to close down houses of prostitution, the prostitutes petitioned the higher court, stating that "prostitution was their traditional occupation, that the order of the lower court to evict them from their ancestral homes was against the fundamental rights of citizens guaranteed by the Constitution of India" (Thomas 1964: 380).

In emphasizing the activist women of India, there is a danger of making the abandonment of purdah seem too easy. Cora Vreede-De Stuers's study of Moslem women in Northern India, *Parda* (1968), brings out both the strength and the helplessness of women bound by the system and also points to its value as an affirmation of cultural autonomy. She uses the concept of *"zenana* modernization" to describe a wholly different concept of modernization than that of Westerners. Other perspectives on the modernization struggles of Indian women will be found in Jain and Banerjee (1985) and Nanda (1976).

Another perspective on the purdah issue relates to the feelings of psychological security that seclusion and the veil afford. Taking the step of leaving the secluded quarters, and, even more, of taking off the veil, may be psychologically agonizing for women. It appears that the equivalent effort for the average U.S. middle-class woman would be to walk down the street stark naked. Socialization to seclusion is powerful and lifelong and cannot easily be abandoned. The level of effort expended and the sheer physical courage displayed by women in leaving purdah should command our profound respect.[7] The not infrequent use of dark glasses by women of the Middle East who have left purdah suggests that a similar practice among some "emancipated" Euro-American women may have common psychological roots.

When English women began coming to India in the 1800s on the wave of the new consciousness about world problems and women's problems, they first found allies among the educated Indian elite and then gradually also among middle-class women who had already left or were about to leave purdah. The Indian suffrage movement was already well equipped to tackle the complex legislative work required to remove the numerous restrictions on women by the time the European allies arrived. The new international organizations the European women brought to India—the YWCA, the WCTU, and others—provided an additional set of tools for Indian women. They were particularly useful for middle- and working-class urban girls in the labor force. Residence and training centers sprang up in many places, linking with the larger enterprise of teacher training and establishing a national education for women.

Yet, one must be realistic and recognize that, in the midst of all this activity, traditional attitudes toward the relative importance of girl and boy babies still operate today to reduce the life chances of Indian baby girls. They are not as important as their brothers, and it is the mothers who enforce these differential values. In Figure 4.1, we find a picture of a young, alert-looking Indian mother and her older son holding 2-year-old twins on their laps. The twin on the left is a girl, on the right, a boy. "The difference in their condition is entirely due to the fact that the boy was nursed first and fed first, his sister getting what was left over. Even here in the clinic, the mother (and the brother) . . . are lavishing their attention on the crying baby, while the apathetic little girl is scarcely noticed" ("Third World Women," 1973).

This is one of the background realities that must be kept in mind as we turn to the all-important involvement of Indian women in world affairs. Hunger at home must be dealt with, yet it is also true that the international participation of women is crucial to the future of the world. The high level of readiness of Indian women to enter international affairs is an important aspect of twentieth-century life. Some of

Figure 4.1. Indian Mother With Twins: A Girl and a Boy
SOURCE: United States Committee for UNICEF, New York; used by permission.

the leading women figures on the world stage in this century have been Indian: Vijaya Lakshmi Pandit, Indian ambassador to both the United States and the former Soviet Union and active in many international organizations, was president of the U.N. General Assembly in its eighth session; Rajkumari Amrit Kaur, former minister of health of India, was president of the World Health Organization; Mrs. Lakshmi Menon, at one time deputy minister of external affairs for India, was former chief of the U.N. Section on the Status of Women. These women, with countless others, gave leadership to the formation of the All-India Women's Conference and the mobilization of many thousands of women into community activity. Among the many examples of this mobilization activity is Tara Bai, former president of a women's college, who has served on the planning boards of many of India's welfare ventures and has developed, with the help of a group of women volunteers, a series of experimental children's villages for homeless children to be extended over as much of India as possible. A second example is a group of Delhi women, both professional educators and community volunteers, who have developed a program of schools on trucks that visit the construction sites all over Delhi where children of the migrant construction workers live and work with their parents. This is the first time education has ever reached the children of these workers, and the plan is to be extended.

Because of the sheer size of India, the basic organizational work for any activity of national scope takes skill, toughness, and endurance unimaginable to the average woman activist of the West. Whatever history's final judgment on Indira Gandhi will be, her decisive rule in a turbulent time for India is another notable example of that toughness.

China

China is giant India's giant sister, with even more massive problems of scale with which to cope. The mutually antagonistic traditions of Confucianism and Taoism have created the same ambiguity about the status of women in China that the Vedic tradition versus the Laws of Manu created in India. The elitist tradition of Confucianism placed women in a position of semislavery with the rule of "thrice-obeying" (*san tsung*), which in practice meant lifelong sequestration within doors and lifelong obedience to men, successively to father, husband, and son. The folk tradition of Taoism on the other hand encouraged the participation of women in community life. China has a long history of secret societies among the peasantry, associated with Taoism, and women have been accepted in these societies as members and as leaders. Some of the women leaders of the twentieth-century revolution in China came directly out of these societies. Another source of strong women's leadership in China has come from the nomadic tribes, which from China's earliest existence have alternated periods of peaceful coexistence with episodes of war and conquest. The roles of Mongol women were described in Chapter 7 in Volume 1. China probably has the same proportion of tribal population as India has, up to 25%. Over the centuries, these peoples have provided a pool of potential women activists. China, like India, still tends to think of its tribal population as "backward" and regards the tribal women as needing emancipation.

Because Confucianism was the belief system of the ruling elite and Taoism the belief system of the peasants, the participation of women stemmed more from peasant than elite traditions. Ancient China was matrilineal. The shamaness and leadership traditions of women were apparently buried in the folk culture, there to stay alive for centuries. I do not have the historical materials for verification of the dates when women's leadership went underground into the folk culture, but reigning empresses in the early centuries of the Common Era have been noted. The status of women went up and down through the centuries depending on the extent of order or anarchy, war or peace. By the end of the first millennium, during the Sung dynasty, there was a period of reform decrees giving greater freedom to women, only to be followed by the Chin dynasty, during which all reforms were abolished and foot binding began. Foot binding was practiced by the middle and upper classes and, as long as the practice was confined to women who had no need to labor, the suffering involved was "minimal." When lower-class families, ambitious to marry a daughter into the middle class, began binding the feet of their girls in hopes of snaring better husbands for them, the full extent of the cruelty of the practice became evident. Few of these girls succeeded in "marrying up," and there are many pitiful accounts of women laborers tottering on stumps in the fields of China, even women drawing canal barges, stumbling along on bound feet. The suffering of working-class women in China was more severe than anywhere else in the world, partly because of the tendency of foot binding to penetrate into working-class culture.

In spite of, or perhaps because of, these widespread atrocities, there seems to have been a women's movement among women of the lower gentry and upper peasantry from the Ming dynasty (1368-1644) on, accompanied by widespread literacy:

> In the sixteenth century widespread female literacy provoked men for the first time to perceive not the equality of women but their comparability, and to ask just how, given these obvious talents, they differed from men. These questions once articulated during the late Ming, continued to worry writers during the Ch'ing. (Handlin, as quoted in Wolf and Witke 1975: 16)

Women of the lower gentry became increasingly active during the Ch'ing dynasty (1644-1911). Not allowed into the clan schools giving special training for the mandarinate, they nevertheless were taught in small family classes for girls only. By the 1880s, they were being reached by the same influences and movements, somewhat differently channeled, that women in the rest of Asia and Africa were experiencing. The birth of the modern women's movement in China may be associated with the 1898 reform movement, which from the beginning linked the "woman question" with nationalism (Rankin, in Wolf and Witke 1975).

It is not easy to explain the strength of the women's movement in China in the 1920s except by postulating some kind of interaction in previous centuries between women in the peasant movements, women of the lower gentry, and women of the upper gentry. In the case of upper-gentry women, their husbands were government officials in the mandarin system and, by the rules of the imperial bureaucracy, were not allowed to serve in their home districts. This meant that the wife of such an official, remaining behind in the clan home, would through most of her adult life be in charge of a large household of hundreds of persons, counting relatives, children, servants, slaves, and concubines (Ayscough 1937). Her household was closely linked with other households in possibly hundreds of other villages within the clan organization. Thus no amount of formal edicts about women being concerned with the indoors only (as stated in the "Record of Rites;" Ayscough 1937: 54) could keep women with that extent of responsibility from being extremely knowledgeable about clan and district affairs and very probably about national affairs.

Women of the lower gentry probably were the schoolteachers for the girls in the households of the upper gentry as well as the counselors and helpers to the women of the peasantry. This counselor-helper role is a traditional role for the lower gentry in China and might be something like the lady-of-the-manor-house role we noted in England. Yung-Teh Chow's *Social Mobility in China* (1966) makes clear how some of the male lower gentry assisted the peasantry during the revolution but scarcely mentions the women of the lower gentry. A study of such women is overdue.

Women who could play go-between roles, either from the upper peasantry or the lower gentry to the peasantry, would include nuns from the Buddhist and Taoist orders, who did a great deal of house to house visiting and teaching as part of their religious role; female professors of divination, professors of spiritual manifestations, and praying women (probably terms for various types of shamanesses); marriage go-betweens; herbalists; and midwives. "In a learned Chinese tome is written: 'Whoever has these mischief-makers about his home is sure to meet trouble' " (Ayscough 1937: 87). This reference suggests that the activities of these more mobile women did not go unnoticed by men.

When Ch'iu Chin, China's "first woman revolutionary," began lecturing against foot binding and started a girls' school in about 1900, she was "standing on the shoulders of giants"[8]—the hundreds of thousands of Chinese women, peasants and gentry, who through the centuries had nourished a vision of women's participation in society. She was a member of a secret revolutionary organization of both men and women, in the old tradition, and trained in sword play. She was also the first woman to join Sun Yat-sen's party, formed in 1904, and did much of the organizing work for it. She set up a headquarters in Shanghai for all the secret societies committed to revolution and was at one time injured by an explosion while supervising the assembly of a bomb. In 1906, she started the *Chinese Women's Journal* to rally women to the revolution. She formed a people's army in the same year, using the secret societies as military contingents. This mother of two young children was beheaded by the Manchu in 1907, at the age of 33, after extreme torture during which she uttered no word but wrote out seven characters as a "confession": "Autumn rain and autumn wind sadden us."

The roster of women revolutionaries in China since 1907 is so immense that there is no possibility of conveying in a few words what has gone on in the past three quarters of a century. By 1925, when Anna Louise Strong visited China, there were already mass organizations of women. One federation of groups was organized under the women's branch of the Kuomintang, Sun Yat-sen's then revolutionary organization; another set was organized within the trade union movement; and the third (and smallest) was organized under the political department of the army. These were in addition to organizations of women and men together. In 1927, there were "nearly a million and a half women in over ten provinces . . . in some kind of organization under the leadership of the Kuomintang" (Strong 1965: 103). How many women were organized into unions it is hard to estimate, but Strong addressed 1,500 union women in Canton in 1925. And 400 noncombatant young women propagandists traveled with the army: "Our work is to organize the women. For this we go into the homes and markets, wherever women are to be found, and talk with them. When we have talked enough, we organize a local women's union and leave it to handle affairs in that district" (Strong 1965: 104).

A study of the work of Helen Foster Snow (1967) on the participation of women in the revolution and in the establishment of the People's Republic of China gives some support to the hypothesis that women from the upper and lower gentry, peasant women, and tribal women shared leadership in the movement. The upper gentry could be represented by Soong Chingling, widow of Sun Yat-sen, "the nearest to a saint that any action has produced since Joan of Arc" (1967: 120) and the first woman Marxist in China. She was one of the famous Soong sisters. Her sisters Mayling and Eling joined the nationalist cause, Mayling as the wife of Chiang Kai-shek and Eling as wife of a conservative Chinese industrialist. All three were ordained to unusual activist roles, although in different causes, and have the double distinction of being directly descended from a sixteenth-century imperial chancellor of Emperor Chung Chen and of coming from Hainan Island. Hainan is a Hakka tribal stronghold, and the sisters are supposed to have inherited some Hakka blood from their father, Charlie Soong. The Hakka tribal traditions are strong on the participation of women, and Soong *père* thus provided the hybrid vigor of tribal traditions for his daughters.

Ts'ai Ting-Li, communist leader in the area of the first Chinese soviet, could stand for the lower gentry. Her family were small landlords and her mother was oppressed by her father's family in typical feudal manner: "My earliest memory is of her reading to me many works of old fiction dealing with the suffering of people. . . . From her I received my own understanding of the problems of people other than myself and a tendency toward Christian humanitarianism" (Wales 1952: 200). In 1926, at 17, Ts'ai Ting-Li went to Hailufeng to do "women's work"—helping organize the Hailufeng Women's Peasant Union, the first all-women's union in China. She spent her life organizing women at the village level. She remarks how hard it is for intellectuals, whether men or women, to endure the physical hardship of the life of the peasant and how often the peasants had to help and protect them (see Ting-Li's autobiography as recounted in Wales 1952).

K'ang K'e-ching, a military commander known as the "Red Amazon," represents the peasantry. She was given away at birth in 1912, for her fisherfolk parents had no food. She joined the village women's peasant union at 14 and became the communist youth inspector in a district of 10 villages at the age of 15, though she was illiterate. At 16, she joined the Red Army and taught herself to read and write by reading billboards and studying slogans while on the march.

The role of tribal women in the revolution is suggested by the fact that Kwangtung Province, the land of the Hakkas, was the home of the T'aip'ing rebellion of 1852 to 1865; the home of the first soviet, organized in 1927; and the home of Sun Yat-sen and of Soong Chingling. Some Chinese are proud of the Hakka tradition and of Hakka women, who did much of the work involved in setting up the first soviet. It was in the Hakka setting that the basis for the alliance of women peasantry and gentry was formed.

From the early 1920s on, intensive work was done among the women of China by leaders from all classes. Tsai Chang, from the leading "great family" of old China and therefore top gentry, coordinated these efforts so that in the spring of 1949 the All-China Democratic Women's Federation was formed, "possibly the largest single mass organization and the most active one ever formed in the history of mankind" (Snow 1967: 230). By 1956, it had 76 million women members, while the Chinese Communist party had fewer than 11 million members.

This federation was almost like a state within a state. It undertook the reform of marriage law and the liberation of slave women before

the new communist state was established. It held courts, passed judgments, and opened training centers for women. When the new government was formed in Peking in the fall of 1949, members of the federation
helped write the new constitution. Tsai Chang and two other women
leaders sat on the presidium that formed the new government. When
the People's Congress met in 1954, women constituted 14% of the
membership elected by popular vote. In northern China, some districts
reported 40% of the elected officials to be women. Some women were
heads of the town governments. (Peking had a woman deputy mayor
in the 1960s.) Land redistribution was a key part of the women's
program, and the fact that land was assigned to *individuals*, women and
men, may be the key to the success of the new society. Women for the
first time had their share of control over significant productive resources.

The development of industrial cooperatives in China in 1938, well
before the revolution, was largely the work of the Soong sisters (and,
apparently, Helen Foster Snow). It was the success of that earlier movement, says Snow, that laid the groundwork for the rapid formation
across China of cooperatives in every factory and workshop, establishing a pattern of local control that saved China from Soviet-style central-
ism. The agricultural commune was also a priority for the women's
movement, and its great success in increasing productivity was only
matched by its success in providing family and community services
that enabled women to work and children to be well and healthy. Like
land redistribution, the commune principle was basic to the liberation
of women. It dealt with them as individuals, paid them as individuals,
and treated the children of the community as a collective responsibility
(Snow 1967: 24-33, 168).

The Chinese women did not do this alone. One kind of support was
the vast complex of Christian missions administered from Western
countries. For all their limitations, these missions brought to China
concerned Western women who contributed substantially to the development of schooling for Chinese women. Margaret Burton's *Women
Workers of the Orient* (1918), written for the Central Committee on the
United Study of Foreign Missions during World War I, shows both the
strengths and the weaknesses of the Western contribution. It was a plea
for the continuation of the labors of peace in the spirit of women's
internationalism of that era: "The world's to build anew—not Europe,
nor America, nor Asia, but the *world*" (1918: 228).

The international women's movement was also active in China. When
the Chinese Women's Federation was formed in 1949, the WCTU and the
YWCA were affiliates. Chinese women were themselves internationally

minded. In December 1949, the Women's Federation had the first "Bandung idea" and called a conference of the women of Asia. Delegates came to Peking from India, Burma, Indonesia, Iran, Israel, Korea, Lebanon, Malaya, Mongolia, Siam, Syria, Vietnam, the Soviet Union, and the Philippines. "Sororal" delegates appeared unofficially from Great Britain, Algeria, Cuba, Czechoslovakia, France, Holland, the Ivory Coast, and Madagascar (Snow 1967: 22-23). The lone visitor from the United States was Eslanda Robeson, wife of the singer Paul Robeson.

With the increasing isolation of China from Western-based internationalism, largely through the influence of the United States, Chinese women had few international contacts outside the Two-Thirds World except through the socialist Women's International Democratic Federation. Western radical women were able to stay in touch with China through this organization and by various means of their own devising. Now that contacts are easier, a broader range of Western women are coming in touch again with Chinese women. The pattern of contact is different, but a few Western women like the American Anna Louise Strong, who edited *Letter from Peking* until she died at the close of the 1960s, helped to bridge the gap between the old and the new.

The women's movement in China had a setback after the first rush of progress. The inevitable male reaction began. What is happening in these decades, particularly to the role of women in the inner circles of power, is not clear at this time. The beautifully produced magazine that was the voice of Chinese women to the women of the world, *Women of China*, stopped publication in 1966. Knowing the history of the women's effort in China, however, and the strength of the local networks involved in the commune form of production, it seems unlikely that the old patriarchal system could ever fully reassert itself.[9]

There are many Asian countries that have not been touched on in this section, but space makes a further survey impossible. I particularly regret leaving out Japan, from which I have so many happy personal memories of the women's movement, and Indonesia, where women participated so actively in the independence movement in ways that paralleled the activities of Indian women. I regret most of all leaving out the remarkable story of the women of Vietnam, who have stayed courageously international throughout the entire tragedy of Western involvement in Indochina. The freer lives of the women of Burma, Thailand, Laos, and Cambodia, first glimpsed through Barbara Ward's *Women in the New Asia* (1963), must also go unrecorded. Because the flavor of life is so different in Asia, it will take another world history of women, one focused on Asia, to do justice to developments that have been sketched so briefly here.

Latin America

Studies of the status of women in Latin America, both before the arrival of the Spanish in 1500 and afterward, are increasingly becoming available.[10] Because Latin American culture is also "American," and therefore supposedly close to North American culture, relatively few social scientists from the North discover and admit the profound gulf. Nora Scott Kinzer's honest description of that gulf in "Sexist Sociology" (1974) comes as a fresh wind into the pretensions of cross-cultural understanding.

General histories of pre-Hispanic Latin America indicate that the Incan and Aztec empires of Peru and Mexico were highly stratified societies with temple-palace complexes not unlike those of Egypt and Sumer. Robert Adams has in fact made a careful study of the similarities and differences between Mesopotamia and Mexico (Adams 1966). Royal women were important in public rituals of ruling, and the Incas practiced brother-sister marriage in the manner of the pharaohs. Women's temples governed by priestesses provided education and convent life for girls who came for brief periods or for a lifetime. There were various categories of priestesses and virgins, some with a special relationship to the ruler, as a part of his harem (Diffie 1945: 176). Associated with the temples were large textile workshops with women workers, again on the pattern of Egypt. In the Incan empire, these workshops ranged in size from 500 women at Caxa to 1,500 women at Cuzco (Wittfogel 1957). Women and men of the lower classes were ranged in a hierarchy of peasants, serfs, and slaves.

In areas not directly ruled by one of the native empires (the Incan hegemony reached from what is currently Ecuador to Chile), tribal life was of a more egalitarian nature. Two glimpses of such tribes from early Spanish accounts show a relatively fluid division of labor, with weaving and pottery engaged in by women and men, depending on the region. Women were active in the markets. A chronicler comments that "the women were the ones who knew most about everything" (Diffie 1945: 122, 129).

The Spanish arrived in Latin America a century before Northern Europeans settled in North America. Although the conquistadors did not bring women with them in the initial invasions, colonists arrived in family groups with women as early as 1502. By 1530, the first of the women religious had arrived—Franciscan tertiaries who opened schools for girls. There was a feeling at first that it was not appropriate to have women from the enclosed orders in the new country, but, by 1550, they were also establishing convents in the New World. By the end of the seventeenth century, there were 80 or more convents from the various Spanish and Portuguese orders. The convents conducted schools for girls and at first accepted all women equally, Spanish, Native American, African, slave, and free. Later, they were compelled by the authorities to be selective and segregate their pupils.

Because the sixteenth century was a time of high culture in the Spanish convents, we can assume that some of these convents were centers of scholarship and culture in the New World. A hint of this is found in the story of Sor Juana Inez de la Cruz (1651-95), sometimes called the first Latin American feminist. According to some accounts, she disguised herself as a boy in order to enter school in Mexico City as a child (Montoya 1975). She entered a Jeronimite convent at 18 and won renown as a painter, composer, scientist, mathematician, dramatist, poet, and theologian before she died at 44. Herbert (1965) ranks her with Leonardo da Vinci, Roger Bacon, and Newton as a scientist. A great synthesizer as well as creator of knowledge, she wrote in Latin, Portuguese, and Aztec as well as Spanish and assembled a library of 4,000 volumes, possibly the largest collection in the Americas at the time. De la Cruz's collected works (1951), available in Spanish, include *La Respuesta*, her spiritual autobiography. At the peak of her productivity, she was commanded by her religious superiors to stop writing and to dismantle her library, an order that she accepted as part of the discipline of the religious life. The ban was lifted eventually, but she died soon after, before she could return to her mental labors.

While Spanish and Portuguese settlers mixed freely with Indians and blacks in both concubinage and marriage, there was also a very clear-cut class society based on largely absentee ownership of haciendas and a nonworking Spanish upper class. While the indigenous peoples were badly exploited, as were the blacks imported as slaves, they were also protected by the missionary orders of priests in a way that did not happen in North America. This was partly because of the bull of Pope Alexander VI in 1493, which conferred on the Spanish and the Portuguese the right to evangelize the territories of the New World according to the line of demarcation he established. Alexander gave the crown the responsibility for "the preaching and diffusion of the Catholic Faith, so that Indians might be educated and live in peace and order" (Philip II, quoted in Houtart and Pin 1965: 4). Blacks were also declared to be "sons of Adam," so that both Native Americans and blacks were treated as humans with souls to save. This modified their oppression, enabling enterprising urban Native Americans and blacks to obtain freedom and middle-class status.

Bowser provides examples of this from colonial Peru. Margareta, a slave freed by Diego de Almajio on his death, became a successful businesswoman who founded a convent in her former master's name and lent money to the Spanish Crown to defeat its enemies in a civil war (Bowser 1974: chap. 9). The general Spanish reluctance to engage in manual labor gave slaves ample opportunity to apprentice into all kinds of skilled crafts and also to open their own businesses. By the seventeenth century, some of them had already become a comfortable middle-class sector of Peruvian society. Spanish, Native American, and African artisans all took each other in as apprentices, male and female. Free black women were particularly successful with large inns and bakeries.

Deep religious sentiments were more common among Native American and black women than among men. Probably the nuns who taught and worked among the women touched their lives more intimately than the monks ever touched the lives of the men of a community. Many women of the poorer classes bequeathed whatever they had to the church.

When Inca-descended Cecilia Tupac Amaru and her brother José led the 1780 Indian revolt against the Spanish, Cecilia must have had women followers. That story has yet to be fully written. The rebellion was unsuccessful, and Cecilia died soon after being captured, whipped, and exiled. Apparently, many women served both on the battlefields and as spies and messengers in Argentina, Colombia, Mexico, Peru, and Brazil during the wars of independence in the early 1800s (Jaquette 1973: 344-53). Gertrudis Bocanegra, a mestiza born in 1765, organized an underground army of women during the 1810 war of independence in Mexico. Taken prisoner by the government, she was tortured and publicly executed in 1817. Her particular contribution to Mexican society was the organization of schools for Native American children (Montoya 1975). Juana Azurduy is one of the most famous of these heroines and fought by her husband's side with her own Amazon corps for the independence of what is now Bolivia. Juana Robles was the slave heroine of Argentinian independence. Women revolutionaries played many different kinds of roles, and each had her own style. Isolated examples of battlefield heroism, and the more general, total-commitment revolutionary activity of Flora Tristan Moscosa, the half-Peruvian Frenchwoman who spent some time in Peru on behalf of the workers' international, represent the two extremes of revolutionary style.

Tristan Moscosa felt very alienated from the Peruvian salonières she found on her visit and denounced these women as not living in the real world. The nineteenth-century *veladas*, or salons, of Lima, Santiago, and

Buenos Aires were widely criticized in their own time and since. It is not clear that they were as totally insulated from pressing social problems as they have been accused of being. According to Chaney (1973: 333-34), the veladas of Lima in the 1870s and 1880s were feminist and dealt with social-justice issues including the situation of the Native American. Many prominent velada women were widows or had remained unmarried, as was true of many of the first university women. One reason they have been so much criticized is that they made a place for themselves outside the familistic structures of Spanish American society.

It will have to be left to the scholars of Latin American history to begin presenting the underside so that we have a better picture of women in that history. A reading of the articles in Pescatello's *Female and Male in Latin America* (1973) suggests that there is a lot of demythologizing to do before the underside becomes clear. On the one hand, there is the conventional picture of the machismo culture, with the women as submissive, dependent creatures who live out their lives in male-dominated cultures. On the other hand, there is the picture of marianismo, the other side of the machismo coin, which suggests that it is the female after all who is dominant. From the marianismo perspective, the macho males are perpetual children and must be protected and cared for by women who strive for an ideal characterized by "semidivinity, moral superiority and spiritual strength. This spiritual strength engenders abnegation, that is, an indefinite capacity for humility and sacrifice" (Stevens 1973: 94). According to the marianismo doctrine, Latin American women are ruthless with their daughters and daughters-in-law to ensure continuance of this ideal of sacrificial moral superiority.

Both machismo and marianismo exist in some form in almost every culture on every continent, distorted remnants of ancient myths. They represent some failure in social maturity with their deliberately maintained distortion of both the male and the female personality in the interests of maintaining a mutual dependency that might be maintained in healthier, more fulfilling ways. Whether Latin American culture represents some unique embodiment of these machismo-marianismo tendencies I very much doubt. Evelyn Stevens sees these culture traits as originating in the Southern European, Middle Eastern, and North African honor and shame cultures and states that "the fully developed syndrome occurs only in Latin America" (1973: 91). I suspect, rather, that the peculiar distorting mirror that keeps northerners from accurately seeing Latin social roles and values gives the machismo-marianismo syndrome a prominence it does not properly deserve.

It is clear that there has been a long history of both political and professional activity on the part of Latin American women. The world feminist movement of the 1880s reached women who had already fought the independence battles their other Two-Thirds World sisters were just beginning to fight. Many writers on economic development have commented on how Latin America seems to be out of rhythm with the world development clock. It started "takeoff" in the 1850s and remains "at takeoff" today. Many things have been invoked to account for this, including the church and the hacienda culture. Domination from the North is rarely included in the standard list of explanations. As this century draws to a close, new patterns are emerging in spite of efforts from the North to keep Latin America as its feudal domain.

Latin American feminism is an intact tradition. Maria Alvarado in Peru and Amanda Labarca in Chile appeared to be carrying on lonely feminist battles in the early part of this century, but the work of mobilization continues. There is a radical network covering the continent, which as yet has few spokeswomen to the outside world. The liberal wing of the women's movement is as important as the radical wing, and its voice is heard through the Latin American women who are active in the world of women's international nongovernmental organizations. The alliance of women of North and South America is a frustrating one, as the League of Women Voters discovered during its program of developing women's centers in certain Latin American countries in recent years. Reports of that project make it clear that the women of the two cultures are speaking different conceptual languages, responding to different aspects of reality. When the Latin American women speak, they are not "heard."

The first Inter-American Congress of Women held in Havana in 1923 used the theme of social motherhood in approaching the problem of women's roles in public life—the extension of women's family role to the community. This is not a special Latino device, stemming from a macho culture, but the lever with which women on every continent have pried themselves loose from privatized roles. As recently as 1965, Margaret Mead and other women, myself included, were speaking to International Cooperation Year audiences of women on the theme of "women as the world's housekeepers," trying to persuade them that the work of opposing militarism and building a peaceful world was but a logical extension of their housewifely roles. This was shortly before the women's liberation movement began. Few U.S. women activists would use that language today.

Time moves faster than before. We have to tune in to all the nuances of the social motherhood theme at the same time that we tune into the Tanias of the guerrilla movements in Latin America and elsewhere. Tania, Argentinian-born Tamara Bunke, was "called" to the revolutionary role in her early teens when her family was living in East Germany. After some years of training to be a guerrilla, training that required keen intelligence, great self-discipline, and much travel in Europe and Latin America, she was in the end trapped and killed in a police ambush with Che Guevara in Bolivia. Her diary and letters (Rojas and Calderón 1971) reveal a great compassion and warmth—traits that do not belong to the guerrilla stereotype. Here is a poem she wrote in April 1966 while waiting for an underground contact somewhere in Latin America:

> *To Leave a Memory*
>
> So I must leave, like flowers that wilt?
> Will my name one day be forgotten
> And nothing of me remain on the earth?
> At least, flowers and song.
> How, then, must my heart behave?
> Is it in vain that we live, that we appear on the earth?
>
> (in Rojas and Calderón 1971: 178)

Some women revolutionaries work and live essentially alone, like Tania, or in small revolutionary circles; others are familistic. There have been many cases of the imprisonment of the wives of guerrilla leaders, from Peru to Chile, and it is usually, although not always, clear that the women were active revolutionary partners. Cuban revolutionaries tend to be familistic. Jaquette (1973: 346-47) points out that the three women most important in the Cuban revolution—Haydee Santamaria, Celia Sanchez, and Vilma Espin—were all "closely linked to important male leaders," Fidel Castro, Raul Castro, and Armando Davalos. There have been revolutionaries who were nuns (Sister Maurina Borgha de Silviera) and revolutionaries who were beauty queens (Rogelia Cruz Martinez). They come from every walk of life. The women revolutionaries of Latin America are perhaps more aware than their middle-class sisters of the realities of everyday life for the masses that keep young girls working in the fields and caring for their younger brothers and sisters, at an age when more fortunate teenage girls are in school. We must freely recognize that women terrorists belong to the women's movement, whatever century or continent they are found in, and that they play a special role in the speeded-up currents of change in the twentieth century.

* * *

This rapid survey of centuries of development of women's history in Africa, Asia, and Latin America, while full of gaps, provides some basis for bringing the reader to women's current moment in history as a prelude to the future. There is no continent on which women do not have an ancient history of working for society from the underside, no continent on which women have not also at times walked freely in the public spaces, and no continent where they have been spared the vicissitudes of alternating recognition and oppression by the male society in which they lived. Wherever a people have accumulated wealth, we have seen the emergence of classes. We have seen that women at the top have had the freedom of that wealth and that women at the bottom have had the burden of poverty—the burden of laboring for bread, whether as artisans, prostitutes, or slaves. In every stratum of these multitiered societies, we have seen children: At the top, little girls of 5 are decked out to marry kings and sit on thrones; at the bottom, fingers of tiny toddlers are put to simple tasks that lighten, however little, their mothers' labor; in the middle, small daughters are "playing house," trying out every nuance of the role their sheltered mothers play.

The feminist movements that have crept across the continents in the past century and a quarter have not been oriented toward the self-assured women at the top, nor toward the laborers at the bottom, nor toward the little girls at every level who strain so hard to learn the lessons of their class. They have tended to be for middle-class women, for the gropers on the underside, equally insulated from both their upper-class and laboring sisters. Now the time has come for the gropers to emerge into the public spaces of the current time, to develop new partnerships with their sisters in poverty as well as with their sisters in privilege, crossing the class, race, and ethnic lines that have so long divided them.

Notes

1. The fact that Jewish as well as Arab merchants engaged in the slave trade is not always mentioned in histories of the period (Shirley Nuss 1974).

2. See Judith Van Allen's " 'Sitting on a Man': Colonialism and the Lost Institutions of Igbo Women" (1972) for a vivid if poignant description of traditional devices for the control of men by women.

3. Freedom must be understood in a relative sense. The recently publicized practices of female circumcision and infibulation in some nomadic and sedentary populations in

Africa hardly seem consonant with "freedom." These practices apparently cause a high mortality rate for women, both in the prepubertal period when the operations are performed and in childbirth, because scar tissue prevents the needed dilation of the cervix during labor. Women, however, are socialized to support these practices and help accomplish them. Dangerous bodily operations performed for a variety of religious and cultural reasons can be found in all societies in all social conditions. Surgical breast building is a contemporary U.S. practice that belongs in this tradition.

4. One of the fascinating things about purdah is how women themselves develop its extreme forms as a status symbol. See Papanek's "Purdah in Pakistan" (1971) for an interesting analysis of this and other aspects of purdah. This pursuit of seclusion by urban Moslem women is very like the pursuit of the domestic role by many middle-class Western women in the nineteenth and twentieth centuries. Purdah is more extreme, of course, creating odd role reversals between mother and child: "The purdah-observing mother may become dependent on her young child when outside the home. The veil hampers her vision and movement so that she may ask the child to lead her" (White 1975: 27).

5. See Cynthia Nelson's "Public and Private Politics: Women in the Middle Eastern World" (1974: 551-63) for a discussion of present-day underlife politics. A number of books are available reporting on women's roles, life ways, and culture in the Middle East. These include Beck and Keddie (1978), Nashat (1983), Abadan-Unat (1981), Abdel-Kader (1987), Fernea (1985), Mernissi (1975; 1991), El Saadawi (1982), and Toubia (1988).

6. These comments on tribal women are based on notes taken during discussions with leading members of women's organizations on a visit to India in 1974 and represent my view, not theirs.

7. At the same time, it is true that the term seclusion can be misleading, in that the zenana may be a crowded, noisy, even raucous place. Elizabeth Cooper describes a scene in the zenana of an Indian lady during a dinner party. In addition to large numbers of women guests, there were about 50 servants and slaves all running around apparently at random. The mistress would direct them from wherever she was in a loud shrill voice. Cooper asked her Indian friend "if Indian ladies generally had such loud voices and commanding tone, and she laughed and said, 'Well, if they have not to begin with they soon acquire them. . . . It takes a strong-minded woman, and one with no mean executive ability, to keep peace and harmony in an Eastern zenana' " (1915: 176). Purdah provides a variety of training for women, some of which is useful in public life.

8. This is a reference to Newton's epigram, "If I have seen farther, it is by standing on the shoulders of giants," delightfully pursued by Robert Merton in a book by that title (1965).

9. A selection of readings from the Chinese press on the women's movement in China from 1949 to 1973 is available in Croll (1974). Other valuable resources on the history and current status of women in China include Kazuko Ono (1989), Wolf and Witke (1975), and Guisso and Johannesen (1981).

10. Note particularly Hahner (1976), Lavrin (1978), Pescatello (1976), Chaney (1979), and Gross and Bingham (1985).

References

Abadan-Unat, Nermin. 1981. *Women in Turkish Society.* Leiden: Brill.
Abdel-Kader, Soha. 1987. *Egyptian Women in a Changing Society, 1899-1987.* Boulder, CO: Lynne Rienner.

Adams, Robert McCormick. 1966. *The Evolution of Urban Society: Early Mesopotamia and Prehispanic Mexico.* Chicago: Aldine.

Afetinan, A. 1962. *Emancipation of the Turkish Woman.* Paris: UNESCO.

Afshar, Haleh, ed. 1985. *Women, Work and Ideology in the Third World.* London: Tavistock.

Ali, Ameer. 1899. "The Influence of Women in Islam." *The Nineteenth Century Magazine* 45(May):755-74.

Altekar, A. S. 1978. *The Position of Women in Hindu Civilization.* 2nd ed. Banaras, India: Motilal Banarsidass.

Amadiume, Ifi. 1987. *Male Daughters, Female Husbands: Gender and Sex in an African Society.* London: Zed.

Ayscough, Florence. 1937. *Chinese Women: Yesterday and Today.* New York: Houghton Mifflin.

Beck, Lois and Nikki Keddie, eds. 1978. *Women in the Muslim World.* Cambridge, MA: Harvard University Press.

Boserup, Ester. 1970. *Woman's Role in Economic Development.* New York: St. Martin's.

Boulding, Elise. 1969. "The Effects of Industrialization on the Participation of Women in Society." Ph.D. dissertation, University of Michigan.

――――. 1977. *Women in the Twentieth Century World.* Beverly Hills, CA: Sage.

――――. 1980. "Women: The Fifth World". Headline series 248, pamphlet. New York: Foreign Policy Association.

Bowser, Frederick P. 1974. *The African Slave in Colonial Peru: 1524-1650.* Stanford, CA: Stanford University Press.

Burton, Margaret E. 1918. *Women Workers of the Orient.* West Medford, MA: Central Committee on the United Study of Foreign Missions.

Burton, Sir Richard. 1966. *A Mission to Gelele: King of Dahome*, edited by C. W. Newbury. New York: Praeger.

Chaney, Elsa M. 1973. "Old and New Feminists in Latin America: The Case of Peru and Chile." *Journal of Marriage and the Family* 35(May):331-43.

――――. 1979. *Supermadre: Women in Politics in Latin America.* Austin: University of Texas Press.

Chow, Yung-Teh. 1966. *Social Mobility in China: Status Careers Among the Gentry in a Chinese Community.* New York: Atherton.

Collins, Robert O. 1971. *Europeans in Africa.* New York: Knopf.

Cooper, Elizabeth. 1915. *The Harem and the Purdah: Studies of Oriental Women.* New York: Century.

Croll, Elizabeth. 1974. *The Women's Movement in China: A Selection of Readings, 1949-1973.* Nottingham, England: Anglo-Chinese Educational Institute.

de la Cruz, Sor Juana Ines. 1951. *Obras Completas de Sor Juana Ines de la Cruz*, edited by Alfonso Mendez Plancarte. Buenos Aires, Argentina: Fondo de Cultura Economica.

Diffie, Bailey W. 1945. *Latin-American Civilization: Colonial Period.* Harrisburg, PA: Stackpole.

Edib, Halide. 1926. *Memoirs of Halide Edib.* New York: Century.

Ekejiuba, Felicia. 1967. "Omu Okwei, the Merchant Queen of Ossomari: A Biographical Sketch." *Journal of the Historical Society of Nigeria* 3(June):633-46.

El Saadawi, Nawal. 1982. *The Hidden Face of Eve: Women in the Arab World*, translated and edited by Sherif Hetata. Boston: Beacon.

Fernea, Elizabeth Warnock. 1985. *Women and Family in the Middle East: New Voices of Change.* Austin: University of Texas Press.

Gordon, David C. 1968. *Women of Algeria: An Essay on Change.* Cambridge, MA: Harvard University Press.

Gross, Susan Hill and Marjorie Wall Bingham, eds. 1985. *Women in Latin America.* Vols. 1 and 2. St. Louis Park, MN: Glenhurst.

Guba, Arun Chandra. 1973. "Gandhian Technique of Revolution" (mimeo).

Guisso, Richard and Stanley Johannesen, eds. 1981. *Women in China: Current Directions in Historical Scholarship.* New York: Philo.

Hahner, June E. 1976. *Women in Latin American History: Their Lives and Views.* Los Angeles: University of California, Latin American Center Publications.

Herbert, Beda. 1965. "The Nun Who Knew Everything." *Capuchin Annual*, pp. 157-62 (Dublin).

Houtart, Francois and Emile Pin. 1965. *The Church and the Latin American Revolution*, translated by Gilbert Barth. New York: Sheed and Ward.

Jain, Devaki and Normala Banerjee, eds. 1985. *Tyranny of the Household: Investigative Essays on Women's Work.* New Delhi: Shakti, Vikas.

Jaquette, Jane E. 1973. "Women in Revolutionary Movements in Latin America." *Journal of Marriage and the Family* 35(May):344-54.

Kamaladevi, Chattopadhyay. 1986. *Inner Recesses Outer Spaces, Memoirs.* New Delhi: Navrang.

Kinzer, Nora Scott. 1974. "Sexist Sociology." *The Center Magazine*, May/June, pp. 48-59.

Lavrin, Asuncion. 1978. *Latin American Women: Historical Perspectives.* Westport, CT: Greenwood.

Lebeuf, Annie. 1963. "The Role of Women in the Political Organization of African Societies." Pp. 93-107 in *Women in Tropical Africa*, edited by Denise Paulme. Berkeley: University of California Press.

Leith-Ross, Sylvia. 1939. *African Women: A Study of the Ibo of Nigeria.* London: Routledge & Kegan Paul.

Levtzion, Nehemia. 1968. *Muslims and Chiefs in West Africa: A Study of Islam in the Middle Volta Basin in the Pre-colonial Period.* Oxford: Clarendon.

Little, Kenneth. 1973. *African Women in Towns.* Cambridge: Cambridge University Press.

Matheson, Alastair. 1970. "A Job for National Importance." *UNICEF News* 65(May):8-10.

Mernissi, Fatima. 1975. *Beyond the Veil: Male-Female Dynamics in a Modern Muslim Society.* Cambridge, MA: Shenkman.

————. 1991. *The Veil and the Male Elite: A Feminist Interpretation of Women's Rights in Islam.* Reading, MA: Addison-Wesley.

Merton, Robert K. 1965. *On the Shoulders of Giants: A Shandean Postscript.* New York: Free Press.

Montoya, David G. 1975. "Perspectives of Women in Mexico." Unpublished student paper, University of Colorado, Boulder, Department of Sociology.

Nanda, B. R., ed. 1976. *Indian Women: From Purdah to Modernity.* New Delhi: Vikas.

Nashat, Guity, ed. 1983. *Women and Revolution in Iran.* Boulder, CO: Westview.

Nelson, Cynthia. 1974. "Public and Private Politics: Women in the Middle Eastern World." *American Ethnologist* 1:551-63.

Nuss, Shirley A. 1974. "Roots of the Middle East Crisis: The Jewish Question and Zionism." University of Colorado, Boulder, Department of Sociology (mimeo).

O'Barr, Jean. 1982. *Perspectives on Power: Women in Africa, Asia and Latin America.* Durham, NC: Duke University, Center for International Studies.

Obbo, Christine. 1980. *African Women: Their Struggle for Economic Independence.* London: Zed.

Oliver, Roland. 1968. "The African Achievement." Pp. 96-103 in *Dawn of African History*, edited by Roland Oliver. 2nd ed. London: Oxford University Press.

Ono, Kazuko. 1989. *Chinese Women in a Century of Revolution 1850-1950.* Stanford, CA: Stanford University Press.

Oppong, Christine. 1974. *Marriage Among a Matrilineal Elite: A Family Study of Ghanaian Senior Civil Servants.* Cambridge Studies in Social Anthropology, no. 8. Cambridge: Cambridge University Press.

————. 1983. *Female and Male in West Africa.* London: George Allen and Unwin.

Papanek, Hannah. 1971. "Purdah in Pakistan: Seclusion and Modern Occupations for Women." *Journal of Marriage and the Family* 33:517-30.

Penzer, N. M. 1935. *The Harem: An Account of the Institution.* Philadelphia: J. B. Lippincott.

Pescatello, Ann, ed. 1973. *Female and Male in Latin America: Essays.* Pittsburgh, PA: University of Pittsburgh Press.

————. 1976. *Power and Pawn: The Female in Iberian Families, Societies and Cultures.* Westport, CT: Greenwood.

Robertson, Claire C. and Martin A. Klein. 1983. *Women and Slavery in Africa.* Madison: University of Wisconsin Press.

Rojas, Marta and Merta Rodriguez Calderón, eds. 1971. *Tania: The Unforgettable Guerrilla.* New York: Random House.

Snow, Helen Foster. 1967. *Women in Modern China.* The Hague, the Netherlands: Mouton.

Stevens, Evelyn P. 1973. "Marianismo: The Other Face of Machismo in Latin America." Pp. 89-102 in *Female and Male in Latin America: Essays,* edited by Ann Pescatello. Pittsburgh: University of Pittsburgh Press.

Strong, Anne Louise. 1965. *China's Millions.* Peking: New World.

Sweetman, David. 1971. *Queen Nzinga: The Woman Who Saved Her People.* London: Longman.

————. 1984. *Women Leaders in Africa History.* London: Heinemann.

Tharpar, Romila. 1963. "The History of Female Emancipation in Southern Asia." Pp. 473-99 in *Women in the New Asia,* edited by Barbara Ward. Paris: UNESCO.

"Third World Women." 1973. *UNICEF News,* pp. 76-17.

Thomas, P. 1964. *Indian Women Through the Ages.* Bombay: Asia.

Toubia, Nahid. 1988. *Women of the Arab World, the Coming Challenge.* Papers of the Arab Women's Solidarity Association Conference. London and New Jersey: Zed Books.

Tuden, Arthur and Leonard Plotnicov, eds. 1970. *Social Stratification in Africa.* New York: Free Press.

Van Allen, Judith. 1972. " 'Sitting on a Man': Colonialism and the Lost Institutions of Igbo Women." *Canadian Journal of African Studies* 6:165-82.

Vreede-De Stuers, Cora. 1968. *Parda: A Study of Muslim Women's Life in Northern India.* Atlantic Highlands, NJ: Humanities Press.

Wales, Nym. 1952. *Red Dust: Autobiographies of Chinese Communists.* Stanford, CA: Stanford University Press.

Ward, Barbara E., ed. 1963. *Women in the New Asia: The Changing Social Roles of Men and Women in South and South-East Asia.* Paris: UNESCO.

White, Elizabeth Herrick. 1975. "Women's Status in an Islamic Society: The Problems of Purdah." Ph.D. Dissertation, University of Denver.

White, Gilbert, David J. Bradley, and Anne U. White. 1972. *Drawers of Water: Domestic Water Use in East Africa.* Chicago: University of Chicago Press.

Wittfogel, Karl August. 1957. *Oriental Despotism: A Comparative Study of Total Power.* New Haven, CT: Yale University Press.

Wolf, Margery and Roxane Witke, eds. 1975. *Women in Chinese Society.* Stanford, CA: Stanford University Press.

Woodsmall, Ruth Frances. 1960. *Women and the New East.* Washington, DC: Middle East Institute.

5

The Journey From the Underside: Women's Movements Enter Public Spaces

I n this chapter, we will not follow the earlier pattern of tracing, for each historical period, the activities of specific categories of women and noting the accomplishments of particular outstanding women. This is not necessary for our own era, because readers of this book will have many other sources of information about women contemporaries. Instead, after a brief update about Euro-North American women in the first half of the twentieth century, we will look at how the new global sisterhood (Morgan 1984) has moved into public spaces through networking. We will particularly examine the agendas that activist women have set for themselves as they emerge from the underside.

Moving Into the Twentieth Century in Euro-North America

We have traced the paths of the Two-Thirds World out of ancient pasts into the current time and now need to bring Euro-North America into the picture as well. In 1920, European and North American women were emerging from World War I with the vote. Some had it well before the war, others got it later, but the decade of the flaming 1920s has a special significance in the history of the underside quite apart from the suffrage issue because of the flamboyant visibility of a few women during the era of the short-skirted, leggy flapper. On the serious side, a greater proportion of women were receiving Ph.D.s at U.S. universities at that time than at any time since.[1] Women scholars were publishing with all the major presses of Europe and the United States. The women from the warring countries who had met at the Hague in 1915 were preparing documents for use in drafting the Covenant of the new League of Nations (Bussey and Tims 1965). Women entered the arena of international politics with zest. By comparison, in the labor movement, this was a time of relative decline, as women felt the backlash against their efforts at self-assertion in the early part of the century beginning with the Triangle Shirtwaist factory strike in 1911 (Maupin 1974).

The contrast between the women of the first quarter-century and women of this last quarter-century of the 1900s comes out in an interesting way in a study comparing samples of women listed in the 1915 and 1973 *Women's Who's Who in America* (Krelle et al. 1975). Allowing for differences due to the fact that the 1915 volume was the first women's *Who's Who* published and that, by 1973, there was a well-developed system for identifying and including women, comparison is nevertheless illuminating. Both populations represent the most educated sector of their respective societies. Between 1915 and 1973, there is a shift in the character of their activities; the category "writer" (authors, poets, journalists, editors) shrinks from 33% to 12%, and the category "educators" from 26% to 20%. There is more specialization in 1973, and there are more women in the paid labor force. The number of career-type activities carried out by individual women ranged from 0 to 46 in 1915 and only 0 to 25 in 1973. The picture is the same for noncareer activities. In 1915, 17% of the women were reported as having six to ten separate civic and volunteer responsibilities and, in 1973, there were 10% of women with that number of community roles. A subjective impression, not verifiable except through further analysis, is that the typical professional woman of 1915 was engaged in more outside activities than the typical professional woman of 1973. More of them stayed without male partners—38% in 1915 as compared with 30% in 1973.

Certainly, there was a tremendous sense of the opening up of new horizons in the first quarter of this century. By the 1920s, idealists everywhere looked to the new social experiments in Russia. Radical innovations in education, in child care, and in the nature of the marriage contract, permitting easy dissolution and recombination of households, were taking place there. This was also the age of the back-to-nature movements in Europe, which took thousands of young people away from the cities and into the mountains.

The Depression cut bleakly into all these movements. Women were pushed out of the labor force, and membership fell off drastically in many women's organizations, never to regain the level of the 1920s. Nazism in Germany wrought further havoc among women. Claudia Koonz (1987) has done a remarkable study of the ways in which German women adapted (and did not adapt) to Nazi repression. The grim story of what happened to the strong early twentieth-century gay and lesbian movement under Nazism is told in *Courage* (1980).

The Hitler youth movement lured young people down from the mountains into Nazism. The mountains, unfortunately, had not been a good training ground for political life. Some of the women who served as administrators of concentration camps during World War II had been part of the 1920s back-to-nature movement.[2] One of the many tragedies of World War II was the number of young people who died as soldiers or victims who had been pupils in the International School in Geneva, a school founded by idealistic parents in the International Labour Office in 1925 to educate their children as world citizens.[3]

There was a death struggle in Europe between the forces of liberalism and the forces of totalitarianism. The European women's movement was at the heart of this struggle. Many movement women were killed, decimating a group that could ill afford to lose members. The story of that struggle has yet to be fully written. It exists in fragments in the records of participating organizations, in private correspondence, and in the heads of an older generation of women activists.[4] Germaine Tillion is one of the few women underground agents to both survive and record a concentration camp experience as a social scientist and a human being. In *Ravensbruch* (Tillion 1975), she describes the human bonds and networks women constructed to protect each other from torture and death.

Another group of women who fought the forces of totalitarianism and war were found within the personalist movement of the Catholic church. Revolutionaries committed to social and personal transformation, they gave strong leadership to social action projects among the urban poor in Europe. Three great Catholic women radicals, all born before 1900, spent the last quarter-century bringing the European spiritual revolution of the 1930s to North America—Russian-born Baroness Catherine de Hueck Doherty, Russian-born Helen Iswolsky, and U.S.-

born Dorothy Day. All three were institution builders for an alternative society—radical activists, writers, saints, and mystics who were equally at home in palaces, slums, and jails. Close friends with separate callings, they supported one another in a powerful and little-recorded change movement countering the regressive militarism of the middle decades of this century.

In a sense, World War II never ended, for the cold war flared quickly after the cessation of hostilities in Europe. The involvements in Korea and Indochina added fuel to cold war flames. It is no wonder that young women born after 1940 cannot easily imagine how promising the world looked to women beginning their careers in the 1920s. The women of the 1920s were world shapers. The women of the 1940s, while they entered the labor force in large numbers as war workers, were already beginning the psychological retreat into the home so graphically described by Betty Friedan (1963). The 1950s were quiet, timid years for many women. But, in some of the countries that had suffered most from the war, in the Soviet Union, Poland, and Japan, the women picked themselves up from their exhaustion and terror and engaged in reconstruction and outreach in those timid 1950s. The luxury of retreat was not for them. I wish I could devote another chapter to the stories of how women went about that reconstruction. How, for example, Russian mothers buried their thousands of babies who died of malnutrition—how they then went back to work and to school, to play their part in every arena of a society so recently feudal. A major international initiative by women after the end of the war came from the women of the Soviet Union, in the founding of the Women's International Democratic Federation (WIDF). It was intended to bridge the gap between socialist and nonsocialist countries. The cold war greatly limited the organization's effectiveness, particularly since women of both the West and the East by and large "supported" the cold war.

I wish I could write about Polish women too—about how the prewar Society of the Friends of Children rose from the ashes of the destruction of Warsaw and began to clear safe underground and aboveground spaces for the surviving children they found in the ruins, and how women whose bodies were severely crippled from medical experimentation in concentration camps used their minds and hands to turn out Europe's most beautiful children's books. The tremendous surge of effort to make a good environment for children developed a momentum that carried women into many other activities and linked with an old Polish tradition of intellectual women taking public responsibility. The Liga Kobiet, the Polish Women's League, operated at a similar level of political sophistication to that of the European women's groups of the early 1920s. Among other things, it actively supported the new postwar peace research movement in its earliest stages. In the early 1960s, the charm, dignity, and intellectual incisiveness of these women left a deep impression on visitors from outside (Boulding 1963).

One "old" Western organization that consistently and carefully responded to the reaching out of the socialist women was the Women's International League for Peace and Freedom (WILPF), reduced in membership though it was. Contact with its members in Eastern European countries had been lost during the war. Although there were continuing efforts at joint WILPF-WIDF activities on disarmament,[5] newer independent peace movements gradually took over some of the roles of Eastern Europe's WIDF. Because the current pace of change in Eastern Europe is so rapid, it is hard to predict what will happen to earlier East-West women's networks in the future. What is certain is that women will find a way to continue networking across whatever barriers the new nationalisms erect and diminish their effect.

After the timid 1950s, the 1960s was the decade when social activism broke out again in the United States and in Europe. Because a new age must have new movements, the 1960s saw the birth of a new international women's peace organization, Women Strike for Peace, in response to the threat to life from the fallout from nuclear testing. Many new national women's peace organizations were also born at this time in Euro-North America.

None of the 1960s movements was really new, however. The commune movement had several antecedents in the 1920s, 1930s, and 1940s. Among the most recent antecedents in the United States were the communities founded by World War II conscientious objectors and their wives. During the war itself, some of these wives lived in rural communes near their husbands' camps, sharing child care while they struggled to support themselves.[6] It was very natural to move from that experience to subsistence agricultural communities after the war. None of these women and men wanted to return to the old society. They wanted to make a new one. Although many of them were gradually reabsorbed into suburbia, the process was never total. They brought up their children to "the sound of a different drummer." Many of these children in turn lived in communes such as the "Life Centers," a loosely organized network known as the Movement for a New Society.[7]

Perhaps the timid 1950s were not so timid after all. The women turned full-time homemakers were breeding a set of revolutionaries who powered the antiwar movement, the civil rights movement, the black liberation movement, and, finally, in the late 1960s, the women's liberation movement. (The Chicano and Native American liberation movements have their own dynamic, not traceable to the middle-class homemakers of the 1950s.) There have been a number of studies of the family life and parent-child relations experienced by middle-class student protesters in the 1960s.[8] Sometimes these are a bit patronizing about the parents who "talked liberal and lived conservative." Given the social forces bearing down on them, one could argue that women were acting in the only way open to them, outwardly conforming but planting the seeds for change in their children. The ones who remained activist and nonconforming have been as much criticized in the literature as their quieter sisters (for being cold, distant mothers who were so busy with social reform that they neglected their children). Both types of critique were wide of the mark.

New Agendas

Women's movements have continued to unfold in highly diverse ways on the five continents and in the 180 countries that comprise the global scene of recent decades. It is well to remember that these movements have a double ancestry: the Eurocentric nineteenth-century women's movements associated with urbanization and industrialization as well as the traditional women's organizations that have long animated the women's culture of tribal societies and among indigenous peoples. What is new in the current movements is that women from the Eurocentric world and the world of the South have started to come to know each other. The process has been painful, instructive, and ultimately rewarding.

Also new is the change from what began as women's reform movements in the nineteenth century to what are now increasingly becoming social change movements in this century. This has been brought about as the analysis of patriarchy as a social institution has brought deeper understandings of the structural nature of the problems that distort the lives of both women and men.

Contemporary women's movements have been classified in many ways. Three different types of emphases, often overlapping, may be noted here: (a) equal opportunity for women with men, politically and economically, within the existing social order (assumption: once equality has been achieved, society will be qualitatively different because of the infusion of women's ways of working); (b) removal of oppressive capitalist structures (assumption: once socialism has been achieved, all forms of social oppression will disappear as men are humanized); and

(c) the creation of a woman-centered culture to replace patriarchy (assumption: this is an end in itself or is an evolutionary step toward a new culture free of all gender dominance).

All three types of movements imply the end of patriarchy—the arbitrary rule of men over women, children, and weaker men—and look to a qualitatively different future social order. But the third is the most rigorous in its analysis of the structures of patriarchy and most emphatic about the need for social transformation.

It must also be said that a women's countermovement has developed, particularly in more affluent societies such as Japan, parts of Western Europe, and the United States, that seeks the re-creation of a mythic golden age when women were "queens of the hearth." While not of major significance, it supports the maintenance of patriarchy and acts as a brake on social changes sought by feminists.

The women's movement, then, is best thought of in the plural, as series of movements. The very term *movement* has many meanings and can be thought of as including (a) a background change of consciousness that makes new perceptions and new behaviors possible, (b) the development of formally structured women's organizations in response to that background change of consciousness, (c) the development of loosely coordinated women's networks oriented to the solution of specific problems, and (d) popular stirrings reflected in public demonstrations and actions of various kinds. Because it is the formally structured women's organizations and the more loosely coordinated networks that are the most specifically related to actual social change, the focus here will be primarily on those two categories, with a secondary emphasis on the background changes of consciousness that have led women to claim new public spaces.

The Rise of Women's International Networking

We saw in Chapter 4 of this volume how women's international networking began. Leadership came from elite European women who could travel. They went to the world's fairs that were so important as gathering places for international interest groups, from the great London exposition of 1851 onward. By 1915, there were 15 international women's organizations; by 1930, there were 31. All had specific agendas of general social betterment as well as gaining political, economic, and legal rights for women. Some were well represented on all continents; others were primarily Eurocentric. On every continent, there remained a great gap between these Western-style internationally minded women's groups, primarily urban in focus, and local women's organizations formed at the grass-roots level. To a degree, this continues today. The educated urban women who came to know one another from all continents did not pay attention to their own local women's associations, particularly those in rural areas. If noticed at all, locals were seen as backward, not modern—a costly reproduction of patriarchal attitudes. The resulting maldevelopment for the world as a whole is only now being recognized.

The modern era for the women's movement started during World War I. This is when a new set of professional women's organizations focused more directly on women's issues, per se, began appearing. Just as the world's fairs helped lay the groundwork for the women-to-women contacts that made the first round of transnational organizations possible, so the League of Nations, through its liaison committees designed to facilitate the new phenomenon of international nongovernmental organizations, helped this new round of women's associations get started. The League, through the International Labor Organization (ILO), the first international agency established prior to World War II to mention women in its constitution, was also directly involved in promoting women's welfare through improving working conditions and related arrangements. The inspiring story of how the ILO has worked for and with women is told in Lubin and Winslow (1990).

Several women's INGOs worked very closely with the League of Nations on disarmament issues, "traffic in women," and women's rights to property and person, education, and employment. As noted earlier, the Depression, the rise of fascism, and World War II brought these developments to a halt. Membership in existing women's organizations fell off drastically, no new organizations were formed, and women apparently disappeared back into the domestic sphere. Community and neighborhood-based women's groups were, however, if anything, strengthened during the Depression years as traditional practices of women helping women across households were reinforced by urgent economic need. Women who had been active internationally only put their activities on temporary hold. After World War II, with the founding of the United Nations and its Commission on the Status of Women, international networks for women resumed development with renewed energy, although with a much-depleted roster of old-timers.

The Post-World War II Era

The most important happening of the early postwar years was the transformation of the international system from the 50 nations signatory to the U.N. Charter to the current 180-nation U.N. system. Women played a key role in the independence movements of all the new nations, both in nonviolent struggles as in India and in wars of liberation as in Algeria. They also played key roles in the rebuilding of war-devastated lands, as already mentioned. The recognition of partnership between women and men, obtained during liberation struggles and postwar recovery processes, was short-lived, however. On every continent, even in the face of massive manpower shortages, women were "sent home to the kitchen" or, at the least, kept out of public decision-making bodies. In Japan, where the U.S. occupation authorities set a high priority on giving public roles to women, the first postwar Diet had 39 women but, by 1970, there were only 8. There were 10 women in the first Algerian parliament after independence; none by 1976. In the postwar France of 1946, there were 40 women in the Assembly, 23 in the Senate. By 1970, there were only 8 women in the Assembly and 5 in the Senate.

Women at the Grass Roots

What is important to bear in mind is that, when women were denied public roles, they did *not* simply return to the kitchen, Betty Friedan (1963) notwithstanding. They continued to be active at the neighborhood level and in their own national networks dealing with a multitude of social problems. Japan is a good example of this process. Women were the primary organizers of the consumer movement, even taking to the streets en masse with their frying pans as a symbol of their determination to establish food safety standards. While women have had their own associations, this was also a men and women's movement. In the joint organizations, women did much of the work, providing both energy and ideas, while letting the men take the formal leadership positions. Over the decades, Japanese women's activities have spread beyond consumer protection to establishing partnership with farmers in the cooperative movement to get better and cheaper food to the cities and to developing a strong environmental protection movement. Most consumer activist women do not see themselves as feminists, but increasingly they have found a public voice as women in the name of family well-being.

Consumer protection, environmental protection, and the formation of producer cooperatives have been grass-roots activities of rural and urban women in many Two-Thirds World countries in the postwar decades. Women's leadership in movements against destruction of forests and savannah have been particularly noted in the world press. One example is the Chipko movement in India, a save-the-trees movement in which women use the strategy of hugging trees to keep men from cutting them down (Shiva 1988). Another is the Greening the Desert Women's Movement in Kenya. Women in Sri Lanka have provided leadership for the sarvodaya shramadana community development movement (Macy 1983), working within traditional Buddhist belief systems but initiating a new level of community self-help. All these activities come out of the concerns of local women for what is happening to their own immediate world.

The movements just mentioned were initially neither feminist nor transformational in orientation. As women continued to gain experience in women's networks beyond the neighborhood level, however, a conscientization process took place that resulted for some in the development of a new kind of feminist awareness. Again, Japan provides an illuminating example. The women's associations founded between 1945 and 1955, except for the socialist women, were moderate to liberal organizations such as the League of Women Voters, the Association of University Women, and Women Lawyers. These associations focused on improving society and the status of women in it. Spread across Japan, they ranged in size from 1,000 to 6 million (Tanaka 1974).

From 1964 to 1980, however, women's groups were forming that had a radically different orientation to society and the role of women. Groups like Agora, the Asian Women's Association, Women's Action Against War, and the International Women's Year Action Group not only tackled issues like sexism, wife abuse, rape, equal rights legislation, union rights, equal employment (and advancement) opportunities for women but also racism, exploitation by Japan of other Asian nations, sex tourism, and militaristic tendencies in the national budget and in textbook revision programs. These organizations are much smaller and more urban, usually with fewer than 1,000 members. Their members march, organize protest demonstrations, hold teach-ins in front of railway stations, run marathons, and do sophisticated research on the social evils they protest as well as carrying on quieter educational work. Unlike most of their sisters, these feminists operate with a very different picture inside their heads of what they would like Japan to be. They particularly stand opposed to the consumerist "my-homeism" of the average middle-class Japanese woman (and consequently frighten their more middle-of-the-road sisters). This makes coalition building across ideological differences an interesting challenge in Japan. Problems of radical versus moderate women's movement strategies are not unique to Japan but are replicated in many countries, most visibly in Western Europe and the Americas.

Bearing in mind that these struggles for social change, and the associated ideological disagreements, are happening locally and nationally in every country, let us now turn to women's international nongovernmental organizations (INGOs). If we were to assess the extent to which women's movements are contributing to transformational change, we have to consider both the local and the transnational aspects, remembering that, for every women's INGO, there are many thousands of women's associations that have remained local or national. They are the backbone of the international women's movement. *Sisterhood Is Global* by Robin Morgan (1984) provides a vivid picture of this backbone.

The Rise of Women's INGOs

Some grass-roots activities translate into national organizations and spread to other countries and continents, so that international headquarters eventually come into being. It is by establishing international headquarters that an organization definitively stakes a claim on public space. It becomes an INGO, so-called because it represents the interests of people in their private capacities and is not answerable to governments. INGOs can be formed around any type of interest: religious, cultural, political, professional, civic, economic, and social (see Boulding 1990: chaps. 3 and 7).

Because organizations take on the forms that the social technologies of the time permit, INGOs have tended to develop on a pattern of hierarchically organized national bureaucracies integrated into an international headquarters. This pattern has worked so well in this century that INGOs have gone from 200 in 1900 to 18,000 in 1986. The women's INGOs that developed in this period followed the same pattern, although their bureaucracies were more flexible, and the international bodies less hierarchically organized, than most men's or mixed organizations. Women's INGOs, like their male counterparts, often represent substantial expertise in their area of interest and so have been able to provide informational inputs that may change the policies of governments. They also have a historical memory, which governments

TABLE 5.1 Women's INGOs in 1973 and 1986

	1973	1986
Public affairs, international understanding	17	61
Professions and occupations	18	58
Research, training, and development	—	35
Religious	9	28
Sports	3	7

SOURCE: Data are from the 1972-73 and 1985-86 editions of the *Yearbook of International Organizations* (Union of International Associations).

rarely do, and so may provide continuity of concern in areas where governments are erratic in their policies. Whether we are talking about the pre-1915 women's INGOs or the post-World War II women's INGOs, there are certain concerns that they have all shared. These can be summarized in three categories:

(a) improving the conditions of women: redistribution of resources toward Two-Thirds World and poor women as well as improvement of education and training, living and working conditions, quality of life, and legal status;

(b) preparation for the participation of women in society: training in leadership, political action, and policy skills as well as general education for activity in the public sphere; and

(c) activation of women's perspectives to create political, social, and economic change as well as the creation of international infrastructures for collaboration across national borders on peace, justice, and human welfare issues.

While the radical critique of patriarchy is soft-pedaled in many INGOs, nevertheless, the empowerment emphasis is universal as is commitment to some degree of social and economic change.

The big spurt of growth of women's INGOs came after 1970. Table 5.1 compares the number and distribution of such organizations in 1973 and in 1986, going from 47 to 189—roughly a fourfold increase.

The most important change from 1973 to 1986 is the shift from Eurocentrism to a broader representation of continental perspectives. The 1986 listing includes 10 all-African women's organizations, 12 Asian, 4 Arab, 1 Buddhist, and 2 that identify themselves as part of the Third World Non-Aligned Movement. Also by 1986, the long-standing traditions of highly effective women's councils in the countries of the South have been translated into INGO formats. During this same period, women's religious orders (now for the first time counted as INGOs but not included under women's organizations because they are answerable to a male hierarchy) have become increasingly innovative and daring in translating religious teachings into work for social justice and peace in the South.

Because some of the newer INGOs call themselves "networks," the distinction between *INGO* and *network* is getting harder to make. Every INGO operates on the basis of networks, but with a defined formal structure, and many activities are administered from a central headquarters. This is changing, however, as the older associations realize the value of the more informal, loosely structured patterns of newer organizations. *Decentralization* is the new watchword. Legislative work, training, and the development of effective information channels are key activities. Good listening, little status consciousness, and awareness of longer time horizons enable new-style women's groups to lay the groundwork for future solutions when impasses arise. Having lived at the margins of the public sphere for so long, they are less emotionally invested in existing ways of doing things and can visualize alternative approaches to the problems more easily.

Because the barriers to women's entry into the public sphere have been so omnipresent and enduring, it has been hard for women to find space in which to organize, platforms from which to speak. Just as the world's fairs in the nineteenth century and the League of Nations in the 1920s provided the earliest of such spaces and platforms, so the United Nations has provided them since 1947. It is not so much what the United Nations per se has done for women—its own record on the employment of women in other than clerical positions continues to be poor (Vajrathon 1985)—but that it has been willing to provide space for women to gather and create their own agendas, their own networks, their own strategies. The U.N. space has been a visible overside space, a legitimizer for those who meet in it, and a support for women to speak to their own governments. Also, the U.N. agency infrastructure has helped—as well as hindered (Waring 1988)—in the slow, painful process of documentation of the situation of women around the world. In what follows, I hope to show both the positive and the negative impact the United Nations has had on the worldwide situation of women.

The United Nations and Public Space for Women

The fact that the U.N. Charter contained an affirmation of "fundamental human rights . . . the dignity and worth of the human person, and . . . the equal rights of men and women"—the first time governments had ever acknowledged equal rights for women—was a direct consequence of the work of the older women's INGOs with the League of Nations in the interwar years. So was the fact that, in 1947, the Economic and Social Council of the United Nations established a subsidiary Commission on the Status of Women; in 1948, the U.N. Declaration of Human Rights included gender as a category in spelling out human rights; in 1949, the United Nations adopted a Convention on Traffic in Women and Prostitution.

But there it all stopped. The attention of men was drawn to other matters, particularly the problem of launching the development decades. True, the United Nations went on turning out conventions on the rights of women—21 in all.[9] But, even in the case of the two most basic conventions in terms of the status of women, the Convention on Elimination of all Forms of Discrimination Against Women and the International Convention on Civil and Political Rights, not more than 45 out of 167 countries have ratified both conventions. For those that did, it has been largely lip service.

A continuing obstacle to improvement in the situation of women that U.N. conventions per se have not corrected has been the male-oriented accounting systems used by national governments, U.N. agencies, and the World Bank, which automatically exclude the bulk of women's activities from the record and therefore from policymaking (Waring 1988).

If the attention of men to women's situation came to a halt, the activity of women did not. In the "silent 1950s," the mobilization of women took place very slowly—it took time to develop the necessary awareness. But, in the 1960s, momentum was rapidly gained. The explosion took place in the 1970s and 1980s.

The first U.N. Development Decade was proclaimed with no mention of women as actors at all. And it was not over economic issues that women first were mobilized after the war but over military ones. While Japanese housewives were demonstrating in the streets of Japan against the U.S.-Japan Mutual Security pact, a call went out from a group of women in Washington, DC, to housewives all over the United States to "strike for peace" over concern for what the strontium 90 from atmospheric testing of nuclear weapons was doing to the teeth and bones of their babies. (No housework for a day!) The Women Strike for Peace movement spread rapidly to Canada and Europe, providing an early example of the new-style network. The strike deliberately eschewed a central headquarters and hierarchical organization. In fact, it got a lot of help in every country from more internationally experienced WILPF members, but it also recruited a new generation of young mothers who had no previous experience with public issues.

One of the young mothers[10] set in motion a process that resulted in the declaration by the United Nations of 1965 as International Cooperation Year. During that year, many women's groups organized traveling teams of women to talk with sisters in other countries about their concerns and to design continuing cooperative projects. International Cooperation Year might be considered a bridge between old and new ways of working. The informal networking style was new, but the language used by the spokespersons (including Margaret Mead and Eleanor Roosevelt) was the earlier language of civic housekeeping.

The important thing was that women had become visible to one another in a new way internationally. Traveling teams soon discovered the deteriorating situation of Two-Thirds World women as development-decade policies directed resources away from women and toward men. In the same period, Ester Boserup of Denmark was investigating what happened to Two-Thirds World women farmers when men were given technical aid to grow cash crops. By 1970, her book had appeared documenting the reality that women were the food producers and that aid given to men not only failed to reach the actual food growers but lengthened their hours of work, as men made new demands on them. This book was carried by women to every continent (Boserup 1970).

When the second Development Decade was declared in 1970, the Commission on the Status of Women saw to it that a phrase about the importance of integrating women into development was included in the development program. The new women's movement seized on this phrase and used it everywhere. By 1972, Helvi Sipila was appointed the first woman assistant secretary general, for humanitarian and social affairs. What followed was an intense two years of work by the Commission on the Status of Women working closely with Sipila, with women's INGOs, and the newer women's networks. What was being created was a women's agenda for the United Nations. The result was the declaration in 1972 by the U.N. General Assembly that 1975 would be International Women's Year.

The 1972 decision was in itself a major turning point for women. Preparations began for the great year. In 1973, the Commission on the Status of Women, wrestling with the meaning of the *status* of women as it wrote drafts for Women's World Plan of Action, defined *status* in terms of the degree of control women had over their conditions of life. "Control over the conditions of life" became a key theme for the women's movement. What became increasingly clear was that nowhere did women have control over the conditions of their lives. They did not even have control over the definition of the problem. Certainly, no one had data about the current situation of women. Women's research committees of the various international social science organizations began forming and became involved in helping assess data needs. The first data handbook on women (Boulding et al. 1976) was a direct result of discussions in the Research Committee on Sex Roles in Society at International Sociological Association meetings in the early 1970s.

The link between development and women's roles had been accepted as a theoretical proposition by governments at the beginning of the second Development Decade, but spelling that out in practice was everywhere resisted. The draft Plan of Action, prepared for the 1974 U.N. World Population Year Conference, contained no mention of women at all! The Committee on the Status of Women and concerned women's INGOs, learning of this, quickly put together a meeting of international women experts on population, and material was presented to the Population Conference in Bucharest with the result that women's roles were taken note of in the resulting World Plan of Action. The same thing happened at the 1974 Rome World Food Conference and at the 1979 Conference on Science and Technology. Initial documents contained no mention of women, but INGO networks were activated, miniconferences of experts held, and the final conference documents incorporated statements about the role of women.

Women developed a new networking strategy at the World Population Conference that they have continued ever since at U.N. conferences, and that has also been adopted by INGOs generally, which is to hold a nongovernmental forum in parallel with any given U.N. intergovernmental conference, in the same city. These forums bring together women with special interest and expertise in the matters before the conference, who are able to spell out the relationship between women's activities and the conference subject for the enlightenment of those who cannot perceive these relationships unaided. As in the case of that initial phrase adopted by the United Nations in 1970, "the integration of women in development," each new formulation accepted by a U.N. meeting was used to build up a more coherent set of policy guidelines for the next issue to come before member states.

The strategy did not always succeed, because women could not always mobilize their networks in time. Even after the 1975 International Women's Year, which produced a World Plan of Action that spelled out a whole range of interconnections between all aspects of social and economic development and women, the 1976 World Habitat Conference made no mention of women. A series of conferences between 1976 and 1978 on economic and technical cooperation among developing countries, desertification, water issues, and primary health care made no mention at all of women in the final documents—even when special advance studies had been made available to them on the gender dimensions of the problem under discussion. Ancient male habits of ignoring women die hard.

Still, the 1975 World Plan of Action became an official U.N. document (United Nations 1976). It spelled out the relationship between the situation of women in each of the world's societies and the global problems of war and poverty. It clarified the issue of equality between men and women in terms of equal rights, opportunities, and responsibilities for each to develop their talents and capabilities both for personal fulfillment and for the benefit of society. It also referred to the conditions of international peace as depending on an end to colonialism and oppression of any category of persons and as requiring the participation of women in all peace processes. Thus the themes of equality, development, and peace were laid down as specific arenas in which progress must be made for women if progress is to be made for society as a whole.

Not only were guidelines for national governments laid down by the World Plan of Action, but two specific new U.N. organs relating to women were recommended and established: The Women's Voluntary Fund (now UNIFEM) and INSTRAW, the International Research and Training Institute for the Advancement of Women. UNIFEM attached itself to the U.N. Development Program and carries out its own small projects as well as pressing UNDP to include women in its major programs. INSTRAW carries out its own research and training program at its headquarters in the Dominican Republic and also tries to influence ongoing U.N. research and training activities. Both serve a lobbying function within the U.N. system for attention to the role of women in development.

Guidelines for national action by governments for the women's decade were a major outcome of the 1975 conference. These guidelines involved very specific recommendations, including (a) involving women in the strengthening of international security and peace through participation at all relevant levels in national, intergovernmental, and U.N. bodies; (b) furthering the political participation of women in national societies at every level; (c) strengthening educational and training programs for women; (d) integrating women workers into the labor force of every country at every level, according to accepted international standards; (e) providing more equitable distribution of health care and nutrition services to take account of the responsibilities of women everywhere for the maintenance of health and provision of food for their families; (f) reordering priorities with regard to social support systems for the family unit; and (g) directly involving women, the primary producers of population, in the development of population programs and other programs affecting the quality of life of individuals of all ages—in family groups and outside them, including housing and social services of every kind.

Every government was strongly urged to establish a specific governmental body to see to the implementation of these recommendations. In fact, 71 governments actually established government ministries or other governmental bodies specifically for women, 33 gave official recognition to an existing national women's organization empowered to work on implementation of the recommendations, and only 24 countries made no response.

The World Plan of Action anticipated a paradigm shift that continues to be glacially slow in coming, but the process has begun. At every step of the way, on every item of the plan, intensive educational, legislative, and research activities have continued to be necessary to coax, cajole, and pressure policymakers to apply what has been agreed to in the plan. The Mexico City meeting in 1975 set goals and timetables. The Copenhagen middecade conference in 1980 (United Nations 1980) reviewed progress to date and set specific targets for the next five years. The 1985 Nairobi Conference (United Nations 1986) set forth "Forward-Looking Strategies" to the year 2000, with plans for a progress-monitoring conference in 1992 and an overall review conference in 2000.

The New Networking Partnership: Expanding the Public Space

While everyone recognizes that progress has been minimal in the women's decade, there has been some movement forward. Perhaps the most important thing that has happened in the decade is the gradual development of an understanding and a degree of partnership between women of the South and North that did not exist in 1975. Corollary to that has been the remarkable growth of women's networks dealing with specific problems relating to equality and development. For an example of the growth in the participation of women's networks during the decade, consider the fact that there were 6,000 women present in Mexico City in 1975 representing nongovernmental groups. In Copenhagen in 1980, there were 7,000, and, at the Nairobi end-of-decade conference in 1985, there were 14,000 women present. Table 5.2 lists 31 women's networks established since 1974, the year in which the explosion of new

text continued on page 325

TABLE 5.2 Some International Women's Networks Founded Between 1974 and 1987

Network	Year Founded	Category	Founding Event	Coordinating Site (1987)
IFN (International Feminist Network)	1974	=, HR	International Tribunal on Crimes Against Women, Brussels, Belgium	Rome, Italy
ISIS International	1974	=, D	International Tribunal on Crimes Against Women, Brussels, Belgium	Santiago, Chile; Rome, Italy; The Philippines
IWTC (International Women's Tribune Centre)	1975	=, D	International Women's Year Nongovernmental Tribune, Mexico City, Mexico	New York, NY, USA
AAWORD (Association of African Women for Research & Development)	1976	R, D	Meeting of Swedish Research Agency with Developing Countries, Lusaka, Zambia	In country where the president resides
GASAT (Girls and Science and Technology)	1979	D	Informal meeting to assist access of girls and women to careers in scientific & technological fields	Ann Arbor, Michigan, USA
WWB (Women's World Banking)	1979	D	Dutch foundation formed to promote women entrepreneurs around the world	New York, NY, USA
Women and Peace Study Group of the International Peace Research Association	1979	P	Special meeting of IPRA women members on sexism in the conduct of peace research	Santiago, Chile
IIC (International Inter-disciplinary Congress on Women)	1980	R	First IIC on Women held in Israel	Dublin, Ireland
ILIS (International Lesbian Information Service)	1981	I, HR	Offshoot of International Gay Association to strengthen lesbian identity	Helsinki, Finland
AWID (Association for Women in Development)	1982	D	Created by a group of scholars, practitioners, and policymakers	Manhattan, Kansas, USA
CAW (Committee for Asian Women)	1982	=, D	Decision to support Asian women workers began in 1977 in Malaysia at the Christian Conference of Asia-Urban Rural Mission	Kowloon, Hong Kong (as of 1985)

Organization	Year	Code	Description	Location
WLD (Women, Law Development Program)	1983	=, D	OEF International decided to support a number of Women's groups working toward women's rights	Washington, DC, USA
Sisterhood Global Institute	1983	=, D	Project of compiling reports and data for *Sisterhood Is Global*	New York, NY, USA
International Feminist Book Fair	1984	D, M	London, 1984	New Delhi, India (as of 1988)
WICS (International Women's Information & Communication Service)	1984	D, M	Grew out of ISIS	Rome, Italy, & Santiago, Chile
Latin American & Caribbean Women and Health Network	1984	D, H	Organized by the Corporacion Regional para el desarrollo Integral de la Mujer y la Familia (Bogota, Colombia)	Santiago, Chile
Women Living Under Muslim Laws	1984	=, HR	Muslim women in Europe met to discuss misinterpretation of Islam by men in Islamic states to suppress women's human rights	Combaillaux, France
DAWN (Development Alternatives with Women for a New Era)	1985	R, D	NGO Forum at U.N. World Women's Conference in Nairobi	Botafago, Brazil (region changes every two years)
GROOTS (Grass Roots Organizations Operating Together for Sisterhood)	1985	D	Network began in Nairobi among low-income rural and urban women workers	Mylapore, Madras, India
IWDA (International Women's Development Agency)	1985	D	Grew from the Australian Women and Development Network	Victoria, Australia
World Women Parliamentarians for Peace	1985	P	Meeting to support initiatives of superpowers toward disarmament	New Delhi, India
Women for a Meaningful Summit, International Liaison Office	1985	P	Began as ad hoc coalition of women & organizations active in arms control	Athens, Greece
CAFRA (Caribbean Association for Feminist Research and Action)	1986	R, D	Seminar, sponsored by University of Sussex, on women and social production in the Caribbean	St. Augustine, Trinidad, and Tobago
Two Thirds World Movement Against the Exploitation of Women	1986	=, HR	Women's campaign launched against Military Prostitution, Camp International	Manila, Philippines
Arab Women's Solidarity Association	1986	=, HR	Created by women professionals in the Middle East	Cairo, Egypt

continued

TABLE 5.2 Continued

Network	Year Founded	Category	Founding Event	Coordinating Site (1987)
Asia Pacific Women's Action Network	1986	=, HR	Bangkok training by the Asian Cultural Forum on Development	Bangkok, Thailand
WINGS (Women's International News Gathering Service)	1986	D, M	Sponsored by Western Public Radio, a nonprofit audio production and training facility	San Francisco, California, USA
Women, Environment and Sustainable Development Network	1986	D, Env	Nairobi NGO Forum established network of women's environmental groups	Amsterdam, The Netherlands
Womenwealth	1986	=, D	After Nairobi in response to calls for North-South cooperation among women	London, England
Feminist Futures International Network	1987	D	Symposium at Siuntio Baths, Finland on "Women and the Military System"	Network by mail, no coordinating center
Global Fund for Women	1987	D	Foundation established in response to the Nairobi Conference call for groups to take specific steps to improve the status of women	California

NOTE: Category Code Key: D—development; =, D—equality and development; =, HR—equality and human rights; R, D—research, development; D, M—development, media; D, H—development, health; D, ENV—development, environment; P—peace.

324

networks began, up until 1987. Information is included about the founding event and location of each network. Some are now regular INGOs, others remain less formal networks but with clearly defined structures and programs. Some of the core public space activity of the women's movement is represented in this type of network.

The list in Table 5.2 is intended to be illustrative, not inclusive. The networks listed are among those most frequently mentioned in activist publications.[11] Coded by type of activity (see Table 5.2 for an explanation of the codes), we find the following distribution of types of networks:

development (D)	7
development, equality (D, =)	6
development, research (D, R)	4
development, media (D, M)	3
development, health (D, H)	1
development, environment (D, ENV)	1
equality, human rights (=, HR)	5
peace (P)	3
human rights, identity (HR, I)	1

What is striking about the organizational emphases indicated in the above list is the overwhelming emphasis on development, either alone or in combination with equality. Equality and human rights are the other major themes. (Only three of these newer networks focus on peace.) What do these themes mean? Are "fix-it" approaches implied or a radical restructuring of society? We will look at each theme and its associated networks in turn, beginning with the peace networks because they are the inheritors of the oldest traditions in women's movement activity.

From War to Peace

The first of this new generation of women's networks addressed not war but violence: the International Tribunal on Crimes Against Women, held in Brussels in 1974. Here we get the first major international statement about patriarchal power as violence against women per se, apart from specific abusive acts. After considering a horrifying array of types of violence experienced by women from all classes on all continents at the hands of men in their families, communities, and places of work, participants joined to establish the international Feminist Network, which continues to deal with that violence. ISIS, the first INGO to devote itself to establishing communication channels and networking skills among women nationally, regionally, and internationally, to mobilize against their own oppression, was also established at that tribunal.

The three new networks specifically targeting peace issues in Table 5.2 are a research group and two political groups. The Women and Peace Study Group represents the women's peace research community whose members have given substantial leadership to the peace research field in the Asia and Pacific region, Europe, and the Americas. A network of women scholars in 30 or more countries who research the conditions of peace, the focus is both on education and gender socialization and on alternative nonpatriarchal models of the world system (Boulding 1981; Brock-Utne 1985, 1989; Reardon 1985). The second, Women for a Meaningful Summit, is a more typical movement organization. It was formed in 1985 to empower women to express themselves on nuclear policies and try to affect disarmament negotiations. The third, World Women Parliamentarians for Peace, follows the same empowerment theme for women legislators as an international body and as members of their respective national parliaments. Both these latter groups have played a valuable dual role in relating women to disarmament issues: (a) by making women's thinking about disarmament part of bilateral and multilateral negotiation processes and (b) by creating a roster of feminist professionals in the field of arms and security who are available to function in decision-making spaces on the "overside," and do. (An example in the United States is Abzug and Kelber's *Women's Foreign Policy Directory*, 1987.)

In general, peace issues received less attention during the formal women's decade conferences than other major "women's" issues. There is an important reason for this, which clarifies a critical difference between earlier and newer women's organizations. The difference has to do with new perceptions about the relationships among patriarchy, violence against women, poverty, and war. In earlier times, women saw a systemic connection between war and poverty and realized that women's lack of rights was an important factor in their inability to improve their lot. But patriarchy, with its legitimation of violence as a means of asserting power, was not perceived as a core institution that distorted and rendered pathological all other institutions. That was perhaps because the earlier women's movement began in a social class that saw men as their allies, having so long accepted the doctrine of "included interest."

While the postwar women's movements at first appeared to pick up from the earlier peace movement traditions, particularly with Women's Strike for Peace, economic development questions quickly moved to center stage as women looked at each other's conditions of life. Women became aware of themselves as victims. The poverty of women in the Two-Thirds World of the South, and in Two-Thirds World enclaves in the North, was not simply due to the failure to modernize quickly enough. It was due to the fact that women and their needs were always considered last. How could women be concerned with men's wars when there had been a war against women going on daily for centuries? The women who went to Brussels in 1974 and heard the testimony of the victims of men's violence from every continent, and those who read the testimony afterward, were never the same again. They began to see the violence in their own lives. Consciousness-raising had begun, and much of it happened outside formal women's peace organizations.

From Inequality to Equality

Next to ending violence and war, the issue of equality with men has been the oldest issue in the women's movement. Earlier, the focus was chiefly on getting the vote, establishing a civic and legal identity, and the right to control property and make contracts. By the 1970s, it was abundantly clear that getting the vote and some associated legal and property rights did little for women's economic situation, little to counter sexual discrimination, and very little toward moving women into policymaking positions in society. Twelve of the new networks in Table 5.2 are concerned with equality.

The equal rights movement has moved ahead on two different fronts. The first has dealt in painstaking detail with legal rights in the areas of family, employment, rights to education and training as well as equal access to other opportunities society offers to men (Schuler 1986). The tremendous increase in the proportion of women graduates from law schools in recent years, as well as in the number of women social scientists who have specialized in equal opportunity issues for women, has enabled the women's networks focusing on this area to draw on a very high level of competence and expertise. For every one of the 21 U.N. conventions on the rights of women mentioned earlier, there has been a growing group of trained women in every country who have spearheaded efforts to make the laws of that country conform to the newly established rights. Because customary law often contravenes new rights, the task is an uphill one.

The other track women have taken has been the political track. To change laws, or make new ones, it is necessary to become involved in the legislative process as elected officials. This has been another uphill task for women. Yet change is occurring, and it is occurring from the bottom up. Data from a study conducted for the Women's Decade (Boulding 1983) indicates that women's political participation is increasing most noticeably at the local level through representation on local government councils—currently that representation is roughly 11% worldwide. Next comes the national level, with approximately 7% of women in national parliaments, and finally there are the appointed officials at the international diplomatic level, where women are a little more than 4% worldwide. We can imagine the global political participation of women as a pyramid, with women most involved at the base in local government and least visible at the top, in international posts.[12]

Some societies have found it easier to include women in the decision-making processes than others, particularly the Nordic countries (Haavio-Manila et al. 1985). When women first enter legislative bodies, they usually confine themselves to women's issues, which have to do with reproduction and human services, but, as their numbers increase and as their experience widens, they become active on a range of social issues, including foreign policy. In 1983, Iceland became the first country in the world to seat candidates from a feminist party, the Women's Alliance, in parliament. In 1987, they doubled their representation, not only winning the right to enter the new government but holding the balance of power in negotiations between center-right and left-wing parties. (For comparison, see Flammang 1984, on women in the U.S. government.)

Given that politics are affairs of nation-states, it is hard for international women's networks to facilitate entry of individual women into national politics. When women do become members of parliament, however, they tend also to be active in international women's organizations and provide both leadership and living role models for younger women.

Two contradictory trends are at work when women enter politics. They are known to vote conservatively and to vote like their husbands (Duverger 1955). But they are also known to hold stronger opinions than men on the necessity for reducing military expenditures and increasing welfare expenditures. "Female men" who become heads of state do not seem to share these nonmilitary preferences, however. Socialized in the male political culture, they can be considered accidents of history rather than products of women's movements. The net effect of women's involvement in law and politics has been to open up new opportunities for women and decrease inequalities at a very slow rate.

From Poverty to Development

Now we turn to the subject that most animates the newer parts of the women's movement worldwide today and focuses the activity of 22 of the 31 networks in Table 5.2. Development seemed like an abstract subject to many women in the 1950s but, in the 1980s and 1990s, it has become the very hinge of change. The facade was gradually stripped from earlier development plans based on "takeoff" or "trickle-down" theories of investing in the development of a country's industrial base and in mechanizing agriculture. Increasing rural and urban poverty for former subsistence farmers and craft workers became the reality to be faced.

The difficulties for the woman subsistence farmer have already been indicated. Traditionally the food provider for her family, she lost her earlier land rights as men were encouraged to grow cash crops with mechanized equipment on expanded acreages. Her troubles multiplied from that point. Women have found themselves working longer and longer hours. Recurring droughts, partly due to mistaken development practices, have stretched women beyond their capacity to manage.

For urban women, the story has been long hours in factories at pittance wages and often under health-destroying conditions. Everywhere the shadow of multinational corporations looms, offering wage labor when subsistence opportunities are gone, leaving formerly autonomous households dependent on a consumer economy, even to the point of leading women to abandon breast-feeding for purchased infant formula (see American Friends Service Committee 1985; Fuentes and Ehrenreich 1985).

Women saw the miserable results of the planning for the first Development Decade. That explains the formation of network after network to deal with specific problems of women in relation to economic processes. Who were the "they" who formed these networks? The process began with the initiatives of European and U.S. women to establish ISIS and the Women's Tribune Centre in 1974 and 1975. But, as the often sharp discussions at the Mexico City Women's Conference between First and Two-Thirds World women made clear, the perspectives on women's problems from the two worlds were very different. As Marie-Angelique Savane pointed out (Savane 1982), inequality between the sexes was the first concern of Euro-North Americans while inequality between the countries of North and South was at least as important as gender inequality for women in the South. Two-Thirds World women were irritated at the preoccupation of Europeans with conjugal relations when life-and-death issues of bride and widow burning, infanticide, and genital mutilation were in question. They saw as patronizing the Europeans' desire to be helpful to the South. They wanted to wage their own struggles in the ways and means that they considered to be fruitful and timely. "We do not need any more champions."

While the distrust and uneasiness that was evidenced in Mexico City has not disappeared, it has been substantially mitigated by the formation of networks by Two-Thirds World Women themselves. The first to be formed was AAWORD, the Association of African Women for Research and Development. Other networks followed in Asia and Latin America. In 1982, the Declaration for the Dakar Conference on Another Development with Women included the following statement: "Feminism is international in defining as its aim the liberation of women from all types of oppression and in providing solidarity among women of all countries; it is national in stating its priorities and strategies in accordance with particular cultural and socio-economic conditions" (Special issue of *Development Dialogue*, 1982: 1-2, p. 15). What has been unifying across cultural differences has been the sense that women everywhere are "foreigners in one's own land" (Awekotuku and Waring 1984).

Respect for one another's cultures has been the key to the increasing levels of cooperation between networks and to the success of the initially Eurocentric ISIS and Women's Tribunal. Both ISIS and the Tribunal provide a wide range of services to women at all levels of skill and literacy and have greatly increased the networking capacity and skills of all women's groups on all continents. New initiatives continue to come from the South, and it is from the women of the South that the language of "development alternatives" and "another development" has come. One of the most recent development networks to be formed is DAWN, Development Alternatives with Women for a New Era. Initially based in Brazil, it will be confined to Two-Thirds World Women and will focus on awareness that other futures are possible and on researching development alternatives, translating them into feasible policy, and involving women more fully into policy and decision processes.

One of the major accomplishments of the development-focused women's networks is to have established among women, by the time of the Nairobi Conference, a genuine sense of sisterhood and involvement with one another across cultural and political differences—although serious differences remain, as eloquently stated in Albrecht and Brewer (1990). There is a feeling that the women's movement is in some sense "global," as Morgan (1984) proclaims.

From Environmental Destruction to
Protection of Earth

Ecology was not one of the themes of the International Women's Decade and is a relatively new issue in the women's movement. It is represented by only one network in Table 5.2. Yet ecofeminism is transformational in ways that encompass both the peace and the development themes of the women's movements. Environmental movements have been under male leadership in this century, but it was a woman, Ellen Swallow, who coined the term *ecology* in 1892 (Davies 1987). It was also a woman, Rachel Carson (*Silent Spring*, [1962] 1987), who gave the signal for the birth of the modern ecology movement. Women's identification with nature has been resisted by parts of the women's movement as a traditionalist stereotype, but awareness of Gaia, or Mother Earth, has for many women opened the way to critiquing industrialization, militarism, and the rule of men.

To the question of whether humans are to rule the earth or be coinhabitants with the rest of nature, feminists answer that ruling the earth is a patriarchal concept. Ecofeminism can be seen as a manifestation of postpatriarchal consciousness. Politically, that consciousness is embodied in the Green movement, which now has political parties in about 10 countries and elected representatives to the national parliaments of several countries, including most notably Germany. It is no accident that women have provided some of the most visible leadership for the Greens. The policies that the Greens espouse involve decentralization, an emphasis on community participation in shaping the conditions of life locally, and a shift to small-scale enterprises and the use of appropriate and resource-conserving technologies in agriculture and industry.

Ecofeminism has a strong spiritual component permeating its political activity, its community development, and its conservation work. Ecofeminism fosters awareness of the feminine aspects of Creation and emphasizes how much a part of nature human beings are. It does not propose to replace a patriarchy with a matriarchy but seeks a blending of the male and female in all aspects of life (Spretnak 1982, 1986; Gray 1979). Ecofeminism, together with lesbian feminism, to be discussed next, are perhaps the most transformational in spirit of all the women's movements that have been discussed.

Beyond the Rule of Men

Lesbian feminism is the least visible internationally of women's movements and has only one entry in Table 5.2. It's theme, human identity, is a poignant one. It encompasses the search for how to be truly human and how to create a world of authentic human beings living at peace with each other and their planet. In that sense, it can be seen as embodying features from all four of the previous themes: peace, equality, development, and ecology. With some type of loose network or structure in over 60 countries (56 in the United States alone) and feminist publications with a lesbian emphasis in at least 10 countries (Alyson Almanac 1990; *Connexions*, Winter, 1982; Morgan 1984), lesbian activism is one of the newest and most rapidly expanding phenomena in feminism.

The movement is often thought of as primarily involving the human right of sexual preference—women loving women. In fact, it is much more. It is the ultimate antipatriarchal movement, demonstrating that women can live independently of men, obtaining love and self-esteem from other women and developing models of social relations not based on power and domination (Myron and Bunch 1975; Ettore 1980). Lesbianism is nonviolent to the core. It embodies an ideal of the equality and dignity of all women (and men), with a strong vision of a postpatriarchal Gaia-conscious world in which men and women will dwell in gentleness, together and separately. Given that homosexuality is punishable by law in most countries of the world, and that homosexuals everywhere live with a constant underlying threat of physical attack by homophobes, the courage and personal nonviolence of lesbian feminists is nothing less than remarkable.

Lesbians have provided significant leadership to the ecofeminism movement (see the essays in Caldecott and Leland 1983). The separatism of the lesbian movement has to do with the perceived necessity of disentangling women from the pathologies of patriarchy and violence so they can learn to be whole and peaceful again. It has to do with reclaiming a women's culture and reclaiming women's powers, stunted by centuries of domination. Lesbian feminism is about love, not hostile rejection. Its visions of the future are strong (Cheatham and Powell 1986).

The Dynamics of Change

Given the societal change/transformation women seek, is there a contradiction between women claiming public, overside spaces for participation with men in societal decision making and developing a stronger women's culture in women-only spaces? There have been times, particularly at midcentury, when serious proposals have been made by leaders in women's organizations to put away the women-only pattern and become "mixed" male-female organizations. Yet most female experience with coparticipation in mixed settings is negative. When it comes to agenda setting, policy planning, and decision making, it has been repeatedly noted not only that women are hesitant in speaking up, but, when they do try, they are rarely acknowledged by male chairpersons. When they do succeed in putting forth creative suggestions, these are not noticed until repeated by a man. The necessary "critical mass" of women that could eliminate this effect is rarely achieved. The distinctive contributions of women's culture cannot be made under such circumstances unless there are coexisting all-women's groups in which that culture can be nurtured, buttressed by strong separatist strategies of social innovation. The significance of these separatist strategies is that they provide working models of how things could be in the future.

The trip to the overside for women has to be a shuttling back and forth between women's and mixed spaces until women are socially strong enough and organizational structures have become open enough to sustain the feminist input into public life in its economic, political, and cultural dimensions. Men's groups that share feminist values and seek the same kind of future society often look to women as role models and support a degree of separatism for women.

The orientation of women's groups has changed very substantially over the past century. The old partnership with men was on male terms, in male space. The new partnership in a shared public space can only be fully developed in a postpatriarchal order. The loss of continuity between the pre- and postwar women's movements has in a way been a blessing, because the accumulation of problems of violence, poverty, and oppression in what was supposed to be a new era under the U.N. Charter has forced women to think more deeply about the nature of the changes required. Institutional transformation has come to be accepted by many of the most articulate and active participants in the women's movements, particularly as reflected in the newly formed networks listed in Table 5.2.

How will transformation work? A highly simplified way of summarizing the dynamics of the oppression of the patriarchal order and the dynamics of transformation from the perspective of women's movements is to place women at the center of the complex of institutions of the old order, as in Figures 5.1 and 5.2. Figure 5.1 shows the patriarchal order encircling the world in which women live and indicates that each institution—church, school, the polity, the marketplace, the workplace, agriculture, and the household—pressures women into a kind of passive conformity with patriarchal expectations.

This is a view of the situation of women that is widely held in the movement: that the institutions of society are stacked against women. There are strong expectations of subservient behavior on their part. These are reinforced by the way girls are brought up in the household of their childhood, by the teachings of church and school, by continuing inequality under the law and a lack of representation in government, by media portrayal of women as consumer queens, and by lack of

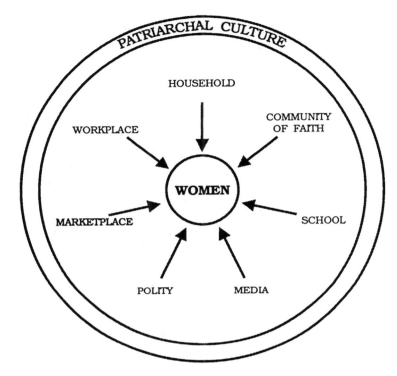

Figure 5.1. The Agents of Oppression for Women

economic opportunities and appropriate tools in the labor force. In Figure 5.1, the woman is shown as the victim of all these pressures.

But this, of course, is not the whole story. Figure 5.2 shows the social order as ringed by a women's culture,[13] a culture handed down from generation to generation even within the patriarchal order. Figure 5.2 reflects the fact that women, out of their own culture, can initiate action to change their life situation and the nature of society itself. Women's individual initiatives are shown by the dashed lines leading to each institution from the woman at the center. Individual initiative alone, however, can be weak and ineffective. The support system for women found in women's organizations and networks acts as a great multiplier of individual effort. Thus the strong mutually reinforcing arrow between the individual woman in the center and the women's networks indicates how that support system empowers individual women, carrying women's transformational energy to each part of society. Note that the United Nations, standing outside all institutions yet acting on

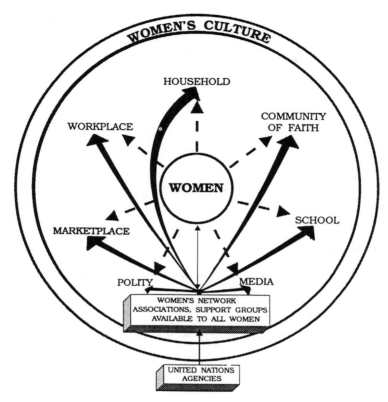

Figure 5.2. The Agents of Social Transformation to the Postpatriarchal Order

behalf of all, feeds resources to the women's networks, which in turn strengthens their transformational effect.

There is something important that the diagrams do not show: that the transformational initiatives of women, strengthened by a variety of separatist strategies, will over time bring them from the underside to become partners with men in new shared spaces, to work together at the shaping of that more humane and peaceful world order for which the human spirit continually longs.

Notes

1. "By 1920 women . . . were receiving roughly 15 percent of the Ph.D.'s. . . . Today women . . . receive about 10 percent of the doctorates" (Graham 1970).

2. This is based on a personal communication regarding an unpublished study of the backgrounds of Germans associated with the extermination camps (Ernst Winter, personal communication, 1973).

3. Madame Marie-Thérèse Maurette, for many years director of this school, spoke with great emotion about these catastrophes at the 1962 Brussels World Forum of Women (Boulding 1962).

4. Women of that period include Gertrude Baer and Gertrud Woker of Germany, Marguerite Thibert and Eugenie Cotton of France, Johanne Reutz Gjermoe of Norway, Alexandra Kollontai of the Soviet Union, Dolores Ibarruri of Spain, Mme Dombska of Poland, Anna Kethly of Hungary, Anna Schustlerova of Czechoslovakia, Aletta Jacobs of the Netherlands, Ellen Wilkinson and Chrystal MacMillan of England, and many many others. During their lifetimes, they carried on the recurring task of reconstruction after war that women have always performed. They were all writers and activists of note.

5. WILPF and WIDF jointly sponsored a seminar on disarmament at the United Nations as part of the program for International Women's Year, the only occasion during the year when problems of peace and war were officially given priority by women.

6. I visited some of these "women's communes" during the war while visiting the camps for conscientious objectors administered by the Quakers, Brethren, and Mennonites. The ruggedness of the living conditions was matched only by the resourcefulness of the women.

7. The movement dissolved by 1980, but a publishing house, New Society Publishers, remains.

8. See the two issues of the *Journal of Social Issues* devoted to this topic (October 1964 and July 1967); the Block, Haan, and Smith study of activism and apathy in adolescents (1968); the Rosenhan study of the civil rights movement activists (1971); and Robert Lifton's analysis of the role of Japanese mothers in the activism of radical Japanese students in the 1950s (1969).

9. The 21 conventions include (a) economic, social, and cultural rights; (b) civil and political rights; (c) optional protocol; (d) elimination of discrimination; (e) political rights; (f) consent to marriage; (g) nationality of married women; (h) recovery abroad of maintenance; (i) racial discrimination; (j) crime of apartheid; (k) refugees; (l) protocol; (m) statelessness; (n) stateless persons; (o) slavery; (p) supplementary slavery; (q) traffic of persons; (r) obscene publications; (s) traffic in obscene publications; (t) discrimination in education; and (u) protocol. A full description of each convention is found in the *Rights of Women* (1983) published by the International Women's Tribune Centre.

10. International Cooperation Year was born in the kitchen of a Kansas mother of two young children, Kathy Menninger, who was thinking one day as she did her chores how millions of mothers around the world were also doing similar chores for their families. Suddenly the idea came to her that the United Nations might declare a year in which ordinary women and men everywhere would be helped to establish links with their counterparts in other countries. It would be a year of thousands of small cooperative international projects, enabling the average person to see everyday acts as part of the building of world community. She immediately telephoned her friend Roger Fisher, professor of international law at Harvard University, to tell him of her idea. He happened at the time to be consulting with the Indian delegation about initiatives they would present to the General Assembly. When he transmitted Kathy Menninger's idea to them, they liked it so well that they sponsored a resolution for a U.N. Year for International Cooperation, which was accepted by the General Assembly. Kathy soon became part of a much larger women's network supporting the idea, and the Canadian-based Voice of Women, the Women Strike for Peace, the Women's International League for Peace and Freedom, and the Women's International Democratic Federation all actively participated in preparing international teams and workshops to mount projects for the year. (This account is based on my own experience and observations.)

11. See the quarterly *ISIS, Women's Journal and Supplement,* and also the quarterly *Tribune,* published by the International Women's Tribune Centre.

12. The European Parliament, with a high percentage of women, is an outstanding exception. See also recent data on increased numbers of women office holders in the 76 countries reporting to the International Centre for Parliamentary Documentation (1985).

13. For a full discussion of women's culture, see Bernard (1987).

References

Abzug, Bella and Mim Kelber. 1987. *Women's Foreign Policy Directory: A Guide to Women Foreign Policy Specialists and Listings of Women and Organizations Working in International Affairs.* New York: Women's Foreign Policy.

Albrecht, Lisa and Rose Brewer. 1990. *Bridges of Power: Women's Multicultural Alliances.* Philadelphia: New Society.

Alyson Almanac. 1990. *A Treasury of Information for the Gay and Lesbian Community.* Boston: Alyson Publications.

American Friends Service Committee. 1985. *Women and Global Corporations* 6(1-2). Philadelphia: AFSC.

Awekotuku, N. and M. Waring. 1984. "Foreigners in Our Own Land." In *Sisterhood Is Global,* edited by Robin Morgan. New York: Anchor/Doubleday.

Bernard, J. 1987. *The Female World from a Global Perspective.* Bloomington: Indiana University Press.

Block, Jeanne H., Norma Haan, and M. Brewster Smith. 1968. "Activism and Apathy in Contemporary Adolescents." Pp. 198-231 in *Understanding Adolescence: Current Developments in Adolescent Psychology,* edited by James F. Adams. Boston: Allyn & Bacon.

Boserup, Esther. 1970. *Women's Role in Economic Development.* New York: St. Martin's.

Boulding, Elise. 1962. "Report to Women's Groups and Educators in the United States on the Brussels Conference on 'The Education of Children and Youth in the Spirit of Friendship and Understanding among Peoples.' " November (mimeo).

———. 1963. "Moscow-Warsaw Journal" (mimeo).

———. 1981. "Perspectives of Women Researchers on Disarmament, National Security and World Order." In *Approaching Disarmament Education,* edited by M. Haavelsrud. Guilford, England: Westbury House.

———. 1983. "Women's Participation in Decisionmaking on Peace, Security and International Cooperation." Unpublished paper for the December 1983 Expert Group Meeting on the Participation of Women in Promoting International Peace and Cooperation of the U.N. Branch for the Advancement of Women.

———. 1990. *Building a Global Civic Culture: Education for an Interdependent World.* Syracuse, NY: Syracuse University Press.

Boulding, Elise, S. Nuss, D. Carson, and M. Greenstein. 1976. *Handbook of International Data on Women.* New York: Sage, Halsted/John Wiley.

Brock-Utne, Birgit. 1985. *Educating for Peace: A Feminist Perspective.* New York: Pergamon.

———. 1989. *Feminist Perspectives on Peace and Peace Education.* New York: Pergamon.

Bussey, Gertrude and Margaret Tims. 1965. *Women's International League for Peace and Freedom, 1915-1965: A Record of Fifty Years Work.* London: Allen & Unwin.

Caldecott, L. and S. Leland, eds. 1983. *Reclaiming the Earth.* London: The Women's Press.

Carson, R. [1962] 1987. *Silent Spring.* Boston: Houghton Mifflin.

Cheatham, A. and M. C. Powell. 1986. *Women's Values and the Future.* Philadelphia: New Society.

Connexions (An International Women's Quarterly). 1982. (Issue reprint no. 3, winter).

Courage (West German Monthly). 1980. July.

Davies, K. 1987. "Historical Associations: Women and the Natural World." Toronto: Women and Environments.

Duverger, M. 1955. *The Political Role of Women.* Paris: UNESCO.

Ettore, E. M. 1980. *Lesbians, Women and Society.* London: Routledge & Kegan Paul.

Flammang, J. 1984. *Political Women, Current Roles in State and Local Government* (Yearbooks in Women's Policy Studies). Beverly Hills, CA: Sage.

Friedan, Betty. 1963. *The Feminine Mystique.* New York: Norton.

Fuentes, A. and B. Ehrenreich. 1985. *Women in the Global Factory.* New York: Institute for New Communications.

Graham, Patricia Alberg. 1970. "Women in Academe." *Science* 169(September 25):1284-90.

Gray, E. D. 1979. *Green Paradise Lost.* Wellesley, MA: Roundtable.

Haavio-Manila, E. et al., eds. 1985. *Unfinished Democracy, Women in Nordic Politics.* New York: Pergamon.

International Centre for Parliamentary Documentation. 1985. *Distribution of Seats by Sex in Parliamentary Assemblies.* Geneva: Inter-Parliamentary Union.

International Women's Tribune Centre. 1983. *Rights of Women: A Workbook of International Conventions Relating to Women's Issues and Concerns.* New York: Author.

Koonz, Claudia. 1987. *Mothers in the Fatherland.* New York: St. Martin's.

Krelle, Janet, Jody Zemel, Judy Reynolds, Karen Garcia, Wendy Speziale, Holley Phelps, and Melinda Lopez. 1975. *Women's Who's Who in America: A Comparative Analysis Between 1915 and 1973.* Unpublished student paper, University of Colorado, Boulder, Department of Sociology.

Lifton, Robert. 1969. *History and Human Survival.* New York: Random House.

Lubin, Carol Riegelman and Anne Winslow. 1990. *Social Justice for Women: The International Labor Organization and Women.* Durham, NC: Duke University Press.

Macy, Joanna. 1983. *Dharma and Development.* West Hartford, CT: Kumarian.

Maupin, Joyce. 1974. *Working Women and Their Organizations: 150 Years of Struggle.* Berkeley, CA: Union WAGE Educational Committee.

Morgan, Robin. 1984. *Sisterhood Is Global.* New York: Anchor/Doubleday.

Myron, N. and C. Bunch, eds. 1975. *Lesbianism and the Women's Movement.* Baltimore: Diana.

Reardon, Betty. 1985. *Sexism and the War System.* New York: Columbia University, Teachers College Press.

Rosenhan, David. 1971. "The Natural Socialization of Altruistic Autonomy." Pp. 251-68 in *Altruism and Helping Behavior*, edited by J. Macauly and L. Berkowitz. New York: Academic Press.

Savane, Maria Angelique. 1982. "Another Development with Women." Special issue of *Development Dialogue*, pp. 1-2 (Uppsala, Sweden).

Schuler, Margaret. 1986. *Empowerment and the Law, Strategies of Third World Women.* Washington, DC: OEF International.

Shiva, Vandana. 1988. *Staying Alive: Women, Ecology and Development in India.* London: Zed.

Spretnak, C., ed. 1982. *The Politics of Women's Spirituality.* Garden City, NY: Anchor.

———. 1986. *The Spiritual Dimension of Green Politics.* Santa Fe, NM: Bear.

Tanaka, Kazuko. 1974. *A Short History of the Women's Movement in Modern Japan.* Tokyo: Femintern.

Tillion, Germaine. 1975. *Ravensbruch: An Eyewitness Account of a Women's Concentration Camp*, translated by Gerald Satterwhite. Garden City, NY: Doubleday/Anchor.

Union of International Associations. 1973. *Yearbook of International Organizations, 1972-73.* Brussels, Belgium: Union of International Associations.

———. 1986. *Yearbook of International Organizations 1985-86.* London: K. G. Saur.

United Nations. 1976. *World Plan of Action, Report of the World Conference of the International Women's Year* (Mexico City, 19 June-2 July, 1975. E/Conf. 66/34). New York: Author.

————. 1980. *Report of the World Conference of the United Nations Decade for Women: Equality, Development and Peace* (Copenhagen, 14-30 July, 1980. A/Conf. 94/35). New York: Author.

————. 1986. *World Conference to Review and Appraise the Achievements of the United Nations Decade for Women: Equality, Development and Peace* (Nairobi, Kenya, 15-26 July, 1985. A. Conf. 116/28). New York: Author.

Vajrathon, Mallica, ed. 1985. *Equal Time* (40th Anniversary Issue). Ad Hoc U.N. Group on Equal Rights for Women. New York: United Nations.

Waring, Marilyn. 1988. *If Women Counted: A New Feminist Economics*. San Francisco: Harper & Row.

Epilogue: Creating Futures

There are few women authors in my futures library. (Margaret Mead is one of the great futurists of this century but is not ordinarily described as such.) The creative imagining work of women does not easily fit into the mold of the professional futurist.[1] We are more likely to encounter it as science fiction[2] than in the "serious" work of spelling out futures. This is nonsense, of course, because every woman with responsibility for a household is a practicing futurist. Families have traditionally depended on the capacity of mothers to hold in their minds the differently rhythmed developments of each person in a household, as they age at their various rates through childhood, adolescence, middle years, and old age. Every family is a constellation of ever-changing individuals and is itself moving through successive stages of a family cycle, each stage with its own social, economic, and political requirements. Families would be in constant chaos if women did not have a grasp of futures and were not able to live mentally ahead of those around them. In fact, all human beings have that capacity. Women develop it to a special degree because they have been given a larger share of the responsibility for family well-being.

Practical futurism is a way of describing not only women's family activities but the entire range of women's activism of the past two centuries. Women have worked into the time spaces of tomorrow to rearrange it in terms of perceived needs of social groups not well served

340

today. From time to time, women have appeared whose minds leaped far into the future, who saw different social constellations entirely. Annie Jiagge, Justice of the Supreme Court of Ghana, is such a person. Soong Chingling of China was such a person. So were Madame Pandit of India, Halide Edib of Turkey, Beatrice Webb of England, Rosa Luxemburg of Poland, Eugenie Cotton of France, Dolores Jimenez y Muro of Mexico, Alva Myrdal of Sweden, and Eleanor Roosevelt of the United States. Of course, there have been women futurists, but they have not been called by that label. And, because they have appeared so far removed from the lives of ordinary women, the gulf between their visioning and the private daydreaming of women who would like to see the world a better place has appeared immense. Yet futurism is only private daydreaming turned public. It is social daydreaming, and social daydreaming is in fact far more widely practiced by women than we generally realize. All we have to do is look at the creative fantasies that have come from the pens of women writers. Carol Kessler (1984) has studied the utopian writings of U.S. women from 1836 to 1919, well before the contemporary women's movement. It should not surprise us that the themes of these utopias—communitarian values, nature awareness, and the spiritual quest—are the themes we find in today's networks, although today's economic and political emphases are not yet present. If we were to study women's utopia writing through history, we would probably find thought experiments involving those themes as far back as we could go. Kessler calls this the "wild zone" of female culture, whose practices may be crucial to the survival of humankind (Kessler 1984: 19).

If the phenomenon of the underlife is a chance detour in the social evolution of the human race, as suggested in Chapter 2 in Volume 1, a detour that "drifted" toward the absurd sex role imbalance we note today, can the evolutionary process be redirected? The basic organizational principle on which the entire set of civilizational enterprises of the past 8,000 years, at least, have been founded, that of hierarchical organization, has played itself out. A planet of 5 to 6 billion people cannot manage with organizational principles that evolved when human aggregates were only counted in hundreds of thousands. It is in fact astounding how well they worked and for how long. The ancient universalistic bureaucracy of China, the mandarin system, in which only the best minds rose to the top and governed the empire; the expanded city-state model the Romans used to govern their empire; the janissary system of the Ottomans, which put ruling entirely in the hands of the trained and the competent, combined with a millet system for local self-government of ethnic minorities; the Cesaro-papism that merged bureaucracies of the old Roman state; and the new Christian church in Byzantium and its successor, Russia—all these have sufficed in their time.[3]

No organizational innovation has touched the basic principle of hierarchical organization in a century that has seen the development of a new science of organization. The twentieth century has witnessed the rise of schools of business management and of public administration as well as of a tradition of empirical studies of the organization of work that brings every principle of mechanical efficiency and human motivation into play. (See Rosabeth Moss Kanter's "Women and the Structure of Organizations," 1975, for a good survey of these innovations.) Nevertheless, although organizational research has emphasized better information processing, varied communication patterns, more feedback systems, and the moving of the locus of decision making as far down the hierarchical structure as possible (the principle of "subsidiarity"), the underlying structural principle has remained intact. By the same token, the structural bases for inequalities of participation by women in all such organizations have also remained intact.

The hierarchical principle is based on the assumption that the higher one climbs, the better the view and the better the capacity to plan and design the future for the social entity in question. Anarcho-decentralists have always questioned this, but their voices went unheard as long as hierarchy worked reasonably well. Today, we face "design problems" for which no perch is high enough to ensure a view of the larger picture. NASA's nonhierarchical technique called "matrix management" came into being to deal with the unimaginable complexities of space missions. Schon (1970) calls it the solar system model, the solution to modern large-scale systems requiring maximum flexibility. The solar system model is also the solution for transnational movement activities (Judge 1971).

Many of today's enterprises are beyond planning in the conventional hierarchical mode: space missions, the administration of large cities, coordination of global projects of all kinds. In the United States—the most social systems-design-oriented country with the most highly trained design capabilities in the world, with system after system under federal administration—is displaying increasingly faulty delivery capabilities: nursing homes for the elderly, food stamp plans for the poor, school lunch programs for the young, and on ad infinitum.

What sectors of society are best equipped to replace hierarchy with decentralist structures based on nonhierarchical communication? The answer is the women's movements we have described in Chapter 5 of this volume. The underlife out of which these movements have grown has equipped them for radically new approaches where current system designs do not work. The plight of cities, of schools, of industry, of the natural environment; the need for alternative energy programs; and, most of all, the need for alternative security programs and policies—all cry out for the fresh perspectives and experience that women can bring from the underside, away from the centers of power and all the investment in the status quo that make power holders resistant to change.

The research frontiers that must be tackled to make a decentralist world work are immense. There must be development of adequate communication, travel, and problem-solving technologies to avoid the traps of neofeudalism and pressures toward reactionary small-town conformity, in a society where neighborhood self-help is an important value. Unless there are active inputs from the women cultures of each society, the new localism could once again be male dominated. Feminist separatist models of community will play a critical role in communicating alternative possibilities. Should women go into large-scale systems research? This is probably the area toward which they are least inclined, the area for which the underside seems particularly inadequate preparation, and also the area where women are most badly needed. Because the world is one ecosystem, interrelationships—both physical and social—must be studied at the planetary level. It is easy to lose one's grounding in reality, however, when studying global systems. This can lead to serious errors in judgment, as military decision makers demonstrate daily.

One of the major challenges that lies immediately ahead for women is to develop a training sequence for people who must work with large-scale systems, a sequence that uses those skills of environmental scanning and of taking feedback from the immediate environment that every person first develops in the family and neighborhood setting. A graduated sequence would involve taking feedback from ever-larger environmental systems, with repeated returns to primary feedback systems. This is necessary to help people gain "grounded" perceptions of global reality. Another set of educational interventions is needed to strengthen the now generally discouraged human capacity for nonlinear, metaphoric thinking to supplement linear thinking. This capacity, less stunted in women than in men, is critical in working with complex systems that cannot be grasped linearly.

There is nothing inherent in global thinking that is antithetical to decentralism. The decentralist world does not represent a retreat from responsibility for global welfare but a new approach to it. Because women have not entered the world-ordering and global-modeling fields to any great extent, they have not had the opportunity to try to spell out the institutional structures of this decentralist world. This spelling out will certainly be coming in the next decades.[4]

Imagining the Future

Unfortunately, images of what a new feminist-inspired social order would look like are not widely available. One reason for this is pointed out by Morgan (1984): "Women face a truly existential tactical dilemma: there are no maps or models for the deep and all-encompassing revolution we are envisioning, and so we must invent them as we go along" (p. 26). Annie Cheatham and Mary Clare Powell, who founded the North American Institute for Women and the Future in 1981, undertook a 30,000-mile journey across North America to see what American women hoped for (Cheatham and Powell 1986). They found hundreds of women acting out visions in concrete terms, locally, where they lived. But the vision stayed out of the public eye.

The women who gathered at the University of Minnesota in 1988 to build bridges and make alliances across the diversity of feminist cultures represented there, including Native American, African American, lesbian, and liberal-to-radical "straight" feminism (note Bunch, Davis, Green and Hall, in Albrecht and Brewer 1990) all had vibrant images of the future that not infrequently clashed with one another. The recognition by these women that their diversity was a source of strength and creativity, not weakness, is one more affirmation of the power of women's cultures.

Indeed, every woman is a futurist and has only to discover her own dreams. Women's organizations are fertile sources of futures thinking. Every network listed in Table 5.2 of in Chapter 5 of this volume, and every one of the roughly 200 women's INGOs encompassed there, are carriers of images of the future implicit in their statements of purpose. Sometimes the futures work of women is more explicit. Workshops on imaging a world without violence, which involve stepping into the future to see how a peaceful and just world could function over time and inventing strategies to achieve such a future, are being carried out by a number of women in Europe and North America (Boulding 1990a: chap. 6). Other activities are happening largely outside the more formally organized networks and women's organizations—in women's encampments, women's peace marches, and other women's public actions directed against militarism. Women's encampments at military installations have been particularly vivid demonstrations of what the new order might look like. Living in tents right up against the barbed wire of military bases, women practice nonviolence, harmony with nature, and mutual nurturance within the community of the encampment (Harford and Hopkins 1984). They are living the future they want in the current time, in the most unlikely locations. The encampments have been found in Greenham Common, England; Seneca Falls, United States; Frauenfeld, Switzerland; Comiso, Sicily; Fita Fuji, Japan; Nevi Shalom, Israel; and elsewhere.

Less dramatically, women teachers are often practicing futurists, offering postpatriarchal role models to the next generation, whether in kindergarten or on the university campus. Teachers whose imaginations can overleap classroom walls help the young discover their real-life environment and how to protect it, change it, reshape it; with kindergartners learning conflict resolution,[5] perhaps the next generation will be gentler, less violence prone.

We have been talking about women who are futures aware. But what about the Jane Doe's of the global sisterhood? Their underlife training inhibits them from using their own skills of imaging and innovating. Yet, if indigenous women in the 10,000 micro societies that inhabit niches within the modern state system are beginning to pick up the fragments of their battered cultures and reweaving living patterns not dependent on state power,[6] why can't the rest of us learn from them?

It doesn't take many encounters with women tribal leaders who have the quiet confidence of centuries of traditional knowledge behind them to realize that here is a network of teachers for Euro-American women stretching from pole to pole. Where does their serenity and self-confidence come from, that quiet sureness, that sense of a life apart that Sylvia Leith-Ross described (in Chapter 4 of this volume)? What do they "know"? Only they can tell us, and they are busy. Many native women are busy with their own problems of injustice, with problems of broken treaties, with their task of creating a world network of indigenous peoples. Elsewhere, Two-Thirds World women are simply struggling to cope with the distorting effects of modernization in their lives. They haven't much time for us, and they don't necessarily think the problems of white women's "liberation" are very important, embedded as these are in a way of life rejected by indigenous and other Two-Thirds World women. A combination of humility and good sense should make it possible for Euro-American women to learn from Two-Thirds World women of the Americas, of Arctic Europe, of the Asia-Pacific region, and of Africa (*Indigenous Women*, Spring 1991; also *Pacific Vision*, June 1991; *INSTRAW News*, No. 16, 1991).

How were Chinese women able to write new family laws that provided for their own liberation from feudalism and see to it that they were enforced? How were they able to design a land distribution scheme that gave land to women for the first time in China's history and see to it that it was enforced? There have been setbacks, and the old China still lives inside the new. But how have they managed to achieve as much as they have? Where does *their* serenity, *their* sureness, come from?

Every part of the world offers teachers—women of quiet self-confidence, with knowledge, with strength. Their skin is all colors, their language all languages, their religion all religions. This is time not only for the multicultural alliances being forged between the articulate and activist women of the countries of the North and the South mentioned earlier, but a time for the rest of us, especially middle-class Western women, to "go to school" to those of our sisters who have the unacknowledged skills, the confidence, the serenity, and the knowledge required for creative social change. Not because other solutions from other traditions are necessarily better, not because women elsewhere are smarter. No, underlife structures exist everywhere and have confined most women. We have walked through 10,000 years of such structures in this book. We have also discovered how strong women are, how steadily and creatively they have built century after century from the underside. This is a time to break through those underside barriers, moving with the strength and confidence our history can give us. We must help each other on every continent. We owe it to each other in the great sisterhood of humanity that embraces both men and women. We owe it to gaia, to earth our mother and earth our daughter.

Notes

1. See, however, the October 1975 issue of *Futures* (7[5]). It is devoted to the future of women, with four women contributors out of a total of nine authors. The reader may be interested in comparing the futures presented there with the approaches in this chapter.

2. We see it in writers such as Ursula Le Guin (for instance, *The Dispossessed*, 1974). See also Gearhart (1981).

3. Cesaro-papism never developed in the same way in the West because the pope and the Holy Roman Emperor never merged into one person as in Byzantium. The more individualistic style of Western bureaucracies stems from centuries of state-church struggles.

4. Donella Meadows, coauthor with Dennis Meadows of *Limits to Growth* (1972), is experimenting with ways to relate localist emphasis to global modeling in her current work at Dartmouth (1985). Schon (1970) and Judge (1971), cited earlier regarding a solar system model of world order, are working in the same direction.

5. Note the program on Children's Creative Response to Conflict supported by the Fellowship of Reconciliation, New York. Note also the approach to education in Brock-Utne (1985).

6. For the concept of "10,000 societies," see Boulding (1990b). There are in fact at least three different types of groups that make up these 10,000 societies: (a) indigenous peoples who have an ancient and very special relationship to the land on which they live; (b) tribal people who may or may not be living on ancestral lands (some are now urban dwellers)

but have a strong sense of common heritage, language, and kinship ties; (c) a variety of Two-Thirds World groups with strong cultural identities but geographically dispersed between urban and rural settings and across national boundaries.

The following are publications concerning indigenous peoples: IWGIA (International Work Group for Indigenous Affairs), Copenhagen, Denmark, publishes a quarterly newsletter, a documentation series, and an annual yearbook (for more information write: IWGIA, the International Secretariat of IWGIA, Fiolstraede 10, KD-1171, Copenhagen K, Denmark); *Cultural Survival* is a quarterly published in Cambridge, Massachusetts, United States (Cultural Survival, Inc., 53 Church Street, Cambridge, MA 02138); *Indigenous Women* is published by Indigenous Women's Network, Lake Elmo, Minnesota, United States (Indigenous Women's Network, P.O. Box 174, Lake Elmo, MN 55042); and *INSTRAW News: Women and Development* is published out of the Dominican Republic (INSTRAW, P.O. Box 21747, Santo Domingo, Dominican Republic).

References

Albrecht, Lisa and Rose M. Brewer. 1990. *Bridges of Power: Women's Multicultural Alliances.* Philadelphia: New Society.

Boulding, Elise. 1990a. *Building a Global Civic Culture: Education for an Interdependent World.* Syracuse, NY: Syracuse University Press.

———. 1990b. "The Challenge of Cultural Development in Industrialized Countries: Learning from the Third World Inside the First World." Paper presented to Committee on Futures Research, International Sociological Association, Madrid, Spain, July.

Brock-Utne, Birgit. 1985. *Educating for Peace: A Feminist Perspective.* New York: Pergamon.

Cheatham, Annie and Mary Claire Powell. 1986. *Women's Values and the Future.* Philadelphia: New Society.

Churchill, Ward, ed. 1991. *Critical Issues in Native North America.* Vol. 2. IWGIA Document 68. Copenhagen, Denmark: International Work Group for Indigenous Affairs.

Gearhart, S. 1981. "Female Futures in Science Fiction." Pp. 41-42 in *Future, Technology and Women: Proceedings of the Conference.* (San Diego University, La Jolla, CA, March 6-8.)

Harford, Barbara and Sarah Hopkins. 1984. *Greenham Common: Women at the Wire.* London: The Women's Press.

Judge, Anthony. 1971. "Matrix Organization and Organizational Networks." *International Associations* 3:154-70.

Kanter, Rosabeth Moss, ed. 1975. "Women and the Structure of Organizations: Explorations in Theory and Behavior." Pp. 34-74 in *Another Voice: Feminist Perspectives on Social Life and Social Science,* edited by Marcia Millman and Rosabeth Moss Kanter. Garden City, NY: Doubleday/Anchor.

Kessler, Carol Farley. 1984. *Daring to Dream: Utopian Stories by United States Women: 1836-1919.* Boston: Pandora.

Le Guin, Ursula. 1974. *The Dispossessed.* New York: Harper & Row.

Meadows, Donella. 1985. *The Electronic Oracle.* New York: John Wiley.

Meadows, Donella and Dennis et al. 1972. *Limits to Growth.* New York: Universe.

Morgan, Robin. 1984. *Sisterhood Is Global.* New York: Anchor/Doubleday.

Schon, Donald. 1970. "B.B.C. Ruth Lectures." *The Listener,* December 3 (London: B.B.C. Publications).

Author Index

Subject Index

About the Author

Elise Boulding is Professor Emerita of Dartmouth College and Senior Fellow in the Dickey Endowment; was Secretary-General of the International Peace Research Association from 1988 to April 1991; and was Professor and Chair at Dartmouth from 1978 until 1985. From 1967 until 1978, she was in the Department of Sociology and Institute of Behavioral Science at the University of Colorado at Boulder. Born in Oslo, Norway, she received her B.A. degree in English from Douglass College; her M.S. in Sociology from Iowa State University; and her Ph.D. from the University of Michigan. She is the wife of Kenneth Boulding, mother of five children, grandmother of fifteen, and a member of the Society of Friends.

A sociologist with a global view, she has undertaken numerous transnational and comparative cross-national studies on conflict and peace, development, and women in society. Her work in the area of future studies dates from 1961, when she translated, from the Dutch, Fred Polak's classic work, *Image of the Future*. She has worked internationally on problems of peace and world order both as a scholar and as an activist. She served as a member of the governing board of the United Nations University, 1980-85, and was a member of the International Jury of the UNESCO Prize for Peace Education and a former member of the U.S. Commission for UNESCO, 1981-87. She has served as a member of the Commission on Proposals for a National Academy of

Peace and Conflict Resolution, which resulted in the establishment by Congress of a U.S. Institute of Peace, and, from 1963-1968 and 1983 to 1987, she served as Editor of the *International Peace Research Newsletter.* Other current international involvements include the World Order Models Project, "Coming Global Civilization," and chairing the International Peace Research Association Commission on Peace Building in the Middle East. From time to time, she has conducted workshops on "imaging a world without weapons."

Her books include *Handbook of International Data on Women* (with Carson, Greenstein, and Nuss; New York: Halsted Press, 1977); *Women in the Twentieth Century World* (Halsted Press, 1977); *From a Monastery Kitchen* (New York: Harper & Row, 1976); *Children's Rights and the Wheel of Life* (Transaction Press, 1979), written especially for the International Year of the child; *Bibliography on World Conflict and Peace* (with Passmore and Gassler; Westview Press, 1979); *The Social System of the Planet Earth* (with K. Boulding and G. Burgess; Addison-Wesley); *Women and Social Costs of Development: Two Case Studies* (with Moen, Lilleydahl, and Palm); *Building a Global Civic Culture: Education for an Interdependent World* (Syracuse University Press, paperback, 1990); *One Small Plot of Heaven* (Pendle Hill Publications, 1989); *Peace Culture and Society: Transnational Research and Dialogue* with Clovis Brigagao and Kevin Clements (eds.) (Westview Press, 1990); and *New Agendas for Peace Research: Conflict and Security Reexamined* (ed.) (Lynne Rienner, 1992).